EMPIRICALLY BASED PLAY INTERVENTIONS FOR CHILDREN Second Edition

EMPIRICALLY BASED PLAY INTERVENTIONS FOR CHILDREN Second Edition

EDITED BY

Linda A. Reddy,

Tara M. Files-Hall,

and Charles E. Schaefer

AMERICAN PSYCHOLOGICAL ASSOCIATION

WASHINGTON, DC

Published by
American Psychological Association
750 First Street, NE
Washington, DC 20002
www.apa.org

To order
APA Order Department
P.O. Box 92984
Washington, DC 20090-2984
Tel: (800) 374-2721; Direct: (202) 336-5510
Fax: (202) 336-5502; TDD/TTY: (202) 336-6123
Online: www.apa.org/pubs/books
E-mail: order@apa.org

In the U.K., Europe, Africa, and the Middle East, copies may be ordered from
American Psychological Association
3 Henrietta Street
Covent Garden, London
WC2E 8LU England

Typeset in Goudy by Circle Graphics, Inc., Columbia, MD

Printer: Bang Printing, Brainerd, MN
Cover Designer: Berg Design, Albany, NY

The opinions and statements published are the responsibility of the authors, and such opinions and statements do not necessarily represent the policies of the American Psychological Association.

Library of Congress Cataloging-in-Publication Data

Empirically based play interventions for children / edited by Linda A. Reddy,
Tara M. Files-Hall, and Charles E. Schaefer. — Second edition.
    pages cm
  Includes bibliographical references and index.
  ISBN 978-1-4338-2039-7 — ISBN 1-4338-2039-0 1. Play therapy. I. Reddy, Linda A. II.
Files-Hall, Tara M. III. Schaefer, Charles E.
  RJ505.P6E567 2016
  618.92'891653—dc23
                            2015004786

British Library Cataloguing-in-Publication Data

A CIP record is available from the British Library.

Printed in the United States of America
Second Edition

http://dx.doi.org/10.1037/14730-000

To my family, Donna, Cailyn, and Ashley, and to my parents,
Thomas Joseph and Geraldine Mary Reddy
—*Linda A. Reddy*

To my husband, Erik; our cherished boys, Ethan and Joshua;
and my parents and brother
—*Tara M. Files-Hall*

To my wife, Anne Weldon Schaefer
—*Charles E. Schaefer*

CONTENTS

CONTRIBUTORS

Martha A. Askins, PhD, Associate Professor, The Children's Cancer Hospital at The University of Texas, MD Anderson Cancer Center, Houston

Sue C. Bratton, PhD, Director, Center for Play Therapy, and Professor, Department of Counseling and Higher Education, University of North Texas, Denton

Meena Dasari, PhD, Assistant Professor, Department of Psychiatry, New York University School of Medicine and Bellevue Hospital Center, and Psychologist, private practice, New York

Katherine S. Davlantis, LCSW, PhD, Associate in Research, Duke Center for Autism and Brain Development, Department of Psychiatry and Behavioral Sciences, Duke University School of Medicine, Durham, NC

Tara M. Files-Hall, PhD, Family C.O.P.E., Center of Psychotherapy/Psychiatry and Evaluation, Sarasota, FL

Eliana M. Gil, PhD, Founding Partner, Gil Institute for Trauma Recovery & Education, Fairfax, VA

Amy D. Herschell, PhD, Associate Professor, Department of Psychology, West Virginia University, Morgantown, and Department of Psychiatry, Western Psychiatric Institute and Clinic, University of Pittsburgh School of Medicine, Pittsburgh, PA

Deborah B. Johnson, EdD, Director of National Services, Children's Institute, Rochester, NY

Susan M. Knell, PhD, Clinical Assistant Professor, Department of Psychological Sciences, Case Western Reserve University, and Psychologist, private practice, Cleveland, OH

Garry L. Landreth, EdD, Regents Professor Emeritus, Department of Counseling and Higher Education, University of North Texas, Denton

Natalya A. Lindo, PhD, Associate Professor, Department of Counseling and Higher Education, University of North Texas, Denton

Cheryl B. McNeil, PhD, Professor, Department of Psychology, West Virginia University, Morgantown

Mary Anne Peabody, EdD, Department of Social and Behavioral Sciences, Lewiston-Auburn College, University of Southern Maine, Lewiston

JoAnne Pedro-Carroll, PhD, Clinical Psychologist and Child Specialist, Rochester, NY

William A. Rae, PhD, Clinical Professor, Department of Educational Psychology, Texas A&M University, College Station

Dee C. Ray, PhD, Professor, Counseling Program, and Director, Child and Family Resource Clinic, University of North Texas, Denton

Linda A. Reddy, PhD, Professor, Graduate School of Applied Professional Psychology, Rutgers University, Piscataway, NJ

Sally J. Rogers, PhD, Professor of Psychiatry and Behavior Sciences, MIND Institute, University of California, Davis Medical Center, Sacramento

Charles E. Schaefer, PhD, Emeritus Professor, Department of Psychology, Fairleigh Dickinson University, Teaneck, NJ

Ashley T. Scudder, PhD, Postdoctoral Associate, Department of Psychiatry, Western Psychiatric Institute and Clinic, University of Pittsburgh School of Medicine, Pittsburgh, PA

Jeremy R. Sullivan, PhD, Associate Professor, Department of Educational Psychology, The University of Texas, San Antonio

Mariska Klein Velderman, PhD, Senior Researcher, Child Health Department, Netherlands Organisation for Applied Scientific Research (TNO), Leiden

Carolyn Webster-Stratton, MSN, MPH, PhD, Professor Emeritus, Department of Family and Child Nursing, The University of Washington, Seattle

Pamela Wolfberg, PhD, Professor, Autism Spectrum Studies, Department of Special Education & Communication Disorders, San Francisco State University, San Francisco, CA

EMPIRICALLY BASED PLAY INTERVENTIONS FOR CHILDREN Second Edition

INTRODUCTION

LINDA A. REDDY, TARA M. FILES-HALL, AND CHARLES E. SCHAEFER

Play is a universal behavior of all children worldwide. It is estimated that by age 6 years, children are likely to have engaged in more than 15,000 hours of play (Schaefer & Drewes, 2014). The benefits of play for healthy cognitive development (Bornstein & O'Reilly, 1993; Piaget, 1962), language development (Lyytinen, Poikkeus, & Laakso, 1997; McCune, 1995; Tamis-LeMonda & Bornstein, 1994), social competence (Howes & Matheson, 1992; Parten, 1932), and physical development (Pellegrini & Smith, 1998) have been well established over decades. As this book demonstrates, positive play experiences also can help alleviate emotional and behavioral difficulties.

For more than 7 decades, play therapy has been recognized as the oldest and most popular form of child therapy in clinical practice (Association for Play Therapy, 2014; Parten, 1932). Play-based assessment and interventions

http://dx.doi.org/10.1037/14730-001
Empirically Based Play Interventions for Children, Second Edition, L. A. Reddy, T. M. Files-Hall, and C. E. Schaefer (Editors)

are routinely taught in master's- and doctoral-level training programs across the nation. The Association for Play Therapy (2014) defined *play therapy* as "the systematic use of a theoretical model to establish an interpersonal process wherein trained play therapists use the therapeutic powers of play to help clients prevent or resolve psychosocial difficulties and achieve optimal growth and development" (p. 20). Play therapy (or play interventions) has been viewed as an effective method for children to communicate their feelings, thoughts, and experiences with peers and/or therapists, as well as to refine skills and/or learn new skills for future social learning opportunities (Reddy, 2012).

For many years, clinicians and researchers have hypothesized factors in play behaviors that may foster therapeutic agents for change. Among the major therapeutic factors are play therapy's communication power (i.e., children naturally express their conscious and unconscious thoughts/feelings better through play than by words alone), its teaching power (i.e., clients attend and learn better when play is used to instruct), its abreaction power (i.e., clients can relive past stressful events and release the associated negative emotions in the safe environment of the play world), and its rapport-building power (i.e., clients tend to like therapists who are playful and fun loving; see Schaefer & Drewes, 2014).

The curative powers of play can be seen in the well-known schools of play therapy (i.e., client-centered, cognitive–behavioral, family, and psychodynamic). The prescriptive-eclectic school of play therapy advocates that play therapists become skilled in numerous therapeutic powers and differentially apply those powers to meet clients' individual needs (Schaefer, 2011). Prescriptive-play therapists tend to use an eclectic approach incorporating different theoretical techniques based on what is best for each child. Thus, therapists who adopt a prescriptive approach often combine different theories and techniques to tailor and strengthen an intervention.

Despite play therapy's rich theoretical foundation, some have questioned its utility and overall efficacy compared with other evidence-based interventions (e.g., Lebo, 1953; Reade, Hunter, & McMillan, 1999). The main criticism of play interventions has been that the field, in general, lacks rigorous research designs and data analytic methods (Phillips, 1985). Scholars have argued that the research on play therapy has been plagued with anecdotal reports or case study designs and includes limitations often found in the general psychotherapy outcome literature (e.g., lack of control and/or alternative treatment groups, small sample sizes, limited or no generalizability of findings to natural settings; LeBlanc & Ritchie, 1999). However, during the past 2 decades, significant innovations in play interventions and validation efforts have been seen. Three meta-analytic studies have examined the effec-tiveness of play therapy with youths (Bratton, Ray, Rhine, & Jones, 2005; LeBlanc & Ritchie, 1999; Ray, Bratton, Rhine, & Jones, 2001), including many well-designed, controlled-play intervention studies. For example, LeBlanc and Ritchie's (1999) meta-analysis included 42 experimental stud-ies conducted from 1947 to 1997; the studies came from multiple sources, such as journals, dissertations, and unpublished studies, and included control- or comparison-group designs, as well as sufficient data and statistical infor-mation. In the studies, the average age of the children was 7.9 years, and no child was older than age 12. Play therapy yielded an overall positive effect size of .66, which reflects that it has a moderate treatment effect. LeBlanc and Ritchie also investigated specific characteristics of treatment related to outcome success. Two factors that significantly related to outcome were parental involvement in the children's therapy and the duration of therapy. Studies that involved the parent as a therapist (e.g., trained parents using therapeutic techniques) resulted in an effect size of .83 (i.e., large positive treatment outcome) compared with an effect size of .56 (i.e., moderate posi-tive treatment outcome) for studies that did not involve parents. Likewise, outcomes appear to have improved with a sustained intervention regimen. The authors noted several factors that were unrelated to outcome, such as the type of presenting problem, treatment context (group vs. individual), and participants' age and gender.

In 2001, Ray et al. (2001) carried out a meta-analysis that included 94 experiment designed studies conducted from 1940 to 2000. The studies came from journal articles, dissertations, and/or unpublished studies, and each study included a control- or comparison-group design and pre- and postmeasures. The child participants ranged in age from 3 to 16 years, with a mean age of 7.1. Findings indicated that play therapy, in general, produced an overall effect size of .80 (i.e., large positive treatment outcome). Different play therapy theoretical models examined outcomes. Investigations were coded as follows: 74 studies were coded as humanistic/nondirective play therapy, 12 studies were behavioral/directive play therapy, and eight were not coded because of a lack of information. The humanistic/nondirective category demonstrated a slightly larger effect size (.93) than the behavioral/directive category (.73); however, the authors cautioned that the difference was likely influenced by the disproportionate number of studies in the two categories. In a comparison of the effect of general play therapy to filial play therapy, the authors found that the filial therapies exhibited a greater effect size (1.06) than general play therapies (.73). Similar to LeBlanc and Ritchie's (1999) findings, routine parental involvement in treatment was a significant predictor of outcome ($p = .008$). In addition, Ray et al. found that the treatment context (i.e., individual vs. group), whether the population was clinical versus analog, and participants' age and/or gender were unrelated to outcome.

Bratton et al. (2005) conducted a meta-analytic review of published and unpublished studies (i.e., control- or comparison-group design with pre- and postmeasures) from 1953 to 2000 to evaluate the efficacy of play therapy. That review examined 93 studies, which included 41 journal articles, two Education Resources Information Center documents, and 50 unpublished dissertations. The average age of children receiving play therapy was 7 years, and two thirds were male. Analyses showed that play therapy was equally effective across age and gender. Across the 93 studies, play therapy, in general, yielded a mean effect size of .80. Characteristics of treatment also were examined. For example, humanistic interventions resulted in a large effect size, whereas nonhumanistic interventions resulted in a moderate effect size. In addition, when a mental health professional conducted play therapy, the result was a moderate-to-large effect size of .72. However, when a paraprofessional (i.e., parent, teacher, peer mentor) conducted play therapy, the result was a large effect size of 1.05. Furthermore, individual and group formats for play therapy were found to be effective, with effect sizes of .79 and .82, respectively. Although the authors also examined target problem behaviors, they found play therapy, in general, to be effective across presenting problem. Although the authors were unable to gain a clear understanding of specific factors that contribute to the efficacy of play therapy, overall results suggested that play therapy is an efficacious intervention method for children.

Collectively, the aforementioned meta-analytic studies revealed that play interventions have moderate-to-large positive effects (0.66–1.05) on outcomes. Play interventions appear to be effective for children across treatment modalities (i.e., group, individual), age groups (i.e., 3–16 years), gender, referred versus nonreferred populations, presenting problem, and treatment orientations (i.e., humanistic/nondirective, behavioral/directive). Thus, these reviews provide substantial evidence for the utility and efficacy of play interventions with children and families.

Since the publication of the 2005 version of *Empirically Based Play Interventions for Children* (Reddy, Files-Hall, & Schaefer, 2005), research on play interventions for children and adolescents has flourished across varied child problems and populations (e.g., darkness phobia, at-risk high school students, homelessness, sexual abuse, political violence in Indonesia, consequences of earthquakes and other natural disasters), treatment models (e.g., child–parent psychotherapy, child parent relationship therapy, kinder training), and treatment agents (e.g., peers, teachers, nurses). Because of this expanding research base, Reddy, Files-Hall, and Schaefer proposed the second edition of *Empirically Based Play Interventions for Children*. Because of space limitations, the authors are unable to cover in detail all of the research and treatment models available in this area, such as filial therapy (see Chapter 12).

PURPOSE OF THIS BOOK

As new health and mental health policies emerge, practitioners increasingly must use well-established, theoretically based, and flexible interventions to meet the growing and diverse needs of children and families in society. Play interventions can play a significant role in the nation's changing policy landscape (Reddy, 2012). For example, in 2013, President Barack Obama launched the early learning proposal in which he put forth an investment of $75 billion over 10 years to support children's access to high-quality preschools (National Women's Law Center, 2013). This proposal was based on the notion that high-quality early education experiences can improve children's academic engagement in later school years and also their social and emotional development (Smith, 2013). This landmark grant will be especially beneficial for increasing low-income families' access to high-quality schools for their children (Smith, 2013). Within this proposal, states will be required to set standards to ensure that preschools include high-quality elements (e.g., well-qualified staff, small class sizes, social–emotional learning opportunities).

Within the Patient Protection and Affordable Care Act, the maternal, infant, and early childhood home visiting program provides support to families with infants and children through age 5 years to implement evidence-based home visiting programs (Smith, 2013). Ultimately, the goal of this initiative is to improve children's overall health, prevent child abuse and neglect, encourage positive parenting, and promote child development and school readiness. Given that studies have shown that paraprofessionals and parents can be effective implementers of play intervention for their children (e.g., Bratton et al., 2005; Ray et al., 2001), it is important to have government support to ensure the success of these interventions.

The goal of this book is to offer practitioners and researchers a unique clinical reference that presents evidence-based and maximally useful play interventions for a variety of child populations and settings. This text illustrates the usefulness of both directive and nondirective approaches and the integration of cognitive–behavioral techniques. To meet the needs of practitioners (e.g., psychologists, social workers, counselors) and researchers, each chapter includes clinical theory and observations, case examples, and research data. Twelve principles guided the authors' selection of intervention programs that

- include well-defined treatment components and processes;
- offer innovative intervention elements;
- are guided by developmental theory;
- demonstrate clinical effectiveness;
- are adaptable for a variety of settings;
- are appropriate for prevention and/or intervention;
- include ongoing comprehensive outcome assessment approaches;
- offer structured and/or time-limited interventions;
- are tailored to the child's developmental level;
- target behaviors and/or competencies in children and/or parents;
- identify and assess quantifiable behavioral goals; and
- include varied intervention agents, such as psychologists, psychiatrists, nurses, counselors, physical therapists, occupational therapists, social workers, paraprofessionals, teachers, and/or parents.

Many of the intervention programs in this book met the guidelines set forth by the American Psychological Association's Task Force on Promotion and Dissemination of Psychological Procedures (Chambless, 1995). Criteria for probably efficacious psychosocial interventions for childhood disorders include

> (a) two studies showing the intervention more effective than a no-treatment control group (or comparison group) OR (b) two studies otherwise meeting the well-established treatment criteria (I, III, IV), but both are conducted by the same investigator, or one good study demonstrating effectiveness by these same criteria, OR (c) at least two good studies demonstrating effectiveness but flawed by heterogeneity of the client samples, OR (d) a small series of single case design studies (i.e., less than 3) otherwise meeting the well-established treatment criteria (II, III, IV). (Chambless, 1995, p. 22)

Weisz and Kazdin (2010) also provided additional criteria for considering an intervention for children as evidence based. Specifically, intervention procedures must be specified and documented, treatment benefits must be demonstrated through well-controlled studies that rule out alternative explanations, and individuals other than the creators of the program must replicate beneficial effects. Our selection of programs does not signify a special status or ranking, nor do we suggest that our choice of interventions is exhaustive. Other excellent programs exist that meet our criteria.

The current authors invited distinguished contributors to present innovative interventions and well-known models. A brief description of each follows.

We conceptualized the book as consisting of five parts: Part I: Empirically Based Play Prevention Interventions, Part II: Empirically Based Play Interventions for Internalizing Disorders, Part III: Empirically Based Play Interventions for Externalizing Disorders, Part IV: Empirically Based Play Interventions for Developmental Disorders and Other Models, and Part V: Final Comments. Each chapter includes a description of the theoretical basis and objectives of the play intervention, key treatment ingredients and processes, detailed intervention session(s) with brief transcripts, brief summary of outcome studies, and recommendations for replication and transportability of the intervention to other settings and populations.

Part I presents three empirically based play prevention programs. Prevention interventions reduce the social, emotional, behavioral, and developmental difficulties faced by children, and prevent the early onset of more severe and costly disorders. In Chapter 1, Johnson and Peabody present a well-researched, school-based preventative play intervention program, the Primary Project (formerly known as the Primary Mental Health Project). Established in 1957, Primary Project targets primary school-age children at risk for adjustment difficulties; it has been implemented in more than 2,000 schools worldwide. Under supervision, trained paraprofessionals (i.e., child associates) are trained in child-centered play therapy (CCPT) principles and skills to conduct individual play sessions. Outcome evaluations of Primary Project have revealed that the children demonstrate improvements in adjustment in the short- and long-term. In Chapter 2, Pedro-Carroll and Velderman present a school-based prevention program that targets the needs of children of divorce in the United States and the Netherlands. Specially trained and supervised mental health professionals and paraprofessionals implement the children of divorce intervention program. Developmentally sensitive play-based activities within a group context are used to help children address the stressful changes that divorce often brings. The chapter synthesizes the Children of Divorce Intervention Program (CODIP)'s evidence for reducing the stress of divorce on children and improving their social, emotional, and school adjustment in the short- and long-term. Also, the chapter presents the adaption and pilot work of CODIP for children in the Netherlands. In the final chapter of Part I, Ray and Bratton present CCPT, one of the longest-standing mental health interventions for ethnically, culturally, and socially diverse populations. CCPT is supported by more than 70 years of research and is grounded in Rogers's (1951) person-centered theory and Axline's (1947) nondirective play therapy models. CCPT aims to help children achieve optimal growth and mental health by developing children's internal resources for self-regulation, self-control creativity, and self-direction.

Part II presents three chapters on play interventions for children with internalizing disorders. In Chapter 4, Knell and Dasari describe the utility and evidence for cognitive–behavioral play therapy for children with anxiety and depressive symptoms. They present the adaption and integration of play therapy with cognitive–behavioral techniques, such contingency management, shaping, exposure, and systematic desensitization. In Chapter 5, Gil presents the combined use of directive and nondirective play interventions for responding to the unique needs of abused and traumatized children: trauma-focused integrated play therapy (TF-IPT). TF-IPT is a prescriptive approach that tailors the type of trauma, intensity of the trauma, and developmental and cultural factors to effectively treat traumatized youths. In the final chapter of this part, Rae, Sullivan, and Askins present a short-term play program for hospitalized children with internalizing symptoms. The authors offer a comprehensive review of the outcome literature on play interventions for hospitalized youths. Based on client-centered, humanistic principles, this proposed approach reduces the psychological distress related to children's illnesses and hospitalization.

Part III presents empirically based play interventions for children with externalizing disorders. This unique group of interventions uses a variety of therapeutic agents, such as professionals, teachers, parents, and paraprofessionals, in play intervention delivery. In Chapter 7, Webster-Stratton presents The Incredible Years, a multimodal play intervention to improve young children's social and emotional competences and behaviors. She details three separate and interlocking evidence-based programs (i.e., parent, teacher, children) to promote social competence in young children and prevent and ameliorate conduct problems. The chapter details how play and coaching methods (i.e., interactive collaborative process of assessing, guiding, and providing feedback toward goals) can build healthy relationships and enhance children's self-regulatory skills and strategies and thus lead to problem solving and academic readiness. In Chapter 8, Scudder, Herschell, and McNeil present parent–child interaction therapy (PCIT), a well-researched intervention designed to treat young children who exhibit externalizing behavior problems. Based on developmental theory, social learning theory, behavioral principles, and traditional play therapy procedures, PCIT is a structured, short-term model that focuses on training parents as therapeutic agents of change. Trained therapists use in vivo coaching methods to help individual parents enhance their child's behavior management. In the final chapter of Part III, Reddy presents the key components and processes of implementing the child ADHD [attention-deficit/hyperactivity disorder] multimodal program (CAMP), an empirically supported program that treats the social and behavioral needs of young children diagnosed with ADHD (Reddy, 2012). Grounded in social learning theory and behavioral principles, this developmental, skill-based program for children integrates cognitive–behavioral methods and developmentally appropriate games to improve social skills, self-control, and anger/stress management within a 10-week, structured group format (e.g., Reddy, 2010, 2012). Parents receive concurrent group training focused on behavioral management techniques in the home, school, and community. Also, individual parent and teacher behavioral consultation services are offered in the home and school.

Part IV presents empirically based interventions for developmental disorders and other models. Unique to the interventions featured in this section is a focus on the value of play interventions for children with autism spectrum disorders. In Chapter 10, Davlantis and Rogers present the early start Denver model, a well-researched, school-based daily play intervention program for fostering the development and growth of young children with autism spectrum disorders. The Denver model is grounded in developmental theory and emphasizes the importance of symbolic, interpersonal, and cognitive aspects of play in the development of children with autism. The Denver model has resulted in improvements in treated children's symbolic play and affective reciprocal exchanges during play with their parents. In Chapter 11, Wolfberg presents the integrated play groups (IPG) model. IPG is an empirically supported play intervention created for children ages 3 to 11 years who have been diagnosed with an autism spectrum disorder. It focuses on enhancing the children's skills, enjoyment, and sustained interactions with adults and typically developing peers during play. The IPG model's primary aim is to target the core challenges faced by children with autism through frameworks of sociocultural theory (Vygotsky, 1933/1967, 1978) and cross-cultural research on guided participation (Rogoff, 1990). A secondary aim is to improve typical peers' understanding and acceptance of children with autism. The integrated play therapy model includes small group training with trained typically developing peers (i.e., expert players), children with autism (i.e., novice players) and trained adult facilitators. In Chapter 12, Lindo, Bratton, and Landreth discuss promoting healthy development of children through child parent relationship therapy (CPRT). The authors outline CPRT's significant theory and research support, and detail the clinical considerations and processes for successful treatment delivery. They briefly discuss filial therapy.

In Part V, Bratton and Ray provide the present status and future directions of play interventions. They briefly synthesize the current outcome research on play interventions and offer recommendations for research, practice, training, and policy.

It is our hope that this volume of innovative, well-designed, and empirically based interventions provides practitioners, researchers, and third-party payers (e.g., insurance) an appreciation of the range of play interventions and programs for children and adolescents. We are grateful to our contributors, who provided a timely, scholarly, and comprehensive presentation of their intervention programs. Their work adds to the growing empirical foundation for this important area. It is our goal that this volume will serve as a springboard for future play intervention development and validation, and will inform new lines of practice and policy for children's healthy development worldwide.

REFERENCES

Association for Play Therapy. (2014). *Why play therapy?* Retrieved from http://www.a4pt.org/?page=WhyPlayTherapy

Axline, V. M. (1947). *Play therapy: The inner dynamics of childhood.* Boston, MA: Houghton Mifflin.

Bornstein, M. H., & O'Reilly, A. (Eds.). (1993). *New directions for child development: The role of play in the development of thought* (Vol. 59). San Francisco, CA: Jossey-Bass.

Bratton, S. C., Ray, D., Rhine, T., & Jones, L. (2005). The efficacy of play therapy with children: A meta-analytic review of treatment outcomes. *Professional Psychology: Research and Practice, 36,* 376–390. http://dx.doi.org/10.1037/0735-7028.36.4.376

Chambless, D. L. (1995). Training in and dissemination of empirically-validated psychological treatments: Report and recommendations. *Clinical Psychologist, 48*(1), 3–24.

Howes, C., & Matheson, C. C. (1992). Sequences in the development of competent play with peers: Social and social pretend play. *Developmental Psychology, 28,* 961–974. http://dx.doi.org/10.1037/0012-1649.28.5.961

LeBlanc, M., & Ritchie, M. (1999). Predictors of play therapy outcomes. *International Journal of Play Therapy, 8*(2), 19–34. http://dx.doi.org/10.1037/h0089429

Lebo, D. (1953). The present status of research on nondirective play therapy. *Journal of Consulting Psychology, 17,* 177–183. http://dx.doi.org/10.1037/h0063570

Lyytinen, P., Poikkeus, A.-M., & Laakso, M.-L. (1997). Language and symbolic play in toddlers. *International Journal of Behavioral Development, 21,* 289–302. http://dx.doi.org/10.1080/016502597384875

McCune, L. (1995). A normative study of representational play in the transition to language. *Developmental Psychology, 31,* 198–206. http://dx.doi.org/10.1037/0012-1649.31.2.198

National Women's Law Center. (2013, April). *President Obama's early learning proposal* [Fact sheet]. Retrieved from http://www.nwlc.org/sites/default/files/pdfs/presidentsproposalfactsheet.pdf

Parten, M. B. (1932). Social participation among preschool children. *Journal of Abnormal and Social Psychology, 27,* 243–269. http://dx.doi.org/10.1037/h0074524

Pellegrini, A. D., & Smith, P. K. (1998). Physical activity play: The nature and function of a neglected aspect of playing. *Child Development, 69,* 577–598. http://dx.doi.org/10.1111/j.1467-8624.1998.tb06226.x

Phillips, R. D. (1985). Whistling in the dark? A review of play therapy research. *Psychotherapy: Theory, Research, Practice, Training, 22*, 752–760. http://dx.doi.org/10.1037/h0085565

Piaget, J. (1962). *Play, dreams, and imitation in childhood.* New York, NY: Norton.

Ray, D., Bratton, S., Rhine, T., & Jones, L. (2001). The effectiveness of play therapy: Responding to the critics. *International Journal of Play Therapy, 10*(1), 85–108. http://dx.doi.org/10.1037/h0089444

Reade, S., Hunter, H., & McMillan, I. R. (1999). Just playing . . . is it time wasted? *British Journal of Occupational Therapy, 62*, 157–162.

Reddy, L. A. (2010). Group play interventions for children with attention deficit/hyperactivity disorder. In A. A. Drewes & C. E. Schaefer (Eds.), *School-based play therapy* (2nd ed., pp. 307–329). Hoboken, NJ: Wiley. http://dx.doi.org/10.1002/9781118269701.ch15

Reddy, L. A. (2012). *Group play interventions for children: Strategies for teaching prosocial skills.* Washington, DC: American Psychological Association. http://dx.doi.org/10.1037/13093-000

Reddy, L. A., Files-Hall, T. M., & Schaefer, C. E. (Eds.). (2005). *Empirically based play interventions for children.* Washington, DC: American Psychological Association. http://dx.doi.org/10.1037/11086-000

Rogers, C. (1951). *Client-centered therapy: Its current practice, implications, and theory.* Oxford, England: Houghton Mifflin.

Rogoff, B. (1990). *Apprenticeship in thinking: Cognitive development in social context.* New York, NY: Oxford University Press.

Schaefer, C. E. (Ed.). (2011). *Foundations of play therapy* (2nd ed.). Hoboken, NJ: Wiley.

Schaefer, C. E., & Drewes, A. A. (Eds.). (2014). *The therapeutic powers of play* (2nd ed.). Hoboken, NJ: Wiley.

Smith, L. (2013, February). *President Obama's plan for early education for all Americans.* Retrieved from http://www.acf.hhs.gov/blog/2013/02/president-obamas-plan-for-early-education-for-all-americans

Tamis-LeMonda, C. S., & Bornstein, M. H. (1994). Specificity in mother–toddler language play relations across the second year. *Developmental Psychology, 30*, 283–292. http://dx.doi.org/10.1037/0012-1649.30.2.283

Vygotsky, L. S. (1967). Play and its role in the mental development of the child. [Original work published 1933]. *Soviet Psychology, 5*(3), 6–18.

Vygotsky, L. S. (1978). *Mind in society: The development of higher psychological processes.* Cambridge, MA: Harvard University Press.

Weisz, J. R., & Kazdin, A. E. (2010). Preface. In J. R. Weisz & A. E. Kazdin (Eds.), *Evidence-based psychotherapies for children and adolescents* (2nd ed., pp. xiii–xv). New York, NY: Guilford Press.

I

EMPIRICALLY BASED
PLAY PREVENTION
INTERVENTIONS

1

PRIMARY PROJECT: A PLAY-BASED INTERVENTION FOR EARLY CHILDHOOD

DEBORAH B. JOHNSON AND MARY ANNE PEABODY

Primary Project, formerly known as the Primary Mental Health Project, began in 1957 and continues decades later as a program based on the theoretical underpinnings of child-centered play. A prevention program designed to help young children adjust to the stresses of the school environment, Primary Project is in more than 2,000 elementary schools today and continues to grow nationally and internationally. With academic demands increasing and time for play decreasing, most classrooms provide limited play for young children (Miller & Almon, 2009). Concurrently, the number of children with mental, emotional, and behavioral health needs continues to grow at an alarming rate. According to the National Research Council and Institute of Medicine (2009), an emotional, behavioral, or mental health diagnosis is as commonplace for a child as a fractured limb—not inevitable, but not at all unusual.

An estimated one in five children in the United States has a diagnosable disorder requiring mental health treatment, yet less than half of those

http://dx.doi.org/10.1037/14730-002
Empirically Based Play Interventions for Children, Second Edition, L. A. Reddy, T. M. Files-Hall, and C. E. Schaefer (Editors)

children receive treatment (U.S. Public Health Service, 2000). The National Center for Health Statistics reported that 4.6% of children between the ages of 4 and 17 years have severe behavioral and emotional difficulties, and 16.2% have minor difficulties (Simpson, Bloom, Cohen, & Blumberg, 2005). These findings illuminate the critical need for early identification, intervention, and prevention efforts for children before problems intensify to a level that requires a diagnosis and mental health treatment (Koller & Bertel, 2006).

Research on potential dropouts has indicated that characteristics associated with such outcomes often can be identified early. Risk factors associated with delinquency also are evident in the early grades (Wasserman et al., 2003). Current studies about the effect of adverse childhood experiences on brain development during the early years of life have continued to point to the critical importance of nurturing environments and interactions for young children (Edwards et al., 2005; Shonkoff & Levitt, 2010). When children at an early age experience nourishing and caring relationships in supportive environments, they develop competencies and resources to adjust and cope with life adversities as they grow older.

CASE EXAMPLE

Sarah is slowly disappearing into the periphery of her first-grade classroom. She is quiet by nature, but with time and encouragement, she usually adjusts to new experiences. However, with the demands of first grade, this new experience has been different. Sarah has found a way to avoid the stress of the classroom by visiting the school nurse with complaints of stomachaches and headaches. During recess, she often plays alone or within inches of adults. Mrs. Smith, Sarah's teacher, has been watching and trying to encourage her since the beginning of the academic year. She is concerned that although the natural adjustment period for most children is over, Sarah is withdrawing more and more. Her parents too are concerned about their daughter.

Mrs. Smith wonders if social and emotional concerns may be at the origin of Sarah's school adjustment difficulty. Because the academic demands of first grade will continue to increase, she worries that Sarah will be unable to maintain good academic standing much longer. In early October, Mrs. Smith met with the school psychologist to review the behavioral and social–emotional needs of her students. During that meeting, it was determined that Sarah could benefit from Primary Project, a school-based program designed to foster the social and emotional wellness of children with emerging school adjustment difficulties. Given her story and profile, Sarah is one of thousands of young students who could benefit from Primary Project.

THE THERAPEUTIC ELEMENTS OF PLAY

For young children, the natural mode of expression and communication is through their play. Therefore, play-based approaches have numerous advantages when working with them, most notably the universal, intrinsic appeal of play as a natural way to safely explore their world. Play enables children to communicate when words are unavailable, inaccessible, or not readily understood. Thus, play provides an opportunity for adults to share the child's inner world on the child's terms and at the child's pace. This approach is at the heart of Primary Project: a trusting, therapeutic relationship in which the child, through play, feels safe to express and explore feelings, deal with stressful experiences, problem solve, and master challenges.

Within the theoretical constructs of Carl Rogers's (1951) client-centered therapy theory, Axline (1969) postulated nondirective or self-directive play therapy. Central to Axline's approach is Rogers's concept that individuals are constantly striving toward personal growth, seeking to fulfill their needs, and self-actualizing. Because children's understanding of reality is the result of their experiences and perceptions of the environment, their adjustment to the environment is directly and greatly affected by the ability of that environment to meet their needs. Internal conflicts and disruptive behavior may arise as the child attempts to fulfill needs not met by the environment. Axline posited that in an optimal environment such as the playroom, the exposure to empathy, implementation of structured limits, and acceptance by the therapist reduces a child's conflict with the environment and facilitates the child's ability to express his or her feelings and to self-actualize and grow. Inherent in Primary Project is the belief that a child experiencing adjustment problems can become more socially and emotionally competent when allowed to lead the play session (Cowen, Hightower, Pedro-Carroll, Work, & Wyman, 1996).

Axline (1969) put forth eight basic principles that guide the facilitation of child-centered play therapy: (a) building a warm rapport with the child, (b) accepting the child unconditionally, (c) establishing a sense of permissiveness, (d) reflecting the child's feelings, (e) maintaining respect for the child, (f) allowing the child to lead the way, (g) not hurrying the child, and (h) establishing only necessary limits (pp. 73–74). Similar to Axline's child-centered play therapy, the Primary Project's intervention depends on warmth, acceptance, empathy, nondirectiveness, and limit setting, when needed. More specifically, the success of Primary Project's training and intervention relies on seven key practices: (a) creating a caring relationship; (b) providing a safe environment; (c) establishing the core conditions of empathy, genuineness, and unconditional positive regard (Rogers, 1957); (d) engaging the child in child-centered play; (e) providing limits in play; (f) using active listening to facilitate children's emotional growth; and (g) supporting child associates (i.e., individuals implementing the play-based intervention) through supervisory sessions with a school mental health professional. In Primary Project, the overarching practice for helping children to become better adjusted to school rests within the child associate's ability to provide a physically and emotionally safe environment through the creation of a warm, caring relationship. The child associate does not provide therapy to the child; rather, Cowen et al. (1996) suggested that the child associates work with the naturally therapeutic elements of a warm and trusting relationship to help a children become better adjusted to the school culture.

PRIMARY PROJECT

Primary Project seeks to enhance and maximize children's school adjustment and other related competencies and to reduce social, emotional, and school adjustment difficulties in preschool through third grade. It is intended for children with emerging school adjustment problems in the mild-to-moderate range and not for children with crystallized, serious concerns. Carefully selected and trained paraprofessionals (i.e., child associates) provide timely, effective help to these children through the mediation of play. What is viewed as a simple construct, however, is one that has been evolving and refined over 55 years.

Schools are important settings for implementing preventive interventions for several reasons. An increasing number of children arrive at school each day with social and emotional needs that affect their ability to learn (Adelman & Taylor, 2006). It is estimated that 70% to 80% of mental health services received by children are provided in schools (Farmer, Burns, Phillips, Angold, & Costello, 2003). If young children do not receive effective interventions, serious consequences that affect learning, social competence, and lifelong health may continue to result (National Scientific Council on the Developing Child, 2008). Young children frequently are referred for mental health services because of difficulties adjusting to the school environment (e.g., classroom behavior, peer relationships). Although some prevention programs primarily aim at changing individual children's behavior, others aim at changing the environment (e.g., instruction strategies, classroom management plans, school climate). Targeting multiple systems by simultaneously enhancing children's competence and promoting effective behavior interactions across school and home settings was identified as a key characteristic of successful school-based prevention programs (Greenberg, Domitrovich, & Bumbarger, 2001).

Primary Project, targeted primarily to young children, uses school-based staff as primary agents of the intervention. The school mental health professional, who supervises the program, is also part of the school structure and, therefore, has a natural consultative relationship with teachers and school administrators. For this reason, school personnel, including teachers and administrators, tend to buy in and feel a sense of "ownership" of the prevention program, which leads them to promote successful referrals to families and high participation levels.

Key Treatment Ingredients

Primary Project has been developed around six structural components, each of which contributes to the program's success:

1. focus on young children;
2. early screening and selection;
3. use of paraprofessionals to provide direct services to children;
4. role change of the school-based mental health professional;
5. ongoing program evaluation; and
6. integration into the school.

Focus on Young Children

Because Primary Project aims to prevent school adjustment difficulties, the delivery of services targets young children in preschool through third grade. With the explosion of research in neuroscience, attachment, early childhood education, and infant/early childhood mental health, it is clear that the earlier the positive mental and physical health of young children and their families can be supported, the better the outcome. Therefore, Primary Project focuses on children from preschool to around age 8 years, or third grade.

Early Screening and Selection

The systematic screening of all children in the target age groups facilitates the consideration of all children for participation in Primary Project. It is particularly helpful in differentiating children who can benefit most from prevention and those needing more intensive intervention. This universal screening also meets response-to-intervention (RtI) screening needs. Data-driven information assists school teams in identifying children who display behavioral and social–emotional difficulties and in guiding decisions regarding appropriate interventions and/or services.

Primary Project targets children who are beginning to show signs of early adjustment difficulties (see Figure 1.1). Although this figure appears to represent four discrete levels of adjustment, those levels are more continuous than discrete. The figure conveys the notion that most children (i.e., those in the lower section of the triangle) are adequately adjusted to school. Next,

Which Children?

Figure 1.1. Primary Project's target population.

it depicts a group of children in whom mild-to-moderate school adjustment problems are evident. These are students like Sarah, who is beginning to show signs that affect her academic and social engagement. These are the youngsters for whom Primary Project services are most appropriate. The third group has more difficulties and is ordinarily served by school mental health professionals. The top group, by far the smallest, depicts children who already have been identified with specific diagnoses and who are—or should be— receiving help through the school's special education system or from clinical mental health professionals.

Use of Paraprofessionals to Provide Direct Services to Children

Primary Project uses carefully selected and trained paraprofessionals (i.e., child associates) to provide direct services to identified children. They work under the direct supervision of certified school mental health professionals. Schools typically seek to identify qualified adults from within the local community because those adults can often provide optimal services to children when they share a similar social, cultural, and racial background, and values and goals. However, more critical factors in the child associate selection are a willingness to enter into a child-centered relationship with young children and an understanding of the social, emotional, behavioral, and school climate needs that affect children.

Child associates are central to the effectiveness of any Primary Project program. Their ability to enter into a meaningful relationship with children is supported and strengthened through ongoing training and supervision by professionally trained mental health personnel. The supervisor becomes the ongoing supporter and facilitator of professional development for the child associate. Initial and ongoing training prepares associates to provide developmentally appropriate, effective intervention services to children. Central to the training are child-centered play and the way in which play mediates the child–associate relationship. In addition to addressing the program's core components, the training program covers topics, such as play and young children, communication skills, effective limit-setting strategies, and cultural and ethnic/racial differences.

The number of children a child associate sees depends on the number of hours that associate works. A part-time (15–20 hours per week) child associate can see 10 to 15 children in a week and have sufficient time for participation in training, supervision, and completion of necessary documents related to program implementation. When feasible, schools have two full-time associates who see a combined 50 to 60 children in a school year.

During a typical school year, schools provide two cycles of 12 to 15 sessions each. Although the intent is to select children who may need only one cycle, occasionally some children may need more sessions. This decision is made on an individual child basis, thus ensuring that if a child needs more intensive services by the school or community mental health system, the child is moved into that level of service and is not kept in Primary Project.

Role Change of the School-Based Mental Health Professional

The role change of the mental health professional to supervisor is another critical program component. These professionals are typically counselors, social workers, or school psychologists. This shift in role requires professionals to increase their clinical supervision, training, and oversight of the Primary Project by focusing their attention on the prevention side of services through their direct work with the child associate. As a result, they can redirect their clinical skills to work with the children who need more intensive intervention. In this way, the effect of their work is geometrically expanded to include a larger number of children.

Ongoing Program Evaluation

Ongoing program evaluation is built into Primary Project. From screening, to pre- and postmeasures, and to reports at the child, class, and school levels, evaluation and data-driven accountability are embedded into Primary Project. Because schools are increasingly relying on data and evidence-based interventions, this component is valuable. All measures and evaluation reports are easily available online, and technical assistance is available to ensure that schools not only collect data but also understand the data so that the schools may continuously improve services to children.

Integration Into the School

Primary Project is not a stand-alone program, and efforts are continuously made to ensure integration into the continuum of services available to children, including normalizing the concepts of school adjustment, and promoting healthy social and emotional wellness as effortlessly as for physical health. Schools integrate Primary Project in numerous ways: involvement at parent open houses, on website pages, in school newsletter columns, and through consideration as an intervention as part of a school's RtI model.

DESCRIPTION OF PRIMARY PROJECT INTERVENTION

Program Services Screening and Selection

The process of child selection starts with procedures to screen children from preschool to third grade to identify those who would benefit from Primary Project. Children experiencing adaptive or interpersonal problems—such as acting out; being mild aggressive, shy, anxious, or withdrawn; and having learning behaviors that interfere with educational progress in school—are typically appropriate for Primary Project. Children may be identified and referred to Primary Project via formal and informal processes, such as the use of behavior rating scales, observation, and/or referral.

The screening process begins with a collection of information 4 to 6 weeks after school starts, which allows time for children to settle into their new environment. This process often is deferred a few months so that kindergarten children may stabilize after their first school experiences. When teachers and other school personnel have some concerns about specific children, they share them at any time with the Primary Project team. Informal information is used to better understand the child's needs. In addition, classroom teachers complete a standardized screening measure, usually the Teacher–Child Rating Scale 2.1 (T–CRS; Perkins & Hightower, 2002). The T–CRS, a behavior rating scale designed specifically for teachers to assess children's school behaviors, consists of 32 items that assess four primary domains of a child's socioemotional adjustment:

1. *Task orientation:* a child's ability to focus on school related tasks.
2. *Behavior control:* a child's skill in adapting and tolerating limits imposed by the school environment or the child's own limitations.
3. *Assertiveness:* a child's interpersonal functioning and confidence in dealing with peers.
4. *Peer social skills:* A child's likeability and popularity among peers, and the child's ability to interact with peers.

The T–CRS serves as a screening measure and as a pre- and postmeasure to evaluate intervention progress. Relevant information is gathered from the T–CRS to identify children who will most likely benefit from involvement in Primary Project and areas of concern.

Selection and Assignment Conferences

Relevant screening data (T–CRS, observation, and teacher report) are reviewed during assignment conferences, which usually start in mid-October and are conducted in ways that best fit the school operation procedures. Primary Project staff, participating teachers, and other relevant school personnel review the assembled information, create composite sketches of children's school adjustment, and identify children who seem most appropriate for Primary Project services. In essence, during the conference, the team reviews the adjustment profile of children identified through the screening process as having some difficulties in school. Based on a child's current level of functioning (i.e., competencies and problems), the team makes recommendations, including Primary Project, to address the child's needs. After children have been identified for participation in Primary Project and the Primary Project team has agreed on that identification, written parental consent for the child's participation is obtained. For example, Sarah was identified during the screening process. Her parents were aware that she was having difficulty in school. They had stayed in contact with Mrs. Smith during the first weeks of school and had worked to support Sarah at home. They were not surprised when Mrs. Smith called and suggested that she participate in Primary Project.

Once parental permission is obtained, an adjustment profile is used to establish goals in collaboration with the teacher, the mental health professional, and, in many schools, the child's parent. Program goals include a dual focus on enhancing competencies and addressing problems. For example, goals for an individual child might include enhancing peer social skills, decreasing the child's aggression through the development of prosocial means of anger expression (i.e., anger identification, developing language for feelings), and increasing frustration tolerance.

WORKING WITH THE CHILDREN THROUGH EXPRESSIVE PLAY

Fundamental to Primary Project is the establishment of a positive, warm, trusting, therapeutic relationship between the child associate and the child through the medium of play. After initial training and selection of children for Primary Project, child associates begin to see children regularly. Children are typically scheduled for weekly, 30-minute individual sessions for a cycle of 12 to 15 weeks—typically one school semester. Depending on the child's needs and the program goals for that child, some children may go through a second cycle (i.e., semester) of sessions. Child associates meet with children in specially equipped playrooms that provide age- and culturally appropriate toys or expressive play medium. Toys and materials within a playroom may include various art supplies, such as crayons, markers, paper, and paints, as well as family dolls, a dollhouse, action figures, a sand table, building blocks, and Lego blocks. Materials should offer opportunities for creative and imaginary play, and they generally facilitate the expression of a child's feelings and thoughts. The playroom provides a safe, welcoming, and supportive environment in which the child and adult can interact.

In a Primary Project session, the child typically engages in self-directed expressive play and sets the pace of the interaction with the child associate. The associate's roles are to support the child's activities using basic listening skills; reflect child's actions, thoughts, and feelings; show acceptance and empathy; and engage in child-led play. The child associate is an active participant in the relationship, but it is the child who regulates the intensity of his or her participation. Child associates have to be flexible in the playroom—to be able to enter into the child's play but not simply as playmates. It is appropriate for a child to direct the child associate in the role he or she wants the associate to take on, within reasonable limits. However, a child associate occasionally may want to capitalize on a particular moment to build skills in a child's specific area of need. Because each child brings his or her uniqueness into the self-directed expressive play activities, it is impossible to convey exact, scripted sessions.

After a child has participated in Primary Project for one cycle, conferences are scheduled to assess the child's progress in meeting program goals. Parents may be invited to attend these meetings. Decisions are made regarding the extent to which goals have been reached and/or need to be changed. If program goals are met, graduation from the program is planned.

Case Example

Sarah followed the traditional pattern of a child participating in Primary Project. She spent time each week with her child associate. For Sarah, this became a safe place for 30 minutes a week when she would have an adult's undivided attention. Within 4 to 5 weeks, her teachers reported that she was beginning to take small risks, such as initiating conversations, raising her hand in class to answer questions, and asserting her needs appropriately. Requests to visit the nurse significantly decreased. Primary Project gave Sarah the opportunity to build another positive school-based relationship and receive the individual attention she needed. Within a few weeks after Primary Project, Sarah began looking forward to school again and increasingly began to positively engage in learning tasks and peer interactions.

SUPERVISION AND TRAINING OF CHILD ASSOCIATES

Because great care is taken to hire child associates with skills and characteristics that provide effective helping services for children, training is intended to build on these positive qualities. Orientation and initial training activities are focused and time limited. The specifics depend in part on a child associate's background experience and needs. Training is designed to impart information and skills that facilitate work with children in a school environment and to clarify basic procedures and intervention strategies. Supporting child associates through supervision by mental health professionals has been considered a necessary component of Primary Project. This process begins with the entrance of a child associate into the program and continues until each associate separates from the project.

Primary Project recognizes two major areas of reflective supervision in work with child associates: child-centered and child associate–centered supervision. *Child-centered supervision* refers to the individual children with whom the associates meet. Primary Project supervisors review the child associates' work with the children; help the associates understand the children's words, behaviors, and feelings; and offer them specific direction in their weekly work with the children in their caseload. *Child associate–centered supervision* focuses on each child associate. Primary Project supervisors explore the child associates' understanding of children's adjustment and mental health issues, and the effect that these difficulties have on children. They offer advice and guidance to each associate as that associate evolves in his or her role emotionally and cognitively. A 2-day supervision of paraprofessionals in Primary Project is offered to all Primary Project supervisors.

GRADUATION FROM PRIMARY PROJECT

Most children will exit Primary Project as a natural course of events. On occasion, some children will transition to more intensive helping services. Whatever the case, a clear transition is important. Approximately 3 weeks before termination, the process of saying goodbye begins.

Case Example

Sarah was told by her child associate from the beginning that they would spend 12 to 15 times together. Around the eighth session, the associate reminded Sarah that her time in the playroom would soon end. After that session, to help with the transition process, the child associate reminded Sarah each week how many times were remaining. A final teacher–parent conference with the child associate was held to describe Sarah's progress to her parents. All agreed that Primary Project had positively affected her behavior, including fewer visits to the nurse. Sarah's parents reported that she was more excited about going to school than earlier.

EVALUATING STUDENT PROGRESS

Children's progress in Primary Project is measured formally and informally. A child's progress is discussed through ongoing individual supervision and in meetings with the classroom teacher. Some programs incorporate a teacher progress report. More formal progress is measured by conducting pre- and post-assessments with the T–CRS and by determining behavior changes.

Case Example

At the conclusion of Sarah's time in Primary Project, Mrs. Smith completed the T–CRS and the school psychologist, who also was the child associate's supervisor, completed a professional summary report. Sarah met her goal of increasing her participation in the classroom and had become more engaged in school. In addition, analysis of the final teacher's rating scale showed positive change in assertiveness and peer social skills.

OUTCOME STUDIES

There is general consensus among experts that Primary Project is an exemplary practice that is based on decades of evaluation and research. It has been recognized at multiple state and national organizational levels (Children's Institute, Inc., 2015). In 1984, the National Mental Health Association awarded Primary Project the Lela Rowland Prevention Award. Four years later, Primary Project was designated as a validated program under New York State's Sharing Successful Programs. In 1993, the American Psychological Association's Section on Clinical and Child Psychology (Section I of the Division of Clinical Psychology) and the Division of Child, Youth, and Family Services awarded Primary Project with the Model Program for Service Delivery for Child and Family Mental Health.

Primary Project was highlighted as an exemplary practice in *Primary Prevention Works* (Albee & Gullotta, 1997), in *Successful Prevention Programs for Children and Adolescents* (Durlak, 1997), and in *Establishing Preventive Services* (Weissberg, Gullotta, Hampton, Ryan, & Adams, 1997). The U.S. Surgeon General's Report on Mental Health (U.S. Public Health Service,

2000) recognized Primary Project as one of the five exemplary research-based prevention programs in the nation for enhancing children's mental health. In 2000, the U.S. Department of Education's Office of Safe and Drug-Free Schools named Primary Project a Promising Program. Primary Project is also listed as an evidenced-based program with the National Registry of Evidence-Based Programs and Practices (Substance Abuse and Mental Health Services Administration, 2012), which includes information about program dissemination, training, and research. As evidence-based programs grow in number, program fidelity becomes a concern.

Primary Project has a national certification process that uses a quantifiable rubric: Certification is based on 3 years' implementation. A national review team evaluates the school's ability to meet the following requirements: systematic screening and review of children; length of children's participation in the program; selection and training of child associates; consistent supervision; appropriate space for the program; active support from administration, teachers, support staff, and community; and a strong commitment to program and child evaluation. In addition, manualized resources and DVDs on supervision and the intervention, and a program development manual (see Replication and Transportability) are available.

Research on Primary Project that started when the program was initially adopted in 1957 has been a continuing, essential part of the program's fabric. Tests of Primary Project's effectiveness as a prevention program have used several evaluation designs. Each has strengths (i.e., methodological or ecological) that provide complementary evidence about program efficacy (Cowen et al., 1996), including a composite evaluation for seven consecutive annual cohorts (Weissberg, Cowen, Lotyczewski, & Gesten, 1983). Primary Project's research efforts have involved the study of elements beyond outcomes, such as factors in children that relate to good and poor school adjustment, specific program elements, and the relationship between the associate–child and associate–supervisor relationship (Cowen & Hightower, 1989; Cowen et al., 1996).

Interest in Primary Project has been renewed, and research studies in various stages include a retrospective review of state adoption of and support for Primary Project, implementation of Primary Project by behavioral health agencies working with school districts, principal mental health supervisors and associates' perspectives on Primary Project, and a randomized controlled study of the intervention.

Evaluation Designs

Controlled Studies

Duerr (1993) randomly assigned children from 18 schools into immediate intervention and delayed treatment groups. Using standard comparison techniques for this design, the study found that children who received Primary Project services relative to those awaiting services showed statistically significant decreases in adjustment problems, such as lower aggression, fewer learning problems, and increased social–emotional competencies, (e.g., frustration tolerance, peer relations). Another evaluation of Primary Project that used a wait-list control design found statistically significant differences between children in an immediate intervention group and those in a wait-list control group (Nafpaktitis & Perlmutter, 1998). These gains were maintained at 3-month follow-up based on teacher ratings.

Comparison Designs

Winer Elkin, Weissberg, and Cowen (1988) evaluated adjustment between children receiving Primary Project services and comparably at-risk children in schools without Primary Project services, and tracked their adjustment over time. Their study compared children in the Primary Project model who received an average of 25 forty-minute contacts over a 5- to 6-month period, and children with similar initial adjustment status identified in non–Primary Project schools. Primary Project–served children were shown, after a school year, to make decreases in adjustment problems and increases in adaptive competencies compared with comparison children. These results were statistically significant.

Longer Term Follow-Up of Primary Project Children

Chandler, Weissberg, Cowen, and Guare (1984) evaluated 61 urban children who had participated 2 to 5 years earlier in the Primary Project model, with 61 matched to the Primary Project sample by gender, grade level, and current teacher. Adjustment ratings by children's current classroom teachers confirmed that children seen in the Primary Project model had, 2 to 5 years later, maintained their initial adjustment gains.

Primary Project was introduced into several elementary schools in Community School District 4 in the East Harlem section of New York City. The implementation of the Primary Project model for children in kindergarten through third grade was evaluated over a 4-year period. Results were that participating children had more positive school adjustment (i.e., fewer adjustment problems, greater competencies) after 1 year in the program (Meller, Laboy, Rothwax, Fritton, & Mangual, 1994). Moreover, children's self-ratings of adjustment showed statistically significant increases in rule compliance, school interest, peer acceptance, and decreased anxiety.

Ongoing Site-Based Evaluations

Evaluations of Primary Project program sites in New York and California included comparison of children's classroom adjustment problems and competencies at referral to and graduation from the program. This method made possible an ecologically valid assessment of children's adjustment status in large numbers of school sites. During the 1997 to 1998 school year, evaluation of children in the New York State Primary Project included more than 1,500 children in 50 schools. These Primary Project sites provided more than 15,000 preventive-focused contacts to children. Overall, 82% of these children had adjustment problems before referral that placed them at "high" or "moderate high" risk. Mental health staff reported that 60% of Primary Project children showed reductions in aggressive behavior and had improved social skills, and 50% had better academic performance (Hightower, 1998).

Replication and Transportability

The Primary Project model has been described in numerous publications, including peer-reviewed journals and books. Primary Project's development and evaluation were summarized in *School-Based Prevention for Children at Risk: The Primary Mental Health Project* (Cowen et al., 1996). A second comprehensive source of information about the Primary Project model and how it can be implemented and evaluated is found in *The Primary Mental Health Project: Program Development Manual* (Johnson, Peabody, & Demanchick, 2013). The key structural components of Primary Project allow for adaptation to local districts/sites while retaining the flexibility to meet the uniqueness of the individual setting. These components make Primary Project applicable to a broad range of children and communities.

Primary Project model programs have been established successfully in 130 school districts across New York State. Nationally, centralized networks of programs in more than 1,000 school districts (Children's Institute, Inc., 2012) have been established: California (Primary Intervention Program), Connecticut (Primary Mental Health Project), Hawaii (Primary School Adjustment Program), Washington (Primary Intervention Program), Arkansas, Florida, Kentucky, Maine, Massachusetts, Michigan, Minnesota, Missouri, and Washington, DC. Primary Project is coordinated in California through the Department of Mental Health via the Early Mental Health Initiatives and in Connecticut, Hawaii, and New York through the Departments of Education. International programs exist in Canada and Nigeria. The newest development in the story of Primary Project implementation is expansion into preschools, Head Start, and child development centers.

Support to districts and sites interested in implementing Primary Project is available through multiple venues: consultation, training, program materials, and internship opportunities. Program materials include *School-Based Prevention for Children at Risk: The Primary Mental Health Project* (Cowen, et al., 1996),

The Primary Mental Health Project: Program Development Manual (Johnson et al., 2013), *Creating Connections: Primary Project* (Children's Institute, Inc., 2012), *Screening and Evaluation Guidelines* (Children's Institute, Inc., 2002), *Primary Project: The Intervention: Basic Skills* (Children's Institute Inc., 2006a), *Supervision Manual* (Children's Institute Inc., 2006b), and *T–CRS 2.1 Teacher–Child Rating Scale Examiner's Manual* (Perkins & Hightower, 2002). On-site consultation and support are available through Children's Institute, Inc., program consultants, and a list of training workshops for state and national programs is available on http://www.childrensinstitute.net.

CONCLUSION

Primary Project is a time-tested early intervention program that helps young children adjust to school during the early years. It has been refined over the past 55 years to a model that is transferable across settings and with children from varied backgrounds and communities. Equally successful in urban, suburban, and rural school districts, Primary Project continues to identify and serve children with mild adjustment difficulties at an early age in an effort to promote social and emotional competence.

Programs with the strongest results adhere to the six key components, with particular emphasis on high-quality child associates who receive systematic training and support from quality mental health professionals. Child-centered play is essential to the ongoing training of child associates. Although the environmental demands and pressures for young children have changed over the years, a deep need for time, attention, and expressive play has not.

REFERENCES

Adelman, H. S., & Taylor, L. (2006). *The school leader's guide to student learning supports: New directions for addressing barriers to learning.* Thousand Oaks, CA: Corwin Press.

Albee, G. W., & Gullotta, T. P. (1997). *Primary prevention works.* Thousand Oaks, CA: Sage.

Axline, V. M. (1969). *Play therapy* (Rev. ed.). New York, NY: Ballantine Books.

Chandler, C. L., Weissberg, R. P., Cowen, E. L., & Guare, J. (1984). Long-term effects of a school-based secondary prevention program for young maladapting children. *Journal of Consulting and Clinical Psychology, 52*, 165–170. http://dx.doi.org/10.1037/0022-006X.52.2.165

Children's Institute, Inc. (2002). *Screening and evaluation guidelines.* Rochester, NY: Author.

Children's Institute, Inc. (2006a). *Primary Project: The intervention: Basic skills.* Rochester, NY: Author.

Children's Institute, Inc. (2006b). *Primary Project: Supervision manual.* Rochester, NY: Author.

Children's Institute, Inc. (2012). *Creating connections: Primary Project* [DVD]. Rochester, NY: Author.

Children's Institute, Inc. (2015). *Primary Project.* Retrieved from https://www.childrens institute.net/programs/primary-project

Cowen, E. L., & Hightower, A. D. (1989). The Primary Mental Health Project: Alternatives in school based preventive interventions. In T. B. Gutkin & C. R. Reynolds (Eds.), *Handbook of school psychology* (2nd ed., pp. 775–795). New York, NY: Wiley.

Cowen, E. L., Hightower, A. D., Pedro-Carroll, J. L., Work, W. C., & Wyman, P. A. (1996). *School-based prevention for children at risk: The Primary Mental Health Project.* Washington, DC: American Psychological Association. http://dx.doi.org/10.1037/10209-000

Duerr, M. (1993). *Early mental health initiative: Year-end evaluation report.* Chico, CA: Duerr Evaluation Resources.

Durlak, J. A. (1997). *Successful prevention programs for children and adolescents.* New York, NY: Plenum Press. http://dx.doi.org/10.1007/978-1-4899-0065-4

Edwards, V. J., Anda, R. F., Dube, S. R., Dong, M., Chapman, D. F., & Felitti, V. J. (2005). The wide-ranging health consequences of adverse childhood experiences. In K. Kendall-Tackett & S. Giacomoni (Eds.), *Child victimization: Maltreatment, bullying, and dating violence prevention and intervention* (pp. 8.1–8.2). Kingston, NJ: Civic Research Institute.

Farmer, E. M. Z., Burns, B. J., Phillips, S. D., Angold, A., & Costello, E. J. (2003). Pathways into and through mental health services for children and adolescents. *Psychiatric Services, 54,* 60–66. http://dx.doi.org/10.1176/appi.ps.54.1.60

Greenberg, M. T., Domitrovich, C., & Bumbarger, D. (2001). The prevention of mental disorders in school-aged children: Current state of the field. *Prevention & Treatment, 4,* 1–59. http://dx.doi.org/10.1037/1522-3736.4.1.41a

Hightower, A. D. (1998). *Primary Project annual report to the New York State Education Department.* Rochester, NY: Children's Institute, Inc.

Johnson, D. B., Peabody, M. A., & Demanchick, S. (2013). *The Primary Mental Health Project: Program development manual.* Rochester, NY: Children's Institute, Inc.

Koller, J. R., & Bertel, J. M. (2006). Responding to today's mental health needs of children, families and schools: Revisiting the preservice training and preparation of school-based personnel. *Education & Treatment of Children, 29,* 197–217.

Meller, P. J., Laboy, W., Rothwax, Y., Fritton, J., & Mangual, J. (1994). *Community school district four: Primary Mental Health Project, 1990–1994.* New York, NY: Community School District #4.

Miller, E., & Almon, J. (2009). *Crisis in the kindergarten: Why children need to play in school.* College Park, MD: Alliance for Childhood.

Nafpaktitis, M., & Perlmutter, B. F. (1998). School-based early mental health intervention with at-risk students. *School Psychology Review, 27*, 420–432.

National Research Council and Institute of Medicine. (2009). *Preventing mental, emotional, and behavioral disorders among young people: Progress and possibilities* (Report Brief). Washington, DC: National Academies Press.

National Scientific Council on the Developing Child. (2008). *Mental health problems in early childhood can impair learning and behavior for life* (Working Paper No. 6). Retrieved from http://www.developingchild.net

Perkins, P. E., & Hightower, A. D. (2002). *T–CRS 2.1 teacher–child rating scale examiner's manual*. Rochester, NY: Children's Institute, Inc.

Rogers, C. R. (1951). *Client-centered therapy: Its current practice, implications, and theory*. Boston, MA: Houghton Mifflin.

Rogers, C. R. (1957). The necessary and sufficient conditions of therapeutic personality change. *Journal of Consulting Psychology, 21*, 95–103. http://dx.doi.org/10.1037/h0045357

Shonkoff, J. P., & Levitt, P. (2010). Neuroscience and the future of early childhood policy: Moving from why to what and how. *Neuron, 67*, 689–691.

Simpson, G. A., Bloom, B., Cohen, R. A., & Blumberg, S. (2005, June 23). U.S. children with emotional and behavioral difficulties: Data from the 2001, 2002, and 2003 National Health Interview surveys. In *Advance data from vital and health statistics* (No. 360). Hyattsville, MD: National Center for Health Statistics.

Substance Abuse and Mental Health Services Administration. (2012). *National Registry of Evidence-Based Programs and Practices*. Retrieved from http://www.nrepp.samhsa.gov/ViewIntervention.aspx?id=39

U.S. Public Health Service. (2000). *Report of the Surgeon General's conference on children's mental health: A national action agenda*. Washington, DC: U.S. Department of Health and Human Services.

Wasserman, G. A., Keenan, K., Tremblay, R. E., Cole, J. D., Herrenkohl, T. I., Loeber, R., & Petechuk, D. (2003, April). Risk and protective factors of child delinquency. In *Child Delinquency Bulletin Series* (No. NCJ 193409). Washington, DC: U.S. Department of Justice, Office of Juvenile Justice and Delinquency Prevention.

Weissberg, R. P., Cowen, E. L., Lotyczewski, B. S., & Gesten, E. L. (1983). The primary mental health project: Seven consecutive years of program outcome research. *Journal of Consulting and Clinical Psychology, 51*, 100–107. http://dx.doi.org/10.1037/0022-006X.51.1.100

Weissberg, R. P., Gullotta, T. P., Hampton, R. L., Ryan, B. A., & Adams, G. R. (1997). *Establishing preventive services* (Vol. 9). Thousand Oaks, CA: Sage.

Winer Elkin, J. I., Weissberg, R. P., & Cowen, E. L. (1988). Evaluation of a planned short-term intervention for school children with focal adjustment problems. *Journal of Clinical Child Psychology, 17*, 106–115. http://dx.doi.org/10.1207/s15374424jccp1702_1

2

EXTENDING THE GLOBAL REACH OF A PLAY-BASED INTERVENTION FOR CHILDREN DEALING WITH SEPARATION AND DIVORCE

JOANNE PEDRO-CARROLL AND MARISKA KLEIN VELDERMAN

This chapter describes the process of translating, adapting, and disseminating the Children of Divorce Intervention Program (CODIP), a play-based preventive intervention developed in the United States, to fit the needs of young children in the Netherlands who are dealing with parental separation and divorce. The chapter describes goals, objectives, and key components of the intervention and offers detailed examples of play activities and approaches tailored to the cultural and developmental characteristics of young Dutch children. Results of the pilot project in the Netherlands replicate outcomes found in controlled studies of CODIP in the United States. Implications for replication and global transportability are discussed.

http://dx.doi.org/10.1037/14730-003
Empirically Based Play Interventions for Children, Second Edition, L. A. Reddy, T. M. Files-Hall, and C. E. Schaefer (Editors)

WHY USE A PLAY-BASED APPROACH?

Play is a fundamental underpinning of prevention programs to promote children's well-being. Primary Project (formerly known as the Primary Mental Health Project), a school-based program to reduce school adjustment problems and promote children's social and emotional well-being, has effectively used play-based approaches to build trusting relationships between children and caring adults since its inception in 1957. Studies have demonstrated the enduring benefits of Primary Project on children's social and emotional adjustment and school engagement (Cowen, Hightower, Pedro-Carroll, Work, & Wyman, 1996; Johnson, Pedro-Carroll, & Demanchik, 2005).

Preventive intervention programs using play-based approaches are an effective format for reducing the stress of marital disruption on children and teaching skills to foster resilience (Pedro-Carroll, 2010). The CODIP is based on shared group support and skills to build and enhance children's capacity to cope effectively with family changes. A sense of safety and shared support is fostered in the groups to give children their "voice" through a variety of interactive play activities, including drawing, puppet play, and therapeutic games. Other international programs use play-based activities in a group setting for children to share feelings and experiences about family changes (Arifoglu, 2006; Cloutier, Filion, & Timmermans, 2012; Klein Velderman, Heinrich, et al., 2011; Marzotto & Bonadonna, 2011). Studies have documented the effectiveness of puppets and games in therapeutic work with children (Burroughs, Wagner, & Johnson, 1997; Pedro-Carroll & Jones, 2005). In CODIP, puppets serve as safe, nonthreatening characters for children to project common divorce-related scenarios and problems to solve. Specially designed games are used in CODIP to promote key program goals and to foster resilience skills and emotional intelligence.

Play-based approaches are ideal for helping children deal with stressful life experiences. The Sesame Workshop, creators of the well-known *Sesame Street* program for young children, launched a resilience project to help children deal with major stressful life events, such as bullying, parental incarceration, parent deployment in the military and separation and divorce (see http://www.sesamestreet.org/parents/topicsandactivities/toolkits/divorce). In a DVD created to help children understand divorce, Muppet characters portray the feelings and concerns young children have about family changes, and demonstrate models of effective coping and examples of resilience skills. In a sensitive and engaging format for young children, Abby Cadabby draws a picture of her two homes. When Muppet friend Elmo sees it, he is puzzled, and Abby explains, in age-appropriate terms, why she has two homes and what divorce means. With these endearing Muppets as coping models, children learn to understand what separation and divorce does mean (i.e., parents have grown-up problems that they could not fix) and does not mean (that she was the cause of the problems).

Family changes such as parent separation and divorce are stressful for children of all ages. Play-based approaches help to make a potentially painful topic more manageable and empower children with a sense of security, competence, and mastery at a time when their world feels shaky and uncertain.

EFFECT OF DIVORCE ON CHILDREN

The risks of divorce know no national boundaries. A large body of research is based on populations in the United States, but other studies have confirmed similar results in Canada, Australia, New Zealand, and Europe. Collectively, these studies have demonstrated that the stresses associated with divorce for children extend across countries and cultures, and in families in every economic bracket; they have shown a link between family structure and psychological adjustment.

Research in the United States confirms that divorce poses specific risks for children socially, emotionally, and academically (Amato, 2000). Large-scale studies have revealed that 10% of children in nondivorced families had severe psychological and social problems. The rate climbed to 20% to 25%—more than double—for children in divorced families (Hetherington & Kelly, 2002). Although not as common as behavior problems, significantly higher rates of anxiety and depression have been found in children from divorced families (Pedro-Carroll, 2010). Often, more internalized difficulties in children go unnoticed in the midst of so many competing demands on even the most attentive parents. All too often, children feel isolated, alone, and "different" from their peers from nondivorced homes. They lack the comfort of knowing that others share their experiences, emotions, and challenges. It was out of an awareness of this need for support and skills to deal with the challenges of family changes that the CODIP was developed.

THEORETICAL BASIS AND OBJECTIVES OF CODIP

Key Treatment Ingredients for CODIP

CODIP is a selective preventive intervention program that is built on the assumption that timely intervention for children of divorce can offer important short- and long-term benefits.[1] CODIP is based on theories of play

---

[1]To purchase copies of the CODIP curricula, contact the Children's Institute, Inc., 274 N. Goodman Street, D103, Rochester, NY 14620 or visit https://www.childrensinstitute.net. For more information about CODIP research or about training and consultation on children and divorce, contact JoAnne Pedro-Carroll at jpcarroll4peace@gmail.com.

therapy, developmental psychology, stress and coping, resilience promotion, and theories of prevention that emphasize the importance of timely supportive outreach to reduce risk across systems that affect children. The program aims at creating a supportive group environment in which children can freely share experiences, establish common bonds, clarify misconceptions, and acquire skills that enhance their capacity to cope with the stressful changes that divorce often poses (Pedro-Carroll, 2005).

CODIP is based on research on risk and protective factors that shape children's adjustment to parent separation, divorce, and remarriage. Studies on risk and resilience in divorce research have provided an important understanding of why some children get back on track after an initial period of adjustment, whereas others struggle with long-term problems. Family factors that influence children's risk or resilience after divorce include parent conflict, parents' psychological well-being, quality of parenting, social support, and family stability (Pedro-Carroll, 2011). Individual child factors that influence adjustment over time are effective coping skills, emotion regulation, age-appropriate understanding of family changes, a realistic sense of control, and positive outlook and hope for the future (Pedro-Carroll, 2010). Many of these factors are incorporated in the CODIP, which has served more than 20,000 children since it began in 1982. Numerous studies have demonstrated that the skills and concepts taught in the program have made a significant improvement in children's adjustment at home and in school, in family and peer relations, in their feelings about themselves and their families, and in their hopes for their future (Pedro-Carroll, 2005). The program uses a combination of group support and resilience skills to address children's needs. The resilience skills described in this chapter have been shown to relate to children's healthy development—socially, emotionally, and academically. For more detailed information about program structure, inclusion criteria, and program objectives, see Pedro-Carroll and Jones (2005).

Program Structure

Groups are co-led by two trained group leaders. CODIP's success depends on their commitment and clinical skills. Their sensitivity and ability to establish a trusting environment and to encourage children's involvement in group activities contribute to the development of a cohesive group. Having two group leaders facilitates responses to sensitive issues, nonverbal cues, and behavior management problems.

Although CODIP is a child-focused program, parents are involved in all stages of the intervention. Before the start of the CODIP group sessions, parents are invited to attend an individual meeting with a group leader on the content of CODIP and common reactions that children experience. During the program, parents receive written resource information and suggestions for reducing the stress of a breakup on their children and ways to reinforce program objectives at home. Three newsletters are sent to parents during the program after the first, fifth, and last session; these newsletters detail ways in which parents can reinforce program objectives at home. At the end of the program, parents attend a one-on-one meeting with group leaders to discuss their child's progress and possible referral for additional family support.

Developmental Factors

CODIP content is tailored to variations in reactions that divorce predisposes in children of different ages. For example, issues of loyalty conflicts, anger, and feelings of stigma and isolation are more predominant responses among 9- to 12-year-olds, whereas sadness, confusion, guilt, and fears of abandonment are prominent among 6- to 8-year-olds. These differing clinical profiles indicate the need to shape the central themes and focal issues of interventions to the special attributes of particular age groups.

Four age-specific versions of CODIP have been developed: (a) versions for kindergarten and first grade, (b) second and third grade, (c) fourth through sixth grades, and (d) seventh and eighth grades. Although the goals and objectives embedded in these CODIP modules remain relatively constant, these versions contain varying topics and techniques according to the developmental differences of the four age groups.

Program Objectives

CODIP has five basic objectives that directly target negative child outcomes of parental divorce or separation.

1. Foster a Supportive Group Environment

A fundamental underpinning of CODIP groups is to provide a safe, supportive environment for children. Contact with peers who have gone through comparable experiences helps participating children to reduce their sense of isolation and develop a sense of shared support and trust. Fostering a comfortable atmosphere in which children can share experiences at their own pace and feel safe that what they say will be respected and kept confidential is a major objective from the first session to the last.

Depending on the age range, different techniques are used within the group process to foster supportive interactions and a sense of belonging. For example, in the first session with young children, a shy turtle hand puppet hesitantly emerges out of its shell, apprehensive and unsure about what to expect from the group. In our experience, young children enjoy being helpers, so group leaders request their assistance in helping the puppet (who is their age and whose parents are recently separated) to feel accepted and more comfortable with the group. They typically respond with suggestions ("Let's tell it our names and what we'll be doing in our group"; "Let's give him/her a name") and reassurances ("I wasn't sure what the group would be like, so I sort of feel like he does"). As group discussion continues and members share common likes and dislikes, favorite foods and TV shows, the puppet, often named Terri Turtle, also shares many of those interests and takes on the role of a group mascot. Thus, when important topics such as confidentiality and coping skills are discussed, the puppet takes an active role in sharing feelings, problems, ideas, and solutions.

2. Facilitate Identification and Appropriate Expression of Feelings

The stressful changes associated with parental divorce cause complex feelings that are difficult for children to identify and understand. Young children are especially vulnerable to being overwhelmed because of their limited cognitive understanding, verbal skills, and coping strategies. CODIP seeks to enhance participants' ability to identify and appropriately express a range of emotions that are associated with the divorce. Thus, group leaders maintain a safe environment in which all feelings are accepted. They carefully balance the need for children to express their feelings while moderating the dose of emotionally laden material with more neutral topics and experiences.

A variety of play techniques are used to help children identify a range of emotions, including the interactive use of books, pictures of facial expression, and the active participation of the group puppet. For example, in the "feelings charades" game, children take turns choosing cards depicting various emotions and silently act out the emotion while group members guess the feelings and share a time when they too felt that way. The group puppet actively participates in this activity and shares times when he has had a similar feeling or experience.

These games have multiple objectives. They help to develop empathy through and awareness and sensitivity to nonverbal signs of how another person feels, expand children's emotional vocabulary with a label for a variety of emotions, promote children's understanding of the universality of emotions, emphasize that all feelings are acceptable, and increase the children's awareness that feelings can change and they can learn healthy ways to help themselves feel better when they are upset.

3. Promote Accurate Understanding of Divorce-Related Concepts,
   and Correct Misconceptions

A third CODIP objective is to help children separate their strong divorce-related fears from reality. Feelings of guilt and responsibility for the separation pose an emotional burden for children, so correcting misconceptions is an essential part of the program. Structured puppet play and games are used extensively to clarify and correct misconceptions. The Daring Dinosaurs board game, developed specifically for CODIP, contains cards that reflect misconceptions children often have about the reasons for family problems; it offers opportunities for group discussion and puppet play to address common fears and problems.

4. Teach Relevant Skills to Enhance Children's Competence and Capacity to Cope

Although the support and solidarity that comes from sharing common experiences is important for children, enhancing coping skills is an equally essential component of this intervention model. Several CODIP sessions are devoted to teaching resilience skills, such as problem solving, communicating effectively, dealing with anger, and asking for help and support. Children are taught to differentiate between problems they can control and those they cannot. This key distinction helps them to master the psychological task of disengaging from interparental conflicts and to redirect their energies into age-appropriate pursuits.

A variety of games and play techniques are used to encourage practice, acquisition, and generalization of skills. Young children are drawn into discussions of problem scenarios and various solutions. They are taught to stop and think in these situations (e.g., "You want to watch your favorite show on TV, but your brother wants to watch something else. What can you do?"). In this way, they are eased naturally into learning relevant problem-solving skills and applying them to personal problems. A team-based Tic-Tac-Toe game helps children learn to generate alternative solutions, evaluate their consequences, and choose the most appropriate solutions to problems. Play-based activities such as the Red Light–Green Light game help children differentiate between favorable (green light) and less favorable (red light) solutions. Puppet play is used to depict common divorce-related problems, such as loyalty conflicts, being caught in the middle of parent conflict, and blended families. Group members then actively participate in generating alternative solutions to help the puppets deal effectively with those problem scenarios.

5. Enhance Children's Perceptions of Self and Family, and Reinforce Coping Skills

This final integrative program objective emphasizes the unique strengths of children and families. Children in the midst of stressful life changes often feel different and defective (e.g., "My friends might think there's something really wrong with me and my family"). Several exercises are used to highlight and reinforce children's unique qualities. For example, children complete an *I Am Special* book detailing their characteristics, likes, feelings, wishes, and contributions to the group. The goal of these activities is to heighten children's awareness of their strengths and the positive family changes that may have occurred.

Building children's resilience skills is so essential to the CODIP intervention that the board game Daring Dinosaurs was specially designed to foster children's sense of self-efficacy and assess their progress in understanding divorce-related issues and developing resilience skills. One of several therapeutic techniques used in the program, the game is designed to address emotion regulation, family and divorce-related issues, social problem solving, communication, and anger control skills, and to promote self-awareness and self-esteem. The game cards incorporated in the board game ask questions about children's thoughts (e.g., "Do you believe you can make your parents get back together?"), their feelings (e.g., "How do kids feel when their parents fight?"), and ways to self-soothe when feeling upset (e.g., "Act like you are feeling lonely. Name two things that you could do to feel better"). If a child cannot answer a question, other children and the group puppet are invited to help. The content of the cards covers most of the topics explored in the previous sessions. Blank cards are included with the game so that leaders can write individualized cards to reflect problems, situations, or feelings specific to their group. Leaders are encouraged to stack the deck so that the most relevant cards for the children in their group are placed on top.

Research on CODIP has provided a solid evidence base for the program's effectiveness with children of different ages and cultural and demographic backgrounds (Alpert-Gillis, Pedro-Carroll & Cowen, 1989; Pedro-Carroll & Alpert-Gillis, 1997; Pedro-Carroll, Alpert-Gillis, & Cowen, 1992; Pedro-Carroll & Cowen, 1985). A follow-up study confirmed that the benefits of CODIP endured for children in their adjustment to family changes, relationships with parents and peers, school engagement, and physical health (Pedro-Carroll, Sutton, & Wyman, 1999). Current research on implementation in other countries has suggested that the CODIP model can be transported effectively to other settings and populations (Arifoglu, 2006; Fthenakis, & Oberndorfer, 1993; Klein Velderman, Pannebakker, et al., 2011; Mireault, Drapreau, Faford, Lapointe, & Clotier, 1991; Pinto, 2008).

CODIP AND CODIP-NETHERLANDS: ADAPTING A PLAY-BASED INTERVENTION TO REDUCE THE NEGATIVE EFFECTS OF DIVORCE ON CHILDREN

The previous section described core components of the CODIP. Next, we focus on an adaptation of the program for 6- to 8-year-old children in the Netherlands, which is referred to in this chapter as CODIP-NL. The following sections describe how the program was modified for young Dutch children with play-based activities and also present implementation and outcome research.

Adaptations for CODIP-NL for 6- to 8-Year-Olds

In the Netherlands, an estimated 70,000 children are involved in parental divorce or separation each year (Spruijt & Kormos, 2014). Available support was highly fragmentized and spread across various organizations in 2007. Accordingly, there was a need for an evidence-based prevention program for children of divorce in the Netherlands, first and foremost for children younger than age 9. The U.S. CODIP was seen as having excellent potential to fill this Dutch lacuna and was the focus of a feasibility study by Klein Velderman, Pannebakker, et al. (2011). Objectives of that early work were to make the second- and third-grade module of CODIP applicable for 6- to 8-year-old Dutch children and to test it in a pilot study to determine the feasibility of national implementation.

The Original Second- and Third-Grade Module

The original U.S. second- and third-grade module of CODIP (Pedro-Carroll, Alpert-Gillis, & Sterling, 1997) consists of 15 weekly group sessions of 45 minutes each. These CODIP module sessions are organized in four primary parts: (a) establishment of the group, feelings, families, and family changes; (b) development of coping skills; (c) child–parent relationships; and (d) children's perceptions of themselves and their families. The module tends to work best with four to seven group members. The CODIP group leader manual provides information about program goals and implementation, including group leader training, group facilitation techniques, and group process issues. For each session, goals, procedures, and needed materials are listed in detail.

CODIP-NL

A first study stage (Klein Velderman, Pannebakker, et al., 2011) focused on the translation and adaptation of CODIP. Thorough translations of the well-developed CODIP program materials were the basis of a first Dutch version of the group leader manual and other written materials. First translations from English into Dutch were done as literally as possible. Some expressions were reconsidered or altered when a literal translation was inappropriate. To prevent a departure of the translated and adapted CODIP-NL from the core elements that constitute the effectiveness of the original program, the conceptual outline of the program was articulated. This outline highlighted theoretical principles of the program from which concrete program activities could be derived—using earlier publications about CODIP—and was developed in close collaboration with the first author of this chapter, Pedro-Carroll, founder and developer of CODIP in the United States. CODIP was to be adapted carefully to meet the characteristics of the Dutch user population, as long as the adaptations were consistent with the theories of change that constituted the original program.

The first versions of the Dutch program materials were designed on the basis of the translated materials and adhered to this conceptual outline. Program materials were designed to be attractive to intermediate users (i.e., organizations and professionals working with the program) as well as end users (i.e., participating children). Dutch alternatives to the children's books used in the original U.S. version of CODIP were sought or designed de novo.

Although CODIP can be implemented in a variety of settings, such as mental health centers, community centers, private practitioners' offices, after-school care programs, and court-connected service groups, schools are regarded as a natural setting for CODIP groups because of the accessibility of large numbers of children sharing similar experiences who can continue their supportive relationships after the groups end. Furthermore, school-based professionals are ideal candidates for group leaders because of the potential continuity of their contacts with program children and their families. However, when considering the size of elementary schools and divorce rates in the Netherlands, it was concluded that it was impossible to form groups of four to seven children in smaller Dutch elementary schools. Instead, Klein Velderman, Pannebakker, et al. (2011) focused on implementation in settings of preventive child mental health care. Prevention workers in these organizations have a higher educational degree (i.e., bachelor's, postgraduate) in the field of behavioral sciences, such as psychology, child and family studies, social work, or a related discipline. They have knowledge about normal and maladaptive cognitive and socioemotional development of children. They are experienced in conducting support groups for children of parents with psychiatric disorders.

Process Evaluation and Final Version of CODIP-NL

The concept version of CODIP-NL was tested in four pilot groups (Klein Velderman, Pannebakker, et al., 2011). Program materials and the intervention process were thoroughly evaluated. Participating children were enthusiastic about the intervention and especially the games and play materials. They liked the atmosphere in the group and mentioned several ways they had profited from the program. CODIP-NL helped them to understand their feelings and made them feel less alone with their family circumstances. Responses heard in the groups were: "I enjoyed being able to talk about things that have happened in my family." "I learned ways to solve problems." "Now I know that fights between my parents aren't my fault." One group leader mentioned a child in her group who had been extremely shy at first had now found the courage to do a class presentation about divorce that emphasized coping skills.

Parents of participating children also were enthusiastic about CODIP-NL. The majority agreed that their child had responded positively to participation in the program. Typical responses from parents were: "My daughter talks more . . . is spontaneous like she used to be, and expresses her feelings more"; and "My son now knows how to keep the divorce in perspective, and knows his father and mother will always be there for him."

Group leaders filled out logbooks during the intervention to report on program materials and intervention process. Leaders rated program materials as effective, engaging, and user friendly. Logbooks and focus group interviews provided specific suggestions for altering certain aspects of the program. Sessions of one of the groups had been interrupted by winter holidays, which led children to be more distracted from the focus of the intervention. Future planning will include this feedback and have sessions end before major holidays.

Half of the group leaders suggested a reduction in the number of sessions. For practical and financial reasons, the decision was considered in consultation with group leaders and Pedro-Carroll, thus resulting in a reduction from 15 to 12 sessions, 45 minutes each. Based on study results and careful clinical considerations of key program content, final changes were made in the program outline, supervision schedule, group leader training, and curriculum for the final (second) version of CODIP-NL for 6- to 8-year-old children (Klein Velderman, Heinrich, et al., 2011).

EXAMPLES OF TRANSCRIPTS AND MATERIALS

Hand Puppet Rex

As in the original version of CODIP (Pedro-Carroll et al., 1997), puppet play is used extensively in CODIP-NL (Klein Velderman, Heinrich, et al., 2011). For the trainers, this was a new but much appreciated way to work with children in groups. In CODIP-NL a dinosaur hand puppet called Rex is introduced from the first group session. The shy dinosaur rests in an egg, where he hesitantly emerges out (as in CODIP, starring the turtle hand puppet called Terri Turtle). Rex shares his family experience with the children: "I am Rex, a dinosaur, 7 years old. My parents and I all lived together in a cave. But my parents broke up [children typically interfere: "They got divorced!" or "That happened to me too!"] and now they live apart. My mum lives in the forest and my dad lives in a cave. I live with my mum, and sometimes I stay with my dad." Children get the opportunity to respond to this introduction. They can ask questions such as "Do you have any brothers or sisters?" or "Are you sad sometimes too?"

In Session 4, children are introduced to problem-solving skills. Rex is used to introduce an example: "When I was playing outside on the street, the neighbor's dog came running and barking at me. I ran inside and didn't dare to get back outside again. I am so scared when I think of the dog and his sharp teeth again!" The trainer reminds the children of the problem-solving steps: (a) "Who knows what the problem is? And the feeling this causes for Rex?" [Children respond]; (b) "Who knows how to help Rex? What are all the things he could he do to solve this problem?" [Children respond]. Rex replies by considering the consequences of each solution (i.e., the third step) and chooses the one that might work best. The puppets act out the solution to cheers and thumbs-up for the solutions that might work best and thumbs-down for behaviors that might make things worse.

Interactive Use of Books

Julia Has Two Houses *Book*

In the U.S. version of CODIP, a selection of reading and picture books are used interactively to engage children in discussion of key concepts and feelings. Instead of translating these books, an alternative was found that was well suited to the intervention: *Julia Has Two Houses* (Wisse Smit, 2008). It has chapters about living in two homes, difficult choices (e.g., missing mum or dad), visiting dad by train (moving back and forth), dad in love, and having a new baby brother. To generate discussion, the trainers can select sections from the book that are most relevant for their group.

Parents and the I Am Special *Book*

CODIP-NL now includes a parent meeting with group leaders to discuss information about children dealing with separation and divorce, and an overview of the program curriculum. In addition to these efforts to reach out to parents, the *I Am Special* book is an effective method for the group leaders to connect with parents. In the original U.S. version of the intervention, this interactive activity is used in the last part of the intervention to detail children's unique strengths, characteristics, likes, feelings, and contributions to the group. This use of the *I Am Special* book was expanded in the Dutch version. In CODIP-NL, every child receives a double-sided page for his or her *I Am Special* book after each session. It summarizes key messages of the intervention sessions and has some fun and educative elements for the child to complete.

Children's Emotions and Reactions in the United States and the Netherlands

Children in the United States and the Netherlands share similar reactions and emotional themes in response to family changes and participation in the group. The stresses and emotions associated with divorce for children extend across cultures. Examples of universal emotions and reactions include sadness; confusion; feelings of guilt, worry, and responsibility for the marital problems; fear of abandonment and fear of replacement; hope of reconciliation; anger; resentment; and common divorce-related stresses, such as going back and forth between homes.

The following are examples of the voices of children in the U.S. program.

Frustration and Sadness

- "Divorce made things better for my mom and dad: They have new partners. But it didn't make it better for me. They still fight with each other or don't speak to each other, and it makes me sad—and mad."
- "Sometimes I feel like I have to choose between my mom and my dad."
- "They say bad things about each other, and it makes my stomach hurt."
- "I look at other kids' families and wish we could be like them."

Anxiety, Guilt and Worry

- "I worry about what will happen to me and my family."
- "I worry we won't have enough money for food."
- "I think the divorce was my fault. I could hear my name come up when they argued. I thought I was the reason for all the yelling."

Fear of Abandonment and Fear of Replacement

- "Maybe if they stopped loving each other, they might not want me anymore either."
- "Something bad might happen to my parents, and I'll be all alone."
- "I'm afraid Dad loves his girlfriend more than he loves me now."
- "I don't see my dad very much since he moved away—and that's really hard. What if he doesn't come back?"

Hope of Reconciliation

- "I wish they could just fix it and live in the same house with me."
- "Someone I know got her parents back together."
- "Maybe if we all try real hard, we can fix the problems."

Divorce-Related Stress: The Hardest Thing About Parents Living Apart

- "When I'm with my mom, I miss my dad. When I'm with my dad, I miss my mom."
- "When they keep arguing and don't get along. Why can't they just get along?"
- "The schedule keeps changing, and I don't know where I'm going that day."
- "When they fight, and the police come. It hurts my heart."
- "I hate it when they ask me lots of questions and make me tell them things the other says."

Dutch children reveal similar themes as American children:

- "I don't know if Dad will still love me if I show how I really feel. When you're mad and you're acting sweet all the time, then you're not being yourself."
- [In response to the question whether divorce has made some things better]: [*growls*] "No, not for me—just for the two of them."
- "When my mum and dad meet up and start talking about money. I really hate that."
- "I am not sure about going to my mom. She has a new boyfriend now and may not want me around as much."
- "My dad is not really interested in me, so what's the point?"
- "I would like to talk about it with my dad, but I can't. I don't even know where he lives."
- "I haven't spoken to my best friend about the divorce. I wanted to, but maybe he would ask questions about what happened? What they've done? I don't know that myself."

Comments About the Group

The comments about participating in the group were similar for American and Dutch children. These are examples of comments by American children:

- "It felt good being in this group because I thought I was the only one. Now I know other kids feel like I do."
- "The group is a safe place to talk about everything!"
- "People in the group listen and care about me."

- "It's not my fault—or any kids' fault."
- "I don't have to choose between my mom and dad. They divorced each other—not me."
- "We learned how to solve problems. That makes me feel good."
- "Some problems can't be solved because they are for the grown-ups to fix. Now I don't have to worry so much".

Dutch children commented:

- "Our group is fun!"
- "Our group is a safe place to talk about my feelings."
- "I made some new friends in our group."
- "Now I worry less about the divorce."
- "I liked that I could tell about the things I experienced."
- "I now know that the fights between your parents aren't your fault!"
- "I learned ways to solve problems."

From these first comparisons of emotions and reactions of U.S. children participating in CODIP and Dutch children participating in the CODIP-NL pilot groups, it is apparent that there are common and universal reactions to divorce and family changes. Children's responses to the group experience in both countries were similarly positive. Results of program evaluation measures are described later.

CODIP is an evidence-based intervention approved by the National Registry of Effective Prevention Programs. Dappere Dinos received comparable scientific validation in a similar Dutch database by the Dutch Youth Institute. In their pilot study, Klein Velderman, Pannebakker, et al. (2011) compared Dutch intervention outcomes with previously reported outcomes in U.S. research (Alpert-Gillis et al., 1989). Child, parent, and trainer reported data were included, and the same questionnaires were used as in the original American study.

Child Self-Reported Family Adjustment

Pretest self-reported adjustment scores of children in the Dutch study were higher than those of U.S. children participating in CODIP (U.S. program), than U.S. children from intact families (U.S. intact controls) or from divorced families but not participating in CODIP (U.S. divorce controls). Thus, child perceptions of their own adjustment were high for the Dutch participants. However, these scores did not increase over time. Dutch posttest scores statistically resembled scores of children participating in the program in the U.S. study, but still statistically significantly exceeded those of U.S. children from intact families and divorce controls in that study.

Parent-Reported Child Adjustment

American parents of children participating in CODIP rated their children's adjustment at pretest significantly lower than Dutch parent ratings. Pre–post comparisons of Dutch children's adjustment revealed a small increase. This increase in mother-reported child functioning was smaller than the increases reported in U.S. research among children participating in CODIP. However, at the posttest, scores of the Dutch program group still exceeded those of the U.S. divorce control group.

Trainer-Reported Child Adjustment

According to the trainers, children in the Dutch study started off at the same level as U.S. children participating in CODIP. Trainer-reported child adjustment of children participating in the CODIP-NL pilot groups increased between pre- and posttest. However, at the posttest, U.S. scores significantly exceed the Dutch scores. So, despite the noteworthy increase in adjustment scores in the Dutch pilot study, the American children were rated higher by CODIP trainers.

RECOMMENDATIONS FOR INTERNATIONAL TRANSPORTABILITY AND EVERYDAY CLINICAL USE

This chapter described the goals, objectives, and key components of an evidence-based, play-based intervention to support children dealing with separation and divorce: CODIP. The effectiveness of this intervention in the United States has been proven previously. A translated CODIP module has been adapted effectively for 6- to 8-year-old children in the Netherlands. The program was based in a child preventive mental health care setting. A process evaluation revealed positive feedback about all aspects of the CODIP-NL module. For the trainers, puppet play was a relatively new but gratifying and effective way to work with children dealing with family changes. The first CODIP-NL pilot study showed that the emotional reactions of Dutch children were quite similar to their peers in America. Results of the Dutch pilot study showed modest but promising first results. With larger sample sizes, it is likely possible to replicate some of the positive effects of the module as found in the United States. Meanwhile, the gap regarding interventions for young children of divorce in the Netherlands has not been completely solved. CODIP-NL has proven to be a promising direction for future intervention in this domain. These results constitute the base for more research into the efficacy of CODIP-NL and future implementation in the Dutch setting. In

2013, the Dutch team developed a Dutch module for 4- to 6-year-olds based on the CODIP kindergarten and first-grade module. First pilot study results for this age module were very much like those for the 6- to 8-year-olds.

This example of CODIP implementation in the Netherlands suggests that the CODIP model can be transported effectively to other settings and populations. Adapting an evidence-based program to a new setting requires careful attention to program fidelity and differences in cultural norms and practice. The experience of adapting a program for children dealing with family changes revealed that children in the United States and the Netherlands share similar emotional reactions and risks that can be alleviated with evidence-based interventions that foster resilience through the universal language of play.

REFERENCES

Alpert-Gillis, L. J., Pedro-Carroll, J. L., & Cowen, E. L. (1989). Children of divorce intervention program: Development, implementation and evaluation of a program for young urban children. *Journal of Consulting and Clinical Psychology, 57,* 583–587. http://dx.doi.org/10.1037/0022-006X.57.5.583

Amato, P. R. (2000). The consequences of divorce for adults and children. *Journal of Marriage and the Family, 62,* 1269–1287. http://dx.doi.org/10.1111/j.1741-3737.2000.01269.x

Arifoglu, B. (2006). *The effects of CODIP on children's adjustment to divorce, anxiety and depression.* Ankara, Turkey: Haceteppe University of Health.

Burroughs, M. S., Wagner, W. W., & Johnson, J. T. (1997). Treatment with children of divorce: A comparison of two types of therapy. *Journal of Divorce & Remarriage, 27,* 83–99. http://dx.doi.org/10.1300/J087v27n03_06

Cloutier, R., Filion, L., & Timmermans, H. (2012). *Les parents se séparent: Mieux vivre la crise et aider son enfant* [Parental separation: Dealing with crises and helping your child] (2nd ed.). Montreal, Quebec, Canada: Éditions du CHU Sainte-Justine.

Cowen, E. L., Hightower, A. D., Pedro-Carroll, J. L., Work, W. C., & Wyman, P.A., (1996). *School-based prevention for children at risk: The Primary Mental Health Project.* Washington, DC: American Psychological Association.

Fthenakis, W. E., & Oberndorfer, R. (1993). Alleinerziehende Vater—eine zu vernechlassigende Minderheit? [Fathers raising children alone: A too-neglected minority?] In R. Reis & K. Fiedler (Eds.), *Die verletzlichen Jahre: Ein Handbuch zur Beratung und Seelsorge an Kindern und Jugendlichen [The vulnerable years: A handbook of counseling and pastoral care with children and adolescents]* (pp. 564–583). Munich, Germany: Chr. Kaiser.

Hetherington, E. M., & Kelly, J. (2002). *For better or for worse: Divorce reconsidered.* New York, NY: Norton.

Johnson, D. B., Pedro-Carroll, J. L., & Demanchik, S. P. (2005). Primary Mental Health Project: A play intervention for school-aged children. In L. A. Reddy, T. M. Files-Hall, & C. E. Schaefer, (Eds.,) *Empirically based play interventions for children.* Washington, DC: American Psychological Association.

Klein Velderman, M., Heinrich, R., Pannebakker, F., Rahder, J., Creemers, J., & De Wolff, M. (2011). *Dappere dinos: Interventieprogramma voor kinderen van 6–8 jaar van gescheiden ouders: Programmabeschrijving voor het leiden van gespreksgroepen voor kinderen van 6–8 jaar van gescheiden ouders [Courageous dinosaurs: Intervention program for children of divorce aged 6–8 years: A procedures manual for conducting support groups for children of divorce aged 6–8 years]* (2nd ed.). Leiden, the Netherlands: TNO Child Health.

Klein Velderman, M., Pannebakker, F. D., De Wolff, M. S., Pedro-Carroll, J. L., Kuiper, R. M., Vlasblom, E., & Reijneveld, S. A. (2011). *Child adjustment in divorced families: Can we successfully intervene with Dutch 6- to 8-year-olds? Feasibility study—Children of Divorce Intervention Program (CODIP) in the Netherlands* (No. TNO/CH 2011.031). Leiden, the Netherlands: TNO Behavioural and Societal Sciences.

Marzotto, C., & Bonadonna, M. (2011). La mediazione familiare e i gruppi di parola per figli di genitori separati: accompagnare la riorganizzazione dei legami familiari [Family mediation and the voice groups for children of divorced parents: Standing by the reorganization of family bonds]. In P. Donati, F. Folgheraiter, & M. L. Raineri (Eds.), *La tutela dei minori: Nuovi scenari relazionali [Child protection: New relational perspectives]* (pp. 243–265). Trento, Italy: Erickson.

Mireault, G., Drapreau, S., Faford, A., Lapointe, J., & Clotier, R. (1991). *Evaluation of an intervention program for children of separated families* [in French]. Quebec, Canada: Department of Community Health: Hospital of Infant Jesus.

Pedro-Carroll, J. (2010). *Putting children first: Proven parenting strategies for helping children thrive through divorce.* New York, NY: Avery/Penguin.

Pedro-Carroll, J., Alpert-Gillis, L., & Sterling, S. (1997). *Children of divorce intervention program: A procedures manual for conducting groups: Second & third grade children* (3rd ed.). Rochester, NY: Children's Institute.

Pedro-Carroll, J. L. (2005). Fostering resilience in the aftermath of divorce: The role of evidence-based programs for children. *Family Court Review, 43,* 52–64.

Pedro-Carroll, J. L. (2011). How parents can help children cope with separation/divorce. In R. E. Tremblay, M. Boivin, & R. D. V. Peters (Eds.), *Encyclopedia on early child development* [online]. Retrieved from http://www.child-encyclopedia.com/sites/default/files/textes-experts/en/630/how-parents-can-help-children-cope-with-separationdivorce.pdf

Pedro-Carroll, J. L., & Alpert-Gillis, L. J. (1997). Preventive interventions for children of divorce: A developmental model for 5 and 6 year old children. *Journal of Primary Prevention, 18,* 5–23. http://dx.doi.org/10.1023/A:1024601421020

Pedro-Carroll, J. L., Alpert-Gillis, L. J., & Cowen, E. L. (1992). An evaluation of the efficacy of a preventive intervention for 4th–6th grade urban children of divorce. *Journal of Primary Prevention, 13*, 115–130. http://dx.doi.org/10.1007/ BF01325070

Pedro-Carroll, J. L., & Cowen, E. L. (1985). The children of divorce intervention program: An investigation of the efficacy of a school-based prevention program. *Journal of Consulting and Clinical Psychology, 53*, 603–611. http://dx.doi. org/10.1037/0022-006X.53.5.603

Pedro-Carroll, J. L., & Jones, S. H. (2005). A preventive play intervention to foster children's resilience in the aftermath of divorce. In L. A. Reddy, T. M. Files-Hall, & C. E. Schaefer (Eds.), *Empirically based play interventions for children* (pp. 51–75). Washington, DC: American Psychological Association. http:// dx.doi.org/10.1037/11086-004

Pedro-Carroll, J. L., Sutton, S. E., & Wyman, P. A. (1999). A two year follow-up evaluation of a preventive intervention program for young children of divorce. *School Psychology Review, 28*, 467–476.

Pinto, R. (2008). *CODIP replication in Portugal.* Lisbon, Portugal: Health Center Vila da Feira.

Spruijt, E., & Kormos, H. (2014). *Handboek scheiden en de kinderen: Voor de beroepskracht die met scheidingskinderen te maken heeft [Handbook divorce and the children: For the professional working with children of divorce]* (2nd ed.). Houten, the Netherlands: Bohn Stafleu van Loghum.

Wisse Smit, N. (2008). *Julia heeft twee huizen: Verhalen voor kinderen van gescheiden ouders* [Julia has two houses: Stories for children of divorced or separated parents] (2nd ed.). Amsterdam, the Netherlands: Uitgeverij SWP.

3

CHILD-CENTERED PLAY THERAPY FOR SCHOOL PREVENTION

DEE C. RAY AND SUE C. BRATTON

Mental health is a prerequisite for children's personal and academic success, yet recent estimates have indicated that one out of five children experiences emotional and behavioral problems that significantly interfere with their development and ability to function at home and school (Centers for Disease Control [CDC], 2013; Mental Health America [MHA], 2013; National Center for Children in Poverty, 2010), and less than one third of these children receive the help they need (MHA, 2013). Over the past decade, numerous government reports have called for action to remedy what has been termed a crisis in the health care of our nation's children (CDC, 2013; New Freedom Commission on Mental Health, 2003; Taras & the American Academy of Pediatrics Committee on School Health, 2004; U.S. Public Health Service, 2000) and have focused on the vital role of schools to address this issue. Recognizing that, for many children, schools

http://dx.doi.org/10.1037/14730-004
Empirically Based Play Interventions for Children, Second Edition, L. A. Reddy, T. M. Files-Hall, and C. E. Schaefer (Editors)

may be the only accessible means of receiving services, recommendations from these reports focused on the school's role in early identification and intervention, and prevention, and the need to identify empirically validated interventions that are developmentally and culturally responsive (Bratton, 2010). The call for an increase in school-based services appears largely unheeded by schools and funding agencies, as evidenced by the rise over the past 10 years in the number of children suffering as the result of a lack of appropriate mental health treatments (CDC, 2013; MHA, 2013). One possible explanation is a lack of empirical evidence to support the cost of expanding school mental health services. In the current climate of accountability and budget constraints, providing evidence for the effectiveness of an intervention is critical to its widespread adoption by school administrators.

Clearly, schools are in a unique position to promote children's mental health and prevent the onset of mental disorders through early screening and assessment, and by providing proven interventions that not only address presenting concerns but also foster children's social and emotional development and resiliency. The importance of early intervention cannot be overstated—not only to respond to early onset behavioral problems but to also mediate the effect of early risk factors, such as poverty and other societal problems, that have been shown to negatively have an impact on children's personal–social and academic success (National Center for Children in Poverty, 2010). Children's early school experiences establish future behavior patterns and interactions with others. Early intervention, particularly for children identified as at risk, can counteract risk factors while enhancing personal strengths, thereby altering a trajectory of increased behavioral problems, low self-esteem, and academic failure (Ackerman, Brown, & Izard, 2003; Bratton et al., 2013; Knitzer, 2000; Webster-Stratton & Reid, 2003).

Child-centered play therapy (CCPT) is a developmentally and culturally responsive early mental health intervention (Bratton, Ray, Edwards, & Landreth, 2009; Gil & Drewes, 2005); it has solid empirical support for its use in school settings with a range of presenting concerns and across ethnically, culturally, and socially diverse populations (Landreth, 2012; Lin, 2012; Ray, 2011). CCPT is unique in its aim to help children achieve optimal growth and mental health through developing the child's internal resources for self-regulation, self-control, creativity, and self-direction—resources that children can continue to draw on to meet life's challenges. This chapter provides an overview of CCPT, including key treatment ingredients, a case illustration of the therapeutic process, and a summary of controlled outcome research published since 2000. It concludes with a discussion of replication and transportability.

THEORETICAL BASIS AND OBJECTIVES

CCPT is a mental health approach to prevention and intervention that recognizes the relationship between therapist and child as the primary healing factor for children who experience challenges. CCPT therapists use a playroom with carefully selected toys to match the developmentally appropriate communication style of children—which is play—thereby supporting the message that the therapist seeks to understand the whole child in the context of his or her world. Within the relationship, the therapist offers the child an environment of acceptance and warmth that helps the child release his or her full potential for growth and reduce harmful ways of meeting personal needs. CCPT is operationalized in several volumes of literature that agree on its basic tenets and structure (Axline, 1947; Cochran, Nordling, & Cochran, 2010; Landreth, 2012; Ray, 2011; VanFleet, Sywulak, & Sniscak, 2010).

CCPT is one of the longest-standing mental health interventions in use today; it is supported by more than 70 years of literature involving research and construct theory. Based on Rogers's (1951) person-centered theory, Virginia Axline (1947) developed nondirective play therapy and operationalized humanistic tenets of philosophy into a structured method of intervention. Nondirective play therapy based on person-centered theory is currently termed CCPT. In the years since the introduction of CCPT, 62 outcome studies have explored its effectiveness and have suggested that CCPT, in general, offers a viable and effective intervention for children (Ray, 2011). CCPT is recognized as the most widely practiced approach to play therapy in the United States (Lambert et al., 2007) and has earned a strong international reputation (see West, 1996; Wilson, Kendrick, & Ryan, 1992).

Theoretical Basis for CCPT

Rogers's (1951) theory of development and change is the basis for the structure and process of CCPT. In his elegant presentation of person-centered theory, he provided a framework for human development and explained in great detail how maladjustment in the human condition occurs. As Rogers (1951) stated, human beings are born to move forward and enhance the organism of the person. The essential concept for growth and change is that personality development lies in the phenomenological experience of the organism. Through interactions with significant others, a concept of self is conceived and developed throughout the life span. Although each person has a personal sense of self, the organism is highly influenced by interaction and a relationship with others. Self-worth may be affected by the perceived expectations of acceptance by others, thereby creating a personal sense of value based on conditions of worth. If a child in a relationship feels that acceptance is only available as a result of certain ways of being or acting, the result is a disruption between the natural organism and construct of self that possibly may lead to harmful ways of being in the environment.

A child's behavior is directly consistent with the view of self and the valuing process, even if the child lacks awareness of this connection. Behavior is seen as an attempt to maintain the organism and have one's needs met, depending on the perceived expectations of the environment, whereas the emotion accompanying behavior is seen as dependent on the perceived need for behavior. Hence, a child will behave and emotionally respond in a way that is consistent with the view of self, even if the view of self does not facilitate the optimal growth of the individual. Rogers (1951) proposed a path on which the person, when given a nonthreatening environment, could examine experiences in a nonjudgmental way and integrate them into a self-structure that is respectful of the intrinsic direction of the organism, thereby enhancing relationships with others.

Based on these basic beliefs about human nature, CCPT therapists seek to establish environments in which a child will feel fully accepted by another (i.e., the therapist) and will learn to develop self-acceptance. The given theoretical outcome of self-acceptance is the resulting movement toward more positive feelings and behaviors. Hence, therapeutic movement depends on several factors, including the person of the therapist, the person of the child, the level of acceptance established in the therapeutic relationship, and the therapist's trust in the child to move naturally toward self-enhancing ways of being.

KEY TREATMENT INGREDIENTS

Conditions for Therapeutic Change in CCPT

The therapeutic path toward self-enhancing growth is identified via six conditions (Rogers, 1951) that must be met in therapy to facilitate change for children. These conditions, which are based on the primacy of the relationship between therapist and child, are: (a) two people are in psychological contact, (b) the first person (client) is in a state of incongruence, (c) the second person (therapist) is congruent in the relationship, (d) the therapist experiences unconditional positive regard for the client, (e) the therapist experiences an empathic understanding of the client's internal frame of reference and attempts to communicate this experience to the client, and (f) communication to the client of the therapist's empathic understanding and unconditional positive regard is, to a minimal degree, achieved (Rogers, 1957).

Three of the conditions—genuineness, unconditional positive regard, and empathic understanding (Conditions 3, 4, and 5)—are labeled as *therapist attitudinal conditions* (Bozarth, 1998). Rogers (1957) described *congruence* as the ability to feel free to be self within the therapeutic relationship and to be able to experience congruence between experience and awareness of self. Unconditional positive regard is a warm acceptance of all aspects of the client's experience without judgment or evaluation (Rogers, 1957). In addition, unconditional positive regard is a therapist-felt condition in which the therapist experiences a feeling of trust in the child's ability to move toward actualization of the organism. Empathic understanding is marked by entering the child's world as if it were one's own without losing a sense of self as the therapist. Ray (2011) cited therapist attitudinal conditions as essential to the provision of CCPT and explored the communication of these conditions in greater detail.

CCPT Intervention Guidelines

Axline (1947, pp. 73–74) offered guidelines operationalizing the provision of conditions in CCPT. They are referred to as the eight basic principles and are paraphrased as follows:

1. The therapist develops a warm, friendly relationship with the child as soon as possible.
2. The therapist accepts the child exactly as is, rather than wishing the child were different in some way.
3. The therapist establishes a feeling of permissiveness in the relationship so that the child can fully express thoughts and feelings.
4. The therapist is attuned to the child's feelings and reflects those back to the child to help gain insight into behavior.
5. The therapist respects the child's ability to solve problems and leaves the responsibility to make choices to the child.
6. The therapist does not direct the child's behavior or conversation. The therapist follows the child.
7. Recognizing the gradual nature of the therapeutic process, the therapist does not attempt to rush therapy.
8. The therapist sets only those limits that anchor the child to reality or make the child aware of responsibilities in the relationship.

These principles provide the structure for play therapy and encourage the therapist to accept, trust, and follow the child. Using the principles to operationalize play therapy, specific types of verbal responses guide the therapist's enactment of the child-centered philosophy. They include reflecting feelings (e.g., you feel angry), reflecting content (e.g., your mom was fighting with your dad), tracking behavior (e.g., you're moving to over there), facilitating decision making (e.g., you can decide), facilitating creativity (e.g., that can be whatever you want), encouraging (e.g., you're trying hard on that), facilitating relationship (e.g., you want to make me feel better), and limit setting (Axline, 1947; Ginott, 1961; Landreth, 2012; Ray, 2004).

Limit setting is used when the child might be a threat to self, others, or the room. For limit setting, Landreth (2012) offered a three-step approach entitled ACT: acknowledge the feeling, communicate the limit, and target an alternative. In ACT, the therapist first and foremost seeks to understand and communicate an understanding of the child's intent by acknowledging the child's feelings (e.g., you're really angry with me). Second, the therapist sets a clear and definitive limit (e.g., but I'm not for hitting). Third, the therapist provides an alternative to allow the child appropriate expression of the feeling (e.g., you can hit the doll). Limit setting allows the child to perceive the playroom as a safe environment.

Procedures for CCPT are clearly outlined in Ray's (2011) treatment manual. Sessions are typically 45 minutes long but range from 30 to 50 minutes, depending on setting constraints. Although there is no definitive number of sessions recommended, 15 to 20 sessions typically yield noteworthy changes that can be measured objectively. Play therapists should have a minimal level of training that includes a master's degree in a mental health field plus at least one 40-hour course on the basics of CCPT. Further education and supervision are highly recommended. Nonverbal skills include matching the child's affect and tone and matching responses to the therapist's internal state (e.g., genuineness). Although CCPT therapists are provided with specific types of verbal responses to help concretely structure CCPT, it should be remembered that the attitudinal conditions provided by the therapist always take precedence over a rigid approach to responding to a child.

Playroom and Materials

The structure of the playroom is the first message sent to the child that all parts of the child are accepted in this environment. Landreth (2012) suggested that toys should facilitate a range of creative expression, facilitate a range of emotional expression, engage children's interests, facilitate expressive and exploratory play, allow exploration and expression without verbalization, allow success without prescribed structure, allow for noncommittal play, and have sturdy construction for active use. Materials for the playroom include toys, craft materials, paints, easel, puppet theater, sandbox, and child furniture. Kottman (2011) categorized materials in five general areas: family/nurturing, scary toys, aggressive toys, expressive toys, and pretend/fantasy toys. In selecting toys, the most fundamental criterion is that the toy serves a purpose in the playroom. Ray (2011) suggested that each therapist should ask the following questions regarding toy selection: What therapeutic purpose will this serve for children who use this room? How will this help children express themselves? How will this help me build a relationship with children? When toys meet a therapeutic purpose, help children express themselves, and help build the therapist–child relationship, they can be considered valuable to the playroom.

INTERVENTION CASE EXAMPLE

Nina was a 5-year-old Latina girl enrolled in kindergarten at a public elementary school. She was referred to play therapy by her mother and teacher, who were concerned about Nina's interactions at home and school. At home, she had become withdrawn and moody, and oppositional and defiant toward her mother and sisters. At school, Nina refused to speak. She was withdrawn and passive in the classroom and had few friends, and the teacher was concerned about her apathy toward schoolwork. In the first play therapy session, the therapist introduced Nina to the playroom:

Therapist: In here is the playroom. You can play with the toys in lots of the ways you like.

Nina: [*walks around the room with her arms crossed, avoiding eye contact with the therapist*]

Therapist: You're not sure about this place.

Nina: [*sits down by the dolls and starts to look at each one*]

Therapist: You're checking those out.

Nina proceeded to sit quietly throughout the session and look at each doll. She then moved around the room to look at the different toys, sometimes picking them up to examine them closely. She never talked, made little eye contact with the therapist, and showed little affect.

For the second session, the therapist arrived at the doorway of Nina's classroom. When Nina saw the therapist, she smiled broadly and ran toward the therapist. As the therapist and Nina walked toward the playroom:

Therapist: You're happy to see me today.

Nina: [*stops walking to show the therapist her shoes; smiles at therapist*]

Therapist: You're showing me your shoes. You want me to see that you like them.

Nina: Yes. They're pink.

Therapist: You like how they're pink.

Nina: Yes. My mom bought them for me.

In the second session, Nina went to the paint easel and painted on the top sheet of paper. She wanted to remove the paper, but needed to unclasp the clamps at the top of the easel. She reached up to clamp but gave up quickly when the clamp resisted. She moved to the sand and tried to fill up a bucket that had holes. When the sand ran through, she looked disappointed and put it down. She continued to try different play activities in the room, but gave up when she encountered difficulties. The following was a typical interaction:

Nina: I want to paint.

Therapist: So, you decided to paint.

Nina: [picks up a paint brush and turns to show it to the therapist] I like yellow.

Therapist: You want me to see the yellow. You like it.

Nina: [looks at the clamp holding the paper; reaches her hand up to clamp]

Therapist: Looks like you want to move that.

Nina: [tries one time to unclasp the paper; she struggles, smiles at the therapist, moves to the kitchen]

Therapist: So, you decided to do something else.

The pattern of giving up with little effort was common for Nina's first five sessions. Once the pattern emerged, the therapist began to focus responses on Nina's tendency to give up on any challenges.

Nina: [tries to reach a puppet in a high place]

Therapist: You're having a hard time reaching that.

Nina: [looks at the therapist as if to say she needs help, but says nothing]

Therapist: Looks like you want something.

Nina: [gives up and moves to sand]

Therapist: You decided that was just too hard and you're not going to try anymore.

The therapist intentionally chose responses that highlighted Nina's decision to give up, thereby emphasizing that she had the choice to not give up. The therapist also intentionally chose not to rescue Nina and help her do things she was capable of doing herself. The therapist made no judgment about Nina's decisions to give up, but accepted that Nina used giving up as a coping skill. Slowly, Nina began to spend more time trying to do things she wanted to do but were challenging for her. The clothes on the dolls and puppets, and dress-up clothes were areas that she began to try and figure out. However, the painting easel continued to be an area on which she gave up quickly. In the eighth session, Nina made a significant turn in her play.

Nina: [goes to the easel] I'm going to add numbers.

Therapist: You want to use that to add numbers. You're writing on it.

Nina: [writes "3 + 4" on the easel paper and looks at it for a long time, then scratches it out] No, I'm going to do another one.

Therapist: You decided you didn't like that one. You're going to do another one.

Nina: [attempts to unclasp the clamp; reaches up and tries hard with the clasp, but it does not open; moves a small chair toward the easel, stands on it, and tries again]

Therapist: You're not giving up. You're trying another way.

Nina: [trying the clamp again and gritting her teeth] This needs to come off.

Therapist: You're trying your hardest. You really want it off.

Nina: [frustrated, she looks around the room]

Therapist: You're trying to figure it out. You really want to find a way to get that off.

Nina: [looks at the therapist and speaks in a determined voice] I know. You come help. You take one side and I'll do the other.

Therapist: [moves toward Nina and the easel] You thought of a way that might work. Tell me what you want me to do.

Nina: You hold one side and I push the other [the therapist holds one side, Nina pushes hard on the other side, the clamp opens, and the paper drops to floor].

Nina: [smiles broadly] Look!

Therapist: You did it. You kept trying until you figured it out. You're really proud.

By continuing to try and use alternate ways to open the clamp, Nina experienced herself as capable and creative. She also figured out a way to involve another person to help her in her struggles instead of isolating or withdrawing. The therapist provided an environment in which the therapist was encouraging, accepting, and allowed Nina to express herself freely and struggle with support. The therapist did not try to rescue Nina, do things for Nina, or direct Nina to accomplish certain goals. In subsequent sessions, Nina prolonged her time to figure out how to accomplish her goals. By the 11th session, Nina was able to simultaneously open both clamps on the easel on her own. She jumped with excitement when she finally unclasped the clamps and said to the therapist, "Look what I can do."

Over the period of 11 sessions, the therapist checked in with Nina's teacher and mother. Nina's mother reported that Nina's defiant behaviors had ceased. Nina's teacher reported that Nina's behavior in the classroom had changed completely: She had many friends and eagerly attempted her homework. The therapist conceptualized that Nina's sense of helplessness and perceived incompetence were the reasons for her refusal to engage at home and school. Once she experienced herself as capable on her own terms and in her own language (play), and motivated internally to accomplish her own goals within an accepting and genuine relationship, she was able to take risks at home and school.

OUTCOME RESEARCH

Research in CCPT spans over 70 years; the first identified study was conducted by Dulsky in 1942. Since then, hundreds of studies have explored the use of CCPT for various presenting problems. Early intervention studies were plagued with design and statistical problems, yet appeared to demonstrate promising results for CCPT. A meta-analysis of 93 controlled-play therapy studies conducted over 6 decades (Bratton, Ray, Rhine, & Jones, 2005) found that humanistic play therapy interventions, identified as CCPT/nondirective play therapy, yielded a large average treatment effect size. In the past few decades, researchers in CCPT have used rigorous experimental designs, manualized protocols, and suitable statistical methods to elevate the credibility of findings. Ray (2011) reviewed CCPT studies and found a total of 62 studies conducted from 1940 to 2010 that showed positive outcomes for CCPT. Of the 62 studies, 29 were categorized as experimental; they used a pre-post randomized control group design. In addition, it appears that CCPT research has increased recently: 19 studies in CCPT were conducted from 2000 to 2010. Ray concluded that CCPT research demonstrated positive results in outcome areas, such as externalizing/disruptive behaviors, attention-deficit/hyperactivity disorder (ADHD), internalizing behavior problems, anxiety, depression, self-concept, social behavior, parent–teacher relationship, sexual abuse/trauma, homelessness, identified disability, academic achievement, and speech/language skills.

For the purpose of providing current empirical support for CCPT in the schools in this chapter, we reviewed experimental CCPT intervention outcome studies conducted since 2000. We used the following inclusion criteria: used a controlled experimental design, conducted in a school, participants were between pre-kindergarten and fifth grade, published since 2000, identified intervention as CCPT or following CCPT procedures, published in peer-reviewed journals or books, and used standardized assessments. Thirteen studies meeting these criteria are summarized in Table 3.1.

Given the comprehensive number of participants (a total of 558 participants across studies, with a mean of 43 participants per study), several conclusions can be drawn from a review of the 13 outcome studies. Research indicated that participation in CCPT resulted in positive outcomes for academic achievement; disruptive behaviors, including aggression and ADHD; internalizing problem behaviors; speech; and functional impairment. The use of active control and comparison groups and procedures to blind assessors to participants' treatment group assignment in several of the CCPT studies lent further credibility to findings. CCPT appeared effective across cultures, including race, ethnicity, gender, and international status. Many of the CCPT outcome studies included a diverse sample of ethnicities and races, and two studies were conducted with samples outside of the United States (see Ojiambo & Bratton, 2014; Shen, 2002). Across the included studies, more than 60% of the participants were non-Caucasian, and the vast majority of participants were identified as low income. The level of multiculturalism addressed in CCPT research is a unique feature of this intervention and may be attributed to the use of CCPT in the real-world setting of schools. Participants' ages ranged from 3 years to 12 years, with a mean age of 7.7 years, which indicated CCPT's responsiveness to the developmental needs of young children through preadolescence. CCPT research studies also indicated that CCPT can be used as a short-term intervention. The mean number of sessions was 15; therapy was often delivered twice a week and resulted in demonstrative change—often in 8 weeks or less. The included studies did not offer a parent or teacher component as part of intervention, thus indicating that children demonstrated change during therapy without a systemic intervention. The finding that young children are capable of change in therapy without direct intervention with caregivers was another distinctive feature of CCPT and made it particularly suitable for school settings. However, previous CCPT research has indicated that the inclusion of parents and teachers in intervention results in stronger outcomes (Bratton et al., 2005).

TABLE 3.1
School-Based Child-Centered Play Therapy Controlled Outcome Research: Selected Studies, 2000 to Present

Authors	Participants/Methods	Findings
Blanco & Ray (2011)	Academically at-risk 1st graders ($N = 43$); random assignment 34% Hispanic, 17% African American, 46% Caucasian C = 20 no treatment waitlist E = 21 16 sessions of CCPT (2/wk, 30 min each) *Experimental design*	Compared with the control group over time, children in the CCPT group demonstrated statistically significant improvement on a standardized achievement test, and the treatment effect was in the medium range.
Bratton et al. (2013)	Head Start children identified with disruptive behavior ($N = 54$); block random assignment 42% African American; 39% Hispanic; 18% Caucasian C = 27 active control–reading mentoring (RM) E = 27 CCPT Both groups: 20 sessions (2/wk, 30 min each) *Experimental design*	According to teachers who were blinded to children's treatment group, children in the CCPT group demonstrated statistically significant improvement on overall disruptive behaviors, attention problems, and aggression, compared with the RM group over time; CCPT demonstrated large treatment effects on all outcome measures; the majority of children receiving CCPT moved from clinical levels of concern to normal functioning.
Danger & Landreth (2005)	Prekindergarten to kindergarten children referred for speech problems ($N = 21$) Random drawing; 19% Hispanic, 81% Caucasian C = 10 weekly speech therapy only E = 11 group CCPT; 25 sessions (1/wk, 30 min), plus weekly speech therapy *Experimental design*	CCPT demonstrated a large treatment effect on improving speech-delayed children's expressive language and a moderate treatment effect on receptive language when compared with the group receiving speech therapy only; between-group differences across time were not statistically significant.
Fall, Navelski, & Welch (2002)	Special education students, ages 6–10 years ($N = 66$); random assignment 98.5% Caucasian C = 23 no-treatment control E = 43 CCPT; six sessions (1/wk, 30 min) *Experimental design*	Teacher reported a decrease in problematic behaviors and social problems for the CCPT group compared with the control group; case manager ratings showed a significant decrease in anxiety for CCPT group but not for the control; between-group differences for self-efficacy were not statistically significant.

Study	Sample and design	Results
Garza & Bratton (2005)	Kindergarten through fifth-grade Hispanic children identified with behavior problems ($N = 29$); random assignment C = 14 small group guidance curriculum E = 15 CCPT Both groups: 15 sessions (1/wk, 30 min) Treatment providers were bilingual *Experimental design*	According to parents who were blinded to the children's treatment group, the CCPT group demonstrated statistically significant improvement (i.e., large treatment effect) on externalizing behavior problems compared with the guidance group; CCPT demonstrated a medium beneficial treatment effect on children's internalizing problems, although not statistically significant.
Ojiambo & Bratton (2014)	Ugandan orphaned students, ages 10–12 years ($N = 60$) Random assignment C = 30 active control–RM E = 30 group CCPT/activity therapy Both groups: 16 sessions (groups of 3; 2/wk, 30 min) *Experimental design*	According to teachers and housemothers who were blinded to the children's treatment group, CCPT demonstrated a statistically significant decrease on children's internalizing and externalizing behavior problems and moderate-to-large treatment effects compared with the active control; the majority of children participating in CCPT moved from a clinical level of behavior concern to normative functioning.
Packman & Bratton (2003)	Fourth and fifth graders identified with learning differences and behavioral difficulties ($N = 24$); random assignment 90% Caucasian; 10% Asian C = 12 no-treatment control E = 12 group CCPT/activity therapy; 12 sessions (1 hr/wk) *Experimental design*	According to parent report, the CCPT group demonstrated statistically significant improvement on internalizing problems and overall behavioral functioning compared with the control group; between-group differences were not significant for externalizing behaviors; CCPT demonstrated medium-to-large treatment effects on all outcome measures. *(continues)*

TABLE 3.1
School-Based Child-Centered Play Therapy Controlled Outcome Research:
Selected Studies, 2000 to Present   *(Continued)*

Authors	Participants/Methods	Findings
Ray, Blanco, Sullivan, & Holliman (2009)	Aggressive children, ages 4–11 years (*N* = 41) 32% Hispanic, 15% African American, 10% Biracial, 44% Caucasian C = 22 no treatment waitlist E = 19 CCPT; 14 sessions (2/wk, 30 min) 32 parents completed pretest and posttest (E = 15, C = 17) Teachers completed pretest and posttest for all 41 children *Quasi-experimental design*	According to parent and teacher report, CCPT demonstrated a moderate treatment effect on aggression compared with the control group, although between-group differences over time were not statistically significant; post hoc analysis revealed children in the experimental group demonstrated a statistically significant decrease in aggressive behaviors, whereas the control group demonstrated no statistically significant difference.
Ray, Schottelkorb, & Tsai (2007)	Kindergarten through fifth graders identified with attention problems and hyperactivity (*N* = 60); random assignment 35% Hispanic, 17% African American, 45% Caucasian C = 29 active control–RM E = 31 CCPT Both groups: 16 sessions (2/wk, 30 min) *Experimental design*	According to teacher report, the CCPT group demonstrated statistically significant improvement on student characteristics, emotional lability, and anxiety/withdrawal over the control group; no statistically significant between-group differences were found on children's ADHD symptoms; post hoc analysis revealed that both groups demonstrated statistically significant improvement in ADHD, student characteristics, anxiety, and learning disability.
Ray, Stulmaker, Lee, & Silverman (2013)	Kindergarten and first and second graders identified with functional impairment (*N* = 37); random assignment 38% Latino/Latina, 32% African American, 30% Caucasian C = 20 delayed-start control E = 17 CCPT; 12–16 sessions (2/wk, 30 min) *Experimental design*	Phase I: CCPT demonstrated a medium treatment effect on children's functional impairment when compared with the control group, although between-group differences were not statistically significant; Phase II (both groups received CCPT): Within group difference indicated that children in both groups showed statistically significant improvement with large effect sizes as a result of CCPT.

68   RAY AND BRATTON

Study	Sample and design	Findings
Schumann (2010)	Aggressive kindergarten through fourth graders (*N* = 37); random assignment 38% Hispanic, 24.4% African American, 37.8% Caucasian C = 17 Second-Step curriculum, small-group guidance E = 20 CCPT; 12–15 individual sessions (1/wk, 30 min) *Experimental design*	No statistically significant differences were found between the CCPT group and the comparison group that received an evidence-based, guidance curriculum intervention; both groups demonstrated statistically significant improvement on aggressive behavior, externalizing problems, and internalizing problems; however, according to parents, more children in the CCPT group demonstrated improvement in aggressive behaviors than in the Second Step group.
Shen (2002)	Taiwanese third through sixth graders identified high-risk for maladjustment (*N* = 30); random assignment C = 15 no-treatment control E = 15 group CCPT; 8–12 sessions (2–3/wk, 40 min) *Experimental design*	Compared with the control group, the CCPT group demonstrated statistically significant decreases in their overall anxiety, physiological anxiety, worry/oversensitivity, and suicide risk; CCPT demonstrated large treatment effects on reducing children's anxiety, worry, and oversensitivity, and small-to-medium treatment effect on reducing suicide risk.
Wang Flahive & Ray (2007)	Fourth and fifth graders identified with behavior problems (*N* = 56); random assignment 62.5% Hispanic, 8.9% African American, 28.6% Caucasian C = 28 no-treatment control E = 28 group sandtray; CCPT procedures; 10 sessions (1/wk, 45 min) *Experimental design*	According to parent and teacher reports, the CCPT group demonstrated statistically significant improvement on externalizing problems compared with the control group over time; teachers also reported a statistically significant between group improvement on the CCPT groups' internalizing and total problems.

Note. Treatment groups: E = experimental; C = control or comparison. CCPT = child-centered play therapy.

REPLICATION AND TRANSPORTABILITY

Current research and practices indicate that CCPT can be used successfully in diverse school settings; with a broad range of ages; with ethnically, culturally, and socially diverse populations; and with different structural formats. CCPT is delivered with very young children in Head Start environments (i.e., Bratton et al., 2013) and with older children in elementary schools (i.e., Packman & Bratton, 2003; Wang Flahive & Ray, 2007). Considerable evidence shows that CCPT is effective throughout the span of childhood with children having a range of issues that prevent them from fully benefitting from the learning environment. The evidence of CCPT's effectiveness cross-culturally is a particular strength and supports its wide applicability. Moreover, CCPT can be modified to meet schools' structural needs. Although it is recommended that schools establish permanent playrooms to increase consistency with children, portable playrooms often are used in schools when play therapists are required to be flexible with space (Landreth, 2012). In addition, CCPT can be delivered in time intervals most suitable to schools. Sessions are typically 30 minutes long and can be delivered once or twice per week. In one single case design study, CCPT was delivered three times per week to meet the needs of lower-functioning intellectually disabled children (i.e., Swan & Ray, 2014).

Because CCPT is well-defined in several volumes of literature (Axline, 1947; Cochran et al., 2010; Landreth, 2012; Ray, 2011; VanFleet et al., 2010), there is ample information on the theory and basics of CCPT. In addition, Ray (2011) provided a manualized protocol that honors the philosophical essentials of CCPT as a relational intervention, yet provides concrete skills on how to deliver CCPT with consistency to maintain treatment integrity. These resources ensure that the effects of CCPT can be replicated in schools across ages, structures, and regions by specially trained mental health professionals. Successful implementation of CCPT by school mental health professionals requires that therapists have adequate graduate education in mental health, CCPT, and supervised experiences facilitating CCPT.

CONCLUSION

The empirical evidence for CCPT in schools supports its efficacy with a range of populations, school settings, and presenting concerns, and holds implications for school counselors, social workers, and psychologists who are accountable to show evidence for the interventions they use. It is our hope that school mental health professionals will present the evidence discussed in this chapter to administrators and funders, and advocate the use of CCPT to expand mental health services in their schools to break the current cycle of neglect in children's care and well-being and to promote optimal development and mental health for the children they serve.

REFERENCES

Ackerman, B. P., Brown, E., & Izard, C. E. (2003). Continuity and change in levels of externalizing behavior in school of children from economically disadvantaged families. *Child Development, 74*, 694–709. http://dx.doi.org/10.1111/1467-8624.00563

Axline, V. (1947). *Play therapy: The inner dynamics of childhood.* Boston, MA: Houghton Mifflin.

Blanco, P. J., & Ray, D. C. (2011). Play therapy in the schools: A best practice for improving academic achievement. *Journal of Counseling & Development, 89*, 235–243.

Bozarth, J. (1998). *Person-centered therapy: A revolutionary paradigm.* Ross on Wye, UK: PCCS Books.

Bratton, S. C. (2010). Meeting the early mental health needs of children through school-based play therapy: A review of outcome research. In A. A. Drewes & C. E. Schaefer (Eds.), *School-based play therapy* (2nd ed., pp. 17–58). New York, NY: Wiley. http://dx.doi.org/10.1002/9781118269701.ch2

Bratton, S. C., Ceballos, P. L., Sheely-Moore, A. I., Meany-Walen, K., Pronchenko, Y., & Jones, L. D. (2013). Head start early mental health intervention: Effects of child-centered play therapy on disruptive behaviors. *International Journal of Play Therapy, 22*(1), 28–42. http://dx.doi.org/10.1037/a0030318

Bratton, S. C., Ray, D., Rhine, T., & Jones, L. (2005). The efficacy of play therapy with children: A meta-analytic review of treatment outcomes. *Professional Psychology: Research and Practice, 36*, 376–390. http://dx.doi.org/10.1037/0735-7028.36.4.376

Bratton, S. C., Ray, D. C., Edwards, N. A., & Landreth, G. (2009). Child-centered play therapy (CCPT): Theory, research, and practice. *Person-Centered and Experiential Psychotherapies, 8*, 266–281. http://dx.doi.org/10.1080/14779757.2009.9688493

Centers for Disease Control. (2013). *Children's mental health—New report.* Retrieved from http://www.cdc.gov/Features/childrensmentalhealth/

Cochran, N. H., Nordling, W. J., & Cochran, J. L. (2010). *Child-centered play therapy: A practical guide to developing therapeutic relationships with children.* Hoboken, NJ: Wiley.

Danger, S., & Landreth, G. (2005). Child-centered group play therapy with children with speech difficulties. *International Journal of Play Therapy, 14*(1), 81–102.

Dulsky, S. G. (1942). Affect and intellect: An experimental study. *Journal of General Psychology, 27*, 199–220. http://dx.doi.org/10.1080/00221309.1942.10544409

Fall, M., Navelski, L. F., & Welch, K. K. (2002). Outcomes of a play intervention for children identified for special education services. *International Journal of Play Therapy, 11*(2), 91–106.

Garza, Y., & Bratton, S. C. (2005). School-based child-centered play therapy with Hispanic children: Outcomes and cultural consideration. *International Journal of Play Therapy, 14*(1), 51–79.

Gil, E., & Drewes, A. A. (Eds.). (2005). *Cultural issues in play therapy.* New York, NY: Guilford Press.

Ginott, H. G. (1961). *Group psychotherapy with children: The theory and practice of play-therapy.* New York, NY: McGraw-Hill. http://dx.doi.org/10.1037/14360-000

Knitzer, J. (2000). Early childhood mental health services: A policy and systems development perspective. In J. P. Shonkoff & S. J. Meisels (Eds.), *Handbook of early childhood intervention* (2nd ed., pp. 416–438). Cambridge, England: Cambridge University Press. http://dx.doi.org/10.1017/CBO9780511529320.021

Kottman, T. (2011). *Play therapy: Basics and beyond* (2nd ed.). Alexandria, VA: American Counseling Association.

Lambert, S. F., LeBlanc, M., Mullen, J. A., Ray, D., Baggerly, J., White, J., & Kaplan, D. (2007). Learning more about those who play in session: The national play therapy in counseling practices project. *Journal of Counseling & Development, 85,* 42–46. http://dx.doi.org/10.1002/j.1556-6678.2007.tb00442.x

Landreth, G. L. (2012). *Play therapy: The art of the relationship* (3rd ed.). New York, NY: Routledge.

Lin, D. (2012). Contemporary research on child-centered play therapy (CCPT) modalities: A meta-analytic review of controlled outcome studies. *Dissertation Abstracts International Section A: Humanities and Social Sciences, 73*(3-A), 891.

Mental Health America. (2013). *Recognizing mental health problems in children.* Retrieved from http://www.mentalhealthamerica.net/recognizing-mental-health-problems-children

National Center for Children in Poverty. (2010). *Children's mental health.* Retrieved from http://nccp.org/publications/pub_929.html

New Freedom Commission on Mental Health. (2003). *Achieving the promise: Transforming mental health care in America. Final Report* (DHHD Pub. No. SMA-03-3832). Rockville, MD: U.S. Department of Health and Human Services.

Ojiambo, D., & Bratton, S. C. (2014). Effects of group activity play therapy on problem behaviors of preadolescent Ugandan orphans. *Journal of Counseling & Development, 92,* 355–365.

Packman, J., & Bratton, S. C. (2003). A school-based play/activity therapy intervention with learning disabled preadolescents exhibiting behavior problems. *International Journal of Play Therapy, 12*(2), 7–29. http://dx.doi.org/10.1037/h0088876

Ray, D. (2004). Supervision of basic and advanced skills in play therapy. *Journal of Professional Counseling: Practice, Theory, & Research, 32*(2), 28–41.

Ray, D. C. (2011). *Advanced play therapy: Essential conditions, knowledge and skills for child practice.* New York, NY: Routledge.

Ray, D. C., Blanco, P. J., Sullivan, J. M., & Holliman, R., (2009). An exploratory study of child-centered play therapy with aggressive children. *International Journal of Play Therapy, 18*(3), 162–175.

Ray, D. C., Schottelkorb, A., & Tsai, M.-H., (2007). Play therapy with children exhibiting symptoms of attention deficit hyperactivity disorder. *International Journal of Play Therapy, 16*(2), 95–111.

Ray, D. C., Stulmaker, H. L., Lee, K. R., & Silverman, W. K. (2013). Child-centered play therapy and impairment: Exploring relationships and constructs. *International Journal of Play Therapy, 22*(1), 13–27.

Rogers, C. (1951). *Client-centered therapy: Its current practice, implications, and theory.* Oxford, England: Houghton Mifflin.

Rogers, C. R. (1957). The necessary and sufficient conditions of therapeutic personality change. *Journal of Consulting Psychology, 21*, 95–103. http://dx.doi.org/10.1037/h0045357

Schumann, B. (2010). Effectiveness of child-centered play therapy on children referred for aggression. In J. N. Baggerly, D. C. Ray, & S. C. Bratton (Eds.), *Child-centered play therapy research: The evidence base for effective practice* (pp. 193–208). Hoboken, NJ: Wiley.

Shen, Y.-J. (2002). Short-term group play therapy with Chinese earthquake victims: Effects on anxiety, depression, and adjustment. *International Journal of Play Therapy, 11*(1), 43–63. http://dx.doi.org/10.1037/h0088856

Swan, K. L., & Ray, D. C. (2014). Effects of child-centered play therapy on irritability and hyperactivity behaviors of children with intellectual disabilities. *Journal of Humanistic Counseling, 53*, 120–133.

Taras, H. L., & the American Academy of Pediatrics Committee on School Health. (2004). School-based mental health services. *Pediatrics, 113*, 1839–1845. http://dx.doi.org/10.1542/peds.113.6.1839

U.S. Public Health Service. (2000). *Report of the Surgeon General's conference on children's mental health: A national action agenda.* Washington, DC: Author.

VanFleet, R., Sywulak, A. E., & Sniscak, C. C. (2010). *Child centered play therapy.* New York, NY: Guilford Press.

Wang Flahive, M., & Ray, D. (2007). Effect of group sandtray therapy with preadolescents. *Journal for Specialists in Group Work, 32*, 362–382. http://dx.doi.org/10.1080/01933920701476706

Webster-Stratton, C., & Reid, M. J. (2003). The incredible years parents, teachers, and children training series: A multifaceted treatment approach for young children with conduct problems. In A. E. Kazdin & J. R. Weisz (Eds.), *Evidence-based psychotherapies for children and adolescents* (pp. 224–240). New York, NY: Guilford Press.

West, J. (1996). *Child-centered play therapy* (2nd ed.). London, England: Hodder Arnold.

Wilson, K., Kendrick, P., & Ryan, V. (1992). *Play therapy: A nondirective approach for children and adolescents.* London, England: Baillière Tindall.

II

EMPIRICALLY BASED PLAY INTERVENTIONS FOR INTERNALIZING DISORDERS

4

COGNITIVE–BEHAVIORAL PLAY THERAPY FOR ANXIETY AND DEPRESSION

SUSAN M. KNELL AND MEENA DASARI

THEORETICAL BASIS AND OBJECTIVES OF COGNITIVE–BEHAVIORAL PLAY THERAPY

Cognitive–behavioral play therapy (CBPT) is a developmentally appropriate treatment that has been developed and used with young children (3–8 years old). CBPT is based primarily on cognitive–behavioral theories of emotional development and psychopathology. The foundation of this approach is based on work of Aaron Beck (e.g., 1964, 1976). Behind cognitive–behavioral therapy (CBT) is the belief that behavior is mediated through cognitive processes and that an individual's thoughts determine how she or he feels and behaves in situations. Emotions are determined in large part from one's perception of events—not the event itself. As a result, the cognitions and emotions determine how a person reacts and responds to such

http://dx.doi.org/10.1037/14730-005
Empirically Based Play Interventions for Children, Second Edition, L. A. Reddy, T. M. Files-Hall, and C. E. Schaefer (Editors)

situations. Thus, when one's perception is inaccurate and/or irrational (i.e., cognitive distortions), CBT interventions focus on challenging and replacing the cognitions with more realistic and adaptive perceptions to alleviate negative emotions. In addition, CBT also works on adding behaviors that allow one to better cope with the negative emotion.

The objective of CBPT is to incorporate cognitive and behavioral techniques within a play therapy paradigm. In the past 20 years, CBT has emerged as the most effective treatment for children and adolescents with a range of disorders (Weisz & Kazdin, 2010). Several protocols are considered the gold standard for treating specific disorders in children ages 8 years and older, such as the Coping Cat (Kendall & Hedtke, 2006) for anxiety disorders and the Treatment for Adolescents with Depression Study (TADS) manual (Curry et al., 2000) for depression. However, with very young children, a more traditional CBT approach is problematic. Because CBT relies on more language-based interventions, a more experiential approach is needed. CBPT offers a novel theoretical approach for young children by integrating empirically based techniques—proven to be effective with older individuals—into an activity consistent with their developmental level (i.e., play) across settings. As noted in this volume, CBT interventions integrated with play interventions can result in promising parent and child outcomes (e.g., see Chapters 7, 8, and 9)

DEVELOPMENTAL ISSUES

Although CBT was conceived originally for work with adults, it has been adapted over time to increasingly younger populations. Among the earliest reports of CBT with youths was Kendall and Finch's (1978) intervention for older, school-age children with impulsive behavior that successfully applied behavioral techniques to increase self-control. However, children younger than age 8 years—in the preoperational stage of cognitive development— were thought to lack the cognitive skills to differentiate between logical and irrational/illogical thoughts. Therefore, they were considered too young for CBT. As a result, one challenge of adapting CBT for young children has been to develop methods of delivering CBT without the complexities of language.

CBPT emerged gradually from the fields of developmental and clinical psychology. In the mid-1980s, Phillips (1985), a developmental psychologist, and Berg (1982), through his clinical work, began describing possible ways of incorporating play and CBT. Knell discussed more specific possibilities and introduced the first published paper on the integration of CBT and play therapy (Knell & Moore, 1990). Building on this case report, Knell (1993a, 1993b, 1994, 1997, 1998, 2003, 2009a, 2009b) and her colleagues (Knell & Dasari, 2009, 2010, 2011; Knell & Ruma, 1996, 2003) argued that play, used historically as a means of communicating with young children in therapy, was a logical approach to a more developmentally friendly CBT. Drawing from the play therapy literature and behavior therapy literature on facilitating behavior through modeling (e.g., Bandura, 1969; Meichenbaum, 1971), Knell (1993a) described an approach using puppets, toys, and books to model and interact with children via a CBT framework. The use of play materials helps the therapist communicate in indirect ways. Also, delivering CBT within a play context helps the therapist to be flexible with the child, use more experiential methods of learning, and decreases the need for more language-based communication on the part of both the child and the therapist (Knell, 1999).

Adapting CBT and play has received increasing attention in the past 20 years. Case studies have described children with diagnoses, such as selective mutism (Knell, 1993b), separation anxiety (Knell, 1999), and anxiety disorders (Knell, 1999; Knell & Dasari, 2006), and children who have been sexually abused (Knell & Ruma, 1996, 2003), have sleep problems (Knell, 2000), and who are experiencing parental divorce (Knell, 1993a). Although more focus has been on clinical case studies, increasing focus has been on more empirical documentation of the effectiveness of CBPT (see the Summary of Outcome Studies of CBPT Effectiveness section for a review of this research).

INTERVENTION

CBPT occurs in four phases: introduction, assessment, treatment (including generalization and response prevention), and termination.

Introduction

The therapist typically meets first with the parent(s) to complete a clinical interview regarding symptoms, developmental history, medical history, and family background. At the session, the CBPT therapist, using short scripts with simple language, helps the parents prepare the child for his or her first session. Although this explanation should be child specific, it usually involves (a) a brief explanation of the child's struggles (e.g., "You know how you worry so much about going to preschool"), (b) an action plan (e.g., "There is a 'feelings' doctor who helps kids learn ways to worry less"), and (c) a general sense of what will happen (e.g., "You will go with us next time and get a chance to talk and play with her"). Other recommendations can be added according to the child's particular presenting problems or concerns about seeing a new professional (e.g., "She is really different than your pediatrician. She doesn't wear a white coat and doesn't give shots!"). In addition, the parents can use supplemental materials, such as *A Child's First Book About Play Therapy* (Nemiroff & Annunziato, 1990) to help with the introduction to therapy.

Assessment

In CBPT, assessment usually begins with the clinical interview with the parent(s). The purpose of the clinical interview is to understand the presenting problems and the family, medical, developmental, learning, and social backgrounds. Also, the therapist's understanding of any specific play interests can be helpful in engaging the child in treatment. The development of an initial case conceptualization (i.e., diagnosis and developmental history) is useful before meeting the child for the first session.

The initial sessions with the child provide an enormous amount of information about the child and his or her difficulties. An assessment of play skills is important because research has shown that play therapy is more effective for children with good pretend play skills (Russ, 2004). The assessment of cognitive, emotional, social, and problem-solving abilities also is important; they are assessed in relationship to the child's developmental level, and information is gleaned from an array of sources (e.g., parent and school reports, behavioral observation). We also recommend adding assessment measures that are specific to the presenting problem. For example, for children who present with obsessive compulsive disorder, therapists should complete a Children's Yale-Brown Obsessive-Compulsive Scale with the parents.

The assessment phase should result in an overall case conceptualization that includes a diagnosis (if applicable), biological factors (e.g., temperament, family history), environmental factors (e.g., school functioning, family functioning), and an understanding of the child's play skills. This conceptualization guides treatment. Assessment is an ongoing process and, thus, this case conceptualization may change as more information is gathered and the therapist develops a richer understanding of the child.

Treatment

CBPT is a combination of structured and unstructured time in which the therapist and child interact, typically in a playroom. The therapist is mindful of specific goals (e.g., helping an anxious child approach new situations, working with a phobic child to master a specific fear). Empirically supported techniques from CBT literature are incorporated into the play and adapted to the child's developmental level. The therapist often presents these techniques through modeling. CBPT techniques are divided into cognitive and behavioral techniques (Tables 4.1 and 4.2 include the techniques and examples of implementation).

TABLE 4.1
Cognitive–Behavioral Play Therapy: Cognitive Techniques

Technique	Example With Sample Script
Psychoeducation	Child is shown feeling flashcards, and therapist says, "Kids and grownups have different feelings that come up at different times. We are going to look at each feeling face together and act out times when the feeling might come up. I will go first and then you can go after me."
Cognitive restructuring	Child who is anxious is shown a puppet with picture of a thought bubble above his head, and therapist says, "When kids get worried, they often have thoughts inside their head. My puppet, X, is afraid of dogs. Here is a picture of a 'thought cloud' above X's head. Let's try to figure out some worry thoughts for X, who sees a dog. I can go first: 'The dog will bite me.' Now, your turn."
Positive self-statements	For a child whose parents are divorcing, the puppet says, "I feel sad about my parents' divorce because my dad moved his stuff out today. I am going to say my helpful thoughts: 'I know that both my parents love me' and 'It will take time but I can have two happy homes.' I feel better when I say helpful things."
Problem solving	The puppet says, "I am going to use my steps to work through this. First, what is the problem? I feel worried when I have to go to my babysitter. What can I do to make this easier? I can remember that I will see Mom when she is done with work. I can tell my babysitter when I am worried so we can play a game together. What else can I do? Let's take turns thinking of ideas. Can you think of one?"

Cognitive techniques include the following:

- *Psychoeducation*: teaching the child about his or her specific disorder, normalizing different emotional states, and explaining the CBT model. Psychoeducation offers the child (and family) accurate and developmentally appropriate information. In addition, the CBT framework that cognitions mediate between events, emotions, and behaviors allows parents to understand how techniques will alleviate his or her child's symptoms.
- *Cognitive restructuring*: identifying, challenging, and modifying maladaptive thoughts (i.e., cognitive distortions) that lead to negative emotions. These techniques can be adapted to the child's developmental level (e.g., having the child be a "thought detective" to find thoughts that are interfering or "unhelpful"). Then, questions related to usefulness, evidence for and against, alternative explanations, and an evaluation of outcomes are introduced and aimed at increasing flexibility in the thoughts.

TABLE 4.2
Cognitive–Behavioral Play Therapy: Behavioral Techniques

Technique	Example
Contingency management	For a puppet that is anxious about reading in front of class, the therapist sets up a play situation with two puppets, a developmentally appropriate book, and a sticker chart. The therapist's puppet reads aloud and stops after each sentence so that the child or therapist can put a sticker on the chart. Cognitive restructuring may be added here (e.g., Puppet saying, "This is hard, but I feel good getting through it and getting a sticker").
Shaping	For a puppet that is anxious about talking to new people, the therapist sets up a play situation with a chart, including a few steps that gradually increase expectations for talking (e.g., saying one word, saying a short sentence, asking a question, starting a conversation). The puppet gets a sticker for each step.
Exposure	For a puppet that is fearful of dogs, the therapist creates a visual "fear ladder" that consists of the least to most anxiety-producing task (e.g., looking at pictures of dogs to petting a dog in the therapy room). Each session, the task is selected and the puppet is placed in the situation while giving "worry" ratings of small, medium, or big. The puppet reports a decrease of anxiety over time from big to small worry.
Systematic desensitization	For a puppet with selective mutism that is anxious about talking at school, the therapist sets up a schoollike setting with toys and activities. The puppet whispers while doing an alternative activity (i.e., playing with selected toy, drawing) to increase comfort and tolerance for anxiety.
Relaxation training	The therapist introduces deep breathing by having a puppet do it first. The child and therapist practice it together by placing puppets on stomachs, counting aloud while breathing in and out, and watching as the object rises and falls.

- *Positive self-statements*: teaching the child to say clear, self-affirming statements that replace cognitive distortions. These statements can be modeled by the therapist or using other toys in play. Positive self-statements can teach coping strategies through active control (e.g., "I can walk past that scary house and be fine"), by reducing aversive feelings (e.g., "I will be able to walk past the house"), using reinforcing statements (e.g., "I am brave") and through reality testing (e.g., "There are really no monsters in the attic").
- *Problem solving*: learning a systematic technique for identifying active ways of coping. The child is shown how to identify the problem, generate a goal, brainstorm strategies, evaluate possible outcomes, and select the best strategy.

Behavioral techniques include the following:

- *Modeling*: learning an adaptive behavior designed to manage a negative emotion by observing a model, such as a puppet or character in book. This technique is used throughout treatment. *Bibliotherapy*, specific to CBPT, refers to reading a book in which the characters provide a coping model to children.
- *Relaxation training*: teaching strategies to calm the body's reactions (i.e., physiological sensations), such as deep breathing, imagery, or muscle relaxation. For child-friendly scripts, Pincus's (2012) chapter "Accepting Physical Feelings" is an excellent resource.
- *Systematic desensitization*: reducing negative emotions by replacing a maladaptive behavior with an adaptive one. Anxiety is reduced when the connection between a particular stimulus and fear or anxiety is broken. Systematic desensitization may be induced through calming play activities or visualization of calming scenes (Knell, 2000). At times, this may look like a form of distraction in that fun activities are identified and used when the child is experiencing difficult emotions.
- *Contingency management*: modifying a behavior by consistently implementing consequences or reinforcement. A number of forms of contingency management are used, but positive reinforcement and shaping are used most frequently:
  - (a) *Positive reinforcement*: targeting a behavior and then using pleasurable or motivating events to increase the likelihood of the behavior. Reinforcement can be social (e.g., praise) or material (e.g., stickers, small prizes).
  - (b) *Shaping*: helping a child get progressively closer to a goal. Positive reinforcement is used as the individual makes closer and closer approximations to the goal. Reinforcing small steps is important and allows the goal to be reached.
- *Exposure*: teaching the child to gradually and systematically confront objects or situations to promote habituation. This technique requires the creation of fear hierarchy (or "fear ladder") and the use of techniques developed through treatment (e.g., deep breathing, positive self-statements, positive reinforcement). The child is introduced to difficult situations in a planned, collaborative manner, often in two steps: (a) preparation (i.e., developing a hierarchy and teaching coping skills) and (b) active exposure (i.e., moving through the hierarchy while using adaptive reactions). The therapist assesses the child's readiness for each task.

Through use of the CBT techniques within play, both cognitions and behaviors change through therapy, and result in adaptive behavior. Specifically with cognitive processes, the child learns to say more self-affirming statements to replace distortions. In addition, the child begins to use coping skills, such as relaxation and positive activities during stressful situations, which allows better management of negative emotions.

Generalization and Relapse Prevention

CBT techniques that are learned and practiced in treatment should be generalized to the "real world" to improve overall functioning and maintain gains. With children, significant adults are typically the individuals who support and reinforce a child's new adaptive skills. CBPT therapists should adapt interventions that address generalization directly, keeping those interventions as similar to real-life situations as possible (e.g., creating play scenarios with settings, people, and events that are similar to those in the child's life). Continuing with interventions past the initial acquisition of skills provides an opportunity for the child to not only learn adaptive skills but to maintain them.

Relapse prevention, as developed by Meichenbaum (1985) and Marlatt and Gordon (1985), focuses on minimizing the risk of symptom return. It can be concretized for children by preparing a book of lessons learned. For example, a child with separation issues might have a book called *What To Do When I Miss Mom* (see the first case example presented later in this chapter). Parents can be assisted in knowing what is a relapse versus what is more likely a normal, developmental reaction to a life event. Anticipating such life events can be helpful in aiding the family toward a smoother path during transitions and major life events.

Termination

Termination is a gradual process so that the child can maintain progress and build up support outside of therapy while the therapeutic relationship is removed. Concrete examples are helpful (e.g., "You will be coming in X more times and then we will say goodbye") as are concrete referents (e.g., marking the sessions on a calendar or making a paper chain of remaining sessions). Some children enjoy having a concrete "transitional" object, such as a picture that the child draws for the therapist that is kept in a special place in the office. Children commonly experience a range of feelings about termination of therapy. It is important for the therapist to identify and normalize these feelings by using any of the following strategies:

- providing direct statements, such as "You seem sad that we won't be meeting anymore";
- providing indirect feedback, such as "Some kids tell me that they are sad about stopping therapy";
- modeling appropriate emotions (e.g., "I will miss seeing you, but I am happy to know that you are doing so well");
- validating mixed emotions, such as sadness and excitement; and/or
- explaining that saying goodbye is hard but part of life (e.g., teachers at the end of the year, counselors at the end of camp).

Parents are included in the termination process and should be provided criteria for returning to therapy.

KEY TREATMENT INGREDIENTS FOR THE INTERVENTION

Integration of Play and CBT

CBPT is completely play focused and integrated with CBT techniques. Several authors have discussed the use of play to facilitate CBT. Games or art projects are used to gather information, teach one specific cognitive or behavioral concept, and improve motivation (Pincus, Chase, Chow, Weiner, & Pian, 2011). Using play in targeted way, though, is different from integrating CBT techniques within a play therapy paradigm.

Materials

CBPT usually takes place in a playroom or office with room for the child and therapist to move and play. Essential CBPT materials include puppets, paper, crayons or markers, family characters, stickers, and books. Ideally, the playroom is well stocked with toys for both genders and for a range of ages and interests. Nonetheless, at times, a specific toy may be needed to help an individual. For example, a child who is having difficulty adjusting to crutches might be able to pretend with crutches created from pipe cleaners.

Therapist's Role

To blend CBT with play therapy techniques, the CBPT therapist relies on a balance between structured, therapist-driven play and less structured, child-driven play. The structured parts of sessions allow the therapist to introduce specific CBT techniques, such as relaxation and cognitive restructuring. Unstructured play is important and is integrated into sessions. The therapist observes the child's spontaneously generated material as a window into the child's thoughts, emotions, and behaviors.

Therapeutic Relationship

Similar to more traditional play therapy, CBPT therapists use empathy and warmth to build a positive relationship with the child (Russ, 2004). Although play is an engaging and enjoyable activity, CBPT builds confidence and mastery over difficult emotions. Therefore, therapeutic relationship allows the child to view adults as empathic and helpful. It also is critical that CBPT take place within the context of a trusting therapeutic relationship because the therapist is encouraging the child to approach the tasks that the child had avoided previously.

Parent/Caregiver Involvement

Because CBPT is used with young children, parents typically are involved in the therapy, although decisions regarding the extent of that involvement are made on a case-by-case basis. Most often, parents, often inadvertently, are reinforcing maladaptive behaviors (e.g., attention). They are taught to use a combination of the following at home: positive reinforcement for adaptive coping, consequences for negative behavior, and ignoring for negative behavior that is annoying but not harmful. Parents also may be involved in assessment and information gathering because they observe the child's behavior in multiple settings. The parents may need support and/or psychoeducation related to the child's presenting problems and normal child development.

CASE EXAMPLES

Case 1: Aaron (6½ Years Old; Separation Anxiety)

Aaron, age 6½ years, was referred because of separation issues. In kindergarten, he cried daily when left at school and began to exhibit fear of separation at dinner on school nights. He woke up during the night with fears, had many somatic complaints, and asked to stay home. He followed his teacher around and often would spend time with a school administrator when very upset. Aaron did not have any traumatic experiences as a young child, but was from a close-knit family and had only been separated from mom in the presence of other family members. He was removed from a preschool because he could not separate from mom.

During play, Aaron was encouraged to talk and play about school and his family. The children's book *The Kissing Hand* (Penn, 1993), whose main character is a raccoon that does not want to separate from his mom to go to school, was used. Aaron happily practiced making the "kissing hand" (i.e., American Sign Language "I love you" sign). At each session, he readily engaged in creating books, such as *What To Do When I Miss Mom*. With the assistance of the therapist, Aaron created positive self-statements and coping statements, and illustrations about going to school and separating from mom. When Aaron struggled with creating a statement, the therapist suggested a positive coping statement. Examples follow:

- "I miss mom, but I will see her after school."
- "She is fine. While I am at school, she is home taking care of my baby brother and the house."
- "Things I like about school: Art, computer, recess, lunch."
- "When I miss mom, I can remember *The Kissing Hand*."

The parents were encouraged to positively reinforce his "brave" behaviors. Stickers were used for separating from mom without crying. Parents were asked to praise Aaron's efforts to be brave (shaping) and ignore behaviors that interfered (extinction). The administrator was encouraged to not remove Aaron from the classroom because it seemed that her attention was providing negative reinforcement for his difficulties. Play included encouraging Aaron to express his feelings through toys (he particularly liked to express his feelings with toy cars).

Aaron's behavior changed markedly. He still expressed that he missed mom, but he began to go to school daily without struggling with his parents and complaining. He stopped crying in the mornings, became much less emotional about his separation issues, and was sleeping better at night.

Case 2: Peter (Age 7 Years; Generalized Anxiety Disorder and Learning Disorder)

Peter is 7-year-old boy who was referred for generalized anxiety and tantrums at home and at school. A recent neuropsychological report indicated diagnoses of dyslexia and expressive language disorder. Peter's anxiety was triggered by perfectionism but initially presented as frustration around his inability to express emotions. When he perceived that an event did not occur as planned or that he was not performing to expectations, he would cry, yell, and refuse to comply with adult requests. Because this behavior was displayed with greater frequency and intensity with parents, family work was added to treatment.

To develop the ability to express emotions (particularly anxiety) using language, Peter was provided psychoeducation on emotions, which was adapted to his learning style and language difficulties. Verbal information, such as emotional labels, was paired with visual information. For example, to illustrate sad, happy, worried, and mad, Peter was shown YouTube videos. When specific emotions were expressed, the video was stopped to discuss the triggering event, facial expressions, and body language. Parents were instructed to complete a feeling chart with Peter each night to generalize the skill.

Once Peter was able to identify emotions in session and at home, a dog puppet named "Pooch" was introduced into play as a character that also "has a hard time with feelings." In session, modeling and shaping were used to develop Peter's ability to describe emotions, thoughts, and behaviors. For each step, Peter was able to earn a reward of game time with the therapist. Initially, Peter and Pooch took turns talking about the events and what emotion was triggered. Then, both took turns talking about thoughts that led to the emotion. Family sessions supplemented individual sessions. With the therapist present, the parents and the child practiced talking through the emotions that triggered the tantrums in the past week. The parents were coached to calmly ask questions, use positive reinforcement (i.e., praise), and normalize emotional reactions.

To lessen his anxiety, Peter was taught CBT techniques of deep breathing, cognitive restructuring, and systematic desensitization using the Coping Cat as a guide (Kendall & Hedtke, 2006). Pooch was present throughout the sessions as visual cue and support when talking about anxiety. For Peter, the majority of sessions focused on cognitive restructuring, which was modified by simplifying language, using visual information, and repeating concepts. Specifically, maladaptive thoughts were labeled "unhappy thoughts" and adaptive thoughts were labeled "happy thoughts." All thoughts were written down on drawings that Peter made or thought bubble worksheets. Here are some examples:

- For the event of switching to a school for learning disorders, "I won't have any friends" was replaced with "It's possible I will make friends and have fun."
- For the event of the babysitter being late for after-school pickup, "My babysitter will never come get me, and I will be stuck here" was replaced with "My babysitter is just running late."
- For the event of dad's saying no to a request, "My dad doesn't love me" was replaced with "My dad loves me but needs to do something important."

Peter learned to express and manage his anxiety, which resulted in a decrease in the frequency and intensity of his tantrums. He talked about feeling anxious when events did not go as planned or when making a mistake. His parents responded by coaching him to use his techniques (i.e., deep breathing, happy thoughts). Also, Peter started to perceive himself to be as competent as other children his age, which was reinforced by his switch to a school for children with learning disorders.

SUMMARY OF OUTCOME STUDIES OF CBPT EFFECTIVENESS

On the basis of the outcome studies to date, CBPT may be an effective intervention for young children. Pearson (2007) explored the outcomes of this approach in preschool children within a school setting by comparing an intervention group with a matched nonplay control group. The children in the cognitive–behavioral play intervention group were seen individually for three sessions that incorporated play with CBT techniques. Teachers reported significantly higher hope, higher social competence, and fewer anxiety withdrawal symptoms in the intervention group. Although more research is needed with clinical populations and with the use of formalized CBPT (i.e., intervention being consistent across children in treatment group), the study was one of the first to empirically support CBPT interventions.

Two lines of related outcome research provide further evidence for CBPT's effectiveness with young children. First, CBT is considered the most effective treatment for children with a range of disorders, especially for internalizing disorders, such as anxiety and depression (Compton et al., 2004; Weisz & Kazdin, 2010). To date, outcomes of the few studies in which individual CBT has been adapted for young children (i.e., ages 3–8 years) have been mixed (Cohen & Mannarino, 1996; Deblinger, Stauffer, & Steer, 2001). However, in a recent meta-analysis, Reynolds, Wilson, Austin, and Hooper (2012) analyzed the existing data to determine whether CBT was effective for young children. Their findings indicated that children aged 4 years to 8 years who received CBT displayed better outcomes than controls but to a smaller degree when compared with children ages 9 to 18 years. Therefore, to increase the effectiveness of CBT for young children, CBPT is likely to be a beneficial approach.

In addition, recent reviews have shown play therapy interventions to be effective in treating children's internalizing and externalizing symptoms (Bratton & Ray, 2000; Bratton, Ray, Rhine, & Jones, 2005; Davenport & Bourgeois, 2008; Leblanc & Ritchie, 2001). Bratton et al. (2005) conducted a meta-analysis of 93 outcome studies with children who were, on average, 7 years old. Results indicated a large effect size for play interventions (i.e., .80), which indicated that children who received the intervention reported better outcomes than children who did not. Overall, given the current support for CBT with children older than age 9 years along with the utility of play therapy interventions in children ages 3 to 8 years, a strong empirical foundation exists that CBPT may increase effectiveness of CBT with young children.

RECOMMENDATIONS

Use in Other Populations

CBPT has been developed for use with young children ages 3 years to 8 years with both internalizing and externalizing disorders. Currently, many case studies have described CBPT with a range of presenting problems. In addition to the presenting problems already cited, CBPT is likely to be a useful treatment modality in a number of other populations that include, but are not limited to the following:

- Learning disorders: CBPT is appropriate due to the low reliance on verbal communication. We recommend integrating visual information (e.g., worksheets) and repetition of concepts with play.
- Older children: CBPT techniques have been effective when blended into treatment for children ages 8 years and older. For example, in the empirically supported manual for anxiety, Coping Cat is a character that is introduced as having anxiety, and modeling is used to help learn techniques (Kendall & Hedtke, 2006).
- Trauma based: Play has been integrated into trauma-focused CBT (e.g., Briggs, Runyon, & Deblinger, 2011; Deblinger, McLeer, & Henry, 1990). Briggs et al. (2011) contended that the success of this approach is based on the therapist's creativity, so that incorporating play into trauma-focused treatment is a natural fit.
- Preventative: Pearson (2007) compared a CBP intervention group with a matched control of preschoolers and found support for a more preventative, nonclinical approach in school settings.

Transporting

CBPT has been developed for use in clinical settings for outpatient therapy (e.g., Knell, 1993a) and has yet to be fully developed and validated for use in alternative settings, such as schools and medical centers. Therefore, it is recommended that CBPT, once provided in clinical settings, be generalized to home, school, or other settings, which is considered a key ingredient to the intervention. The steps should be as follows:

1. The therapist identifies the most useful CBT techniques for each child.
2. The therapist creates a plan with parents, caregivers, teachers, or school staff to transfer the techniques to the specific setting. Depending on the child's level of mastery, the techniques can

be practiced with play objects or in the situations that trigger symptoms.

3. Adults are asked to track successful implementation so that progress is reported back to the therapist.

For example, with a child with separation anxiety, parents are instructed to give stickers for doing adaptive behavior (e.g., relaxation, positive self-statements) and for gradually being able to stay with other trusted adults (e.g., teachers, babysitters). Meanwhile, teachers are taught to give stickers for adaptive behavior in the classroom. Both parents and teachers are asked to report number of stickers earned per week.

Future Research

Because it integrates play and CBT, CBPT is a valuable intervention for young children. Although play therapy and CBT independently have been shown to be highly effective interventions for children, research is needed to determine the effectiveness of CBPT in particular. One recommendation is for the development of a manualized approach. However, the challenge is that the manual must maintain a balance between structured sessions for consistent implementation and flexibility for an individual approach that allows for spontaneous play. Once developed, a manual can provide the foundation for conducting randomized clinical intervention studies to establish effectiveness.

It is also recommended that research be designed to explore alternative settings and modalities for CBPT. To date, of the published clinical case studies, CBPT has been provided in outpatient settings for clinical populations only. CBPT may be effective in schools, medical settings, and residential treatment facilities. Also, CBPT should be studied when delivered in a group format or preventatively (i.e., nonclinical populations). Based on the outcome of these lines of research, CBPT would have a wider scope and more guidelines for use outside of clinical settings. Although more research is needed on the effectiveness of standardized CBPT, it is a developmentally sensitive intervention that integrates CBT and play therapy and is useful for treatment of internalizing and externalizing disorders in young children.

REFERENCES

Bandura, A. (1969). *Principles of behavior modification*. New York, NY: Holt, Rinehart and Winston.

Beck, A. T. (1964). Thinking and depression. II. Theory and therapy. *Archives of General Psychiatry*, 10, 561–571. http://dx.doi.org/10.1001/archpsyc.1964.01720240015003

Beck, A. T. (1976). *Cognitive therapy and the emotional disorders*. New York, NY: International Universities Press.

Berg, B. (1982). *The changing family game: A problem-solving program for children of divorce*. Dayton, OH: Cognitive–Behavioral Resources.

Bratton, S., & Ray, D. (2000). What the research shows about play therapy. *International Journal of Play Therapy, 9*(1), 47–88. http://dx.doi.org/10.1037/h0089440

Bratton, S. C., Ray, D., Rhine, T., & Jones, L. (2005). The efficacy of play therapy with children: A meta-analytic review of treatment outcomes. *Professional Psychology: Research and Practice, 36*, 376–390. http://dx.doi.org/10.1037/0735-7028.36.4.376

Briggs, K. M., Runyon, M. K., & Deblinger, E. (2011). The use of play in trauma-focused cognitive–behavioral therapy. In S. W. Russ & L. N. Niec (Eds.), *Play in clinical practice: Evidence-based approaches* (pp. 168–200). New York, NY: Guilford Press.

Cohen, J. A., & Mannarino, A. P. (1996). A treatment outcome study for sexually abused preschool children: Initial findings. *Journal of the American Academy of Child & Adolescent Psychiatry, 35*, 42–50. http://dx.doi.org/10.1097/00004583-199601000-00011

Compton, S. N., March, J. S., Brent, D., Albano, A. M., Weersing, V. R., & Curry, J. (2004). Cognitive–behavioral psychotherapy for anxiety and depressive disorders in children and adolescents: An evidence-based medicine review. *Journal of the American Academy of Child & Adolescent Psychiatry, 43*, 930–959. http://dx.doi.org/10.1097/01.chi.0000127589.57468.bf

Curry, J. F., Wells, K. C., Brent, D. A., Clarke, G. N., Rohde, P., & Albano, A. M, . . . March, J. S. (2000). *Treatment for adolescents with depression study (TADS): Cognitive Behavior Therapy Manual*. Durham, NC: Duke University Medical Center.

Davenport, B. R., & Bourgeois, N. M. (2008). Play, aggression, the preschool child, and the family: A review of the literature to guide empirically informed play therapy with aggressive preschool children. *International Journal of Play Therapy, 17*(1), 2–23. http://dx.doi.org/10.1037/1555-6824.17.1.2

Deblinger, E., McLeer, S. V., & Henry, D. (1990). Cognitive behavioral treatment for sexually abused children suffering post-traumatic stress: Preliminary findings. *Journal of the American Academy of Child & Adolescent Psychiatry, 29*, 747–752. http://dx.doi.org/10.1097/00004583-199009000-00012

Deblinger, E., Stauffer, L. B., & Steer, R. A. (2001). Comparative efficacies of supportive and cognitive behavioral group therapies for young children who have been sexually abused and their nonoffending mothers. *Child Maltreatment, 6*, 332–343. http://dx.doi.org/10.1177/1077559501006004006

Kendall, P. C., & Finch, A. J., Jr. (1978). A cognitive–behavioral treatment for impulsivity: A group comparison study. *Journal of Consulting and Clinical Psychology, 46*, 110–118. http://dx.doi.org/10.1037/0022-006X.46.1.110

Kendall, P. C., & Hedtke, K. A. (2006). *Coping Cat workbook* (3rd ed.). Ardmore, PA: Workbook.

Knell, S. M. (1993a). *Cognitive–behavioral play therapy*. Lanham, MD: Jason Aronson.

Knell, S. M. (1993b). To show and not tell: Cognitive–behavioral play therapy in the treatment of elective mutism. In T. Kottman & C. Schaefer (Eds.), *Play therapy in action: A casebook for practitioners* (pp. 169–208). Northvale, NJ: Jason Aronson.

Knell, S. M. (1994). Cognitive–behavioral play therapy. In K. O'Connor & C. Schaefer (Eds.). *Handbook of play therapy: Vol. 2. Advances and innovations.* (pp. 111–142). New York, NY: Wiley.

Knell, S. M. (1997). Cognitive–behavioral play therapy. In K. J. O'Connor, & L. M. Braverman (Eds.), *Play therapy: Theory and practice—A comparative presentation* (pp. 79–99). New York, NY: Wiley.

Knell, S. M. (1998). Cognitive–behavioral play therapy. *Journal of Clinical Child Psychology, 27,* 28–33. http://dx.doi.org/10.1207/s15374424jccp2701_3

Knell, S. M. (1999). Cognitive behavioral play therapy. In S. W. Russ & T. Ollendick (Eds.), *Handbook of psychotherapies with children and families* (pp. 385–404). New York, NY: Plenum Press. http://dx.doi.org/10.1007/978-1-4615-4755-6_20

Knell, S. M. (2000). Cognitive–behavioral play therapy with children with fears and phobias. In H. G. Kaduson & C. E. Schaefer (Eds.), *Short-term therapies with children* (pp. 3–27). New York, NY: Guilford Press.

Knell, S. M. (2003). Cognitive–behavioral play therapy. In C. E. Schaefer (Ed.), *Foundations of play therapy* (pp. 175–191). New York, NY: Wiley.

Knell, S. M. (2009a). Cognitive–behavioral play therapy. In K. J. O'Connor & L. D. Braverman (Eds.), *Play therapy: Theory and practice—Comparing theories and techniques* (2nd ed., pp. 203–236). New York, NY: Wiley.

Knell, S. M. (2009b). Cognitive behavioral play therapy: Theory and applications. In A. A. Drewes (Ed.), *Blending play therapy with cognitive behavioral therapy: Evidence-based and other effective treatments and techniques* (pp. 117–133). Hoboken, NJ: Wiley.

Knell, S. M., & Dasari, M. (2006). Cognitive–behavioral play therapy for children with anxiety and phobias. In H. G. Kaduson & C. E. Schaefer (Eds.), *Short-term therapies with children* (2nd ed., pp. 22–50). New York, NY: Guilford Press.

Knell, S. M., & Dasari, M. (2009). CBPT: Implementing and integrating CBPT into clinical practice. In A. A. Drewes (Ed.), *Blending play therapy and cognitive behavioral therapy: Evidence-based and other effective treatments and techniques* (pp. 321–352). Hoboken, NJ: Wiley.

Knell, S. M., & Dasari, M. (2010). Cognitive–behavioral play therapy for preschoolers: Integrating play and cognitive–behavioral interventions. In C. E. Schaefer (Ed.), *Play therapy for preschool children* (pp. 157–178). Washington, DC: American Psychological Association. http://dx.doi.org/10.1037/12060-008

Knell, S. M., & Dasari, M. (2011). Cognitive behavioral play therapy. In S. W. Russ & L. N. Niec (Eds.), *An evidence-based approach to play in intervention and prevention: Integrating developmental and clinical science* (pp. 236–262). New York, NY: Guilford Press.

Knell, S. M., & Moore, D. J. (1990). Cognitive–behavioral play therapy in the treatment of encopresis. *Journal of Clinical Child Psychology, 19,* 55–60. http://dx.doi.org/10.1207/s15374424jccp1901_7

Knell, S. M., & Ruma, C. D. (1996). Play therapy with a sexually abused child. In M. A. Reinecke, F. M. Dattilio, & A. Freeman (Eds.), *Cognitive therapy with children and adolescents: A casebook for clinical practice* (pp. 367–393). New York, NY: Guilford Press.

Knell, S. M., & Ruma, C. D. (2003). Play therapy with a sexually abused child. In M. A. Reinecke, F. M. Dattilio, & A. Freeman (Eds.), *Cognitive therapy with children and adolescents: A casebook for clinical practice* (2nd ed., pp. 338–368). New York, NY: Guilford Press.

Leblanc, M., & Ritchie, M. (2001). A meta-analysis of play therapy outcomes. *Counselling Psychology Quarterly, 14,* 149–163. http://dx.doi.org/10.1080/09515070110059142

Marlatt, G. A., & Gordon, J. R. (1985). *Relapse prevention: Maintenance strategies in the treatment of addictive behaviors.* New York, NY: Guilford Press.

Meichenbaum, D. (1985). *Stress inoculation training.* New York, NY: Pegamon Press.

Meichenbaum, D. H. (1971). Examination of model characteristics in reducing avoidance behavior. *Journal of Personality and Social Psychology, 17,* 298–307. http://dx.doi.org/10.1037/h0030593

Nemiroff, M. A., & Annunziato, J. (1990). *A child's first book about play therapy.* Washington, DC: Magination Press.

Pearson, B. (2007). *Effects of a cognitive behavioral play intervention on children's hope and school adjustment* (Unpublished doctoral dissertation). Case Western Reserve University, Cleveland, OH.

Penn, A. (1993). *The kissing hand.* Washington, DC: Child Welfare League of America.

Phillips, R. D. (1985). Whistling in the dark? A review of play therapy research. *Psychotherapy: Theory, Research, Practice, Training, 22,* 752–760. http://dx.doi.org/10.1037/h0085565

Pincus, D. B. (2012). *Growing up brave: Expert strategies for helping your child overcome fear, stress, and anxiety.* New York, NY: Little, Brown.

Pincus, D. B., Chase, R. M., Chow, C., Weiner, C. L., & Pian, J. (2011). Integrating play into cognitive–behavioral therapy for child anxiety disorders. In S. W. Russ & L. N. Niec (Eds.), *Play in clinical practice: Evidence-based approaches* (pp. 218–235). New York, NY: Guilford Press.

Reynolds, S., Wilson, C., Austin, J., & Hooper, L. (2012). Effects of psychotherapy for anxiety in children and adolescents: A meta-analytic review. *Clinical Psychology Review, 32,* 251–262. http://dx.doi.org/10.1016/j.cpr.2012.01.005

Russ, S. W. (2004). *Play in child development and psychotherapy: Toward empirically supported practice.* Mahwah, NJ: Erlbaum.

Weisz, J. R., & Kazdin, A. E. (2010). *Evidence-based psychotherapies for children and adolescents.* New York, NY: Guilford Press.

5

USING INTEGRATED DIRECTIVE AND NONDIRECTIVE PLAY INTERVENTIONS FOR ABUSED AND TRAUMATIZED CHILDREN

ELIANA M. GIL

Traditionally, when people think of play therapy, they tend to think of child-centered (or nondirective) play therapy. This default setting anchored in psychoanalytic tradition was rightfully earned through a historical foundation set in the 1900s by Anna Freud and Melanie Klein (Schaefer, 1999). The development of play therapy theories has been well documented (O'Connor & Braverman, 1997, 2009), and contemporary play therapists enjoy an array of meaningful choices that guide their clinical work. The theories and approaches are so varied that when people say they are "trained in play therapy," it is prudent to explore what theoretical framework guides their work.

Charles Schaefer, one of the pioneers in play therapy theory and education, used the term *prescriptive* in reference to a tailored play therapy approach

http://dx.doi.org/10.1037/14730-006
Empirically Based Play Interventions for Children, Second Edition, L. A. Reddy, T. M. Files-Hall, and C. E. Schaefer (Editors)

that fits the intervention to clients' unique needs. Schaefer (2001) stated that the prescriptive approach

> espouses as its core premise the "differential therapeutics" concept (Frances, Clarkin, & Perry, 1984), which holds that some play interventions are more effective than others for certain disorders and that a client who does poorly with one type of play therapy may do well with another (Beutler, 1979). (p. 58)

Therefore, the prescriptive therapist explores the research literature for evidence-based treatments that have outcome data showing effectiveness for target problems. Integrated play therapists tailor their approach to clients by drawing on a wealth of supportive evidence- and practice-based literature (Bratton, Ray, Rhine, & Jones, 2005; Christophersen & Mortweet, 2001; Reddy, Files-Hall, & Schaefer, 2005), and are not limited to a single treatment approach.

Abused and traumatized children, in particular, are in need of integrated treatment because trauma affects a multitude of facets of development and functioning, and children can present with varied symptomology, depending on the type of trauma and the individual child.

CHILDHOOD TRAUMA

According to the U.S. Department of Health and Human Services (DHHS) 2010 report, child protective services received around 3.3 million reports of child maltreatment (DHHS, 2011). Of those, 695,000 were judged to be victims of maltreatment—a number that may underestimate true occurrences. Of those reports, 78% were of neglect; 18%, physical abuse; 9%, sexual abuse; and 8%, emotional abuse. In addition, 34% of victims were younger than age 4 years (DHHS, 2011).

All forms of abuse and neglect, especially complex trauma, affect many aspects of children's development, including physical, emotional, and behavioral regulation, and social and relational development (Anda et al., 2006; Cicchetti & Toth, 1995; Cook et al., 2005; van der Kolk et al., 2009). The effects of abuse and trauma are compounded when experienced in childhood and can manifest themselves in other common psychological symptoms and diagnoses (Anda et al., 2006; van der Kolk et al., 1996). Therefore, it is imperative that practitioners are trained on trauma-informed, evidence-based assessment and intervention for abused and traumatized children.

Complex trauma is a relatively new term that refers to situations of interpersonal violence with family members or trusted caretakers, or with multiple perpetrators. It is punctuated by chronicity (i.e., it crosses developmental ages and stages) and occurs with families that are enduring multiple stressors in their lives. van der Kolk and Courtois (2005) suggested that this is a better term for describing the pervasive negative effect of chronic trauma, including loss of sense of safety and sense of self, trust and self-worth difficulties, the tendency to be revictimized, and psychological fragmentation.

Trauma model proponents have pointed to specific critical domains that clinicians must address in their treatments (Ford & Cloitre, 2010; Goodyear-Brown, 2012). Cook et al. (2005) found that children exposed to complex trauma had impairment in the following domains: attachment, biology, affect or emotional regulation, dissociation, behavioral control, cognition, and self-concept. Those domains are consistently viewed as relevant in the treatment of traumatized children and suggest areas for focused attention (i.e., attachment, self-regulation, trauma processing, and identity enhancement). Ford and Cloitre (2010) and Saunders (2012) have advocated for the selection of evidence-based practices for sexually abused children and have listed several well-tested programs, including trauma-focused cognitive–behavioral therapy (TF-CBT), the current treatment of choice for complex trauma in children.

An integrated play approach is a useful alternative when traditional cognitive behavioral therapy (CBT) treatment is ineffectual because of children's young age or style of noncompliance. Integrative play therapy (in the context of systemic/contextual approaches) is uniquely suited to young children's mode of expression.

INTEGRATED PLAY THERAPY

An integrated approach is consistent with the literature on integrated psychotherapy, which boldly promotes incorporating theories and approaches for the client's benefit. Norcross (2005) noted that integrated psychotherapy is "characterized by dissatisfaction with single-school approaches and concomitant desire to look across school boundaries to see what can be learned from other ways of conducting psychotherapy." (p. 4). Several authors have advocated for integration, blending, and incorporating approaches and techniques (Drewes, Bratton, & Schaefer, 2011; Gil, 2006; Kenney-Noziska, Schaefer, & Homeyer, 2012; Shelby & Felix, 2005). However, each of these approaches differs in its choices and use of techniques as determined by its theoretical foundation.

Play therapy has curative factors that include its inherent communication and self-expression potential (Schaefer, 1992), and ability to accessing problem-solving capacities, role-playing, and attachment formation. In addition, Gil (2010), Schaefer (1994), Terr (1981), and others have chronicled a unique type of play that tends to emerge in the play of traumatized children: posttraumatic play, an organic choice for young children who have a desire to externalize their worries and distress. In doing so, anchored in what we know about posttrauma play, namely, its mastery intent, children may become willing and able to use this form of reparative play strategically to externalize their concerns, thus exposing themselves gradually to feared experiences and subsequent thoughts and emotions. Play therapists may then witness how the child's posttrauma play facilitates the child's self-inherent healing process through the therapist–child relationship (i.e., modeling secure attachment), or they may directly stimulate the child's participation in posttrauma play in a variety of ways: by providing them with symbol triggers reminiscent of the traumatic events and/or by leading the play toward sense of control over and mastery of feared stimuli.

An integrated play therapy approach would use nondirective and directive techniques, and would focus simultaneously on relational, emotional, and cognitive mastery, as directed by the individual child's needs. This approach also would address relational dynamics that surround conditions of abuse in families. The integrated play therapy model proposed in this chapter is specifically based on the concept of assimilative integration, which Norcross (2005) described as a form of integration which "entails a firm grounding in one system of psychotherapy, but with a willingness to actively incorporate (assimilate) practices and views from other systems" (p. 10).

THEORETICAL BASIS OF INTEGRATED TRAUMA-FOCUSED INTEGRATIVE PLAY THERAPY

Child-Directed Play Therapy

The foundational treatment ingredient for this model is curative child-directed play (Gil, 2012). Therapists provide children with opportunities for self-expression and communication alternatives that are not limited to verbal therapy. Examples of communication alternatives include puppets, art, or sandplay. These modes allow children to externalize their worries or preoccupations, process traumatic events, and explore and reflect on their play to gain insight, and give children opportunities for mastery and to restore personal power and control.

Throughout this process, the therapist may use cognitive–behavioral interventions, another key ingredient. As reviewed previously, a wealth of evidence supports the treatment efficacy of TF-CBT (Chaffin & Friedrich, 2004; Mannarino, Cohen, Deblinger, Runyon, & Steer, 2012). Within the play metaphor, the therapist may reframe and challenge cognitive distortions stemming from the traumatic or abusive experiences processed by the child. The therapist may facilitate cognitive exploration of the child's play to help the child gain insight. As the child communicates more directly and literally about the trauma or abuse, the therapist may take a literal and directive role in educating the child about safety, personal boundaries, and healthy relationships. The therapist also teaches and practices positive coping strategies with the child.

Attachment-Based Therapy

Another influential ingredient in children's healing from trauma and abuse is secure attachment relationships. Parent–child interaction therapy (PCIT) is based on both CBT and attachment theories. It was designed for children who experience a range of behavioral, emotional, or family problems, and has been shown to be effective with cases of child maltreatment (Timmer, Urquiza, Zebell, & McGrath, 2005). Parents are trained in warmth, positive attention, discipline, limit-setting, consistency, and other parenting skills. Parents then practice, in a play setting with their child, skills that are characteristic of secure parent–child attachment relationships (Eyberg, Nelson, & Boggs, 2008; Kaminski, Valle, Filene, & Boyle, 2008).

Dozier et al.'s (2009) attachment and biobehavioral catch-up (ABC) model has a distinguishing feature of providing attachment work in which parents are coached to be "co-regulators" of children's emotions through responsive, nurturing interactions. In clinical trials of the effect of this intervention on maltreated foster children, it was shown to lower cortisol levels (Dozier, Peloso, Lewis, Laurenceau, & Levine, 2008) and was associated with reduced avoidant behavior of children (Dozier et al., 2009).

Dyadic developmental psychotherapy (DDP) is another attachment-based therapy that has been tested with children with histories of maltreatment against a control group (Becker-Weidman & Hughes, 2008). Children in treatment experienced clinical significant improvement in secure attachment with caregivers and decreases in symptomatic behavior, as measured by the child behavior checklist (CBCL). Those improvements extended up to 4 years posttreatment (Becker-Weidman & Hughes, 2008). The effectiveness of these three treatments, namely, PCIT, ABC, and DDP, provides evidence for the importance of involving attachment figures and fostering the quality of children's attachment relationships in an integrated model of treatment. In addition, the integration of Theraplay (Booth & Jernberg, 2009), Circle of Security (Cassidy, Woodhouse, Sherman, Stupica, & Lejuez, 2011; Hoffman, Marvin, Cooper, & Powell, 2006) and filial therapy (Van Fleet, 2005) with the client population (i.e., primarily complex trauma cases) has had a huge effect on establishing or enhancing parent–child attachments, which, in turn, contributes to a more secure, stable, protective, and nurturing environment. Furthermore, many child clients have witnessed domestic violence, and child–parent psychotherapy (Lieberman & Van Horn, 2005, 2008) has been found to provide guidance for dyadic work that seeks to restore mother to a protective parent in the child's eyes and that makes discrete efforts to strengthen and support the parent's role. Each of these models works directly with parents (alone or in dyads) in diverse ways to encourage them to view their children's needs differently and to use nurturing, safe, and positive interactions with their children.

Systemic/Contextual Dynamics

The final treatment ingredient is addressing systemic or contextual dynamics that contribute to or maintain the possibility of abuse. In addition to the aforementioned family-based models that focus primarily on younger children, multisystemic therapy (MST) is an empirically supported treatment—tested mostly with older, physically abused children or children in the juvenile justice system (Littell, Popa, & Forsythe, 2005)—that uses systems theory and intervenes with patterns in the family and between the family and outside systems, such as relatives, schools, or other involved agencies (Brunk, Henggeler, & Whelan, 1987; Swenson, Schaeffer, Henggeler, Faldowski, & Mayhew, 2010).

Thus, significant evidence supports the inclusion of a range of interventions in an integrated play approach to therapy with abused and traumatized children. With child-directed play as a foundation, the integrated play therapy approach described in this chapter also uses cognitive–behavioral, attachment-based, and systemic/contextual interventions, as determined by the individual child's needs, to promote healing. The following case example illustrates the practical application of this integrated treatment approach.

KEY TREATMENT INGREDIENTS FOR TRAUMA-FOCUSED INTEGRATIED PLAY THERAPY

It is difficult to estimate a precise number of sessions for integrated play therapy approaches; however, 3 to 6 months (12–24 sessions) might be an adequate time frame to consider to accommodate a good assessment and treatment of initial symptoms within stable environments. Toy and art supplies are necessary to provide children with ample alternative communication strategies. This model is best provided by registered play therapists or child therapists with specialized training in art, sand, play, and other expressive therapies. An integrated approach presumes an easy and smooth shifting from nondirective to directive techniques designed to promote specific goals.

PROPOSED MODEL CASE EXAMPLE

Rodrigo, a 4-year-old Hispanic child, was adopted at age 2 years when his birth mother's parental rights were terminated because of pervasive and persistent child neglect. Rodrigo had been in three foster homes before placement with his current adoptive parents, Stefan and Angela. He was separated at age 3 years from his older brother, Patricio, who systematically physically abused Rodrigo. Patricio had been diagnosed with reactive attachment disorder and was referred to a residential treatment center with no contact with Rodrigo subsequent to his placement.

Rodrigo was referred to treatment because of his history and some unique symptoms that had emerged in the past 6 months. Angela had given birth to her first child, Carlos, now close to age 1 year. Around the time of Carlos's birth, Rodrigo had become more clingy and had showed regressive behaviors: He sucked his thumb, wanted to sleep with his adoptive parents, and touched his penis excessively and publicly. Angela also was concerned that Rodrigo wanted to breast-feed; he became extremely disruptive whenever she breast-fed Carlos.

Angela also shared that she was concerned about her own "postpartum depression" and her lack of patience. She said she was fatigued most of the time and found herself irritated by Rodrigo's babyish behaviors, which she understood intellectually but felt unable to respond to in the way she had hoped. Angela stated that because her husband was currently working two jobs to send money home to his ailing mother, she felt that she should not burden him with child care and carefully protected his rest time.

This assessment information indicated that complex factors potentially were contributing to Rodrigo's symptoms. Clearly, the parents were seeking behavioral intervention for distinct symptoms (i.e., sucking his thumb, bedtime routine, touching his penis). In addition, attachment and family systemic dynamics were contributing to Rodrigo's behavior. At this point, Rodrigo's perspective had yet to be assessed, which is the core premise of the integrated play therapy approach.

In my first session with Rodrigo, he looked around excitedly. He separated easily from Angela after asking what she would be doing with Carlos while he came into the play therapy room. Angela told him that, because Carlos was sleeping, she would simply be reading. I asked Rodrigo what he had been told about coming to see me, and he replied, "You like children and have toys for them!" That was a pretty good description, and I added, "Yep, I like children and toys." I also said to him, "Lots of kids come to see me who have things happen that make them feel worried, or sad, or confused, or any other feelings." He asked if he could play with the puppets.

He chose the kangaroo puppet with the joey inside. He took the joey out and threw it across the room; he found a squirrel to fit in the pouch.

Rodrigo: I want him to be inside the bag.

Therapist: Sure, you want him to be inside the kangaroo's bag!

Rodrigo: Yeah, and now the kangaroo is going for a walk. [grabs the kangaroo by the hand and looks around the office]

Therapist: There are lots of things here for you to play with.

Rodrigo: Did you buy all these toys?

Therapist: You're wondering if I bought all these toys.

Rodrigo: Wow. You're rich.

He did not let go of the kangaroo the entire first session, and, at one point, he stuck the kangaroo inside the front of his pants: "I'm going to carry the kangaroo in my bag." "I see that," I responded. He then played with the following toys in the playroom: toy trucks that drove in circles, magnetic puzzles that were put together into long lines, miniature snakes that he hid underneath the sand in the sandbox, and a king and queen who stood erect in the sandtray.

This child-directed approach, the foundational ingredient of integrated play therapy, allowed me to learn a few things about Rodrigo's perspective: From an ample array of puppets, including some that might have had more appeal to a boy his age, such as a dinosaur, crocodile, or bear, he chose a mother and child puppet and began his play. He did not pick a single puppet; he picked two and immediately brought a relationship into the room. His first brisk movement was to take the baby from the mother's pouch and throw him across the room, clearly bringing a ruptured attachment theme into the session. In addition, he picked a baby from a different species, a squirrel (despite the option of another small kangaroo sock puppet in the room), to relocate inside the pouch. My interpretation was that Rodrigo had asserted the issue of adoption: a mother's not taking care of her own child but one of a different species. In addition to this interpretation, I wondered if Rodrigo was also showing his desire for one baby to be replaced with another (i.e., throwing the baby kangaroo, Carlos, out of his mother's pouch, and putting the squirrel, or himself, inside the pouch).

The sandplay also introduced relevant symbols and relationships. The king and queen could be symbols of authority or parents. Snakes were covered with sand and left covered in the end, which could indicate feelings and material yet to be uncovered. Rodrigo also was interested in objects of movement, not unusual for children of his age and gender. Noticeably, his cars did not get from point A to point B; rather, they simply went in circles without a destination or goal. This movement could suggest exploring for the sake of exploring and playing for the sake of playing without a specific goal. I was thrilled with Rodrigo's ability to externalize, communicate, and express himself.

As treatment progressed, I continued to follow Rodrigo's lead in determining when and how to integrate supplementary directive, cognitive–behavioral, attachment, or systemic interventions. The thematic material in Rodrigo's play was as rich and diverse as the way that he structured his time in the play therapy office: using mostly the objects he had chosen in the first session, adding bits and pieces of variety, but not straying too much from his initial play.

Angela told me with great concern that she had found Rodrigo kissing his baby brother's erect penis. She seemed horrified, and I told her that babies' penises get erect with a full bladder and any light stimulation, and that it was inappropriate for Rodrigo to be kissing his brother's penis and that he needed guidance from his parents to learn this boundary. She stated that her husband told her it was not a big deal. Angela was concerned, however, that Rodrigo was still touching himself, and she felt he was overly-focused on his own penis and his brother's. Thus, I opted to integrate a directive, behavioral component to our play therapy sessions in this way:

Therapist: Rodrigo, we are going to do something a little different today. [*I had his attention*] We are going to spend half the time like we always do—with you playing with the things you choose to play with. The other half of the time, I will take the lead and we will work on some problems that mom has told me about.

Rodrigo [looks at therapist]: I know. [*therapist asks what he knows*] Mom is mad at me because I kissed Carlos's *palomita.*

Therapist: I see. So, you kissed Carlos's palomita. What is a palomita? [It is a Spanish slang word for "penis."]

Rodrigo: You know, down here [*points to and touches his penis*].

Therapist: Yes, your mom told me that she saw you doing that and also that sometimes you touch your own palomita so much that it gets hurt and bleeds.

Rodrigo: My dad said my palomita belongs to me and I can do what I want with it.

Therapist: Oh, so that's what your dad says. How about your mom?

Rodrigo: She gets mad.

Therapist:	Okay, so we'll talk about this so that you can learn some rules about touching so that it doesn't turn into a problem for you with mom or anyone else. [*therapist and Rodrigo shake hands*] Do you want to play first or work on the touching problem first?
Rodrigo:	Play. [*runs over to the sandtray to play*]

I set a timer and said that when the bell went off, we would talk about touching and touching problems. Rodrigo made an easy adjustment to this transition in the time we spent together. I then began a series of sessions in which we talked about boundaries, private parts of the body, and what to do when ideas about touching come to mind, and used a workbook that talks about touching in general and touching of private parts (Gil & Shaw, 2012).

It was unclear whether Rodrigo had been exposed to inappropriate sexual behaviors in his early experiences before coming to live with Angela and Stefan. What was clear is that Rodrigo had intense curiosity about body parts, and his family was conflicted and anxious in determining what was normal versus concerning behavior.

I worked with Rodrigo and his mother to directly teach and communicate about boundaries. I also worked with Rodrigo and his adoptive father to strengthen engagement between father and son and provide opportunities for Stefan to teach lessons unique to fathers and sons. This component of treatment was not only educational and behavioral, but sought to increase secure parent–child attachment and readjust family system norms and communication about taboo subjects.

We put Hula-Hoops on the floor and sat inside them. In an effort to teach the child about physical boundaries, I labeled this as "private space" that we all have. Sitting inside the Hula-Hoop seemed to clarify that people have acceptable physical distances between them. We talked together about circumstances when those boundaries are crossed with people you know (to say hello or goodbye, when kissing your parents goodnight, and so on). "There is lots and lots of loving touching between people who know each other or belong to the same family," I said. We also talked about strangers, peers at school, and neighbors, and what touching was and was not okay in those relationships. Rodrigo walked outside with the Hula-Hoop held around his middle. "Mami, look. This is my private space. I can carry it with me in my imagination." He then wanted to put the Hula-Hoop around his brother, Carlos, to show him about private spaces. His mother patiently helped him succeed. Over time, mother's anxiety about protecting Carlos was parallel to her comfort with working with Rodrigo on boundaries and safe contact, and with her and Stefan's being on the same page about rules to avoid confusion in Rodrigo.

Stefan attended therapy sessions, and he talked with Rodrigo about what he had learned about being a boy and a man (Carlos was also present, but wandered around the room playing, except when dad wanted both of them to hear). I had asked Stefan to talk to Rodrigo about being a boy and to facilitate this dialogue, I used the sandtray that Rodrigo loved so much. I took my finger and divided the tray in half: "On this side, I would like you to show what it was like for you as a boy and the touching lessons you learned from your dad." I continued, "On this side, Rodrigo, I would like you to show your dad what it's like for you to be a boy and what touching lessons you've learned already from your mom and dad." Rodrigo had a big smile on his face as he showed his dad the shelves with the miniatures and began to collect his toys. Stefan, likewise, took this activity seriously and seemed to be interested in taking his time and finding precisely the things he wanted.

Stefan was quick to tear when Rodrigo asked about Stefan's mother. Stefan responded that his mother was now very sick and might join his father in heaven fairly soon. He chose about six miniatures that he then described to Rodrigo. Each object seemed to represent fond memories of his childhood and his father. Stefan picked a king, a canoe and fish, a cave, a ring, and several colorful "worry people." The lesson he discussed was: "Man is the king of his castle," and this brings much responsibility and obligation. Quality time fishing was his father's preferred activity with his son, and Stefan pledged to make time to take Rodrigo fishing with him. The cave was Stefan's way of talking about exploration. He remembered going many places with his father—holding his hand, stepping carefully, and learning about spiders and trees, and how things thrive in the tropics. He had picked the ring because of a ring his father gave him when he was a teenager, and he still wore on his finger (it looked as if it never came off). Stefan said his father had used the ring to talk about never-ending love. Stefan talked about the worry people and how, in his country, people keep them in a box so that they do not bother us as much. Unfortunately, Stefan said, his worries pushed out of the box sometimes and caused him problems. He then put the queen in the tray next to the king and told Rodrigo that because his mother was old and sick, she soon would go to heaven to be with the king. Rodrigo added, "Maybe my mom and dad will be there too," suggesting his confusion about whether his parents were dead or alive.

Rodrigo chose a man sitting at a computer, a plate with burritos, a medical doctor, a joey (from a miniature gray kangaroo), and a jester. He also chose a statue of a man and a boy. Rodrigo talked about how Stefan has to work all the time and has his face looking at the computer (I noted that it was clear that Rodrigo missed his father). He talked about how dad loves to cook and loves to eat: "I know how to make burritos with my mom," he offered. I asked if he had ever made burritos for his dad. His dad said that they were delicious, and Rodrigo smiled.

Stefan was intrigued by the miniature of the medical doctor and asked Rodrigo about it. Rodrigo said that he wanted a doctor to make his grandmother better so that his dad would not need to worry so much. Stefan gratefully accepted the doctor's help placing it in his half of the sandbox next to the king and queen. When Rodrigo picked up the little joey, I was interested to hear what he would say. He surprised me when he said, "Dad, this is you! You are going to be a joey without a mother soon." He said it in a matter-of-fact way, and then took the joey and made a little bed for it by covering up some of the body with sand. "He will sleep now. I covered him up." Rodrigo then picked up a soldier, stood him next to the little joey, and called it the joey's guard. "He can really sleep, Dad; he's got a guard to protect him." Rodrigo picked up the jester and said he liked it when Dad did fun things, such as going trick-or-treating with him. This session was sublime and is firmly planted in my memory bank of tender exchanges between a father and his son.

Treatment continued to proceed in an integrated fashion: following the child's need to integrate behavioral, attachment, or systemic components and providing freedom for child direction. In our individual sessions, Rodrigo processed more about the loss of his grandmother by using the joey and kangaroo puppets. In addition, Rodrigo acted out a lot of dangerous situations in which superheroes saved the day by protecting everyone from danger. His play was rigorous and active, and his energy often exploded and then retreated in what appeared to be his growing ability to self-regulate.

As part of the behavioral and family component, Rodrigo and his parents participated in the Boundary Project, a young children's group for those with sexual preoccupation (Gil & Shaw, 2013).

SUMMARY OF THE EVIDENCE BASE FOR INTEGRATED PLAY THERAPY

Briggs, Runyon, and Deblinger (2011), in a discussion of their trauma-focused cognitive–behavioral therapy (TF-CBT) evidence-based model, stated:

> The use of play in TF-CBT is structured and educational play versus free, nondirective, or pretend play. Play is used as a way to engage children and their parents in the therapy process, to create a fun therapeutic environment, to facilitate clinician communication, and to teach specific skills. (p. 174)

As these authors explained, CBT is their basic psychotherapy foundation, and play techniques are used to advance those goals. TF-CBT has substantial research to validate its effectiveness (Chaffin & Friedrich, 2004; Cohen, Mannarino, Kliethermes, & Murray, 2012; Mannarino et al., 2012).

The integrated model proposed in this chapter has a distinguishing feature: It is not using play therapy to advance another goal, for example, to relax the child so the child can talk about his or her problems. Invitations to play are provided to traumatized children because of an unwavering commitment to the idea that children have within them the capacity to self-repair, as eloquently stated by Landreth (2002), and that play therapy allows them to access those reparative capacities, in most cases. Play therapy is the foundation, and other theories and approaches are incorporated because they have the capacity to promote positive healing. This is quite different than viewing play as a way to break the ice with children, as a way to distract them so they will answer questions, or as a way to make the chosen therapy more palatable.

This integrated approach draws on the supporting evidence of the effectiveness of play therapy (Bratton et al., 2005) and the effect of trauma on young children's development (Osofsky, 2004). In addition, other effective therapies are integrated as determined by the child's individual treatment needs. Cognitive–behavioral strategies (Cohen et al., 2012), attachment-based intervention (Becker-Weidman & Hughes, 2008; Chaffin & Friedrich, 2004; Chaffin et al., 2004), and systemic/contextual components (Borduin, Schaeffer, & Heiblum, 2009; Swenson et al., 2010) are evidence-based elements composing the proposed integrated play therapy. In addition, a variety of innovative strategies, such as animal-assisted therapies, (Van Fleet, 2008), can contribute greatly to children's development and growth, and to scientific data about the effect of stress on the brain that becomes highly relevant in treatment (Perry, 2006).

Furthermore, this trauma-focused integrative play therapy approach has preliminary evidence supporting its effectiveness with clinical populations. In an unpublished pilot study funded by the National Children's Alliance, the effectiveness of TF-CBT was compared with this integrated play approach for treatment of child sexual abuse victims. Both treatments were effective in reducing child overall symptomology and internalizing problems and posttraumatic stress, as measured by the CBCL. There was no significant difference between treatment effectiveness for the two approaches. This study offers preliminary empirical evidence that supports the effectiveness of an integrative play approach.

RECOMMENDATIONS FOR REPLICATION AND TRANSPORTABILITY

Challenges in applying this approach to settings in which treatment is more short term (e.g., many agencies, hospitals, schools) are that clinicians may not have the privilege of time to build important therapy relationships

and may have to shift orientations more abruptly to address urgent symptoms in as brief a manner as possible. However, the general principle is to
believe and facilitate the direction of the child to lead therapy. Agencies,
schools, and hospitals can do so by stocking their offices with basic toys and
symbols that will facilitate the expression of the child. Even if the mode of
treatment required by the agency is more directive and structured in that
it requires verbal interviews with children, clinicians may find their verbal
interviews enhanced by the provision of toys and symbols. A child may not
verbally answer an inquiry but may eye a toy on the shelf or fiddle with a
figurine (e.g., the kangaroo and joey in the aforementioned case example).
In addition, clinicians' integrated practice will be enhanced by their willingness to and comfort with occasionally including other family members
in assessment and treatment sessions, and in parent education (Siegel &
Bryson, 2012).

This integrated play approach also is well suited to children of diverse
social and cultural backgrounds. Seponski, Bermudez, and Lewis (2013)
noted that culturally sensitive therapy is client-centered and seeks to understand the client's subjective, socially-constructed world. Symbolic expression
seems to tap into the client's subjective world and can transcend miscommu-
nications that can occur with language and cultural barriers. It is important
for clinicians to include in their play materials a range of cultural, ethnic,
socioeconomic, and other symbols that provide children with options for
externalizing and playing out cultural and social themes that are relevant to
their presentation in treatment (Gil & Drewes, 2006; Vicario, Tucker, Smith
Adcock, & Hudgins-Mitchell, 2013).

CONCLUSION

This integrated play therapy approach is applicable in any clinical setting or with varied client populations precisely because it is sensitive and
directed by the child's individual needs. However, play therapists have to
be acquainted with the research base and feel confident in more than one
primary orientation. This increased security will allow for a more facile transition from one mode to another. This integrated approach presumes that
clinicians have a strong theoretical grounding and can shift to and incorporate ideas and approaches as supported by theory and research. Boundaries
between approaches can be flexible and interactive, fluid and purposeful,
and attuned to the benefits and counter-indications of varied approaches
when the therapist first fosters a belief and interest in the world and expression of the child.

REFERENCES

Anda, R. F., Felitti, V. J., Bremner, J. D., Walker, J. D., Whitfield, C., Perry, B. D., . . . Giles, W. H. (2006). The enduring effects of abuse and related adverse experiences in childhood. *European Archives of Psychiatry and Clinical Neuroscience, 256,* 174–186. http://dx.doi.org/10.1007/s00406-005-0624-4

Becker-Weidman, A., & Hughes, D. (2008). Dyadic developmental psychotherapy: An evidence-based treatment for children with complex trauma and disorders of attachment. *Child & Family Social Work, 13,* 329–337. http://dx.doi.org/10.1111/j.1365-2206.2008.00557.x

Beutler, L. E. (1979). Toward specific psychological therapies for specific conditions. *Journal of Consulting and Clinical Psychology, 47,* 882–897. http://dx.doi.org/10.1037/0022-006X.47.5.882

Booth, P. B., & Jernberg, A. M. (2009). *Theraplay: Helping parents and children build better relationships through attachment-based play* (3rd ed.). San Francisco, CA: Jossey-Bass.

Borduin, C. M., Schaeffer, C. M., & Heiblum, N. (2009). A randomized clinical trial of multisystemic therapy with juvenile sexual offenders: Effects on youth social ecology and criminal activity. *Journal of Consulting and Clinical Psychology, 77,* 26–37. http://dx.doi.org/10.1037/a0013035

Bratton, S. C., Ray, D., Rhine, T., & Jones, L. (2005). The efficacy of play therapy with children: A meta-analytic review of treatment outcomes. *Professional Psychology: Research and Practice, 36,* 376–390. http://dx.doi.org/10.1037/0735-7028.36.4.376

Briggs, K. M., Runyon, M. K., & Deblinger, E. (2011). The use of play in trauma-focused cognitive–behavioral therapy. In S. W. Russ & L. N. Niec (Eds.), *Play in clinical practice: Evidence-based approaches* (pp. 168–200). New York, NY: Guilford Press.

Brunk, M. A., Henggeler, S. W., & Whelan, J. P. (1987). Comparison of multisystemic therapy and parent training in the brief treatment of child abuse and neglect. *Journal of Consulting and Clinical Psychology, 55,* 171–178. http://dx.doi.org/10.1037/0022-006X.55.2.171

Cassidy, J., Woodhouse, S. S., Sherman, L. J., Stupica, B., & Lejuez, C. W. (2011). Enhancing infant attachment security: An examination of treatment efficacy and differential susceptibility. *Development and Psychopathology, 23,* 131–148. http://dx.doi.org/10.1017/S0954579410000696

Chaffin, M., & Friedrich, B. (2004). Evidence-based treatments in child abuse and neglect. *Children and Youth Services Review, 26,* 1097–1113. http://dx.doi.org/10.1016/j.childyouth.2004.08.008

Chaffin, M., Silovsky, J. F., Funderburk, B., Valle, L. A., Brestan, E. V., Balachova, T., . . . Bonner, B. L. (2004). Parent–child interaction therapy with physically abusive parents: Efficacy for reducing future abuse reports.

Journal of Consulting and Clinical Psychology, 72, 500–510. http://dx.doi.org/10.1037/0022-006X.72.3.500

Christophersen, E. R., & Mortweet, S. (2001). *Treatments that work with children: Empirically supported strategies for managing childhood problems.* Washington, DC: American Psychological Association. http://dx.doi.org/10.1037/10405-000

Cicchetti, D., & Toth, S. L. (1995). A developmental psychopathology perspective on child abuse and neglect. *Journal of the American Academy of Child & Adolescent Psychiatry, 34,* 541–565. http://dx.doi.org/10.1097/00004583-199505000-00008

Cohen, J. A., Mannarino, A. P., Kliethermes, M., & Murray, L. A. (2012). Trauma-focused CBT for youth with complex trauma. *Child Abuse & Neglect, 36,* 528–541. http://dx.doi.org/10.1016/j.chiabu.2012.03.007

Cook, A., Spinazzola, J., Ford, J. D., Lanktree, C., Blaustein, M., Cloitre, M., . . . van der Kolk, B. (2005). Complex trauma in children and adolescents. *Psychiatric Annals, 35,* 390–398.

Dozier, M., Lindhiem, O., Lewis, E., Bick, J., Bernard, K., & Peloso, E. (2009). Effects of a foster parent training program on young children's attachment behaviors: Preliminary evidence from a randomized clinical trial. *Child & Adolescent Social Work Journal, 26,* 321–332. http://dx.doi.org/10.1007/s10560-009-0165-1

Dozier, M., Peloso, E., Lewis, E., Laurenceau, J. P., & Levine, S. (2008). Effects of an attachment-based intervention on the cortisol production of infants and toddlers in foster care. *Development and Psychopathology, 20,* 845–859. http://dx.doi.org/10.1017/S0954579408000400

Drewes, A. A., Bratton, S. C., & Schaefer, C. E. (Eds.). (2011). *Integrative play therapy.* New York, NY: Wiley. http://dx.doi.org/10.1002/9781118094792

Eyberg, S. M., Nelson, M. M., & Boggs, S. R. (2008). Evidence-based psychosocial treatments for children and adolescents with disruptive behavior. *Journal of Clinical Child & Adolescent Psychology, 37,* 215–237. http://dx.doi.org/10.1080/15374410701820117

Ford, J. D. & Cloitre, M. (2010). Best practices in psychotherapy for children and adolescents. In C. A. Courtois & J. D. Ford (Eds.), *Treating complex traumatic stress disorders: An evidence based guide* (pp. 59–81). New York, NY: Guilford Press.

Frances, A., Clarkin, J., & Perry, S. (1984). *Differential therapeutics in psychiatry: The art and science of treatment selection.* New York, NY: Brunner/Mazel.

Gil, E. (2006). *Helping abused and traumatized children: Integrating directive and non-directive approaches.* New York, NY: Guilford Press.

Gil, E. (2010). Children's self-initiated gradual exposure: The wonders of post-traumatic play and behavioral reenactments. In E. Gil (Ed.), *Working with children to heal interpersonal trauma: The power of play* (pp. 44–66). New York, NY: Guilford Press.

Gil, E. (2012). Trauma-focused integrated play therapy. In P. Goodyear-Brown (Ed.), *Handbook of child sexual abuse: Identification, assessment, and treatment* (pp. 251–279). New York, NY: Wiley.

Gil, E., & Drewes, A. (2006). *Cultural issues in play therapy*. New York, NY: Guilford Press.

Gil, E., & Shaw, J. (2012). *A book for kids about private parts, touching, touching problems, and other stuff*. Royal Oak, MI: Self-Esteem Shop.

Gil, E., & Shaw, J. (2013). *Working with children with sexual behavior problems*. New York, NY: Guilford Press.

Goodyear-Brown, P. (Ed.). (2012). *Handbook of child sexual abuse: Identification, assessment, and treatment*. New York, NY: Wiley.

Hoffman, K. T., Marvin, R. S., Cooper, G., & Powell, B. (2006). Changing toddlers' and preschoolers' attachment classifications: The circle of security intervention. *Journal of Consulting and Clinical Psychology, 74*, 1017–1026. http://dx.doi.org/10.1037/0022-006X.74.6.1017

Kaminski, J. W., Valle, L. A., Filene, J. H., & Boyle, C. L. (2008). A meta-analytic review of components associated with parent training program effectiveness. *Journal of Abnormal Child Psychology, 36*, 567–589. http://dx.doi.org/10.1007/s10802-007-9201-9

Kenney-Noziska, S. G., Schaefer, C. E., & Homeyer, L. E. (2012). Beyond directive and nondirective: Moving the conversation forward. *International Journal of Play Therapy, 21*, 244–252. http://dx.doi.org/10.1037/a0028910

Landreth, G. L. (2002). *Play therapy: The art of the relationship*. New York, NY: Brunner-Rutledge.

Lieberman, A. F., & Van Horn, P. (2005). *Don't hit my mommy: A manual for child–parent psychotherapy with young witnesses of family violence*. Washington, DC: Zero to Three.

Lieberman, A. F., & Van Horn, P. (2008). *Psychotherapy with infants and young children: Repairing the effects of stress and trauma on early attachment*. New York, NY: Guilford Press.

Littell, J. H., Popa, M., & Forsythe, B. (2005). *Multisystemic therapy for social, emotional, and behavioral problems in youth aged 10–17 (Cochrane Review)*. New York, NY: Wiley.

Mannarino, A. P., Cohen, J. A., Deblinger, E., Runyon, M. K., & Steer, R. A. (2012). Trauma-focused cognitive–behavioral therapy for children: Sustained impact of treatment 6 and 12 months later. *Child Maltreatment, 17*, 231–241. http://dx.doi.org/10.1177/1077559512451787

Norcross, J. (2005). A primer on psychotherapy integration. In J. C. Norcross & M. R. Goldfried (Eds.), *Handbook of psychotherapy integration* (2nd ed., pp. 3–23). New York, NY: Oxford University Press.

O'Connor, K. J., & Braverman, L. M. (Eds.). (1997). *Play therapy theory and practice: A comparative presentation*. New York, NY: Wiley.

O'Connor, K. J., & Braverman, L. M. (Eds.). (2009). *Play therapy theory and practice: Comparing theories and techniques* (2nd ed.). New York, NY: Wiley.

Osofsky, J. D. (2004). *Young children and trauma: Intervention and treatment.* New York, NY: Guilford Press.

Perry, B. D. (2006). Applying principles of neurodevelopment to clinical work with maltreated and traumatized children: The neurosequential model of therapeutics. In N. B. Webb (Ed.), *Working with traumatized youth in child welfare* (pp. 27–52). New York, NY: Guilford Press.

Reddy, L. A., Files-Hall, T. M., & Schaefer, C. E. (Eds.). (2005). *Empirically based play interventions for children.* Washington, DC: American Psychological Association. http://dx.doi.org/10.1037/11086-000

Saunders, B. (2012). Determining best practice for treating sexually victimized children. In P. Goodyear-Brown (Ed.), *Handbook of child sexual abuse: Identification, assessment, and treatment* (pp. 173–198). New York, NY: Wiley.

Schaefer, C. E. (Ed.). (1992). *The therapeutic powers of play.* New York, NY: Jason Aronson.

Schaefer, C. E. (1994). Play therapy for psychic trauma in children. In K. J. O'Connor & C. E. Schaefer (Eds.), *Handbook of play therapy. Vol. 2: Advances and innovations* (pp. 297–318). New York, NY: Wiley.

Schaefer, C. E. (Ed.). (1999). *Innovative psychotherapy techniques in child and adolescent therapy.* New York, NY: Wiley.

Schaefer, C. E. (2001). Prescriptive play therapy. *International Journal of Play Therapy, 10*(2), 57–73. http://dx.doi.org/10.1037/h0089480

Seponski, D. M., Bermudez, J. M., & Lewis, D. C. (2013). Creating culturally responsive family therapy models and research: Introducing the use of responsive evaluation as a method. *Journal of Marital and Family Therapy, 39,* 28–42. http://dx.doi.org/10.1111/j.1752-0606.2011.00282.x

Shelby, J. S., & Felix, E. D. (2005). Post-traumatic play therapy: The need for an integrated model of directive and nondirective approaches. In L. A. Reddy, T. M. Files-Hall, & C. E. Schaefer (Eds.), *Empirically based play interventions for children* (pp. 79–103). Washington, DC: American Psychological Association. http://dx.doi.org/10.1037/11086-005

Siegel, D. J., & Bryson, T. P. (2012). *The whole-brain child: 12 revolutionary strategies to nurture your child's developing mind.* New York, NY: Delacorte Press.

Swenson, C. C., Schaeffer, C. M., Henggeler, S. W., Faldowski, R., & Mayhew, A. M. (2010). Multisystemic therapy for child abuse and neglect: A randomized effectiveness trial. *Journal of Family Psychology, 24,* 497–507. http://dx.doi.org/10.1037/a0020324

Terr, L. C. (1981). "Forbidden games": Post-traumatic child's play. *Journal of the American Academy of Child Psychiatry, 20,* 741–760. http://dx.doi.org/10.1097/00004583-198102000-00006

Timmer, S. G., Urquiza, A. J., Zebell, N. M., & McGrath, J. M. (2005). Parent–child interaction therapy: Application to maltreating parent–child dyads. *Child Abuse & Neglect, 29,* 825–842. http://dx.doi.org/10.1016/j.chiabu.2005.01.003

U.S. Department of Health and Human Services, Administration for Children and Families, Administration on Children, Youth and Families, Children's Bureau. (2011). *Child Maltreatment, 2010*. Washington, DC: Author.

van der Kolk, B. A., & Courtois, C. A. (2005). Editorial comments: Complex developmental trauma. *Journal of Traumatic Stress, 18*, 385–388.

van der Kolk, B. A., Pelcovitz, D., Roth, S., Mandel, F. S., McFarlane, A., & Herman, J. L. (1996). Dissociation, somatization, and affect dysregulation: The complexity of adaptation of trauma. *The American Journal of Psychiatry, 153*(7), 83–93. http://dx.doi.org/10.1176/ajp.153.7.83

van der Kolk, B. A., Pynoos, R. S., Cicchetti, D., Cloitre, M., D'Andrea, W., Ford, J. D., . . . Teicher, M. (2009). *Proposal to include a developmental trauma disorder diagnosis for children and adolescents in DSM-V.* Unpublished manuscript. Retrieved from http://www.traumacenter.org/announcements/DTD_papers_oct_09.pdf

Van Fleet, R. (2005). *Filial therapy: Strengthening parent–child relationships through play* (2nd ed.). Sarasota, FL: Professional Resource Series.

Van Fleet, R. (2008). *Play therapy with kids and canines: Benefits for children's developmental and psychosocial health.* Sarasota, FL: Practitioner's Resource Series.

Vicario, M., Tucker, C., Smith Adcock, S., & Hudgins-Mitchell, C. (2013). Relational-cultural play therapy: Reestablishing healthy connections with children exposed to trauma in relationships. *International Journal of Play Therapy, 22*, 103–117. http://dx.doi.org/10.1037/a0032313

6

PLAY INTERVENTIONS FOR HOSPITALIZED CHILDREN

WILLIAM A. RAE, JEREMY R. SULLIVAN, AND MARTHA A. ASKINS

According to recent statistics, approximately 1.8 million children ages 1 year to 17 years are hospitalized in the United States each year for a variety of medical conditions (Yu, Wier, & Elixhauser, 2011). The average age of children hospitalized (excluding newborn infants) is 6.7 years. The majority of these children are hospitalized for acute illnesses and typically stay as an inpatient for 3 to 4 days. Children with chronic illnesses, on the other hand, typically have much longer hospital stays. For example, children with cancer have a mean length of stay of 12 days per hospitalization (Price, Stranges, & Elixhauser, 2012). Given the nature of chronic illnesses, children with these conditions often require long-term psychological care commensurate with the seriousness of their medical issues.

Hospital-based therapeutic play programs are designed for children between ages 3 years and 13 years who may be at risk for experiencing stress

http://dx.doi.org/10.1037/14730-007
Empirically Based Play Interventions for Children, Second Edition, L. A. Reddy, T. M. Files-Hall, and C. E. Schaefer (Editors)

associated with their illnesses, diagnostic procedures, and treatment interventions. Psychological intervention may be especially important for children who have preexisting psychological conditions or family difficulties that complicate adjustment to medical treatment and/or compliance with prescribed treatment regimens. When managing medical crises, children and their families are exposed to a variety of potentially traumatic events that can have untoward psychosocial consequences (Kazak, Schneider, & Kassam-Adams, 2009). The child's perception of physical illness or injury and the experience of hospitalization present potentially significant areas of psychotherapeutic focus. Play therapy programs hold much potential for enhancing the psychological well-being of children and families affected by medical conditions.

Fortunately, not all children manifest ongoing symptoms of emotional or psychological distress as a result of their hospital or illness experience (Thompson & Snow, 2009). Much more common are situational anxiety and discomfort with physical pain. When children are able to master negative internal states (e.g., anxiety) and learn to cope with invasive, painful medical procedures, they experience positive psychological growth and enhanced confidence (e.g., Siegel & Conte, 2001).

Children often "play through" their worries, in the same way that adults talk through their concerns, to achieve psychological resolution. The goals of play therapy in a medical setting are to prepare a child psychologically for the potentially negative effects of hospitalization and illness with the accompanying traumatic stress. Therapeutic play is one of several methods designed to help a child cope with the difficulties inherent in pediatric hospitalization. Other methods of preparation for hospitalized children may include providing information, increasing familiarity with the hospital environment, preparing parents, providing emotional support to the family, developing trust, and providing coping strategies (e.g., Goldberger, Mohl, & Thompson, 2009). These traditional preparation programs for children undergoing elective surgery and/or hospitalization are common in pediatric hospital settings and have been shown to be effective at ameliorating untoward emotional reactions (Li & Lopez, 2008; Siegel & Conte, 2001). Therapeutic play interventions are especially useful with children who may be unable or unwilling to express attitudes, fears, or feelings verbally and directly (Ellinwood & Raskin, 1993), and who may be unable to benefit from a traditional education-based preparation program.

This chapter describes a therapeutic play program for hospitalized children. It focuses on medical play, preparation, and unstructured play interventions in which the content and process of the play sessions may be seen as at least somewhat child-directed, as opposed to completely therapist-directed. First, the theoretical basis and objectives of the intervention are described, then the key treatment ingredients of the intervention are discussed. Second, the empirical basis for the effectiveness of the program is illustrated, as is the replicability of the program in other settings. Third, brief transcripts of two typical play sessions are provided. Although the terms *play therapy* and *therapeutic play program* are used interchangeably throughout this chapter, the authors recognize that the focused, short-term therapeutic play program described herein is different from long-term play therapy.

THEORETICAL BASIS AND OBJECTIVES OF THE INTERVENTION

Although a clear-cut causal relationship between pediatric hospitalization and maladaptive psychological functioning has not been empirically established, numerous authors have cogently argued that pediatric hospitalization can adversely affect a child's psychological development (e.g., Harbeck-Weber & McKee, 1995; Kazak et al., 2009; Siegel & Conte, 2001; Thompson & Snow, 2009). In their review of the research on preparation for hospitalization and the effects of chronic illness in children, Harbeck-Weber and McKee (1995) identified five factors that can influence the outcome of preparation. First, previous negative experiences with hospitalization are associated with the need for more extensive preparation. Second, the child's coping style also affects the outcome. For example, a child who copes by avoiding information about his or her illness may do worse when confronted with medical information or the treatment situation at hand than a child who actively seeks out medical information. Third, the timing of the intervention may affect the outcome. Fourth, parents may influence the child's coping because their own emotional status can influence that of the child. That is, parents who are very anxious about the child's illness and/or hospitalization can communicate their distress to their child (whether verbally or nonverbally), which in turn can cause the child to feel anxious. Conversely, when parents feel confidence in the medical staff and treatment plan, children feel trust and are more assured. Fifth, the child's developmental level affects how the child conceptualizes his or her hospitalization or illness. Interventions congruent with the child's developmental skills have been more effective than approaches that have not considered development. In general, younger children tend to be at greater risk for developing behavioral and emotional problems during and after hospitalization (Siegel & Conte, 2001).

A distinction can be made between medical preparation and medical play. *Medical play* can occur either before or after a procedure and provides information to the child while also allowing the child to process and express his or her feelings with regard to the procedure or event. In contrast, *medical preparation* occurs before the medical procedure and primarily serves an information-giving function (Bolig, Yolton, & Nissen, 1991). Thus, preparation approaches primarily attempt to educate the child and may or may not involve actual play. Inherent in this distinction is the difference in the therapist's role. Preparation interventions that include a play component entail the therapist's providing information to the child while also facilitating play with certain medically themed objects, and thus may be seen as therapist-directed. Medical play interventions, with their greater emphasis on emotional expression, give greater control to the child with regard to the objects that are used during play and the content of the play sessions, and place great importance on the therapist–child relationship. An example of medical play may involve a child's rehearsing a magnetic resonance imaging (MRI) scan with a doll and play model of an MRI machine. As a child prepares the doll and pretends to administer the scan, he or she may gain an enhanced sense of familiarity and control with the procedure, desensitizing the child to anxiety that is commonly associated with diagnostic scans, especially when they are new to the child. The therapist's role in this situation is key because he or she can clarify the child's feelings, positively reinforce progress, and serve as a supportive presence, thereby adding to the child's confidence. Thus, these interventions may be seen as more child-directed than preparation interventions, although degrees of adult direction within both types of interventions may vary widely.

Although the distinction between medical play and preparation interventions is a useful one to make, some overlap exists between the two definitions. For example, a medical play intervention also could be considered a preparation intervention if it occurs before the medical procedure, focuses on providing information, focuses on processing and expressing emotions, and allows the child some freedom in determining the direction of therapy. Indeed, this combination of play and preparation would appear to be a common version of the hospital-based play intervention.

Bolig, Fernie, and Klein (1986) theorized that unstructured or child-directed play in the hospital setting provides more opportunity for the child to develop a sense of competence, internal locus of control, and mastery than do structured medical play and preparation interventions. Unstructured play allows children to assume different roles (e.g., the medical professional instead of the patient) and determine the outcomes of events. More structured interventions are primarily concerned with providing information and reducing anxiety and distress associated with specific illnesses and treatment procedures, thereby giving the child less opportunity for creativity and control in determining the content of sessions.

Medical play therapy was derived from more traditional play therapy techniques. Webb (1995) thoughtfully applied Axline's (1969) principles of play therapy to the context of hospital-based interventions. Several important concepts have arisen from that work. The development of rapport and the therapeutic relationship is of special significance because the play therapist represents one of the few people within the hospital setting who is not associated with painful or unpleasant medical procedures. Many children, especially those who are severely or terminally ill, need a safe and confidential setting in which they can express their fears and emotions without having to be concerned about upsetting or worrying their parents. The therapist must be prepared to process the child's emotions with regard to illness and death, which may present a great challenge to the therapist.

Hospital-based play interventions differ in goals and purposes from traditional play therapy interventions. During a short-term hospitalization, the child's play is semistructured, whereas in most common forms of play therapy, the child's play is unstructured and child-directed. At the same time, play interventions in the hospital setting do allow the child to decide with what to play, but the therapist influences the content of sessions by providing the child with medically related toys and materials. The therapist's verbalizations and behaviors are not scripted and depend on what the child says or does. In this way, the therapist follows the child's lead.

Play is seen as a method by which a child can master his or her environment and cope with the stressful effects of hospitalization. Furthermore, hospital-based play programs are believed to help the child gain a sense of control within a stressful environment. In this context, therapeutic play may serve to give the child a sense of normalcy and familiarity because play is associated with the normal daily life of the child outside the hospital (Petrillo & Sanger, 1980). General play interventions have been credited with providing children with a sense of mastery because they can manipulate the process and outcomes of situations through play, thereby changing their role from passive observer to active participant. In a health care context, supervised play with syringes and other medical equipment may give children a sense of mastery over the threatening environment and may reduce anxiety and fears associated with medical equipment and procedures (Klinzing & Klinzing, 1987). Furthermore, play activities provide a context within which children can make decisions and feel in control that, intuitively, would be adaptive for children who may have little control over their illness or over what happens to them in the hospital (Bolig et al., 1986; Klinzing & Klinzing, 1987; Webb, 1995).

KEY TREATMENT INGREDIENTS

Several caveats must be provided before implementing a therapeutic play program for hospitalized and/or physically ill children. First, as with any psychological intervention, the person implementing the program must be competent to work with children, pediatric medical disorders, and play interventions. Second, the clinician should take into account empirically supported factors that could influence the outcome of the play intervention. For example, he or she should consider the previously described factors important to hospitalization preparation programs, such as the child's developmental level, previous hospital experience, coping style, timing of intervention, and inclusion of parents (Harbeck-Weber & McKee, 1995). In addition, the clinician must be intimately familiar with the child's history so he or she can craft the play intervention program to meet the child's specific needs. The clinician must consider individual child-risk and resilience factors when shaping the intervention, including premorbid psychological functioning, coping style, invasiveness of medical procedures, length of hospitalization, degree of disability, seriousness of illness, family support and resources, cognitive functioning, temperament, and motivation. The therapeutic play program should be individualized based on each child's unique needs.

The therapeutic play program for hospitalized and physically ill children described in this chapter is modeled after the program described and evaluated by Rae, Worchel, Upchurch, Sanner, and Daniel (1989). It is designed as a time-limited, brief intervention because most children are only hospitalized for short periods. Although a child may be hospitalized for an extended period (e.g., stem cell transplant), the general elements of the program would function in the same way. The program is designed to provide daily intervention during pediatric hospitalization. Although not specifically designed for outpatient treatment, the elements of the program could be adapted easily to the needs of a nonhospitalized child who is experiencing adaptation problems to illness or medical interventions. Four key treatment ingredients for a treatment program with hospitalized and physically ill children are described as follows.

Client-Centered Approach

A slightly modified client-centered, nondirective, humanistic approach is seen as the most basic element of the therapeutic play program for hospitalized children. The basic elements of a client-centered, humanistic play therapy approach are well documented elsewhere (see Landreth, 2012). The client-centered approach uses three essential elements: unconditional positive regard, empathic understanding, and congruence of feelings (Ellinwood & Raskin, 1993). Bolig et al. (1986) suggested that this approach provides more opportunity for the child to develop an internal locus of control and a sense of competence and/or mastery because he or she can choose to assume different roles during the play sessions.

Using a child-centered approach, Axline (1969) developed the basic principles that most play therapists use. The first principle requires that the therapist develop a warm, supportive relationship with the child. The therapist accepts the child unconditionally. Furthermore, within the therapeutic relationship, the therapist's duty is to create a permissive atmosphere in which the child is free to express his or her feelings. By reflecting feelings back to the child, the therapist helps the child to understand his or her feelings and to develop insight. Within this philosophy, the therapist only puts limitations on the child that are necessary to ensure safety in the play therapy setting and to help the child become aware of the social responsibility involved in the relationship with the therapist.

Although these elements are generally consistent with the play therapy program for hospitalized children, Axline (1969) posited two other principles that require a slight modification. First, she stated that because therapy is a gradual process, the therapeutic intervention should not be rushed or hurried. This may be impossible in the medical setting because the therapeutic intervention may be time limited corresponding to the child's hospitalization. During a brief hospitalization, not enough time is available to allow the child's feelings to unfold in a gradual manner; however, this traditional model can be followed for children who are hospitalized regularly or who can be seen with a combination of inpatient and outpatient care by the same therapist. Second, Axline (1969) stated that the child's behaviors or conversation should never be directed because the child has the capacity to solve his or her problems and make appropriate choices. Although we believe this to be the case in most therapy situations, within a therapeutic play program for hospitalized children, there is some allowance for the therapist's giving the client direction. For example, the child is invited to play with hospital equipment or the child can be invited to talk about his or her illness and/or hospitalization. Being mildly directive allows the therapist to talk about the child's concerns, the child's coping style, and possible misconceptions that the child might have about the hospital setting or medical environment.

Focus on Mastery and Coping

Within the context of this modified client-centered approach, the therapist helps the child cope with his or her illness and hospitalization by mastering negative emotions. Because of the time-limited nature of the intervention, the therapist gently exposes the child to potentially distressing material during the therapeutic play program. This exposure takes place with the play materials, play activities, and verbal content of the interaction between the therapist and the child. At the same time, the therapist is careful to be attuned to the child's emotional status to be sure he or she is not emotionally overwhelmed because that could be countertherapeutic. The therapist continues to provide unconditional positive regard and empathic understanding within a supportive relationship. As the child expresses negative emotions about the hospitalization and/or illness, the therapist helps the child process these feelings and provides an atmosphere within which the child's coping strategies can emerge. Within this context, the child also may wish to process feelings concerning separation from family (e.g., siblings) and friends.

Miller, Sherman, Combs, and Kruus (1992) extensively reviewed the empirical literature on children's coping with medical stressors and described the relationship between coping and adaptation. Children tend to adapt better when they prepare for a stressful event and are able to master it. In addition, children tend to show increased benefit if they seek out threat-relevant information and are able to actively cope with the stressor. Children who are less emotionally defended and are more open also tend to adapt more positively. Those children who use psychological defenses of intellectualization, intellectualization with isolation, or a mixed pattern tend to cope more adaptively with stressors (Miller et al., 1992).

Although it is acknowledged that coping with hospitalization and illness involves a number of divergent components, these results are consistent with using a child-centered, mastery-focused play therapy approach during hospitalization. Therapeutic play provides a platform for the therapist to gently introduce the child to stressful hospital-based and/or procedure-based equipment in a nonthreatening, supportive therapeutic environment in which the child can master his or her emotions. The therapeutic relationship provides an atmosphere in which defensiveness is deescalated and, as a result, the child is more open to dealing with negative emotions. In addition, during the play intervention, the child can be helped to deal with his or her psychological defenses and aided in the use of more adaptive cognitive coping strategies. The therapist may be required to confront the child's coping style directly if the child is avoiding important material or information, or is using other maladaptive coping strategies.

Mastery and coping are usually accomplished by a concurrent combination of therapeutic play techniques and verbal processing (i.e., cognitive behavioral) techniques. The therapeutic play techniques involve the use of play materials—often in the form of medical and nonmedical play materials—selected to facilitate the expression of aggression, fantasies, and fears associated with hospitalization and illness. Medical play materials might involve medical equipment (e.g., syringe, stethoscope, gauze, bandages) and hospital-related representational materials (e.g., doctor and nurse puppets, hospital bed, hospital dollhouse, toy ambulance). Nonmedical play materials would involve toys often used in traditional play therapy programs. Having a variety of toys is helpful, including manipulatives (e.g., art supplies), family puppets or dolls, dollhouse, vehicles, building materials (e.g., blocks, Legos), and board games. In addition, toys that might evoke aggressive play (e.g., dinosaurs, lions) also can be useful. By presenting the child with a variety of play materials, the therapist can maximize the likelihood that the child will find materials appropriate and relevant to the expression of a variety of ideas and feelings. Furthermore, this variety allows the therapist to ease the child into play and discussions specifically related to the hospital and illness by starting with the more neutral toys and gradually encouraging play with the medically themed materials.

Dynamic Formulation and Therapeutic Insight

Whereas behaviors are observable and provide important points of psychotherapeutic intervention within the play therapy context, it is also important to consider what is happening within the child from an interpersonal and intrapsychic developmental perspective. From a psychodynamic perspective, the importance of the therapeutic relationship is paramount. To have the confidence to face one's fears, the child needs to perceive the therapist as strong enough to remain present and to support the child through reviewing and reworking worrisome or traumatic events. Reworking of the traumatic event often entails playing through the same or similar scenarios over and over again until the child resolves the psychological issues associated with a particular distressing event. During the play scenarios, the therapist offers reflection of feelings, carefully timed interpretation of conflicts, and clarifications to help the child understand and work through the dilemma. The child may borrow ego strength from the therapist while developing his or her own internal emotional strength to heal and cope with future challenges. Not only are benefits gained within the session, but, with successful treatment, the child will generalize the trust and positive regard developed within the psychotherapeutic relationship outside to other health professionals and caregivers in the child's life, which should help buffer the child during future stressful situations.

Parent Support and Involvement

Although not a component of the original study (Rae et al., 1989), parental involvement is seen as crucial to facilitating the child's positive adjustment to hospitalization. A strong positive relationship has been found between treatment effectiveness of the play intervention and the inclusion of parents in the therapeutic process (Bratton, Ray, Rhine, & Jones, 2005; Leblanc & Ritchie, 2001). Parents usually can help their children emotionally unless they themselves are emotionally stressed by the hospitalization, which may make them psychologically unavailable to their children. Parents may be intimidated by the hospital environment, anxious for their child, financially stressed, and unable to use more typical soothing and coping strategies with their child; these issues may be exacerbated if parents have their own negative histories of illness and hospitalization. Having parents who can support their child can have overall positive effects on the child. Within the therapeutic play program, parents need to understand the meaning of the child's anxiety or distress. Also, the parents must not only be educated about their child's illness and hospitalization, but helped to facilitate appropriate emotional coping. Parental understanding of and involvement with the therapeutic play program with hospitalized children are seen as crucial aspects contributing to the program's success.

OUTCOME STUDIES OF EFFECTIVENESS

Play therapy has clearly been shown to be an effective overall intervention with children. An abundance of books have been written on the positive therapeutic effects of play (e.g., Landreth, 2012; McMahon, 2009), but only a few provide empirical support. In contrast, in a meta-analysis of 42 empirical studies on play interventions, Leblanc and Ritchie (2001) concluded that the average treatment effect of play therapy was comparable to the treatment effect of nonplay interventions (e.g., verbal psychotherapy) with both children and adults. The treatment effect was enhanced by having lengthy treatment duration and by including parents in the child's therapy. In the same way, Bratton and others (2005) conducted a meta-analysis on 93 controlled outcome studies that yielded 0.80 standard deviation effect size. Play therapy was equally effective across gender, age, and presenting issue. In addition, effects were more positive when humanistic approaches were used and when parents were actively involved.

In a review of the effects of play therapy on hospitalized children's distress, Thompson (1985) noted that research on play therapy in hospital settings through the mid-1980s was limited by a paucity of experimental studies and by poor research methodology for the few studies completed. More recently, Thompson and Snow (2009) concluded that there was support for play interventions in medical settings. Specifically, although hospitalization tends to temporarily suppress children's play, children tend to engage in spontaneous play that is related to their medical or emotional condition. In addition, systematically providing opportunities for play may provide benefits (e.g., reduction of distress), but the results may be limited.

On reviewing the literature on therapeutic play with hospitalized children, we found no methodologically rigorous empirical articles published during the past decade that evaluated medical play programs using the aforementioned key treatment ingredients. There are likely several reasons for the lack of articles in this area. First, children are hospitalized for far shorter periods than in decades past. Fifty years ago, it was common for a child to be routinely hospitalized for several weeks, but currently the average length of stay in the hospital is far shorter (Yu et al., 2011). Second, because of the desire to conduct most pediatric care on an outpatient basis, only the most ill and/or medically involved children are hospitalized. Third, although psychosocial interventions are the duty of all health care professionals in a pediatric inpatient setting (e.g., nurses), frequently little time is available to implement such programs. These pragmatic, real-world factors have likely contributed to the recent lack of interest in conducting empirical evaluations of hospital-based play interventions.

With that said, the literature has suggested that hospitalized children can benefit from play therapy interventions. Clatworthy (1981) examined whether a therapeutic play intervention reduced anxiety among hospitalized children. The intervention consisted of a daily, individual 30-minute therapeutic play session and was described as child-directed, with the therapist providing reflection and interpretation as the child played with materials of his or her choice. Using a pre–post design, anxiety scores among children in the experimental groups did not decrease following the intervention; rather, scores among children in the control groups increased between admission and discharge. Thus, the play intervention may not have helped children reduce their anxiety, but it may have helped them to keep their anxiety from increasing.

Rae et al. (1989) conducted an empirical study that attempted to address the limitations of previous research by including random assignment to different treatment conditions. They assessed the effects of a therapeutic play intervention on children who were hospitalized for diagnosis and treatment of acute illnesses. Following the preassessment phase, participants were randomly assigned to one of four groups or conditions: (a) therapeutic play (i.e., client-centered medical play), (b) verbal support (i.e., talking about feelings, but no play), (c) diversionary play (i.e., nonsymbolic play with board or card games without therapeutic discussion), and (d) control group (i.e., no intervention). The results suggested that children in the therapeutic play group reported significantly greater reduction of hospital-related fears than children in the other three groups. However, children in the therapeutic play group reported a slight increase in somatization. Furthermore, the study used methodologically sound procedures, such as random assignment to treatment conditions and consistent administration of experimental conditions by the same research assistant.

Other researchers also conducted empirical investigations of hospital-based play interventions during the 1980s and early 1990s. Gillis (1989) evaluated the use of a play therapy intervention with hospitalized children who were immobilized. Immobilized children in the hospital represent a special population in that immobility limits the child's capacity for exploration and physical activity, which may threaten his or her self-esteem and self-concept. The intervention consisted of four sessions of individual assisted play between the child and either the researcher or research assistant, although the exact nature of the intervention is not clearly specified. Following the intervention, children in the intervention group reported significantly higher self-esteem than children in the control group.

Fosson, Martin, and Haley (1990) examined the effect of a single 30-minute play session on the anxiety of hospitalized children. The content of the session included exploration of the medical equipment, needle play, and play medical procedures. The same therapist administered the experimental and comparison conditions, and parents usually were present in both conditions. Results indicated that following the intervention, anxiety among children within the experimental group decreased to a greater extent than anxiety among children within the comparison group, but the group mean difference was not great enough to reach statistical significance. In the study, child participants were accompanied by a parent throughout the hospitalization experience, which may account for the failure to detect a greater intervention effect. In the same way, Young and Fu (1988) examined the effects of a needle play intervention on children's perceptions of pain following a blood test. Participants were randomly assigned to one of four groups: (a) pre–blood test needle play, (b) post–blood test needle play, (c) pre– and post–blood test needle play, and (d) no needle play. Thus, there were three intervention groups and a control group. Results indicated that children in the three intervention groups produced pulse rates statistically significantly lower than those produced by children in the control group 5 minutes after the blood test. Although the intervention did appear to influence children's pulse rate and nervous behaviors, participation in the intervention did not influence children's subjective pain appraisals.

More recently, Li, Chung, and Ho (2011) looked at the effectiveness of therapeutic play to promote the well-being of children with cancer. They hypothesized that using a virtual reality computer would help these children cope more effectively with the stress of hospitalization. In the experimental intervention, the children received a 30-minute therapeutic play intervention using virtual reality computer games for 5 days out the week. The children in the experimental group reported fewer depressive symptoms than the control group by Day 7. Thus, the use of computer games seemed to help the children cope more effectively with their hospitalization.

These studies suggest that psychosocial play interventions are probably efficacious for hospitalized children, particularly with regard to decreasing anxiety and hospital-related fears, preventing anxiety from worsening, improving self-esteem, and reducing behaviors indicative of distress (e.g., depression). A number of case studies evaluating play therapy interventions in hospital settings also have provided anecdotal support for the interventions' effectiveness (e.g., Atala & Carter, 1992; Landreth, Homeyer, Glover, & Sweeney, 1996).

REPLICATION AND TRANSPORTABILITY

The replicability of the previously described hospital-based play interventions in nonhospital settings is difficult to determine. Because the therapeutic interventions involved nondirective play, it might be difficult to replicate the therapeutic trajectory. Within the context of hospital-based interventions, different children will present with different fears, coping styles, illnesses or injuries, and resources. Thus, the direction that a child takes within a play therapy session will vary as a function of these and other (e.g., temperament, propensity to disclose) factors. In the same way, each study tended to have a slightly different treatment approach. Although common features exist, exact replication might be difficult. At the same time, it is suspected that these approaches can be replicated in outpatient clinics and other settings in which medically related issues are important. Although not specifically designed for this purpose, the elements of the play interventions could be adapted easily to meet the needs of a nonhospitalized child who is experiencing adaptation problems to illness, medical interventions, or outpatient treatment.

Although the therapist must be trained in play therapy theory and techniques, other health care professionals might be able to implement aspects of this program. Hospital personnel implementing this kind of program must be trained in the delivery of psychological interventions with children. Clearly, knowledge of childhood medical conditions and diseases, and how these conditions can affect children's psychosocial development, is desirable (see, e.g., Clay, 2004). Child Life personnel within hospital settings routinely conduct similar interventions (Thompson, 2009).

TRANSCRIPTS OF TWO CASES

Psychological Preparation of a Child for Major Surgery

Catherine was 6 years old when she was diagnosed with a low grade sarcoma of the right face, orbit, and jaw. Because the tumor was unresponsive to chemotherapy, a craniofacial surgery was planned. The surgery was not expected to affect cognitive functioning but would involve the loss of her right eye and cause facial changes. Catherine was bright and verbal. The following is a transcript from a hospital play therapy session during which Catherine and the therapist worked closely together to prepare for Catherine's planned surgery:

Therapist [*therapist and child are sitting on the carpeted floor, facing one another*]: I'm glad we have time to talk and play together today. [*Catherine quietly nods in agreement*] I notice that you are quiet now. Is there something you are thinking about?

Catherine: I am worried about my surgery.

Therapist: You have an important surgery coming up, and it's okay to feel worried. Your doctors, nurses, family, and I are going to be here for you and will take very special care of you all along the way. What do you think may be bothering you the most right now?

Catherine: I'm worried about losing my eye. I love my eye and do not want the doctors to take it out. [*holds a favorite stuffed dinosaur named "Rex" close to her chest, protecting his eyes*]

Therapist: I understand. Your eyes are a very special part of you and you will miss your eye very much. [*a few tears run down Catherine's face, so the therapist moves closer in empathy and to show her support*] You know, after you have surgery, some things change, but the most important things stay the same. First, let's work on what will change. What do you think will be hard about not having your right eye?

Catherine: I'm not sure how well I will be able to see.

Therapist: That's an important worry. Let's see if we can figure that out. First, let's look around the room, from side to side, with both of our eyes open. Maybe Rex would like to try this with us. [*therapist and child turn their heads slowly and moderately, from side-to-side together; Catherine turns Rex's head in the same fashion*] Notice what all you see.

Catherine: I see all of the fun things we usually play with like the doll-house, the puppets, and art stuff.

Therapist: Great. Me too. Now, let's cover our right eye with our hand and see what we can see. [*both turn their heads together again, but stretch further both ways to accomplish the same visual field range*] What do you notice?

Catherine: I can still see everything, but I have to turn my head further to each side to see all around. [*Catherine talks to Rex*] Like this, Rex.

Therapist: What does Rex think?

Catherine:	Rex thinks he can still see most things fine.
Therapist:	Rex is right. You will still be able to see very well after surgery, but you will depend on your left eye. You will have to get used to turning your head more, especially to the right, to see everything on your right side, but all in all, you will be able to do everything you enjoy and still do a great job at school. [Catherine smiles and hugs Rex]

Psychological Support for a Child in the Intensive Care Unit

José was an 11-year-old boy who had fallen while riding his bike. Although rare, his primary injury was a pneumothorax that caused his lung to collapse. He was brought to the children's hospital via ambulance and was stabilized in the emergency center, where a chest tube was placed. José was then recovering in the pediatric intensive care unit. A referral was made to the behavioral health team because José was observed to be crying frequently and having difficulty with sleep.

Therapist:	Hi, José. I am glad to meet you and your family. I am a therapist with the children's hospital and I visit and play with many of the children who come here for their care. [José looks at the therapist and nods] How are you feeling today? [José uses a hand gesture to indicate that he is feeling so-so] So just so-so right now?
José:	Yeah.
Therapist:	You have been through a lot in the last couple of days. Would you like to play a game or make art together while we visit?
José:	I like to draw.
Therapist:	Great. I have some new colored pencils and markers. Would you like to use these? [José nods and smiles] Is this your first time to ever stay in a hospital?
José:	Yeah. [José nods and begins to draw]
Therapist:	So everything here is probably very new to you. [José nods] Is there anything that you are especially curious about, or even worried about? [José points to his chest tube and frowns] I see— you are worried about your chest tube. That's understandable. Do you know what it's for? [José shakes his head] When you came in, one of your lungs was weak and not filling with air fully, so the doctors made a decision to insert a chest tube to help your lung inflate and to help it heal. The chest tube is actually soft and flexible and kind of small. Would you like to feel a tube like the one that's in your chest now?

José: Sure. [*Therapist hands José a piece of tubing*] Wow, it is softer than I thought it was.

Therapist: That's right—it is soft. You can squeeze it easily with your fingers. The doctors say that it will be there about another 2 days, but then they will be able to remove it because your lung should be working well on its own by then. [*José smiles and looks relieved*]

CONCLUSION

Research has suggested that therapeutic play programs for hospitalized children can reduce psychological distress related to the experience of illness and hospitalization. Bolig (1990) correctly predicted that trends related to health care may serve to reduce the use of unstructured, child-directed play interventions and increase the use of more structured and directive interventions that relate specifically to the child's illness and associated treatment procedures (e.g., medical play and preparation). In light of these trends, it will be necessary to determine the effectiveness of these more directive interventions in comparison with the relatively more unstructured interventions, such as those described in the present chapter.

More than 25 years ago, Phillips (1988) noted that a determination of whether play therapy interventions would reach their lofty goals with regard to facilitating children's adjustment to hospitals and medical procedures (e.g., enhancing autonomy, mastery, and control; reducing anxiety and fear) awaited more rigorous empirical support than was currently available. Presently, the child health care literature is replete with case studies and anecdotal accounts attesting to the utility of play therapy in hospital settings, in addition to theoretical, conceptual, and position papers. What is needed, however, is a shift from descriptive and anecdotal papers to methodologically sound research. Hospital-based play interventions hold the potential to make hospitalization less threatening for children, but more convincing data will be necessary to communicate the value and importance of these programs to parents and hospital administration.

REFERENCES

Atala, K. D., & Carter, B. D. (1992). Pediatric limb amputation: Aspects of coping and psychotherapeutic intervention. *Child Psychiatry and Human Development*, *23*, 117–130. http://dx.doi.org/10.1007/BF00709754

Axline, V. M. (1969). *Play therapy* (Rev. ed.). New York, NY: Ballantine Books.

Bolig, R. (1990). Play in health care settings: A challenge for the 1990s. *Children's Health Care, 19*, 229–233. http://dx.doi.org/10.1207/s15326888chc1904_6

Bolig, R., Fernie, D. E., & Klein, E. L. (1986). Unstructured play in hospital settings: An internal locus of control rationale. *Children's Health Care, 15*, 101–107. http://dx.doi.org/10.1207/s15326888chc1502_8

Bolig, R., Yolton, K. A., & Nissen, H. L. (1991). Medical play and preparation: Questions and issues. *Children's Health Care, 20*, 225–229. http://dx.doi.org/10.1207/s15326888chc2004_5

Bratton, S. C., Ray, D., Rhine, T., & Jones, L. (2005). The efficacy of play therapy with children: A meta-analytic review of treatment outcomes. *Professional Psychology: Research and Practice, 36*, 376–390. http://dx.doi.org/10.1037/0735-7028.36.4.376

Clatworthy, S. (1981). Therapeutic play: Effects on hospitalized children. *Children's Health Care, 9*, 108–113.

Clay, D. L. (2004). *Helping schoolchildren with chronic health conditions: A practical guide.* New York, NY: Guilford Press.

Ellinwood, C. G., & Raskin, N. J. (1993). Client-centered humanistic psychotherapy. In T. R. Kratochwill & R. J. Morris (Eds.), *Handbook of psychotherapy with children and adolescents* (pp. 258–277). Boston, MA: Allyn & Bacon.

Fosson, A., Martin, J., & Haley, J. (1990). Anxiety among hospitalized latency-age children. *Journal of Developmental and Behavioral Pediatrics, 11*, 324–327. http://dx.doi.org/10.1097/00004703-199012000-00009

Gillis, A. J. (1989). The effect of play on immobilized children in hospital. *International Journal of Nursing Studies, 26*, 261–269. http://dx.doi.org/10.1016/0020-7489(89)90007-2

Goldberger, J., Mohl, A. L., & Thompson, R. H. (2009). Psychological preparation and coping. In R. H. Thompson (Ed.), *The handbook of child life: A guide for pediatric psychosocial care* (pp. 160–198). Springfield, IL: Charles C Thomas.

Harbeck-Weber, C., & McKee, D. H. (1995). Prevention of emotional and behavioral distress in children experiencing hospitalization and chronic illness. In M. C. Roberts (Ed.), *Handbook of pediatric psychology* (2nd ed., pp. 167–184). New York, NY: Guilford Press.

Kazak, A. E., Schneider, S., & Kassam-Adams, N. (2009). Pediatric medical traumatic stress. In M. C. Roberts & R. G. Steele (Eds.), *Handbook of pediatric psychology* (4th ed., pp. 205–215). New York, NY: Guilford Press.

Klinzing, D. G., & Klinzing, D. R. (1987). The hospitalization of a child and family responses. *Marriage & Family Review, 11*, 119–134. http://dx.doi.org/10.1300/J002v11n01_08

Landreth, G. L. (2012). *Play therapy: The art of relationship* (3rd ed.). New York, NY: Routledge/Taylor & Francis.

Landreth, G. L., Homeyer, L. E., Glover, G., & Sweeney, D. S. (1996). *Play therapy interventions with children's problems*. Northvale, NJ: Jason Aronson.

Leblanc, M., & Ritchie, M. (2001). A meta-analysis of play therapy outcomes. *Counselling Psychology Quarterly, 14*, 149–163. http://dx.doi.org/10.1080/09515070110059142

Li, H. C. W., Chung, J. O., & Ho, E. K. Y. (2011). The effectiveness of therapeutic play, using virtual reality computer games, in promoting the psychological well-being of children hospitalised with cancer. *Journal of Clinical Nursing, 20*, 2135–2143. http://dx.doi.org/10.1111/j.1365-2702.2011.03733.x

Li, H. C. W., & Lopez, V. (2008). Effectiveness and appropriateness of therapeutic play intervention in preparing children for surgery: A randomized controlled trial study. *Journal for Specialists in Pediatric Nursing, 13*, 63–73. http://dx.doi.org/10.1111/j.1744-6155.2008.00138.x

McMahon, L. (2009). *The handbook of play therapy and therapeutic play*. New York, NY: Routledge/Taylor & Francis.

Miller, S. M., Sherman, H. D., Combs, C., & Kruus, L. (1992). Patterns of children's coping and short-term medical and dental stressors: Nature, implications, and future directions. In A. M. La Greca, L. J. Siegel, J. L. Wallander, & C. E. Walker (Eds.), *Stress and coping in child health* (pp. 157–190). New York, NY: Guilford Press.

Petrillo, M., & Sanger, S. (1980). *Emotional care of hospitalized children: An environmental approach*. Philadelphia, PA: Lippincott Williams & Wilkins.

Phillips, R. D. (1988). Play therapy in health care settings: Promises never kept? *Children's Health Care, 16*, 182–187. http://dx.doi.org/10.1207/s15326888chc1603_9

Price, R. A., Stranges, E., & Elixhauser, A. (2012). Pediatric cancer hospitalizations, 2009: Statistical brief #132. In *Healthcare Cost and Utilization Project (HCUP) statistical briefs*. Retrieved from http://www.ncbi.nlm.nih.gov/pubmed/22787680

Rae, W. A., Worchel, F. F., Upchurch, J., Sanner, J. H., & Daniel, C. A. (1989). The psychosocial impact of play on hospitalized children. *Journal of Pediatric Psychology, 14*, 617–627. http://dx.doi.org/10.1093/jpepsy/14.4.617

Siegel, L. J., & Conte, P. (2001). Hospitalization and medical care of children. In C. E. Walker & M. C. Roberts (Eds.), *Handbook of clinical child psychology* (3rd ed., pp. 895–909). New York, NY: Wiley.

Thompson, R. H. (1985). *Psychosocial research on pediatric hospitalization and health care: A review of the literature*. Springfield, IL: Charles C Thomas.

Thompson, R. H. (Ed.). (2009). *The handbook of child life: A guide for pediatric psychosocial care*. Springfield, IL: Charles C Thomas.

Thompson, R. H., & Snow, C. (2009). Research in child life. In R. H. Thompson (Ed.), *The handbook of child life: A guide for pediatric psychosocial care* (pp. 36–56). Springfield, IL: Charles C Thomas.

Webb, J. R. (1995). Play therapy with hospitalized children. *International Journal of Play Therapy*, 4(1), 51–59. http://dx.doi.org/10.1037/h0089214

Young, M. R., & Fu, V. R. (1988). Influence of play and temperament on the young child's response to pain. *Children's Health Care*, *16*, 209–215. http://dx.doi.org/10.1207/s15326888chc1603_13

Yu, H., Wier, L. M., & Elixhauser, A. (2011). Hospital stays for children, 2009: Statistical Brief #118. In *Healthcare Cost and Utilization Project (HCUP) statistical briefs*. National Center for Biotechnology Information website. Retrieved from http://www.ncbi.nlm.nih.gov/books/NBK65134/

III

EMPIRICALLY BASED PLAY INTERVENTIONS FOR EXTERNALIZING DISORDERS

7

THE INCREDIBLE YEARS: USE OF PLAY INTERVENTIONS AND COACHING FOR CHILDREN WITH EXTERNALIZING DIFFICULTIES

CAROLYN WEBSTER-STRATTON

Children derive unique benefits when their parents and teachers give them undivided, focused, regular, and responsive attention during child-directed play interactions. During adult–child play, the child develops a trusting emotional bond and important physical, cognitive, social, and language skills. Attentive playtimes also play a critical role in shaping the way children think, learn, react to challenges, and develop relationships throughout their lives (Raver & Knitzer, 2002). Children who are not supported to develop these prosocial and emotional regulation skills are more likely to continue to exhibit immature behaviors typically seen in toddlers, such as aggression, oppositional behaviors, and tantrums (Tremblay et al., 1999). Such children with "early-onset" conduct problems or oppositional defiant disorder (ODD) are subsequently at high risk for recurring conduct disorders, underachievement, school dropout, violence, and eventual delinquency (Loeber et al., 1993). Thus, early intervention efforts designed to assist parents, teachers, and child

http://dx.doi.org/10.1037/14730-008
Empirically Based Play Interventions for Children, Second Edition, L. A. Reddy, T. M. Files-Hall, and C. E. Schaefer (Editors)

therapists with the strategies to promote children's optimal social, emotional, and problem-solving competencies can help lay a positive foundation for optimal brain development.

RATIONALE AND DESCRIPTION OF THE INCREDIBLE YEARS PARENT, TEACHER, AND CHILD PROGRAMS

The Incredible Years (IY) Parents, Teachers and Children's Series is a set of three separate, but interlocking, evidence-based programs designed to promote social and emotional competence in young children and to prevent and treat conduct problems. First is the IY BASIC parenting series, which consists of five curricula versions designed for different age groups (infant–12 years). These programs are offered weekly for nine to 20 sessions (program length varies by target age) to groups of eight to 12 parents; they emphasize developmentally age-appropriate parenting skills that help children accomplish key developmental milestones. The primary goals of these programs are to strengthen parent–child attachment through nurturing relationships, increasing positive discipline (i.e., rules, predictable routines, effective limit-setting, problem solving), decreasing critical or harsh parenting (i.e., logical consequences), and building relationships with day care providers and teachers. The foundation of the IY program Parenting Pyramid rests on parents' ongoing investment of their attention and time in the use of child-directed play and coaching strategies to strengthen their attachment with their children. Through child-directed play interactions, parents learn how to coach their children's social, emotional, and language growth, and, for early school-age children, how to build their academic readiness and beginning problem-solving steps.

The second program is the IY teacher training series, a 6-day training program for teachers, school counselors, and psychologists who work with children aged 3 to 8 years. This training is offered monthly to groups of 10 to 15 teachers who complete classroom assignments between training sessions. The foundation of this IY program Teaching Pyramid is also to promote positive teacher classroom management skills and relationships with students through social, emotional, academic, and persistence coaching. In addition, topics for teachers include praise, incentives, proactive discipline, behavior planning, and development of partnerships with parents.

The third program in the series is the IY Dina Dinosaur's social skills, emotion, and problem-solving curriculum (also known as Dinosaur School). Both a classroom prevention version of this curriculum and a treatment pull-out small-group version are available. The treatment version is offered for 20 weeks in 2-hour sessions to groups of six children with conduct or social problems, or attention-deficit/hyperactivity disorder (ADHD), usually in conjunction with the IY parent program. The prevention classroom version of the program is offered twice weekly to the whole class throughout the school year. Topics include teaching children social skills and ways to talk with peers, understanding and expressing feelings, managing anger, and problem solving. Material is taught to the children during circle time lessons, small group experiential activities, and free play, and through the use of large puppets.

All three programs (parent, teacher, and child) rely heavily on relationship building; performance training methods, including presentation of video vignettes; observational learning through video or live modeling; active experiential role-plays and practices; assigned home and classroom practice activities; and live feedback and coaching from trained group leaders and group participants. (For further information and a description of these programs, please see the following articles: Webster-Stratton, 1999, 2012b, 2012c, 2013; Webster-Stratton & Reid, 2010).

THEORETICAL UNDERPINNINGS

The use of child-directed play and coaching strategies with children draws from underlying theories of social learning, modeling, and relational theories, such as attachment and psychodynamic theories. In addition, extensive research regarding children's social, emotional, and cognitive development has provided interventions with a developmental framework of empirically based models of normal and pathological child development.

Contributions From Social Learning Theory

IY child training philosophy has its roots in applied behavior analysis, models of operant behavior (Baer, Wolf, & Risley, 1968), and cognitive social learning theory (Bandura, 1989). A key assumption is that children's behaviors are learned from their interactions with significant people in their lives, particularly their parents, teachers, and peers. Child problem behaviors—whether internalizing or externalizing problems—are believed to be maintained by environmental reinforcers. The focus of training from this perspective is on changing maladaptive child behaviors by changing the environmental contingencies that maintain these problem behaviors.

Cognitive social learning theory (Bandura, 1977) posits that behavior is learned not only by experiencing the direct consequences of those behaviors but also by children's observing similar behavior and its consequences. The IY programs incorporate modeling theory by emphasizing the importance of parents, teachers, and therapists modeling of appropriate social interactions, emotional regulation, and appropriate expression of emotions for children. In accordance with a cognitive social learning model, then, each of the three intervention programs in the series is aimed at identifying children's prosocial (or appropriate) and maladaptive (or inappropriate) behaviors, emotions, and thoughts, and changing the reinforcement contingencies by prompting and reinforcing positive opposite behaviors and ignoring or instituting brief consequences for negative behavior.

Contributions From Relational Theories

The IY programs also draw from relational approaches of attachment and psychoanalytic theory (Ainsworth, Bell, & Stayton, 1974; Belsky & de Haan, 2011; Cicchetti, Rogosch, & Toth, 2006; Sroufe, Carlson, Levy, & Egeland, 1999) because of their central concern with emotion, affective processes, and the quality of relationships. Social learning and behavioral theory suggests that a more positive child relationship will occur when parents and teachers use child-directed and coaching skills with children because their use of attentive and sensitive responding, and praise, makes them more reinforcing. However, it is the developer's hypotheses that these coaching strategies with children also influence the affective and relational aspects of adult–child interactions, as separate from behavioral management. Within a relational focus as espoused by Axline (1969), child-directed play is seen as a way to promote positive parenting and adult–child bonding or attachment and is a goal in itself. Therefore, the IY programs emphasize the importance of the adult's increased expression and communication of positive affect, including love, affection, acceptance, enjoyment, and empathy during play interactions. Another therapy component that grows out of relational theory is training parents, teachers, and therapists to label, encourage, and respond to children's expression of emotions, including a focus on teaching adults and children to process and manage strong emotions. This renewed interest in affective processes reflects a growing recognition that a parent or teacher's emotional expression and self-regulation ability are likely to affect the quality of children's emotional expression, which, in turn, affects the quality of their social relationships and ability to self-regulate in the face of conflict.

Developmental Theory

The IY programs also draw heavily on developmental cognitive learning stages and research in regard to brain development (Belsky & de Haan, 2011; Piaget & Inhelder, 1962). Children must be developmentally ready to learn from specific training approaches. The IY program addresses the major developmental milestones for toddlers versus preschoolers versus school-age children.

RESEARCH EVIDENCE SUPPORTING IY PROGRAMS

All the IY programs (parent, teacher, and child) have been evaluated extensively in multiple randomized controlled trials (RCTs) by the developer and by independent investigators. Separate evaluations of each program have been done for the treatment versions of the programs (i.e., for children with diagnosed problems) and for the prevention versions of the programs (i.e., for high-risk populations). These RCTs have included families from socio-economically and ethnically diverse populations. A detailed review of the specific outcomes of each of these evaluations can be found in the library of the IY website (Webster-Stratton, 2012a).

Briefly, the parenting intervention has been shown to improve paren-tal attitudes and parent–child interactions and reduce harsh discipline and child conduct problems compared with waitlist control groups. The results were consistent for early childhood and school-age versions of the pro-grams, and were sustained at 1 year to 3 years postintervention (Webster-Stratton, 1990) and in a 10-year follow-up (Webster-Stratton, Rinaldi, & Reid, 2011).

The teacher intervention showed that teachers who received the intervention used more proactive classroom management strategies, praised their students more, used fewer coercive or critical discipline strategies, and placed more focus on helping students to problem solve than teachers who had not received this training. Intervention classrooms were rated as having a more positive classroom atmosphere, increases in child social compe-tence and school readiness skills, and lower levels of aggressive behavior. Prevention and treatment studies have suggested there is an added effect when the IY teacher classroom management program is combined with the child Dinosaur School treatment program and/or IY parent program in terms of peer relationship improvements, school readiness outcomes, and reduction of aggressive behaviors in the classroom (Webster-Stratton & Hammond, 1997; Webster-Stratton, Reid, & Beauchaine, 2013; Webster-Stratton, Reid, & Hammond, 2004).

The child intervention, when offered alone, led to improvements in children's problem-solving and conflict management skills with peers compared with those who did not receive the intervention. At the 1-year follow up, combining child training with parent training led to the most improvement (compared with either training in isolation). The classroom prevention version of the child program with Head Start families and primary grade classrooms indicated significant improvements in school readiness, emotional regulation, and social skills, and reductions in behavior problems in the classroom (Webster-Stratton, Reid, & Stoolmiller, 2008).

PLAY AND COACHING: FOUNDATIONAL COMPONENTS OF ALL THREE PROGRAMS

One of the key therapeutic aspects of all three IY programs in the series is training in child-directed play interactions using academic, persistence, social, and emotional coaching skills, and training in using imaginary play to teach children's self-regulation and problem-solving skills. These coached child-directed play components compose at least half of all the intervention program's content and the time spent training, although the specific play coaching methods on which the program focuses vary according to the child's developmental stage. These play coaching skills form the foundation for building children's relationships with their parents, teachers, and peers. The IY program research summarized earlier was evaluated as a complete intervention that includes the play and coaching skills in combination with the limit-setting and positive discipline components. No research has evaluated individual components of the program in isolation. It is the developer's belief that teaching the play relationship-building and coaching components before training in the discipline components is essential to the therapeutic behavior change model; however, the positive discipline is also believed to be a core component of the program. It is not recommended that the program be shortened to deliver parts of the program separately. The origins of parent–child interaction therapy (PCIT) developed by Sheila Eyberg, are theoretically compatible with those of the IY program, and PCIT also has had positive outcomes in randomized trials (Eyberg et al., 2001; Funderburk et al., 1998).

The remainder of this chapter focuses primarily on describing the child-directed play interaction, coaching strategies, and problem-solving components of each of the three IY series. It describes their rationale, theories, practical uses, and how the approaches are tailored to meet the particular developmental needs of each child and family circumstances. More information on the full program, including the praise, incentives, and discipline sections, can be found in other chapters and articles (see Webster-Stratton, 2006a, 2012b; Webster-Stratton & Herbert, 1994).

Child-Directed Play

All three IY series start by building a foundation of positive adult–child relationships through child-directed play interactions. This style of interacting during play means that parents, teachers, and therapists avoid giving unnecessary commands, corrections, or instructions, or asking questions during play. Instead, these adults follow the children's lead and ideas, enter with the children into their imaginary and pretend world, express their joy and playfulness in being with the children, and help the children feel special by being an appreciative audience to their play. Because one of the major developmental tasks for young children is to become more autonomous, program participants come to understand how their time spent playing with children in child-directed ways is a valuable way to help them feel some independence and develop an individual sense of self. In addition, a second major developmental task for young children is to form secure attachments with parents and teachers. Child-directed play strategies help build safe and secure relationships that eventually lead to fewer difficulties for children separating from their parents and easier transitions to school settings.

Descriptive Language Coaching

Parents, teachers, and therapists are taught how to coach children during child-directed playtimes using *descriptive language coaching* (Hanf & Kling, 1973). Descriptive commenting is a running commentary during play that describes the children's behaviors and activities. Descriptive commenting indicates to the child how focused and responsive the parent, teacher, or therapist is on what the child is doing, which further strengthens their relationship bond. It is also an invaluable teaching tool that encourages language development because this approach bathes the child in language by providing direct, important verbal information about behavior and actions or the names of objects. It also provides positive attention (and reinforcement) to whatever aspect of the play that the commenting is focused on, which encourages children's exploration and sense of discovery. In this kind of coaching, sometimes called *academic readiness coaching*, parents and teachers focus their comments on academic concepts, including the names of objects, shapes, colors, sizes, numbers, textures, and position (e.g., on, under, inside, beside, next to). For example, when the parent or teacher says, "You have three yellow rectangles on top of the red fire truck," the child is learning about shape, colors and numbers, and the language to describe these concepts. Thus, descriptive language coaching can be delivered strategically and can be tailored to meet a number of relationship, language, and learning goals, according to children's needs and developmental levels.

Persistence Coaching

Persistence coaching is when the adult comments on the child's cognitive and behavioral states while the child is playing. For example, a teacher interacting with a student working on a project will comment on the child's being focused, or concentrating well, or trying hard, or persisting and staying patient, even though the activity is difficult. Recognizing the child's internal state of mind and the physical behaviors that go along with that state is especially important for children who are inattentive, easily frustrated, impulsive, or hyperactive. Labeling the times a child is focused and persisting patiently and calmly with a difficult task helps the child to recognize that internal state, what it feels like, and to put a word to it. Attention and coaching help the child to stick with the task longer then he or she might have otherwise, and builds confidence by teaching that, with patience and persistence, the child will be able to eventually navigate a difficult situation.

Emotion Coaching

A major developmental task for young children (ages 3–6 years) is the development of emotional self-regulation skills, such as the recognition and expression of emotions, ability to wait and accept limits, development of empathy, and self-control over aggression. *Emotion coaching*, that is, labeling feelings as children experience them, helps children link a word to a feeling-state, which helps them develop a vocabulary for recognizing and expressing emotions. Once children are emotionally literate, they will be able to express their feelings to others and more easily regulate their emotional responses. In addition, they will begin to recognize emotions in others—the first step toward empathy.

Parents, teachers, and therapists are encouraged to give more attention to positive emotions than negative emotions during play interactions. However, when children do exhibit negative or uncomfortable emotions, such as anger, fearfulness, or sadness, the adult playing with them will coach them by pairing the negative emotion with the positive coping response. For example, a teacher or parent might say to a child whose tower is knocked over, "You look frustrated about that, but you are staying calm and concentrating hard to try to solve the problem," or to a fearful child, "I could tell that you felt shy about asking her to play. It was really brave of you to try it!" In this way, the adult validates the angry or shy feeling without giving it too much attention, and also expresses faith that the child will be able to cope with the feeling to produce a positive outcome. Emotional and persistence coaching are combined, and this approach may even preempt an escalation of angry tantrum.

As children begin to recognize and express their feelings, parents and teachers can begin to teach them self-calming strategies. Because children are visual thinkers and love imaginary play, it is highly effective to use stories, puppets, pictures, and role-plays to help them practice calming thoughts, images, and words. For example, parents and teachers learn in the IY training programs how to use Tiny Turtle's secret to calming down through deep breaths, positive self-talk, and happy visualizations. During playful interactions with the help of a calm-down thermometer and turtle puppet, children practice these cognitive strategies.

One-on-One Social Coaching

Another major developmental task for young children is forming social and friendship skills that include beginning to share, helping others, initiating conversations, listening, and cooperating. *Social coaching* involves adults playing with children in a way that models, prompts, and reinforces these skills. The first step in social coaching is for the teacher, parent, or therapist to model and label appropriate social skills whenever they occur in the child. For example, a teacher or parent might model social skills during play interactions by saying, "I'm going to be your friend and share my truck with you." Next, the teacher can prompt a social behavior by asking for the child's help to find something or asking the child for a turn. If the child does share or help, then the teacher responds to this behavior by describing it and praising. For example, "Thank you! You found the blue block I was looking for. That was so helpful. You are a good friend!" On the other hand, if the child does not share or help when prompted, the adult models waiting and being respectful by saying, "I guess you are not ready to share. I am going to wait patiently for a turn and do something else right now." Through modeling, prompting, and scaffolding social skills with social coaching and praise during one-on-one playtimes, children are learning positive play social interactions.

There is a wide range of developmental variation in the development of children's social skills. Most toddlers and some preschoolers are in what is called *parallel play*. Parallel play is when children may be playing next to another child but are totally involved in their own exploration and discovery process and rarely, if ever, initiate interaction or seem aware of the child sitting next to them. Next, children begin to be interested in other children but lack the social skills to initiate and sustain these interactions on their own. At ages 4 to 5 years, children progress to some sustained interactions with peers but still need coaching to maintain these interactions in a positive way and to solve interpersonal peer issues during the play.

Peer Social Coaching

For children who have moved beyond parallel play to peer interactions, parents, teachers, and therapists can do *social coaching* with several children playing together. This time the adult prompts, models, and describes the social skills that occur among the children, for example, commenting on times the children share, wait, take turns, say thank you, help each other, ask before grabbing a toy, and give a friendly suggestion. They also encourage interactions among children by providing words for a child to use to ask for something he or she wants, or praising a child who is waiting patiently when another child is not ready to share, or prompting a child to praise another child. Individual or peer social coaching strengthens children's friendships and makes it clear what the desired social skills are. However, it is important to assess children's developmental readiness for social play with peers. Children who are primarily engaged in parallel play and do not initiate play with peers or seem interested in peers will benefit from individual practice with an adult before entering into situations with a peer. Then, when they do play with peers, intense scaffolding by adults will be necessary for them to be successful. Children who are interested and motivated to play with other children but who lack the impulse control or skill to do so successfully also will benefit from individual coaching because an adult can patiently help a child to practice and fine-tune social skills. Then, when playing with peers, the adult can continue to prompt and praise social behaviors as they happen. For example, the teacher might say, "You shared with Mary. That was so friendly! Look at how happy your friend seems now." Helping children make the connection between their positive social behavior and another child's feelings is important for them in developing empathy, as well as peer relationships.

TEACHING CHILDREN TO PROBLEM SOLVE THROUGH PLAY INTERACTIONS

As children move from toddlerhood to the preschool and early school-age years, they are helped through play to learn how to express their feelings and begin to use calm-down self-regulation strategies, and to practice appropriate social behaviors, such as sharing, waiting, helping, and taking turns. These are the bedrock cognitive and behavioral skills needed for eventually solving problems. During the preoperational stage of cognitive development (ages 4–6 years), when children's imaginary play is exploding, parents, teachers, and therapists use puppet play and pretend scenarios during play interactions to teach children problem-solving strategies for managing conflicts through a five-step process.

The first step is to help them define and recognize a problem by having a puppet present children with a common childhood problem (e.g., being teased) that is signaled by an uncomfortable feeling. Then children are asked to help the puppet come up with a solution to the problem by showing what the solution looks like (e.g., staying calm and ignoring). Next, the children are asked to help the puppet think of other solutions in case the first solution does not work. Each time, the children demonstrate and practice one of these solutions with the puppet. As children move into the operational stage of cognitive development, they eventually are able to learn the fourth and fifth problem-solving steps of evaluating solutions and choosing the best solution. All of this problem-solving learning takes place in fun, imaginary, creative, and playful situations so that children can learn the language and emotional self-regulation behaviors before they are encouraged to use this approach in the midst of real-life conflict.

ADDRESSING BARRIERS AND MEETING CHILDREN'S DEVELOPMENTAL NEEDS

When parents and occasionally some teachers are first trained in the child-directed play, coaching, and problem-solving methods, it can seem foreign to them—almost like learning a new language. Parents and teachers are used to asking children questions and telling them what to do, not describing their actions, cognitions, or feelings, and many parents believe in just the opposite approach: that children should be *parent-directed*, that is, obedient to and respectful of them. They may respond negatively to a child's bid for autonomy or curious exploration. Parents learn in the program about normal developmental milestones for children and about the *modeling and attention principles*; that is, behaviors parents model and give attention to are what their children learn. Understanding these principles helps parents to see the value of their positive child-directed play and coaching language for achieving their goals of a more cooperative relationship and increasing their children's social competence. Parents who speak a language other than English are encouraged to speak using their native language and to share and participate in role-play scenarios that represent their culture and childhood experiences. In doing so, such parents experience the joy of their children's happy responses and learn that they are helping their children to be more respectful and more attached to their family and culture.

Parents living in stressful environments due to poverty and unemployment may be overwhelmed and depressed with life stressors and find it difficult to find time to play with their children, perceiving it as a less important priority. In the parent programs, group facilitators acknowledge these barriers and problem solve creative ways in which parents can practice the play and coaching methods within their hectic schedules, such as during bath times, meals, or when they are doing laundry. Practices are set up for parents in groups with each other so they can learn the new language scripts for their play interactions. Moreover, the group-based approach to this learning helps parents build support networks and decrease their sense of isolation as they discover other families in similar situations.

In the remainder of this chapter, case examples are used to demonstrate the ways in which the child-directed play, coaching methods, and problem-solving puppet play are tailored to meet a particular child's goals and cognitive developmental stage. In all examples, parents received the IY parenting group specific to the age of their children while their children were in the 20-week Dinosaur School (i.e., the treatment model). School consultation and teacher training in coaching and problem-solving methods also was provided. In this way, the child's and family's goals were worked on by parents, therapists, and teachers in a coordinated effort.

Children With Oppositional Behavior

Children with conduct problems are difficult because they are non-compliant and oppositional to adult's requests. When adults cannot get children to do what they want, they cannot socialize or teach them new behaviors. Sometimes parents, teachers, and other caregivers respond to this defiant behavior by criticizing, yelling, or hitting them to try to make them comply. Other times, the intensity of a child's defiant response causes adults to give in to the child's demands, resulting in inconsistent responses. These unpredictable responses lead to children's feeling insecure in their relationships. In addition, hitting or yelling at a child models aggressive and disrespectful behavior, and gives the children's oppositional behavior powerful emotional attention, thereby reinforcing its occurrence. In turn, parents of such defiant children feel helpless and do not want to play with their children because they find their interactions stressful.

Parents are helped to understand that child-directed play helps children who are oppositional to be more compliant because parents are modeling compliance and respect for their children's ideas and requests, thereby teaching them what this behavior looks like. This approach also gives the children some legitimate opportunities to exercise control and autonomy (as long as they are behaving appropriately), which is important because it is one of children's developmental tasks. Moreover, this child-directed play helps shift a coercive parent–child dynamic into a more nurturing relationship and promotes positive attachment. Often, parents are feeling angry with such defiant children because of their disruptive behavior, and they have experienced few positive times together. These regular, daily, child-directed coaching playtimes will begin to build up the positive bank account in the relationship between the parent and child. When this bank account of positive feelings is full, then discipline is more likely to be effective.

Children who are oppositional with adults are usually aggressive with peers and have few friends. Other children do not like to play with them because they are uncooperative, bossy, and likely to criticize their ideas and suggestions. These negative responses and rejection by peers further compound the oppositional child's problems and reinforce his or her negative reputation. The resulting social isolation results in even fewer opportunities to make friends and in low self-esteem and loneliness.

Teachers can use social coaching with oppositional children during play to help them use appropriate friendship skills with peers and to stay emotionally regulated. The teacher may comment on how the target child is sharing, being a good team member in play, or helping another. The teacher also can help the oppositional child to use coping strategies when the child is frustrated, which will help him or her solve peer problems in a more positive way. This teacher coaching and attention for the targeted prosocial child behaviors during unstructured playtimes or small group projects not only reinforces the appropriate social behavior for the child with behavior difficulties but also helps to change the child's negative reputation with his or her peers. As the teacher comments on the target child's friendly behaviors and points out how the child is working hard to help or share with others, peers will begin to see the child as more friendly.

Case Example

Dylan, age 5 years, is a bright, articulate child with ODD. At the onset of therapy, he was noncompliant with approximately 90% of parent or teacher requests, he had multiple tantrums each day at home and at school, and his parents felt as if they were "held hostage" by his manipulative behavior. He was aggressive with adults and peers. He was extremely volatile, easily irritated, and had dramatic mood swings during which here he became enraged with little provocation or warning. Teachers and parents reported that they walked on eggshells around Dylan because they were afraid of his extreme reactions.

Because almost all adult–child interactions with Dylan involved a power struggle, and because his negative behaviors had placed such great strain on the parent–child relationship, the first goal of therapy was to use child-directed play to begin to change the dynamic of this relationship. Dylan's parents were encouraged to let him orchestrate the play. Their job was to be an appreciative audience, follow his lead, comply with his ideas, and not to make demands as long as his behavior was appropriate. This style of play with Dylan was designed to give him some power in the relationship in an appropriate setting, to show him that his parents valued him, and to give his parents a time when they could just enjoy his creativity and playfulness without feeling as if they had to make him behave in a certain way. At first, Dylan's parents reported that he rejected even their attempts to play with him. They were encouraged to be persistent and to make regular attempts each day to engage with him in this way, and to use persistence and positive emotion coaching. Gradually, Dylan became used to these interactions, first tolerating them, and then looking forward to this time with his parents. Dylan began to invite his parents into his play and seemed excited that they were willing to play on his terms. His parents reported that he seemed calmer after play sessions and that they had moments of feeling connected and appreciative of his strengths.

As part of the play interactions and at other times during the day, Dylan's parents learned to avoid giving attention to or commenting about his negative behaviors (e.g., angry outbursts, arguments) while strategically responding with positive attention when he was calm, happy, and patient. They modeled compliance to his requests when reasonable and gave him attention when he was compliant by praising his cooperation and helpfulness. As these playtimes and interactions became more enjoyable, they began to use some puppet scenarios to teach him calm-down strategies.

Children With ADHD

Children with ADHD also have difficulty playing with peers and making friends (Coie, Dodge, & Kupersmidt, 1990). Because of their impulsivity and distractibility, it is hard for them to wait for a turn when playing or to concentrate long enough to complete a puzzle, game, or building project. They are more likely to grab things from another child or disrupt a carefully built tower or puzzle because of their activity level and lack of patience. Research has shown these children are significantly delayed in their play skills and social skills (Barkley, 1996; Webster-Stratton & Lindsay, 1999). For example, a 6-year-old with ADHD plays more like a 4-year-old and will have difficulty focusing on a play activity for more than a few minutes; sharing with peers; or even being aware of a peer's requests for help, suggestions, or feelings. Such children are more likely to be engaged in solitary or parallel play. Other typically developing 6-year-olds will find such children annoying to play with, so frequently these inattentive children experience peer rejection—a problem that further compounds their social difficulties and their self-esteem. For children with ADHD, persistence coaching is key to helping them sustain focus or attention for longer periods, emotion coaching is crucial in teaching them to regulate strong emotions, and social coaching helps to build their friendship skills. These coached play interactions not only enhance children's skills but also have the added advantage of helping parents and teachers understand and accept the developmental, temperament, and biological differences in these children, such as variation in their distractibility, impulsiveness, and hyperactivity. Previous research also has shown that teaching children how to play games that are developmentally appropriate has been effective in successfully treating children with ADHD and with conduct problems (Reddy, Spencer, Hall, & Rubel, 2001; Reddy et al., 2005).

Case Example

Kevin is an 8-year-old boy with ADHD. His primary difficulties occur at school and with his peers. Kevin is eager to please adults, but he is unable to wait for the teacher's attention, blurts out answers in school, has trouble sitting still in class, and is easily drawn into off-task behavior of others. With friends, Kevin is eager to play and has many friendly social skills in his repertoire. He knows how to share, ask, trade, and even make suggestions and negotiate with friends. However, he has difficulty sustaining play because of his impulsivity. For example, he inadvertently messes up the play with expansive body movements, has difficulty waiting for a turn, impulsively grabs toys, and sometimes cannot maintain attention long enough to listen and respond to peers ideas. He is also occasionally aggressive, usually in reaction to something another child says or does.

For Kevin, the first emphasis during child-directed play was on persistence and emotion regulation. Kevin's mother and teachers used focused coaching to comment when they saw Kevin being persistent, calm, or patient with an activity. For example, teachers commented when he was engaged in academic tasks (i.e., circle time and seat work): "Kevin, I know that you want a turn to talk. I'm proud of you for waiting until I call on you" and "I think that you're frustrated with that math problem, but you are staying so focused and you are trying to figure it out."

In addition, his mother used persistence, social, and emotional coaching when he was playing with his sibling or peers. The key in these situations was to monitor carefully and notice when Kevin was beginning to become dysregulated. At these moments, Kevin's mother would intervene with reminders of how his body could stay calm: "Kevin, I see that you want to use that toy too. I think you can stop your body and take a deep breath." Then she would provide Kevin with words to use to facilitate the interaction. "Can you ask Bill if you can borrow it?" Kevin was responsive to this type of coaching. Because he already had many of the skills in his repertoire, these simple prompts were enough to keep his play on track. In addition, emphasis was on describing times when he was waiting, sharing with his brother, listening to a friend, playing calmly, and keeping his body slow and careful. Kevin continued to be quite impulsive and needed much structure in his school and play environments. However, with this coaching, his behaviors at school with peers and with his brother became more controlled and manageable. After a time, teachers and Kevin's mother were able to use more brief verbal reminders, and Kevin was able to respond to some non-verbal cues as a trigger for exerting impulse control in challenging situations.

Children With Attachment Problems

Children with conduct problems and/or ADHD also may have ambivalent or avoidant attachment patterns with their biological, foster, or adoptive parents for a variety of reasons (Bakermans-Kranenburg, van IJzendoorn, & Juffer, 2003). Insecure attachment may develop because children have experienced abandonment, neglect, death of a parent, trauma, or physical abuse during their early childhood years. It also may occur because parents' responses have been unpredictable, inconsistent, harsh, neglectful, and dismissive of children's emotional needs. Children who have experienced such stressful, inconsistent, and nonnurturing parenting learn not to trust the world or their relationships with others. Their insecure attachment, in turn, affects how they process information, solve problems, and behave with others. For example, children with insecure attachment may be angry with adults and oppositional, suspicious, or rejecting of caregiver nurturing. Children also may experience sadness, anxiety, and withdrawal. In some cases, these feelings have been ignored or invalidated by caregivers and, consequently, children may be unable to label or discuss their feelings easily and may not believe that it is safe to share these feelings with others. Children may have an insatiable need for adult attention and be resentful and clingy whenever adult attention is given to someone other than themselves. Still other children with insecure attachment may be frightened of adults and become emotionally absent or disassociated as a way of escaping their fears. Children's attachment classifications are not permanent and may become more secure if parent and other adult relationships become more predictable and consistent, sensitive to their cues, calming and nurturing when they are distressed, and accepting of their emotions (van IJzendoorn, Juffer, & Duyvesteyn, 1995).

Case Example

Michelle is a 4-year-old girl who lives with her single mother. Michelle's father left when she was 2 years old, and her mother is clinically depressed. She tries to meet Michelle's needs, and there are times when she lavishes attention on Michelle. However, she treats Michelle like a peer, engaging in activities that are age inappropriate (e.g., makeovers, adult music, watching adult movies, sharing personal aspects of her adult life). At other times, she does not have the energy to engage with Michelle at all. At the onset of treatment, Michelle had difficulty separating from her mother at the beginning of each Dinosaur School small group therapy session, and she was then clingy and almost inappropriately attached to the two child group therapists that she had just met. At times, she was withdrawn and sad, and at other times, she seemed angry, defiant, oppositional, and noncompliant. She was interested in other children and seemed to want to make friends but was easily jealous of any attention that other children were getting from the therapists. She had little sense of appropriate physical boundaries and hugged and kissed therapists and other children without tuning in to their responses. She often was pouty or weepy when she did not get her way.

Therapy for this family involved using the parent group to help Michelle's mother to provide regular and predictable child-directed playtimes during which she consistently gave Michelle positive attention, consistent responses, and positive emotional coaching. The goal of providing this predictable, undivided, focused attention was to help Michelle feel valued, respected, and more secure in her relationship with her mother. Michelle's mother also was encouraged to let Michelle be a child and to follow Michelle's lead in imaginary play. This allowed Michelle's mother to develop empathy and learn to appreciate Michelle's ideas, feelings, fears, and a 4-year-old's point of view. It also provided a new and more age-appropriate way for Michelle and her mother to interact. As Michelle's mother continued parent group sessions, her confidence in her parenting skills began to increase. She was helped to develop more positive self-talk and how to provide herself with some pleasurable activities. She reported that, for the first time in her life, she believed that she had good things to offer Michelle. Although she still struggled with her own depression and with Michelle's behavior, she felt more hopeful about her ability to cope.

Therapists played with Michelle in ways that would model healthy relationships. Using puppets, therapists modeled setting boundaries on physical touch by teaching Michelle how to ask before hugging or touching someone else. They paid little attention to Michelle's sulky or pouty behavior, but continued to encourage her to engage in activities with other children. For example if Michelle was sulking, no direct attempts were made to cajole her out of her mood. Rather, therapists might say to another child, "John, I'm really enjoying working on this art project with you. I bet that when Michelle is ready to join us, she'll have some great ideas about what we should add to our drawing. She's a great artist." Puppets were an important part of Michelle's treatment plan. She seemed much more willing to share feelings and experiences with the puppets than directly with the therapists. Through puppet play, Michelle also began to establish close and healthy relationships with the therapists. Therapists also showed Michelle that they would continue to be positive and engage with her, even after she had rejected their attention or been oppositional. This attention was given strategically so that Michelle received little attention when her behaviors were negative but was quickly supported as soon as she was neutral or positive. Gradually, Michelle began to seem happier and more secure in the group.

IMPLEMENTATION WITH FIDELITY

An important aspect of a program's efficacy is fidelity or delivery proficiency of implementation. Indeed, if the IY program protocol is not rigorously followed (e.g., if components are dispensed with, or if the parents, teachers, or therapists do not receive authorized training by accredited mentors), then the absence of effects may be attributed not to the inefficacy of the program but to a lack of fidelity in its implementation (Schoenwald, Sheidow, & Letourneau, 2004). Recent research with IY programs has shown that implementation with a high degree of fidelity not only preserves the anticipated behavior change mechanisms but is predictive of cognitive, emotional, and behavioral changes in parents, teachers, or therapists, which, in turn, are predictive of positive outcomes for children as a result of the treatment (Eames et al., 2009).

In the context of implementation with fidelity, the training, ongoing supervision, and accreditation of IY group facilitators all warrant great attention (Webster-Stratton, 2006b, 2012a; Webster-Stratton, Reinke, Herman, & Newcomer, 2011). Consequently, IY group facilitators initially receive 3 days of structured, active, experiential training workshops by accredited IY mentors before leading their first groups; they are then subject to ongoing supervision through video recordings of their sessions and to expert coaching and consultation. Considerable emphasis is on peer coaching through the joint viewing of the video recordings of their sessions and using self-reflection inventories to be filled in by the group facilitator or teacher and by the peer. The process of group facilitator accreditation is demanding; it involves the leadership of at least two sets of groups, peer review and supervision, a positive final video group assessment by an accredited trainer, and satisfactory completion of facilitator group session protocols and participant evaluations. A network of national and international accredited IY mentors and trainers carry out the entire process of coaching, consultation, and accreditation of new facilitators, which means the programs are readily transportable. A recent RCT showed that providing group facilitators with ongoing consultation and coaching following the 3-day workshop leads to increased facilitator proficiency, treatment adherence, and delivery fidelity compared with those who do not get ongoing coaching (Webster-Stratton, Reid, & Marsenich, 2014).

SUMMARY AND CONCLUSIONS

This chapter has highlighted how the IY Parents, Teachers and Children's Series uses four types of coaching and problem-solving role plays—modeling, coaching, guided practice, and encouragement—during child-directed play as integral components in the prevention and treatment of behavior problems, and the promotion of children's social and emotional competence. These focused, regular, child-directed play, coaching, and role-plays are thought to be necessary or critical ingredients to the IY's successful outcomes. They are theorized to result in building a more positive and loving relationship between the parent, teacher, therapist, and child and setting the foundation for later success with the discipline components of the program. In addition, these play interactions have the advantage of teaching children key social skills, such as how to take turns, wait, share, make a suggestion, give an apology or compliment, share a feeling, or learn to cooperate and compromise. The case examples showed how important it is that these play interventions be tailored to the particular developmental level of each child, target the specific goals for each child, and take into account the parents' or teacher's particular needs and home or classroom situation.

As with any therapy, there is no "magic moondust," and changing feelings, thoughts, and behaviors is hard work for parents, teachers, therapists, and children. Progress is often measured in small steps, and participants are counseled to expect setbacks as well as improvements. At any time throughout the program, those working with children are encouraged to go back to the pyramid foundation of child-directed play and coaching methods when they are feeling stuck or frustrated with the progress that the child is making. Reconnecting through strengthening the adult–child relationship is often the key to making progress in difficult areas.

Case Example

A final case example: In the 19th week of therapy, Kevin approached another child who was building a complicated Lego model. He watched for a minute, and then said, "That's cool. Can I help?" The other child did not respond, and Kevin waited. He then asked again. For a child as impulsive as Kevin, this ability to pause and ask to join the play was a remarkable change in his behavior. Even more impressive was his next response. The child who was building the model said that he did not need help, and Kevin looked disappointed but turned to a therapist and asked, "Would you help me build a model just like that?" In this interaction, Kevin was able to use his social skills to initiate a positive social interaction and then stay calm and regulated when his overture was rejected. The ability to control his impulses in a difficult social interaction is a huge step for a child like Kevin and is the beginning of the kind of self-control and self-regulation that is necessary for successful school and life experiences.

REFERENCES

Ainsworth, M. D. S., Bell, S. M., & Stayton, D. J. (1974). Infant–mother attachment and social development: 'Socialization' as a product of reciprocal responsiveness to signals. In M. Richards (Ed.), *The integration of the child into the social world* (pp. 99–135). Cambridge, England: Cambridge University Press.

Axline, V. M. (1969). *Play therapy*. New York, NY: Ballantine Books.

Baer, D. M., Wolf, M. M., & Risley, T. R. (1968). Some current dimensions of applied behavior analysis. *Journal of Applied Behavior Analysis, 1*, 91–97. http://dx.doi.org/10.1901/jaba.1968.1-91

Bakermans-Kranenburg, M. J., van IJzendoorn, M. H., & Juffer, F. (2003). Less is more: Meta-analyses of sensitivity and attachment interventions in early childhood. *Psychological Bulletin, 129*, 195–215. http://dx.doi.org/10.1037/0033-2909.129.2.195

Bandura, A. (1977). *Social learning theory*. Englewood Cliffs, NJ: Prentice Hall.

Bandura, A. (1989). Regulation of cognitive processes through perceived self-efficacy. *Developmental Psychology, 25*, 729–735. http://dx.doi.org/10.1037/0012-1649.25.5.729

Barkley, R. A. (1996). Attention deficit/hyperactivity disorder. In E. J. Mash & R. A. Barkley (Eds.), *Child psychopathology* (pp. 63–112). New York, NY: Guilford Press.

Belsky, J., & de Haan, M. (2011). Annual Research Review: Parenting and children's brain development: The end of the beginning. *Journal of Child Psychology and Psychiatry, 52*(4), 409–428. http://dx.doi.org/10.1111/j.1469-7610.2010.02281.x

Cicchetti, D., Rogosch, F. A., & Toth, S. L. (2006). Fostering secure attachment in infants in maltreating families through preventive interventions. *Development and Psychopathology, 18*, 623–649. http://dx.doi.org/10.1017/S0954579406060329

Coie, J. D., Dodge, K. A., & Kupersmidt, J. B. (1990). Peer group behavior and social status. In S. R. Asher & J. D. Coie (Eds.), *Peer rejection in childhood* (pp. 17–59). New York, NY: Cambridge University Press.

Eames, C., Daley, D., Hutchings, J., Whitaker, C. J., Jones, K., Hughes, J. C., & Bywater, T. (2009). Treatment fidelity as a predictor of behaviour change in parents attending group-based parent training. *Child: Care, Health and Development, 35*, 603–612. http://dx.doi.org/10.1111/j.1365-2214.2009.00975.x

Eyberg, S. M., Funderburk, B. W., Hembree-Kigin, T. L., McNeil, C. B., Querido, J. G., & Hood, K. K. (2001). Parent–child interaction therapy with behavior problem children: One and two year maintenance of treatment effects in the family. *Child & Family Behavior Therapy, 23*, 1–20. http://dx.doi.org/10.1300/J019v23n04_01

Funderburk, B. W., Eyberg, S. M., Newcomb, K., McNeil, C. B., Hembree-Kigin, T., & Capage, L. (1998). Parent–child interaction therapy with behavior problem children: Maintenance of treatment effects in the school setting. *Child & Family Behavior Therapy, 20*, 17–38. http://dx.doi.org/10.1300/J019v20n02_02

Hanf, E., & Kling, J. (1973). *Facilitating parent–child interactions: A two-stage training model*. Unpublished manuscript, University of Oregon Medical School, Portland.

Loeber, R., Wung, P., Keenan, K., Giroux, B., Stouthamer-Loeber, M., Van Kammen, W. B., & Maugham, B. (1993). Developmental pathways in disruptive child behavior. *Development and Psychopathology, 5*, 103–133. http://dx.doi.org/10.1017/S0954579400004296

Piaget, J., & Inhelder, B. (1962). *The psychology of the child*. New York, NY: Basic Books.

Raver, C. C., & Knitzer, J. (2002). *Ready to enter: What research tells policy makers about strategies to promote social and emotional school readiness among three- and four-year-old children*. New York, NY: National Center for Children in Poverty.

Reddy, L. A., Spencer, P., Hall, T. M., & Rubel, D. (2001). Use of developmentally appropriate games in child group training program for young children with attention-deficit/hyperactivity disorder. In A. A. Drewes, L. J. Carey, & C. E. Schaefer (Eds.), *School-based play therapy* (pp. 256–274). New York, NY: Wiley.

Reddy, L. A., Springer, C., Files-Hall, T. M., Benisz, E. S., Hauch, Y., Braunstein, D., & Atamanoff, T. (2005). Child ADHD multimodal program: An empirically supported intervention for young children with ADHD. In L. A. Reddy, T. M. Files-Hall, & C. E. Schaefer (Eds.), *Empirically based play interventions for children* (pp. 145–167). Washington, DC: American Psychological Association. http://dx.doi.org/10.1037/11086-009

Schoenwald, S. K., Sheidow, A. J., & Letourneau, E. J. (2004). Toward effective quality assurance in evidence-based practice: Links between expert consultation, therapist fidelity, and child outcomes. *Journal of Clinical Child and Adolescent Clinical Psychology*, *33*, 94–104. http://dx.doi.org/10.1207/S15374424JCCP3301_10

Sroufe, L. A., Carlson, E. A., Levy, A. K., & Egeland, B. (1999). Implications of attachment theory for developmental psychopathology. *Development and Psychopathology*, *11*, 1–13. http://dx.doi.org/10.1017/S0954579499001923

Tremblay, R. E., Japel, C., Pérusse, D., McDuff, P., Boivin, M., Zoccolillo, M., & Montplaisir, J. (1999). The search for the age of "onset" of physical aggression: Rousseau and Bandura revisited. *Criminal Behaviour and Mental Health*, *24*, 129–141.

van IJzendoorn, M. H., Juffer, F., & Duyvesteyn, M. G. C. (1995). Breaking the intergenerational cycle of insecure attachment: A review of the effects of attachment-based interventions on maternal sensitivity and infant security. *Child Psychology & Psychiatry*, *36*, 225–248.

Webster-Stratton, C. (1990). Long-term follow-up of families with young conduct problem children: From preschool to grade school. *Journal of Clinical Child Psychology*, *19*, 144–149. http://dx.doi.org/10.1207/s15374424jccp1902_6

Webster-Stratton, C. (1999). *How to promote children's social and emotional competence*. London, England: Sage.

Webster-Stratton, C. (2006a). *The Incredible Years: A trouble-shooting guide for parents of children ages 3–8 years*. Seattle, WA: Incredible Years.

Webster-Stratton, C. (2006b). Treating children with early-onset conduct problems: Key ingredients to implementing The Incredible Years programs with fidelity. In K. T. Neill (Ed.), *Helping others help children: Clinical supervision of child psychotherapy* (pp. 161–175). Washington, DC: American Psychological Association. http://dx.doi.org/10.1037/11467-009

Webster-Stratton, C. (2012a). *Blueprints for violence prevention, book eleven: The Incredible Years—Parent, Teacher, and Child Training Series*. Seattle, WA: Incredible Years.

Webster-Stratton, C. (2012b). *Collaborating with parents to reduce children's behavior problems: A book for therapists using The Incredible Years programs.* Seattle, WA: Incredible Years.

Webster-Stratton, C. (2012c). *Incredible teachers: Nurturing children's social, emotional, and academic competence.* Seattle, WA: Incredible Years.

Webster-Stratton, C. (2013). Incredible Years: Parent and child programs for maltreating families. In S. Timmer and A. Urquiza (Eds.), *Evidence-based approaches for the treatment of maltreated children* (pp. 81–104). New York, NY: Springer.

Webster-Stratton, C., & Hammond, M. (1997). Treating children with early-onset conduct problems: A comparison of child and parent training interventions. *Journal of Consulting and Clinical Psychology, 65,* 93–109. http://dx.doi.org/10.1037/0022-006X.65.1.93

Webster-Stratton, C., & Herbert, M. (1994). *Troubled families—problem children: Working with parents: A collaborative process.* Chichester, England: Wiley.

Webster-Stratton, C., & Lindsay, D. W. (1999). Social competence and conduct problems in young children: Issues in assessment. *Journal of Child Clinical Psychology, 28,* 25–43. http://dx.doi.org/10.1207/s15374424jccp2801_3

Webster-Stratton, C., & Reid, M. J. (2010). The Incredible Years Parents, Teachers and Children Training Series: A multifaceted treatment approach for young children with conduct problems. In A. E. Kazdin & J. R. Weisz (Eds.), *Evidence-based psychotherapies for children and adolescents* (2nd ed., pp. 194–210). New York, NY: Guilford Press.

Webster-Stratton, C., Reid, M. J., & Beauchaine, T. P. (2013). One-year follow-up of combined parent and child intervention for young children with ADHD. *Journal of Clinical Child & Adolescent Psychology, 42,* 251–261.

Webster-Stratton, C., Reid, M. J., & Hammond, M. (2004). Treating children with early-onset conduct problems: Intervention outcomes for parent, child, and teacher training. *Journal of Clinical Child & Adolescent Psychology, 33,* 105–124. http://dx.doi.org/10.1207/S15374424JCCP3301_11

Webster-Stratton, C., Reid, M. J., & Stoolmiller, M. (2008). Preventing conduct problems and improving school readiness: Evaluation of The Incredible Years Teacher and Child Training Programs in high-risk schools. *Journal of Child Psychology and Psychiatry, 49,* 471–488. http://dx.doi.org/10.1111/j.1469-7610.2007.01861.x

Webster-Stratton, C., Reinke, W. M., Herman, K. C., & Newcomer, L. (2011). The Incredible Years teacher classroom management training: The methods and principles that support fidelity of training delivery. *School Psychology Review, 40,* 509–529.

Webster-Stratton, C., Rinaldi, J., & Reid, J. M. (2011). Long-term outcomes of Incredible Years parenting program: Predictors of adolescent adjustment. *Child and Adolescent Mental Health, 16,* 38–46. http://dx.doi.org/10.1111/j.1475-3588.2010.00576.x

Webster-Stratton, C. H., Reid, M. J., & Marsenich, L. (2014). Improving therapist fidelity during implementation of evidence-based practices: Incredible Years program. *Psychiatric Services, 65,* 789–795. http://psycnet.apa.org/doi/10.1176/appi.ps.201200177

8

PARENT–CHILD INTERACTION THERAPY FOR CHILDREN WITH DISRUPTIVE BEHAVIOR DISORDERS

ASHLEY T. SCUDDER, AMY D. HERSCHELL, AND CHERYL B. McNEIL

Parent–child interaction therapy (PCIT; Eyberg, Nelson, & Boggs, 2008; McNeil & Hembree-Kigin, 2010) is an evidenced-based intervention originally designed to treat disruptive behavior problems in children aged 2½ years to 7 years. It is also considered an evidence-based intervention for the treatment of harsh parenting practices associated with child physical abuse (Chadwick Center for Children and Families, 2004). Although this has been less extensively examined, the use of PCIT for other presenting problems (e.g., separation anxiety) also has demonstrated empirical support. Typically, parents and their child meet with a PCIT clinician in approximately 12 to 20 one-hour weekly sessions. Outcome studies have demonstrated that completion of the treatment program results in increased parent skill, decreased child behavior problems, decreased parent distress, and generalizations of outcomes to home and school settings and to untreated siblings (Herschell, Calzada, Eyberg, & McNeil, 2002).

http://dx.doi.org/10.1037/14730-009
Empirically Based Play Interventions for Children, *Second Edition*, L. A. Reddy, T. M. Files-Hall, and C. E. Schaefer (Editors)

This chapter updates an original chapter that Herschell and McNeil (2005) included in the first edition (Reddy, Files-Hall, & Schaefer, 2005) of the current book. First, we provide a brief overview of PCIT (e.g., theoretical basis, objectives, structure) and research updates. We then use a clinical case vignette to illustrate the implementation of PCIT in community settings.

OVERVIEW OF PCIT

Theoretical Underpinnings

PCIT was developed based on Hanf's two-stage operant conditioning model and is one of several Hanf-derived behavioral parent training programs designed to treat young children with disruptive behavior difficulties (Reitman & McMahon, 2013). PCIT emphasizes coaching of specialized skills with the parent and child together in session and the inclusion of criteria for skills mastery. During PCIT, the parents' role in shaping their child's behaviors is emphasized, and PCIT clinicians assist parents in adopting an authoritative parenting style (Baumrind, 1967) through direct coaching of parent behavior, which emphasizes the importance of a balance between parent warmth and firm limit-setting to achieve optimal child outcomes. Social learning theory, which posits that child behavior problems can be inadvertently established and maintained by parent–child relationships (Patterson, 1975), also is incorporated. Patterson's (1982) coercive interaction theory asserts that each member of the parent–child pair influences the other's behavior, which creates a coercive cycle that is maintained by negative reinforcement. Parents are assisted in managing these situations by teaching consistent and fair limits; predictably following through with directives; and providing reasonable, age-appropriate consequences for child misbehavior within the context of a positive parent–child relationship.

Treatment Objectives

PCIT emphasizes enhancing specific parent and child skills. The goal for parents is to develop a set of skills that will enable them to balance a warm, positive relationship with healthy and consistent discipline. The child's goals are to increase prosocial behaviors (e.g., gentle play, sharing) and decrease inappropriate behavior, particularly noncompliance and aggression. Both the parent and child goals are quantifiable and measured at each session, and PCIT treatment progression depends on how quickly these skills are acquired.

Structure of PCIT

Treatment Structure

In PCIT, adult caregivers who have frequent, ongoing contact with the child (e.g., biological parent, foster parent, grandparent, adult sibling) and who take on a parenting role are considered "parents" and can participate in treatment. Both parent and child are actively involved in each session, and parents are taught "specialized" skills to affect the child's positive social, emotional, and behavioral development. PCIT treatment consists of two treatment phases: child-directed interaction (CDI) and parent-directed interaction (PDI). Both CDI and PDI phases are necessary; however, CDI should precede PDI to most effectively decrease problematic child behavior (Eisenstadt, Eyberg, McNeil, Newcomb, & Funderburk, 1993). Treatment generally includes (a) a pretreatment assessment of child, parent, and family functioning; (b) a CDI teach session, when parents are taught selective attention skills; (c) CDI coaching sessions, when parents receive in vivo coding and coaching of the CDI skills; (d) a PDI teach session, when parents are taught effective commands, and consistent and predictable consequences following child compliance or noncompliance; (e) PDI coaching sessions, when parents receive in vivo coding and coaching in their use of the discipline sequence; and (f) posttreatment assessment of child, parent, and family functioning (see Eyberg & Funderburk, 2011, for protocol).

Assessment

The treatment program begins with a clinic-based, comprehensive, multimethod assessment that includes a semistructured clinical interview, parent rating scales, and structured behavior observations of the parent and child as they interact during three situations: child-led play, parent-led play, and cleanup. Intake assessments are designed to determine the appropriateness of PCIT for the family and often include standardized assessment measures, such as a broadband measure of child behavior and functioning (e.g., the Child Behavior Checklist [CBCL]: Achenbach & Rescorla, 2001; Behavior Assessment System for Children: Reynolds & Kamphaus, 2002), a detailed parent report of child externalizing behaviors (e.g., Eyberg Child Behavior Inventory [ECBI]: Eyberg & Pincus, 1999), a measure of parenting stress (e.g., Parenting Stress Index: Abidin, 1995), and the structured behavior observations using the Dyadic Parent–Child Interaction Coding System–III (DPICS-III; Eyberg, Nelson, Duke, & Boggs, 2005). Clinical decisions regarding the focus and outcome of treatment are guided throughout the treatment process using the ECBI and the DPICS-III, which are completed at each treatment session so that the clinician has a weekly measure of child behavior and parent skill.

ECBI. The ECBI, a 36-item parent-report measure of disruptive behavior problems, is appropriate for use with families of children ages 2 years to 16 years (Eyberg & Pincus, 1999). This measure takes parents approximately 10 minutes to complete and provides the clinician with a list of specific child behaviors to target in treatment. For each item, parents are asked to rate the intensity (i.e., 1–7 scale) and whether that behavior is problematic (i.e., yes or no). The intensity scale provides a score of the parent's perception of the severity of child's behaviors. The problem scale provides a score of the parent's perception of how problematic the child behavior is for the parent.

DPICS-III. The DPICS-III (Eyberg et al., 2005), a behavioral coding system, is designed to assess the quality of parent–child social interactions. The DPICS has empirical support for use in interaction with children ages 3 years to 6 years. The DPICS is used in PCIT and other parent training interventions for children with disruptive behaviors to guide treatment and assess change over time. In PCIT, the DPICS is used during the pretreatment assessment and during the majority of treatment sessions to measure the quality of the parent–child interaction and to assess treatment progress across the course of treatment.

EFFICACY AND EFFECTIVENESS OF PCIT

PCIT delivered in university-based clinics has well-establish efficacy. Treatment outcome studies have shown large effects related to child outcomes and family functioning (Thomas & Zimmer-Gembeck, 2007). Change in parents' use of positive and negative responding occurs over treatment; rapid change is demonstrated in the first three sessions (Hakman, Chaffin, Funderburk, & Silovsky, 2009). Outcomes following PCIT demonstrate superiority over control conditions: wait-list controls (e.g., Schuhmann, Foote, Eyberg, Boggs, & Algina, 1998), classroom controls with normative behavior, classroom controls and peer groups with varying levels of disruptive behavior (e.g., Funderburk et al., 1998), modified treatment groups (e.g., Nixon, Sweeney, Erickson, & Touyz, 2003), parenting group didactic trainings (e.g., Chaffin et al., 2004), wraparound services (e.g., Chaffin et al., 2004), and treatment dropouts (e.g., Boggs et al., 2004). Furthermore, PCIT treatment gains have been demonstrated up to 6 years after treatment completion (Hood & Eyberg, 2003).

Several prior reviews have examined university-based outcome studies. Kaminski, Valle, Filene, and Boyle (2008) reviewed 77 published studies of behavioral parent training programs conducted with children birth to 7 years. PCIT has demonstrated large effects and contains each of the three components consistently related to larger effects across programs: (a) increasing positive parent–child interactions and emotional communication skills, (b) teaching parents to use time-out, and (c) teaching parenting consistency. In their review of 13 PCIT studies, Thomas and Zimmer-Gembeck (2007) also found large effects for changes in child outcomes and parenting stress. Gallagher (2003) completed a review of 17 PCIT outcome investigations and found child behavior improvements for PCIT to be statistically significant across all studies and in the clinically significant range (i.e., clinical range at pretreatment to within normal ranges at posttreatment) in 82% (14 of 17) of studies.

Studies have demonstrated improvement in family functioning, with specific enhancement of the parent–child relationship and parent, child, and sibling functioning. After completing treatment, parents have demonstrated increases in their use of reflective listening and praise, decreases in use of sarcasm, and increases in physical proximity between the parent and child (Eisenstadt et al., 1993; Schuhmann et al., 1998). Parents and teachers have reported statistically and clinically significant reductions in the intensity of child behavior problems (i.e., pre- to posttreatment difference scores of parent ECBI and teacher Sutter–Eyberg student behavior inventory intensity scores [Eyberg & Pincus, 1999]) and increases in classroom compliance rates from 40.7% to 70.4% (McNeil, Eyberg, Eisenstadt, Newcomb, & Funderburk, 1991). Gains also have been found to generalize to untreated siblings (e.g., Brestan, Eyberg, Boggs, & Algina, 1997). Furthermore, parents have reported statistically significant decreases in marital distress (Eyberg & Robinson, 1982), increases in confidence in their parenting skills (Schuhmann et al., 1998), and improvements in parental psychopathology (e.g., mild depressive symptoms; Timmer et al., 2011). With regard to social validity, parents have reported high satisfaction with the content and process of treatment (e.g., Brestan, Jacobs, Rayfield, & Eyberg, 1999).

Treatment gains have been shown to maintain over time. Gallagher (2003) found that 75% of studies ($n = 17$) included in the meta-analyses reported that treatment gains were maintained during follow-up. Eyberg et al. (2001) found treatment gains in the home setting at 1 year and 2 years after completion of treatment. In a small sample of children ($n = 10$), Funderburk et al. (1998) found classroom improvements maintained up to 1 year, but to a lesser extent at 18 months. Families that dropped out of PCIT before treatment completion functioned the same after 1 year to 3 years as before treatment had started, yet families who completed PCIT maintained their treatment gains. In a long-term follow-up study of functioning 3 years to 6 years after PCIT, Hood and Eyberg (2003) found that parent-reported child behavior problems were less frequent and less problematic than their reports of behavior before the initiation of PCIT. In addition, child behavior problems decreased further as the length of time from treatment increased, which suggests not only that PCIT treatment gains are maintained but also that children continue to improve.

Using PCIT With Other Populations

PCIT was originally developed to treat children with disruptive behavior disorders (i.e., oppositional defiant disorder [ODD]; conduct disorder; or disruptive behavior disorder, not otherwise specified) and their biological parents. However, PCIT is now established as an evidenced-based treatment for children with a history of child physical abuse (Chaffin et al., 2004; Thomas & Zimmer-Gembeck, 2007). In addition, PCIT has been explored in numerous empirical research and case studies involving children and parents with other clinical presentations. PCIT has been examined with children with comorbid internalizing and externalizing symptoms (Chase & Eyberg, 2008), such as separation anxiety disorder (e.g., Pincus, Santucci, Ehrenreich, & Eyberg, 2008) and depression (e.g., Luby, Lenze, & Tillman, 2012). It also has been examined in toddlers and young children born premature (e.g., Bagner, Sheinkopf, Vohr, & Lester, 2010) and children with chronic illness (Bagner, Fernandez, & Eyberg, 2004), mental retardation (e.g., Bagner & Eyberg, 2007), attention-deficit/hyperactivity disorder (ADHD; Matos, Bauermeister, & Bernal, 2009; Wagner & McNeil, 2008), and developmental disabilities (e.g., McDiarmid & Bagner, 2005) such as autism spectrum disorders (Hatamzadeh, Pouretemad, & Hassanabadi, 2010). PCIT typically is not indicated for children under age 2 years or older than age 7 years; however, preliminary work has been conducted with children outside of the typical age range (e.g., Bagner et al., 2010; Dombrowski, Timmer, Blacker, & Urquiza, 2005).

PCIT has been examined in families with a history of general maltreatment (Fricker-Elhai, Ruggiero, & Smith, 2005) and domestic violence (e.g., Borrego, Gutow, Reicher, & Barker, 2008; Timmer, Ware, Urquiza, & Zebell, 2010), and in families with mild parental psychopathology (e.g., depressed mothers; Timmer et al., 2011). Studies have also examined the use of PCIT with adoptive and foster parents (i.e., kin and nonkinship care; e.g., Timmer, Urquiza, & Zebell, 2006). It has been demonstrated as an effective and acceptable treatment with African American (e.g., Fernandez, Butler, & Eyberg, 2011) and Latino families (e.g., Mexican Americans: McCabe & Yeh, 2009; Spanish-speaking families: Borrego, Anhalt, Terao, Vargas, & Urquiza, 2006; Puerto Ricans: Matos et al., 2009), and families in countries outside of the United States, such as Australia (e.g., Nixon et al., 2003; Phillips, Morgan, Cawthorne, & Barnett, 2008), China (e.g., Yu, Roberts, Wong, & Shen, 2011), Iran (Hatamzadeh et al., 2010), the Netherlands (Abrahamse et al., 2012), and Norway (Bjørseth & Wormdal, 2005).

Research findings and clinical experience have suggested that PCIT is less successful with certain populations, such as families currently experiencing extreme marital discord or family chaos, or parents who have chronic and severe psychopathology (e.g., borderline personality disorder, psychotic disorders, substance dependence, major depressive disorder). In addition, it is potentially harmful to conduct PCIT with parents who have perpetrated child sexual abuse (McNeil & Hembree-Kigin, 2010).

Tailoring, Adapting, and Modifying the Model

Although tailoring, adapting, or modifying PCIT is not frequently required or clinically implicated, modifications should be made with clinical and empirical consideration (Eyberg, 2005). As highlighted by Eyberg (2005, p. 200): (a) "*Tailoring* refers to changes made in the focus or delivery style of essential elements in an established treatment, based on the unique features of the individual case," (b) "[t]reatment *adaptations* refer to changes in the structure or content of an established treatment," and (c) "[t]reatment *modifications* refer to universal changes in established treatments, made by the treatment developer." Slight modifications to the clinic-based PCIT protocol have been made to transport it to settings in which the bug-in-the-ear, one-way mirror, and/or time-out backup are unavailable. These restrictions require PCIT clinicians to do *in-room coaching*, which involves structuring the playroom so that the parent and child sit side by side and the PCIT clinician positions himself or herself slightly behind the parent on the side opposite to the child. As the parent and child interact, the PCIT clinician works to provide the same intensity and quality of feedback by subtly whispering comments to the parent just as would be provided in coaching behind the one-way mirror. Parents and children are instructed to avoid conversations with the PCIT clinician until the coaching part of the session is complete. In-room coaching has been shown to be effective within the larger PCIT protocol.

More substantial modifications have been made to PCIT by adapting it to fit home- and school-based settings or to provide it as a group-based intervention. In-home PCIT has been clinically and conceptually explored to address barriers to treatment, such as transportation, and, to aid in generalization of skills, has been used in combination with clinic-based services for children with extreme behavior problems and or families with low resources. PCIT clinicians have gone to family homes and conducted PCIT with the same treatment and session structure as the clinic-based model, but have used in-room coaching. Few studies have been published about the effectiveness of this approach. In one, the in-home PCIT and clinic-based PCIT with an in-home component did not demonstrate added benefit in reducing the amount of child misbehavior or increasing the level of parent skill performance compared with standard PCIT without a home component (Lanier et al., 2011). However, studies showed that in-home PCIT led to a decrease in the level of stress reported by parents (Lanier et al., 2011; Timmer, Zebell, Culver, & Urquiza, 2010) and an increased parent tolerance of child misbehavior (Timmer, Ware, et al., 2010).

PCIT also has been examined in a group format (Niec, Hemme, Yopp, & Brestan, 2005), and adaptations have been made to incorporate a group-based motivational engagement component before using PCIT with families with child welfare involvement (e.g., Chaffin, Funderburk, Bard, Valle, & Gurwitch, 2011). PCIT has been adapted to the classroom setting by training teachers in teacher–child interaction therapy/training (TCIT), which has shown reductions in the number of classroom time-outs and teacher-provided criticism, and increases in labeled praise and teacher-reported manageable behavior (e.g., Lyon et al., 2009; Stokes, Tempel, Chengappa, Costello, & McNeil, 2011). Although these innovations in PCIT are exciting and appear promising, they do not have the same level of empirical support that clinic-based PCIT has acquired.

Transporting PCIT to Other Settings

PCIT has been provided primarily in university training centers (e.g., University of Florida, West Virginia University) or university-affiliated medical centers (e.g., University of Oklahoma Health Sciences Center, UC Davis Medical Center). In recent years, PCIT clinics have been established at other universities (e.g., Auburn University, Central Michigan University, Texas Tech University) and university-affiliated medical centers (e.g., Duke Medical Center, University of Iowa, University of Pittsburgh School of Medicine, University of Tennessee Health Sciences Center). Historically, PCIT training has been conducted using an apprenticeship model. Clinical psychology doctoral students have trained and conducted PCIT in a cotherapy model with more experienced clinicians while receiving intensive individual and group supervision by an expert PCIT trainer. However, as PCIT has been implemented more broadly, other modalities of training and supervision have been tried.

Introductory workshops and presentations have been conducted at national conferences (e.g., American Psychological Association, Association for Behavioral and Cognitive Therapies), and a biennial PCIT convention and numerous state and regional-level conferences also have been established. PCIT has been implemented within a system of care (Franco, Soler, & McBride, 2005) and within numerous grant-funded initiatives (e.g., Duke Endowment Learning Collaborative). States such as California, Delaware, Iowa, and Pennsylvania have had large-scale dissemination efforts sponsored by a variety of funding sources. As PCIT has been implemented more broadly, PCIT International was developed to provide additional support and guidance about implementation. PCIT International training guidelines (PCIT International Training Committee, 2013), which outline requirements of training at all levels, have been published, and subcommitees have been formed to address concerns, such as training issues, continuing education, research, PCIT master trainers, international development, communications, and advertising.

Training

Although no standardized model for PCIT training in community settings currently exists, the PCIT International guidelines (PCIT International Training Committee, 2013) outline clinician competencies to be assessed across the training process. Training generally involves at least 40 hours of in-person training that includes (a) intensive didactic presentations containing information on PCIT's theoretical basis, assessment, treatment protocol, and session structure; (b) videotape review of relatively straightforward to complex cases; and (c) interactive discussions, modeling, role-plays, and live demonstrations with children and families. Training manuals, workshops, and seminars alone have been shown to be insufficient to achieve reliable and competent skill transfer from training to service provision (Herschell et al., 2009). Following the initial in-person training, clinician trainees are required to complete clinical case consultation with a PCIT trainer until they have graduated at least two families from PCIT and to continue consultation until they have met all required training competencies. Several authors have begun examining the use of technology to support aspects of the training process, such as using telemedicine technology for consultation (Funderburk, Ware, Altshuler, & Chaffin, 2008) and the video analysis tool for providing feedback during clinical case review (Wilsie & Brestan-Knight, 2012). Herschell and colleagues are in the process of empirically evaluating training methods with a statewide trial to compare three training models for implementing PCIT (National Institute of Mental Health Grant No. R01 MH095750).

Evaluating PCIT Clinicians' Implementation of the Treatment Protocol

Empirical support for evidence-based treatments such as PCIT has been provided by treatment outcome studies that follow clearly outlined treatment protocols. If PCIT clinicians provide the intervention without integrity to the treatment model, there is less certainty about the effectiveness of their services. Improved client outcomes have been demonstrated when clinicians adhere closely to a treatment protocol (Henggeler, Melton, Brondino,

Scherer, & Hanley, 1997). Treatment integrity checklists are included in the PCIT training protocol and were developed to be used across settings (e.g., community-based agencies, university-based clinics) to assess fidelity to the treatment protocol and to support training, supervision, consultation, and case review. To date, few studies have focused specifically on the effect that therapist behavior has on PCIT treatment outcomes; however, the existing studies have suggested that elements of the therapist–parent interactions are key. Therapist verbal behavior and communication styles early in treatment have been shown to be related to family success in skill development and treatment completion (Harwood & Eyberg, 2004; Herschell, Capage, Bahl, & McNeil, 2008). In training, initial clinician attitudes have been shown to be related to their participation and satisfaction with varying levels of post-workshop training support and case enrollment for PCIT (Nelson, Shanley, Funderburk, & Bard, 2012), and therapist characteristics and attitudes toward the adoption of evidence-based practices have been shown to affect dissemination and implementation efforts (Herschell, McNeil, & McNeil, 2004).

Considerations From a Community-Based Agency Perspective

When implementing PCIT in community-based clinics, consideration must be given to understanding how PCIT fits into the larger service system. This may entail securing start-up support, building a referral base, balancing treatment fidelity with state and federal regulations, establishing billing, and understanding the cost–benefit of the program at multiple levels of effect (e.g., family, agency, state service systems). Start-up requires infrastructure, such as informing administrative and referring staff about PCIT (e.g., target population, clinical outcomes, treatment format) and outlining an agency referral and intake process to support the PCIT clinical services. As with any service, it is essential to identify a referral base specific to PCIT. Other professionals within the agency (e.g., caseworkers) and community (e.g., child welfare agencies, schools, pediatricians' offices) typically welcome new PCIT services given the high demand for effective early childhood services for disruptive behavioral difficulties that exists in most, if not all, communities.

Further support also may be needed to coordinate ordering materials (e.g., ECBI), installing technical equipment (e.g., bug-in-the-ear, one-way mirror), and making modifications to existing therapy rooms (e.g., removing unnecessary furniture and toys, constructing a time-out backup space). Although these startup costs must be considered, PCIT is estimated to be more cost-effective than standard care alternatives ($1,441/child) and the total benefits minus costs are estimated to be $3,749 per child (Lee, Aos, & Miller, 2008). Community programs vary in their billing of PCIT to Medicaid (Children's Hospital of Philadelphia, 2009). In some areas, PCIT may be billed at an enhanced service rate; however, others continue to bill PCIT more standardly as individual child or individual family outpatient therapy. Additional knowledge of state and federal regulations can be helpful in working with regulating bodies, such as The Joint Commission and states' Office of Mental Health and Substance Abuse Services (OMHSAS), to ensure that PCIT may be used with fidelity. In Pennsylvania, for example, OMHSAS produced a service bulletin (Hodas, Herschell, & Mrozowski, 2013) to communicate how components of the treatment program, such as the use of a time-out room, are considered important to effectiveness and can be used in compliance with the existing regulations.

CASE EXAMPLE

Referral

The Gold family recently became involved in child protective services (CPS) following a report of child physical abuse. According to the records provided by CPS, Ms. Gold was observed using her body weight to restrain her son and smacking him several times across the face. As part of the family's CPS safety plan, Ms. Gold was referred to parenting classes. Given the concern for family safety, the CPS caseworker scheduled an appointment for Ms. Gold and her son, Jayden, at a local clinic that specialized in evaluating and treating families of young children and that is known for providing PCIT services. The caseworker had previously observed the success of other families whom he had referred to this agency's PCIT clinic.

Evaluation

At the intake appointment, Ms. Gold was asked to complete several standardized measures, including the CBCL (Achenbach & Rescorla, 2001), the ECBI (Eyberg & Pincus, 1999), and the Parenting Stress Index (PSI; Abidin, 1995). She also participated in a clinical interview and a structured behavior observation with Jayden that consisted of three 5-minute situations (child-led play, parent-led play, and cleanup) that were coded using the DPICS-III.

From the intake information gathered, the PCIT clinician learned that Jayden was a 4-year-old African American boy who was one of four children. He lived with his biological mother, Ms. Gold (age 24 years), and Jayden's three siblings: Jordan (8 years), Jeremiah (2 years) and Makayla (7 months). Until recently, Ms. Gold's fiancé also lived in the household. Jayden was described as always having been a challenging child to parent. As an infant, he cried a lot and was difficult to soothe. As a toddler, Jayden experienced light sleep, with patterns of awakening in the middle of the night. For more than 2 years, he has exhibited a pattern of overactive, aggressive, defiant, and destructive behavior.

According to Ms. Gold, the family's case was opened after she had tried to discipline Jayden for leaving the family home while Ms. Gold and the other children were asleep. At the time of the intake, Ms. Gold reported exhaustion—her own sleep difficulties resulting from Jayden's demanding behaviors and her need to balance her parenting responsibilities among her four children. She reported little family support and difficulty with child care. Although Jayden had been assessed and reported to have speech delays, he was not accepted into a developmental preschool because of concerns about his disruptive (e.g., running from the teacher) and aggressive (e.g., hitting and biting) behaviors. Ms. Gold reported that he previously had been removed from several child care settings as a result of his behavioral difficulties and that family and friends had refused to keep him, which added a great deal of stress and had required Ms. Gold to leave her job to stay at home and care for Jayden. When asked about how Jayden's behavior was at home, she described it as clingy to the extent that she would allow him into the bathroom with her to prevent "a fit." She also described reliance on a great deal of physical control to manage Jayden's behaviors, such as holding him while sleeping to know that he was "not misbehaving."

Ms. Gold also reported that Jayden would frequently hit her or Makayla for no apparent reason, and, when upset, he often destroyed his toys or other things in the family's apartment. In juggling her other children's needs and safety, Ms. Gold reported that she typically tried to move the other children to another room when Jayden had a tantrum or that she would give in to Jayden's behaviors as she saw them escalating. When the family's case-worker approached her with concerns, Ms. Gold reported that she felt like she was "failing as a parent" and that she felt a lot of guilt about parenting her children the same "bad" way that she had been parented. Although she recognized problems that needed to be addressed, she felt skeptical that the required parenting class could be of benefit to her family's needs.

Standardized assessment measures confirmed that Jayden was exhibiting a clinically significant level of disruptive behavior. Ms. Gold's CBCL T-scores were clinically elevated on the externalizing (T = 97) and total problems (T = 92) scales. On the ECBI, Ms. Gold obtained an intensity score of 203 (T = 80) and a problem score of 31 (T = 81), which indicate clinically significant, intense, and problematic disruptive behaviors. During the pretreatment behavioral observations, Ms. Gold demonstrated positive parenting behaviors, such as reflections. She tended to use low levels of praise and high levels of questions and commands. In the child-led play observations, Ms. Gold gave zero praise statements, two reflective statements, zero descriptive statements, 12 questions, nine indirect commands, and seven direct commands.

Similar patterns were noted during observation of the parent-led play and cleanup situations. Jayden complied with approximately 30% of Ms. Gold's instructions. He had no opportunity to comply with approximately 40% of her instructions. This is far less than the normative level of compliance (i.e., approximately 62%; Eyberg & Robinson, 1982) for children within this age range. Considering all the information gathered, the PCIT clinician diagnosed Jayden with ODD, noted a V-code of parent–child relational problems, and recommended that Ms. Gold and Jayden participate together in PCIT.

Child-Directed Interaction

As discussed at the initial intake, Ms. Gold returned alone the following week to begin learning PCIT by attending the CDI teach session with the PCIT clinician. During this 1-hour meeting, the PCIT clinician presented each skill individually, provided its description and rationale, and offered examples of how to apply each skill to Jayden's specific behaviors. Throughout the session, the PCIT clinician highlighted Ms. Gold's parenting strengths. She also described how the skills would further enhance Ms. Gold's existing skills and her relationship with Jayden, provide a safer way to interact as a family, reduce Jayden's disruptive behaviors, and improve his language. Ms. Gold agreed to complete 5 minutes of one-on-one special time at home (i.e., CDI) with Jayden each day. She was given a form for recording her completion of at-home practice and noting questions or concerns that might arise during the special time or throughout the week.

Ms. Gold and Jayden were brought to the next session by the family's CPS caseworker. After a brief explanation for Jayden, the PCIT clinician reviewed the completed at-home practice sheet with Ms. Gold. She reported practicing 4 of 7 days and indicated that Jayden continued to be very physical during the play. The PCIT clinician discussed with Ms. Gold that behavioral improvements would occur but would take some time. Ms. Gold's effort to complete the at-home practice was acknowledged, and the PCIT clinician emphasized that this regular completion of special time would help Jayden's behavior improve more rapidly.

After assisting Ms. Gold in the correct placement of the bug-in-the-ear device, the PCIT clinician left the playroom and went into the observation room to conduct the 5-minute DPICS-III coding. This coding indicated that Ms. Gold had increased her use of labeled praise and slightly decreased commands from the initial assessment. Because Ms. Gold also mentioned that she felt labeled praises would be most difficult for her, she and the PCIT clinician decided to work on increasing labeled praises during the session. Over the bug-in-the-ear, the PCIT clinician highlighted this improvement and focused on assisting Ms. Gold to increase her use of labeled praises throughout the coaching period. Because of the family's reasons for referral and Jayden's observed rough play, the PCIT clinician also focused on recognizing calm, gentle, and safe behaviors by both Jayden and Ms. Gold throughout the coaching session. At one point, Jayden began knocking the toys to the floor to prevent Ms. Gold from playing. The PCIT clinician coached Ms. Gold to use selective attention and redirection by not attending to the disruptive behavior and directing her attention to her own appropriate modeling of play behavior. Immediately after Jayden picked up a block and began helping, Ms. Gold was coached to provide a specific labeled praise for gentle hands. After 30 minutes of coaching, the PCIT clinician met briefly with Ms. Gold while Jayden continued to play with the toys. Together they reviewed the session and a graph depicting Ms. Gold's use of the parent mastery skills, and discussed the at home practice for the upcoming week.

After the session, the PCIT clinician sought further supervision from her on-site PCIT supervisor regarding Jayden's aggressive behaviors during the CDI play. On her biweekly PCIT consultation call, she also sought feedback from the PCIT trainer and other PCIT clinicians in her training group. She was encouraged to hear that others had successfully problem-solved these difficulties and that they agreed with her approach in coaching the parent to remove and redirect her attention during the rough play behaviors in the first CDI session. Using the recommendations of others, the PCIT clinician continued to coach Ms. Gold in the use of selective attention skills while she made modifications to her playroom setup, such as selecting soft toys for play until Jayden developed more calm play behaviors. Ms. Gold and Jayden participated in five additional CDI coaching sessions until Ms. Gold met mastery criteria for the CDI skills (i.e., 10 labeled praises; 10 behavioral descriptions; 10 reflections; and three or fewer questions, commands, and criticism in a 5-minute observation). Each session followed a similar format, including a 10- to 15-minute check-in, 5-minute behavior observation, 30-minute coaching period, and 10-minute review of Ms. Gold's skill use during the session and homework planning.

Parent-Directed Interaction

Similar to the CDI phase of treatment, PDI began with an interactive PDI teach session that Ms. Gold attended alone. During this time, the PCIT clinician provided an overview of PDI, described the use of effective commands, and explained how to differentiate child compliance versus noncompliance. Labeled praise was recommended following compliance and a brief, highly-structured, time-out sequence was recommended following noncompliance. The PCIT clinician reviewed, modeled, and role-played each component of the PDI time-out sequence with Ms. Gold, emphasizing the importance of practicing the sequence together in-session before practicing at home. Together, they discussed the utility of the PCIT clinician's coaching Ms. Gold through the procedure the first time so that the therapist could help Ms. Gold remain calm and confident during discipline and could support problem solving as difficult behaviors occurred. Ms. Gold agreed not to use the PDI skills with Jayden during the next week.

Ms. Gold returned the following week with Jayden. At the start of this first PDI coaching session, the PCIT clinician briefly reviewed the PDI procedure with Ms. Gold, and then, through the bug-in-the-ear, coached Ms. Gold while she explained the PDI procedure to Jayden. Ms. Gold was noticeably nervous, so the PCIT clinician emphasized how well prepared Ms. Gold was, how quickly she learned the CDI skills, and that the PCIT clinician would be there to support her. The PCIT clinician's coaching style during this session was supportive, directive, proactive, fast paced, and matched the level of child behavior to ensure that the child and parent were successful and to prevent any unnecessary escalation in behavior. During the session, Jayden experienced one time-out; however, by the end of the session, he was complying with his mother's instructions. At the end of the session, the PCIT clinician congratulated Ms. Gold on her perseverance, processed the session with her, and emphasized the importance of continuing CDI practice with Jayden every day. Together, they decided that they would continue to work together in the next session—until Ms. Gold felt more confident—before practicing time-out at home.

During the remaining seven PDI sessions, Jayden's behavior, particularly his compliance, continued to improve, and he rarely went to time-out. Once Jayden was more compliant and better able to regulate his emotions and Ms. Gold was more confident and skillful, PDI sessions were devoted to practicing real-life situations, such as establishing "house rules," including Jayden's siblings in sessions to practice sharing, and using the skills in public places.

Treatment Completion

During the 16th session, Ms. Gold demonstrated mastery criteria of CDI and PDI skills. The PCIT clinician asked Ms. Gold to complete the same standardized measures she had completed during the initial evaluation (i.e., CBCL, ECBI, and PSI). Ms. Gold reported scores within normal limits on previously elevated scales on both the CBCL and ECBI: CBCL externalizing (T = 55), CBCL total problems scales (T = 56), ECBI intensity score 108 (T = 53), and ECBI problem score of 9 (T = 52). Ms. Gold and Jayden were invited back to the clinic to attend a "graduation session." The PCIT clinician, Ms. Gold, and Jayden watched the behavior observations (which Ms. Gold had consented to have videotaped) from their initial and final sessions, and reflected on the family's successes. Together, the PCIT clinician, Ms. Gold, the CPS case-worker, and Jayden highlighted the gains that had been made by pointing out on the videotape notable improvements in parent skill and child behavior. Ms. Gold was presented with a treatment completion certificate, and Jayden was given an award for good behavior.

CONCLUSION

PCIT originated as a treatment for disruptive behavior disorders in early childhood. Scientist–practitioners have examined the treatment program through clinical application and empirical investigation. Subsequently, PCIT is now considered an evidence-based treatment for families with a history of child physical abuse. PCIT has been modified over time to include meaningful research findings. It remains a 12- to 20-week treatment program that guides parents in managing their children's difficult behavior through teaching specialized skills to jointly focus on enhancing the parent–child relationship while also providing consistent and predictable consequences for child behaviors. As PCIT has been implemented and disseminated more widely, the standard PCIT model has demonstrated robustness. Use of PCIT in community-based settings has the potential to improve families' access to treatment and to provide more comprehensive and effective care.

REFERENCES

Abidin, R. R. (1995). *Parenting stress index: Professional manual* (3rd ed.). Odessa, FL: Psychological Assessment Resources.

Abrahamse, M. E., Junger, M., Chavannes, E. L., Coelman, F. J. G., Boer, F., & Lindauer, R. J. L. (2012). Parent–child interaction therapy for preschool children with disruptive behaviour problems in the Netherlands [Advance online publication]. *Child and Adolescent Psychiatry and Mental Health*, 6, 24. http://dx.doi.org/10.1186/1753-2000-6-24

Achenbach, T. M., & Rescorla, L. A. (2001). *Manual for ASEBA school-age forms & profiles*. Burlington, VT: University of Vermont, Research Center for Children, Youth, & Families.

Bagner, D. M., & Eyberg, S. M. (2007). Parent–child interaction therapy for disruptive behavior in children with mental retardation: A randomized controlled trial. *Journal of Clinical Child & Adolescent Psychology*, 36, 418–429. http://dx.doi.org/10.1080/15374410701448448

Bagner, D. M., Fernandez, M. A., & Eyberg, S. M. (2004). Parent–child interaction therapy and chronic illness: A case study. *Journal of Clinical Psychology in Medical Settings*, 11, 1–6. http://dx.doi.org/10.1023/B:JOCS.0000016264.02407.fd

Bagner, D. M., Sheinkopf, S. J., Vohr, B. R., & Lester, B. M. (2010). Parenting intervention for externalizing behavior problems in children born premature: An initial examination. *Journal of Developmental and Behavioral Pediatrics, 31,* 209–216. http://dx.doi.org/10.1097/DBP.0b013e3181d5a294

Baumrind, D. (1967). Child care practices anteceding three patterns of preschool behavior. *Genetic Psychology Monographs, 75,* 43–88.

Bjørseth, A., & Wormdal, A. K. (2005). Parent–child interaction therapy in Norway. *Tidsskrift for Norsk Psykologforening, 42,* 693–699.

Boggs, S. R., Eyberg, S. M., Edwards, D., Rayfield, A., Jacobs, J., Bagner, D., & Hood, K. (2004). Outcomes of parent–child interaction therapy: A comparison of treatment completers and study dropouts one to three years later. *Child & Family Behavior Therapy, 26*(4), 1–22. http://dx.doi.org/10.1300/J019v26n04_01

Borrego, J., Jr., Anhalt, K., Terao, S. Y., Vargas, E., & Urquiza, A. J. (2006). Parent–child interaction therapy with a Spanish-speaking family. *Cognitive and Behavioral Practice, 13,* 121–133. http://dx.doi.org/10.1016/j.cbpra.2005.09.001

Borrego, J., Jr., Gutow, M. R., Reicher, S., & Barker, C. H. (2008). Parent–child interaction therapy with domestic violence populations. *Journal of Family Violence, 23,* 495–505. http://dx.doi.org/10.1007/s10896-008-9177-4

Brestan, E. V., Eyberg, S. M., Boggs, S., & Algina, J. (1997). Parent–child interaction therapy: Parent perceptions of untreated siblings. *Child & Family Behavior Therapy, 19*(3), 13–28. http://dx.doi.org/10.1300/J019v19n03_02

Brestan, E. V., Jacobs, J., Rayfield, A., & Eyberg, S. M. (1999). A consumer satisfaction measure for parent–child treatments and its relation to measures of child behavior change. *Behavior Therapy, 30,* 17–30. http://dx.doi.org/10.1016/S0005-7894(99)80043-4

Chadwick Center for Children and Families. (2004). *Closing the quality chasm in child abuse treatment: Identifying and disseminating best practices.* San Diego, CA: Author.

Chaffin, M., Funderburk, B., Bard, D., Valle, L. A., & Gurwitch, R. (2011). A combined motivation and parent–child interaction therapy package reduces child welfare recidivism in a randomized dismantling field trial. *Journal of Consulting and Clinical Psychology, 79,* 84–95. http://dx.doi.org/10.1037/a0021227

Chaffin, M., Silovsky, J. F., Funderburk, B., Valle, L. A., Brestan, E. V., Balachova, T., . . . Bonner, B. L. (2004). Parent–child interaction therapy with physically abusive parents: Efficacy for reducing future abuse reports. *Journal of Consulting Clinical Psychology, 72,* 500–510. Retrieved from: http://www.ncbi.nlm.nih.gov/pubmed/15279533

Chase, R. M., & Eyberg, S. M. (2008). Clinical presentation and treatment outcome for children with comorbid externalizing and internalizing symptoms. *Journal of Anxiety Disorders, 22,* 273–282. http://dx.doi.org/10.1016/j.janxdis.2007.03.006

Children's Hospital of Philadelphia. (2009). *States billing parent–child interaction therapy to Medicaid.* Philadelphia, PA: PolicyLab.

Dombrowski, S. C., Timmer, S. G., Blacker, D. B., & Urquiza, A. J. (2005). A positive behavioural intervention for toddlers: Parent–child attunement therapy. *Child Abuse Review, 14*, 132–151.

Eisenstadt, T. H., Eyberg, S. M., McNeil, C. B., Newcomb, K., & Funderburk, B. (1993). Parent–child interaction therapy with behavior problem children: Relative effectiveness of two stages and overall treatment outcome. *Journal of Clinical Child Psychology, 22*, 42–51. http://dx.doi.org/10.1207/s15374424jccp2201_4

Eyberg, S. M. (2005). Tailoring and adapting parent–child interaction therapy to new populations. *Education & Treatment of Children, 28*, 197–201.

Eyberg, S. M., & Funderburk, B. (2011). *Parent–child interaction therapy protocol.* Gainesville, FL: PCIT International.

Eyberg, S. M., Funderburk, B. W., Hembree-Kigin, T. L., McNeil, C. B., Querido, J. G., & Hood, K. K. (2001). Parent–child interaction therapy with behavior problem children: One and two year maintenance of treatment effects in the family. *Child & Family Behavior Therapy, 23*(4), 1–20. http://dx.doi.org/10.1300/J019v23n04_01

Eyberg, S. M., Nelson, M. M., & Boggs, S. R. (2008). Evidence-based psychosocial treatments for children and adolescents with disruptive behavior. *Journal of Clinical Child & Adolescent Psychology, 37*, 215–237. http://dx.doi.org/10.1080/15374410701820117

Eyberg, S. M., Nelson, M. M., Duke, M., & Boggs, S. R. (2005). *Manual for the dyadic parent–child interaction coding system* (3rd ed.). Gainesville, FL: PCIT International.

Eyberg, S. M., & Pincus, D. (1999). *Eyberg child behavior inventory and Sutter–Eyberg student behavior inventory—revised professional manual.* Odessa, FL: Psychological Assessment Resources.

Eyberg, S. M., & Robinson, E. A. (1982). Parent–child interaction training: Effects on family functioning. *Journal of Clinical Child Psychology, 11*, 130–137.

Fernandez, M., Butler, A., & Eyberg, S. M. (2011). Treatment outcome for low socioeconomic status African American families in parent–child interaction therapy: A pilot study. *Child & Family Behavior Therapy, 33*(1), 32–48. http://dx.doi.org/10.1080/07317107.2011.545011

Franco, E., Soler, R. E., & McBride, M. (2005). Introducing and evaluating parent–child interaction therapy in a system of care. *Child and Adolescent Psychiatric Clinics of North America, 14*, 351–366, x. http://dx.doi.org/10.1016/j.chc.2004.11.003

Fricker-Elhai, A. E., Ruggiero, K. J., & Smith, D. W. (2005). Parent–child interaction therapy with two maltreated children in foster care. *Clinical Case Studies, 4*, 13–39. http://dx.doi.org/10.1177/1534650103259671

Funderburk, B. W., Eyberg, S. M., Newcomb, K., McNeil, C. B., Hembree-Kigin, T., & Capage, L. (1998). Parent–child interaction therapy with behavior problem children: Maintenance of treatment effects in the school setting. *Child & Family Behavior Therapy, 20*(2), 17–38. http://dx.doi.org/10.1300/J019v20n02_02

Funderburk, B. W., Ware, L. M., Altshuler, E., & Chaffin, M. (2008). Use and feasibility of telemedicine technology in the dissemination of parent–child interaction therapy. *Child Maltreatment, 13*, 377–382. Retrieved from http://cmx.sagepub.com/content/13/4/377.short

Gallagher, N. (2003). Effects of parent–child interaction therapy on young children with disruptive behavior disorders. *Bridges: Practice-Based Research Syntheses, 1*(4), 1–17. Retrieved from http://sc-boces.org/english/IMC/Focus/parent-child_interaction_theory.pdf

Hakman, M., Chaffin, M., Funderburk, B., & Silovsky, J. F. (2009). Change trajectories for parent–child interaction sequences during parent–child interaction therapy for child physical abuse. *Child Abuse & Neglect, 33*, 461–470. http://dx.doi.org/10.1016/j.chiabu.2008.08.003

Harwood, M. D., & Eyberg, S. M. (2004). Therapist verbal behavior early in treatment: Relation to successful completion of parent–child interaction therapy. *Journal of Clinical Child & Adolescent Psychology, 33*, 601–612. http://dx.doi.org/10.1207/s15374424jccp3303_17

Hatamzadeh, A., Pouretemad, H., & Hassanabadi, H. (2010). The effectiveness of parent–child interaction therapy for children with high functioning autism. *Procedia: Social and Behavioral Sciences, 5*, 994–997. http://dx.doi.org/10.1016/j.sbspro.2010.07.224

Henggeler, S. W., Melton, G. B., Brondino, M. J., Scherer, D. G., & Hanley, J. H. (1997). Multisystemic therapy with violent and chronic juvenile offenders and their families: The role of treatment fidelity in successful dissemination. *Journal of Consulting and Clinical Psychology, 65*, 821–833. http://dx.doi.org/10.1037/0022-006X.65.5.821

Herschell, A. D., Calzada, E. J., Eyberg, S. M., & McNeil, C. B. (2002). Parent–child interaction therapy: New directions in research. *Cognitive and Behavioral Practice, 9*, 9–16. http://dx.doi.org/10.1016/S1077-7229(02)80034-7

Herschell, A. D., Capage, L. C., Bahl, A. B., & McNeil, C. B. (2008). The role of therapist communication style in parent–child interaction therapy. *Child & Family Behavior Therapy, 30*(1), 13–35. http://dx.doi.org/10.1300/J019v30n01_02

Herschell, A. D., & McNeil, C. B. (2005). Parent–child interaction therapy for children experiencing externalizing behavior problems. In L. A. Reddy, T. M. Files-Hall, & C. S. Schaefer (Eds.), *Empirically based play interventions for children* (pp. 169–190). Washington, DC: American Psychological Association. http://dx.doi.org/10.1037/11086-010

Herschell, A. D., McNeil, C. B., & McNeil, D. W. (2004). Child clinical psychology's progress in disseminating empirically supported treatments. *Clinical Psychology: Science and Practice, 11*, 267–288. http://dx.doi.org/10.1093/clipsy.bph082

Herschell, A. D., McNeil, C. B., Urquiza, A. J., McGrath, J. M., Zebell, N. M., Timmer, S. G., & Porter, A. (2009). Evaluation of a treatment manual and workshops for disseminating, parent–child interaction therapy. *Administration and Policy in Mental Health and Mental Health Services Research, 36*, 63–81. http://dx.doi.org/10.1007/s10488-008-0194-7

Hodas, G., Herschell, A. D., & Mrozowski, S. (2013). *The use of time-out in parent–child interaction therapy in Pennsylvania: Policy statement clarification from Pennsylvania Office of Mental Health and Substance Abuse Services.* Unpublished manuscript.

Hood, K. K., & Eyberg, S. M. (2003). Outcomes of parent–child interaction therapy: Mothers' reports of maintenance three to six years after treatment. *Journal of Clinical Child & Adolescent Psychology, 32,* 419–429. http://dx.doi.org/10.1207/S15374424JCCP3203_10

Kaminski, J. W., Valle, L. A., Filene, J. H., & Boyle, C. L. (2008). A meta-analytic review of components associated with parent training program effectiveness. *Journal of Abnormal Child Psychology, 36,* 567–589. http://dx.doi.org/10.1007/s10802-007-9201-9

Lanier, P., Kohl, P. L., Benz, J., Swinger, D., Moussette, P., & Drake, B. (2011). Parent–child interaction therapy in a community setting: Examining outcomes, attrition, and treatment setting. *Research on Social Work Practice, 21,* 689–698. http://dx.doi.org/10.1177/1049731511406551

Lee, S., Aos, S., & Miller, M. (2008). *Evidence-based programs to prevent children from entering and remaining in the child welfare system: Interim report.* Olympia, WA: Washington State Institute for Public Policy.

Luby, J., Lenze, S., & Tillman, R. (2012). A novel early intervention for preschool depression: Findings from a pilot randomized controlled trial. *Journal of Child Psychology and Psychiatry, 53,* 313–322. http://dx.doi.org/10.1111/j.1469-7610.2011.02483.x

Lyon, A. R., Gershenson, R. A., Farahmand, F. K., Thaxter, P. J., Behling, S., & Budd, K. S. (2009). Effectiveness of teacher–child interaction training (TCIT) in a preschool setting. *Behavior Modification, 33,* 855–884. http://dx.doi.org/10.1177/0145445509344215

Matos, M., Bauermeister, J. J., & Bernal, G. (2009). Parent–child interaction therapy for Puerto Rican preschool children with ADHD and behavior problems: A pilot efficacy study. *Family Process, 48,* 232–252. http://dx.doi.org/10.1111/j.1545-5300.2009.01279.x

McCabe, K., & Yeh, M. (2009). Parent–child interaction therapy for Mexican Americans: A randomized clinical trial. *Journal of Clinical Child and Adolescent Psychology, 38,* 753–759. http://dx.doi.org/10.1080/15374410903103544

McDiarmid, M. D., & Bagner, D. M. (2005). Parent–child interaction therapy for children with disruptive behavior and developmental disabilities. *Education and Treatment of Children, 28,* 130–141.

McNeil, C. B., Eyberg, S., Eisenstadt, T. H., Newcomb, K., & Funderburk, B. (1991). Parent–child interaction therapy with behavior problem children: Generalization of treatment effects to the school setting. *Journal of Clinical Child Psychology, 20,* 140–151. http://dx.doi.org/10.1207/s15374424jccp2002_5

McNeil, C. B., & Hembree-Kigin, T. L. (2010). *Parent–child interaction therapy* (2nd ed.). New York, NY: Springer. http://dx.doi.org/10.1007/978-0-387-88639-8

Nelson, M. M., Shanley, J. R., Funderburk, B. W., & Bard, E. (2012). Therapists' attitudes toward evidence-based practices and implementation of parent–child interaction therapy. *Child Maltreatment, 17*, 47–55. http://dx.doi.org/10.1177/1077559512436674

Niec, L. N., Hemme, J. M., Yopp, J. M., & Brestan, E. V. (2005). Parent–child interaction therapy: The rewards and challenges of a group format. *Cognitive and Behavioral Practice, 12*, 113–25. http://dx.doi.org/10.1016/S1077-7229(05)80046-X

Nixon, R. D. V., Sweeney, L., Erickson, D. B., & Touyz, S. W. (2003). Parent–child interaction therapy: A comparison of standard and abbreviated treatments for oppositional defiant preschoolers. *Journal of Consulting and Clinical Psychology, 71*, 251–260. http://dx.doi.org/10.1037/0022-006X.71.2.251

Patterson, G. R. (1975). *Families: Application of social learning to family life*. Champaign, IL: Research Press.

Patterson, G. R. (1982). *Coercive family process*. Eugene, OR: Castalia.

PCIT International Training Committee. (2013). *Training guidelines for parent–child interaction therapy*. Gainesville, FL: PCIT International. Retrieved from http://www.pcit.org/training-guidelines/

Phillips, J., Morgan, S., Cawthorne, K., & Barnett, B. (2008). Pilot evaluation of parent–child interaction therapy delivered in an Australian community early childhood clinic setting. *Australian & New Zealand Journal of Psychiatry, 42*(8), 712–719. http://dx.doi.org/10.1080/00048670802206320

Pincus, D., Santucci, L., Ehrenreich, J., & Eyberg, S. M. (2008). The implementation of modified parent–child interaction therapy for youth with separation anxiety disorder. *Cognitive and Behavioral Practice, 15*, 118–125. http://dx.doi.org/10.1016/j.cbpra.2007.08.002

Reddy, L. A., Files-Hall, T. M., & Schaefer, C. E. (Eds.). (2005). *Empirically based play interventions for children*. Washington, DC: American Psychological Association. http://dx.doi.org/10.1037/11086-000

Reitman, D., & McMahon, R. J. (2013). Constance "Connie" Hanf (1917–2002): The mentor and the model. *Cognitive and Behavioral Practice, 20*, 106–116.

Reynolds, C. R., & Kamphaus, R. W. (2002). *The clinician's guide to the Behavior Assessment System for Children (BASC)*. New York, NY: Guilford Press.

Schuhmann, E. M., Foote, R. C., Eyberg, S. M., Boggs, S. R., & Algina, J. (1998). Efficacy of parent–child interaction therapy: Interim report of a randomized trial with short-term maintenance. *Journal of Clinical Child Psychology, 27*, 34–45. http://dx.doi.org/10.1207/s15374424jccp2701_4

Stokes, J. O., Tempel, A. B., Chengappa, K., Costello, A. H., & McNeil, C. B. (2011). Teacher–child interaction training: Description, historical underpinnings, and case example. In R. J. Newley (Ed.), *Classrooms, management, effectiveness and challenges* (pp. 77–92). New York, NY: Nova Science.

Thomas, R., & Zimmer-Gembeck, M. J. (2007). Behavioral outcomes of parent–child interaction therapy and triple p-positive parenting program: A review and meta-analysis. *Journal of Abnormal Child Psychology, 35,* 475–495. http://dx.doi.org/10.1007/s10802-007-9104-9

Timmer, S. G., Ho, L. K., Urquiza, A. J., Zebell, N. M., Fernandez, Y., Garcia, E., & Boys, D. (2011). *The effectiveness of parent–child interaction therapy with depressive mothers: The changing relationship as the agent of individual change.* Retrieved from http://www.ncbi.nlm.nih.gov/pubmed/21479510

Timmer, S. G., Urquiza, A. J., & Zebell, N. (2006). Challenging foster caregiver–maltreated child relationships: The effectiveness of parent–child interaction therapy. *Children and Youth Services Review, 28,* 1–19. http://dx.doi.org/10.1016/j.childyouth.2005.01.006

Timmer, S. G., Ware, L. M., Urquiza, A. J., & Zebell, N. M. (2010). The effectiveness of parent–child interaction therapy for victims of interparental violence. *Violence and Victims, 25*(4), 486–503. http://dx.doi.org/10.1891/0886-6708.25.4.486

Timmer, S. G., Zebell, N., Culver, M. A., & Urquiza, A. J. (2010). Efficacy of adjunct in-home coaching to improve outcomes in parent–child interaction therapy. *Research on Social Work Practice, 20,* 36–45. http://dx.doi.org/10.1177/1049731509332842

Wagner, S., & McNeil, C. B. (2008). Parent–child interaction therapy for ADHD: A conceptual overview and critical literature review. *Child & Family Behavior Therapy, 30,* 231–256. http://dx.doi.org/10.1080/07317100802275546

Wilsie, C. C., & Brestan-Knight, E. (2012). Using an online viewing system for parent–child interaction therapy consulting with professionals. *Psychological Services, 9,* 224–226. http://dx.doi.org/10.1037/a0026183

Yu, J., Roberts, M., Wong, M., & Shen, Y. (2011). Acceptability of behavioral family therapy among caregivers in China. *Journal of Child and Family Studies, 20,* 272–278. http://dx.doi.org/10.1007/s10826-010-9388-1

9

CHILD ADHD MULTIMODAL PROGRAM: USE OF COGNITIVE–BEHAVIORAL GROUP PLAY INTERVENTIONS

LINDA A. REDDY

Attention-deficit/hyperactivity disorder (ADHD), a heterogeneous neurocognitive disorder, is one of the most common disorders for which children are referred to mental health professionals. Current estimates suggest that 3% to 5% of all school-age children have the disorder, which translates to approximately two children per classroom (DuPaul & Stoner, 2014). Children with ADHD experience executive deficits in planning, attention, organization, and self-control, which negatively affect their academic, social, and/or behavioral functioning in the home and school (DuPaul & Stoner, 2014; Reddy, Weissman & Hale, 2013b). ADHD is confounded by high rates of comorbidity, such as specific learning disabilities, disruptive behavior disorders, mood disorders, anxiety disorders; and tic disorders (Perou et al., 2013). The disorder's complexity challenges the identification, education, and treatment process for practitioners (Reddy, Weissman, & Hale, 2013a). However, most scholars and practitioners agree with the recommendation of developmentally

http://dx.doi.org/10.1037/14730-010
Empirically Based Play Interventions for Children, Second Edition, L. A. Reddy, T. M. Files-Hall, and C. E. Schaefer (Editors)

sensitive, multimodal interventions that incorporate child, teacher, and parent components (Reddy, Newman, & Verdesco, 2015a, 2015b).

PURPOSE

This chapter describes the Child ADHD Multimodal Program (CAMP), an empirically supported group intervention for children younger than 8½ years who have been diagnosed with ADHD. CAMP is designed to train children, parents, and teachers. CAMP training is conducted for 10 consecutive weeks in 90-minute sessions, during which children and their parents are trained separately but concurrently. The children's group training integrates cognitive–behavioral techniques and group play interventions (cognitive–behavioral group play interventions, or CB-GPI) that target prosocial and self-control skills (Reddy, 2012). Behavioral consultation (BC) is offered to parents and classroom teachers individually in the home and at school. To this end, this chapter presents an overview of the value and evidence of group play interventions, CAMP intervention components and an example child group training session, and a synopsis of the evidence and replication strategies for CAMP.

VALUE AND EVIDENCE OF GROUP PLAY INTERVENTIONS

Scholars have advocated ADHD interventions that focus on "the performance of particular behaviors at the points of performance in the natural environment where and when such behaviors should be performed" (Barkley, 1998, p. 65). Thus, interventions are most likely to be effective when skills are taught in the contexts in which children work and play, such as the school, home, and playground. Group play interventions are one effective way to capture ADHD children's interest and motivation while teaching them important skills in natural settings (Reddy, 2010, 2012). Group play interventions (also known as developmentally appropriate games, or DAGs) provide children with an opportunity to interact naturally with peers and learn appropriate behaviors. DAGs offer practitioners valuable information on when and how social problems or opportunities occur among children. Treating children in a natural play setting also increases the likelihood of maintaining treatment gains over time and generalizing treatment gains to other settings, such as school, home, or community (Hoag & Burlingame, 1997; Reddy et al., 2005). For children with ADHD, DAGs offer an important means to acquire new skills, practice previously learned information, and experience an enjoyable learning environment with other children (Reddy, 2010, 2012).

DAGs are gross motor activities that are based on four principles:

a. Each child has the opportunity to participate at his or her own ability level.
b. As each child plays the game, opportunities to participate increase.
c. Elimination of a group member is impossible. As a result, children become more active members of the group and exhibit greater cooperation, cohesion, and problem solving.
d. Children who vary in ability can interact positively with each other. (Reddy, 2012)

Therefore, children who participate in DAGs share an affiliation through which they can encourage others' growth via positive social interactions. DAGs also will present social, academic, and behavioral/physical challenges that encourage children to persist and try alternative solutions.

Research has shown that DAGs improve participation, cooperation, social skills, self-concept, aggression, and visual motor skills of regular education, emotionally disturbed, and perceptually impaired students more so than traditional school-based games (Ferland, 1997; Reddy, 2012; Reddy et al., 2005). A synthesis of some of the evidence for DAGs is presented to enhance practitioners' appreciation of the range of DAGs. For example, Baggerly and Parker (2005) examined the application of child-centered group play therapy (9–11 sessions, once a week) with 22 African American boys in elementary school. Results revealed improvements in self-confidence, behavior, social skills, expression of feelings, and acceptance of self and others.

Bay-Hinitz and Wilson (2005) examined the effectiveness of a cooperative games intervention for 70 aggressive preschool children (ages 4–5 years). This intervention used teacher-directed cooperative board games and other cooperative activities to reduce aggressive behavior. Results indicated that children who participated in the intervention exhibited more participation and prosocial behavior than those in traditional competitive games. Orlick (1988) and Garaigordobil and Echebarria (1995) reported similar findings. With a sample of 178 children (ages 6–7 years), Garaigordobil and Echebarria implemented a cooperative games program (22 sessions) that resulted in significant improvements in classroom behavior (e.g., leadership skills, cheerfulness, sensitivity/respect to others, aggression, apathy, and anxiety). Also, Schneider (1989) compared the effects of DAGs versus free play on the self-esteem of 36 kindergarten students across 17 sessions. Teacher and child self-report indicated higher levels of social behavior and self-esteem among students who participated in DAGs.

Several investigations have found symptom improvements for children with special needs. In an experimental study with 30 Taiwanese children (ages 8–12 years) who were earthquake victims, Shen (2002) investigated the effectiveness of short-term, child-centered group play therapy. Children in the intervention group displayed significantly lower anxiety and suicide risk behaviors than controls. Also, Rennie (2000) explored the effectiveness of individual and group play therapy in treating kindergarten children with adjustment difficulties (e.g., withdrawn, anxious, depressed). Children received 12 to 14 forty-five-minute group play therapy sessions in 14 weeks and 10 to 12 thirty-minute individual play therapy sessions in 12 weeks in an elementary school. Results revealed that children who participated in group and individual play therapy exhibited more significant reductions in behavior problems than did controls. In addition, Hand (1986) found that group play interventions (16 weeks) resulted in greater reductions in verbal and physical aggression than traditional recess games for children (ages 10–12 years) classified as emotionally disturbed. In a sample of children (ages 6–12 years) with perceptual disabilities and aggression, a parent–child group training program with DAGs (1-hour sessions, twice a week, for 16 weeks) resulted in enhancements in social skills and specific perceptual motor skills (e.g., visual motor skills, visual acuity, body awareness). Likewise, parent ratings revealed improved peer interactions, group participation, and rule-following at home and school (Reed, Black, & Eastman, 1978).

Other programs in this volume have demonstrated substantial evidence for the utility of DAGs (e.g., Chapters 2, 7, and 10). Using experimental and quasi-experimental design studies, Reddy and associates have found reduced disruptive and aggressive behaviors in children with ADHD who received CB-GPIs with parent and teacher training sessions (CAMP; Reddy, 2010, 2012; Reddy, Spencer, Hall, & Rubel, 2001; Reddy et al., 2005; Springer & Reddy, 2010).

CHILD ADHD MULTIMODAL PROGRAM

CAMP includes two training components: separate (concurrent) child and parent group training, and individual parent and teacher BC. Because of space limitations, only an example of a child group training session is detailed in this chapter.

Child Group Training

The ADHD child group training is designed to promote social skills, self-control, and anger and stress management through the integration of cognitive–behavioral techniques and group play skills and interventions. The children's program is based in part on social learning theory and the behavior-deficit model (Bandura, 1973), anger replacement training (Goldstein, 1988; Reddy & Goldstein, 2001), and cooperative games literature (Torbert, 1994).

Children's training is run for 90 minutes per session, once per week, for 11 training sessions. Each group includes approximately eight to 10 children. One adult therapist for every two children is recommended. Child group training follows: an introduction (teaching) and reinforcement of group structures and behavior motivation systems, group play skill sequences, and group play interventions. The final session serves as a graduation ceremony for the children and parents in the program. A carpeted room that accommodates about 15 people is used.

At the beginning of each session, the group rules (e.g., raise hand before talking) and the group structure (e.g., review of group goals, sticker awards, use of time-out or bathroom passes) are reviewed. A token economy system is used to monitor and reinforce positive behaviors during each training session. The children are provided rewards for following three goals: (a) follow directions, (b) use my words to express my thoughts and feelings, and (b) keep my hands and feet to myself. Children can earn one sticker/point for achieving each of the three goals during a group session. A group sticker chart is displayed. At the end of every group, each child is asked to evaluate, with adult assistance, how well he or she achieved each goal during the session. A star for each goal the child attained is then placed by the child's name on the group sticker chart. Next, the child selects stickers (i.e., that correspond with the number of goals attained) and places them in his or her sticker book. The sticker book is given to the child at the program graduation (i.e., Session 11).

Time-out is used as a positive self-control technique in the group. Children are instructed that taking a time-out is not a punishment but, rather, a positive technique for regaining self-control. In this program, children are not placed in time-out for a set time (e.g., 1 minute multiplied by the child's age). Instead, children are instructed to remain in time-out until they demonstrate positive control over their hands, feet, and mouth. For example, some children will be in time-out for 45 to 60 seconds, whereas others may remain in time-out for 2 to 3 minutes. Therapists model time-out. Children are encouraged to monitor their behavior and self-initiate time-out. Children are verbally praised for self-initiating time-out and for compliance with adult direction to take time-out. The procedure for taking a time-out includes (a) raising your hand, (b) waiting to be called on, (c) requesting a time-out, and (d) taking the "time-out pass" to the time-out chair. A time-out pass is used to nonverbally communicate to others that the child is taking a break and needs to be left alone. After a few minutes (i.e., 1 minute or 2 minutes) in time-out, a therapist approaches the child, validates him or her for taking a time-out, and then helps the child assess whether he or she is ready to return to the group.

Three levels of time-out are used. *Level one time-out* is designated by a specific chair placed on the far side of the group room. This level distances the child from being directly involved in the group's activity. *Level two time-out* is a chair located directly outside of the group room. This level further distances the child from the group activity and decreases the level of visual and auditory stimulation for the child. *Level three time-out* is a chair in a separate room. Level three time-out eliminates the visual and auditory stimulation of the group activity. A therapist accompanies the child when a level two or three time-out is implemented. Children in level two or three time-out are required to return to the group activity gradually by spending a few minutes in each of the successively lower levels of time-out (e.g., the child in level two time-out must go to level one time-out before returning to the group activity).

Group Play Skill Sequences

Group play skill sequences are a step-by-step behavioral approach used to teach children prosocial skills through modeling, role-playing, and feedback with adults and peers. Group play skill sequences are designed to train and prepare children to successfully participate in group play interventions. Collectively, the behavioral steps illustrate the implementation of the skill (see the skill sequences Asking for Help and Helping Others in the Example Child Group Session section).

Group play skill sequences are taught and reinforced through four methods: (a) written and verbal description, (b) modeling (i.e., adult demonstration of skills), (c) role-playing (i.e., guided opportunities to practice and rehearse skills), and (d) performance feedback (i.e., frequent specific labeled praise and corrective feedback on skill performance). The behavioral steps for each skill are written on an easel that is placed in front of the group. A child or therapist reads each step aloud and then the step is explained and discussed. Each skill sequence is modeled and role-played in three ways: (a) modeled by two therapists, (b) modeled by a therapist and child, and (c) modeled by two children who are assisted by a therapist. Skills taught are role-played in the social contexts of home, school, and peer group. During role-plays, children are encouraged to praise, by clapping, other children for their role-play efforts (see other skill transfer and maintenance-enhancing procedures in Reddy, 2012).

Group Play Interventions

Group play skill sequences are further learned through the implementation of group play interventions (i.e., DAGs). Group play interventions adhere to the previously described four principles. For the child group training, several skill sequences and DAGs are included to promote social skills, impulse control, and anger/stress management. The skill topics taught include using nice talk; following directions; sharing with others; helping others; asking for help; identifying and coping with scared, sad, and angry feelings in oneself and others; using self-control; ignoring provocation managing stress and anger; dealing with boredom; using brave talk (i.e., saying no and accepting no); not interrupting others; joining in; dealing with being left out; and being a good sport. A total of 10 DAGs are implemented across 10 sessions. See Reddy (2012) for a description of 43 group play skill sequences and 67 group play interventions.

Training

This program can be implemented by teachers, paraprofessionals, and/ or professionals with appropriate supervision. Depending on the knowledge and skills of the group trainers, training may take approximately 6 hours and focuses on the behavioral, social, and neurocognitive features of ADHD; structure of the group; behavioral techniques to promote positive behavior and group cooperation; implementation of group play skill sequences and DAGs; time-out procedures; behavior motivation system; and team building among trainers. It is recommended that all group training elements be discussed, modeled, and role-played before group training and that the implementation process and group responses are discussed after the group. An example 60-minute child group training session is outlined next.

Example Child Group Session

Therapists welcome the children to the group and introduce themselves. Name tags are used for all children and group therapists. Therapists then describe the structure of the group and the day's agenda. As part of this discussion, therapists review the group goals: (a) follow directions, (b) keep my hands and feet to myself, and (c) use my words to express my thoughts and feelings. Therapists also discuss the use of stickers as awards: One sticker is awarded for reaching each goal. If three stickers are earned in a session, an additional sticker is awarded for the child to take home. This discussion also includes the use of bathroom passes and time-out passes (*time-out* is a positive break to improve the children's self-control skills). Therapists role-play time-out for the children by spontaneously taking a time-out sometime during the group. Therapists introduce and review the games that will be played.

The group play skill sequences of Asking for Help and Helping Others are introduced as "practice" games to the children. The training, modeling, and practice of Asking for Help and Helping Others are completed before the group game of Islands is introduced and played. Islands requires children to ask for help, help others, share, cooperate, control their hands and feet (i.e., self-control), and manage stress effectively. The following are specific instructions and steps for therapists for implementing the group play skill sequences (i.e., Asking for Help, Helping Others) and group play intervention (i.e., Islands).

Teaching Module: Asking for Help and Helping Others

Purpose

The purpose of this module is to teach children ways to identify situations in which they require help, obtain appropriate help, identify situations when others need help, and help others. Accessing help and helping others are two powerful protective factors (strengths) related to academic and social success in children (Ryan & Patrick, 2001). Five teaching methods are recommended: (a) group play skill sequences provide structured play activities that promote specific prosocial skills; (b) modeling, in which the adult facilitator demonstrates specific behaviors and skills; (c) role-playing provides guided opportunities to practice and rehearse appropriate interpersonal behaviors; (d) performance feedback (i.e., coaching, corrective feedback, praise)—adult facilitators frequently praise and provide children with feedback on how well they modeled the skills and behavior that were demonstrated, and the facilitators also assist children in correcting any mistakes that are made; and (e) group play interventions allow children to use the skills and behaviors in a fun, practical, real-world context that enhances and promotes skill use and generalization.

Suggested Group Play Skill Sequences: Asking for Help and Helping Others

Required materials for group play skill sequences. Materials include an easel with a large poster board, dry-erase board, or blackboard.

Room setup for group play skill sequences. Boards should be set up in front of the room with group play skill sequences written on them. Children should sit facing the boards.

Group play skill sequence: Asking for Help. (Emphasize the underlined words.) (a) <u>Decide</u> what the problem is and if you need help: "I am having a problem with my math homework." (b) <u>Decide</u> who to ask: "I will ask my mom." (c) <u>Choose</u> what to say: "Mom, can you help me with my math homework?" (d) <u>Wait</u> until you get the other person's attention and say, "Excuse me." (e) <u>Tell</u> the person what you need in a friendly way: "Mom, can you please help me with my math homework?"

Other examples to consider. (a) You cannot reach something that you need/want (e.g., book, game boy, snack), (b) someone hit you and you do not know what to do, and (c) you received a bad grade on a test and need help to do better next time.

Group play skill sequence: Helping Others. (a) <u>Decide</u> what the problem is: "A friend tells you that he is mad at Jeff [another classmate] for cheating during a basketball game." (b) <u>Decide</u> if someone needs your help. (c) <u>Ask</u> your friend if you can help him or her: "Can I help?" (d) If your friend says yes, <u>offer</u> help: "You can tell Jeff that you will not play with him if he does not follow the rules. If he still cheats, we can play basketball together instead."

Other examples to consider. (a) A mother is having trouble carrying the groceries, (b) a friend was teased by another classmate during recess, and (c) your sister is having difficulties playing a video game.

Steps for Implementing Group Play Skill Sequences

Step 1. Write each skill sequence on a large poster board so that each step is listed numerically. Underline the action words for each skill sequence.

Step 2. Introduce group play skill sequences as a game to the group. It is important for group facilitators to introduce and reinforce the group play skill sequences in a playful manner. For example, it is recommended that before performing a group skill sequence, the children pretend it is a movie set. Explain that the observing children are directors and the children/group facilitators who are role-playing the skill sequence are actors. The children should be told that when the actors indicate they are ready, the directors should put their arms apart in the air and count "1-2-3-action!" and close their arms and hands on the word *action*. This gesture will signify that the actors should begin role-playing the skill sequence.

Step 3. Explain that the game requires each member to follow directions, take turns, and clap for each other. The game also requires each member to listen and remain quiet while group members are "acting."

Step 4. Initially, group facilitators should act out the group play skill sequence for the children. Next, with encouragement and feedback from a group facilitator, one or two child volunteers are invited to demonstrate the group skill sequence to the group. After several demonstrations of the skill sequence, facilitators may wish to split the group up into smaller ones so that all children will have an opportunity to practice and correctly demonstrate the skill sequence. Once the skill sequences for Asking for Help and Helping Others have been successfully practiced, the following group play intervention can be introduced and implemented with the children. Group play interventions offer fun, real-world contexts for children to learn targeted prosocial skills and generalize their skills to other settings.

Group Play Intervention: Islands

Overview

The Islands game places children in an imaginary dangerous situation. This game requires children to ask for help, help others, share, cooperate, control their hands and feet (i.e., self-control), and manage stress effectively.

Group play intervention skills taught. The skills are primary—asking for help and helping others; and secondary—following directions, self-control, and stress management.

Prerequisite skills. Before playing this game, children should possess basic abilities to follow a sequence of simple directions and keep their bodies in control with redirection/reminders.

Required materials. Have ready three or four bath towels and a radio/tape/CD player.

Room setup. Towels should be placed on the floor of the group room, spread out, and evenly spaced apart. Make ample room for children to comfortably move in between the towels. Set up a radio near a group facilitator so that he or she can easily and slowly turn the volume up and down. The radio should not be shut off abruptly as in the game musical chairs because doing so will induce unnecessary anxiety and impulsivity in the children. An age-appropriate radio station/tape/CD with dance music should be identified before playing the game. As the game progresses, towels are gradually folded and later removed.

Game synopsis. Islands is an interactive game in which children are told to pretend that they live on islands, which are represented by towels. Imaginary crocodiles share the islands and water with the children. The facilitator instructs the children on how to live peacefully with the crocodiles and how to avoid being bitten or eaten. While the music is playing, the crocodiles go to sleep on the islands, allowing the children time to swim freely in the water. However, when the volume of the music slowly turns down, the crocodiles wake up, go into the water, and become aggressive. As a result, the children should swim around the islands while the music is playing and go onto an island when the music turns down and stops. However, if a child is found to be in the water for more than a couple of seconds after the music stops, that child must ask one of the other children for help getting onto an island. As the game progresses, the tide comes in and the islands get smaller (towels are folded and are eventually removed), therefore increasing the number of children asking for help.

Steps for Implementing Islands

Step 1. Introduce the game Islands to the children in a positive playful manner. Children should be told that they are about to play a special game that involves following directions, asking for help, helping others, controlling their hands and feet, and managing their stress.

Step 2. Read the following "Story of the Islands" to the children:

> You are islanders who live on a beautiful group of islands, and the water around the islands is warm and blue. You like to swim every day, but there is one problem: There are crocodiles that travel together that also live in the water and on the islands. When the wind blows over the water and through the trees, a musical sound starts. The music causes the crocodiles to go onto the islands and fall asleep, leaving the waters peaceful. But when the music slowly turns down, the crocodiles wake up [*make a yawning gesture and sound*], go into the water, and look for food. So, when the music is playing, you should swim around in the water by walking, floating, or dancing slowly around the islands. Make sure that when the music is playing, you are not on an island because you do not want to disturb the peaceful crocodiles. When the music turns down, you must leave the water and climb onto an island. If you are not on an island right away, you need to ask someone on an island for help. One of the other islanders will help you onto an island. If you are on an island and someone asks you for help, you should put out your arm and help them onto the island. When the tide comes in, the water covers some of the beaches on the islands and you will need to share the island with more of your friends or find another island to stay on. Sharing islands and helping others will keep you safe and happy.

Step 3. Review the rules for playing Islands with the group. Instruct children that they need to (a) keep their arms in control, not hit or push others; (b) keep their feet in control and walk, but no running, and avoid bumping into objects and other group members; (c) listen for the music to start or stop; (d) walk over to an island and step onto it as soon as the music stops (children may not run or jump onto islands); (e) freeze (if they are not on an island right away) and ask a person on an island for help; and (f) (if the child is already on the island) give someone who is asking for help your arm.

Step 4. Have everyone repeat the directions aloud before beginning the game.

Step 5. Begin playing the music. Children should be encouraged to walk slowly, (pretend) swim, or dance around the islands without stepping on them while the music is playing. After approximately 1 minute, slowly turn the music down. Once the music has stopped, tell the children to freeze and remind them that they should now be on an island. Children who are not on an island should ask someone on an island for help. Children on an island who are asked for help should extend one of their arms to help others onto the island. If children jumped onto an island after they were told to freeze, tell those children to step off the island and ask others for help onto one. The children asking for help should do so loud enough for the entire group to hear.

Step 6. Repeat Step 5. After a couple of times, fold the towels to signify that the tide is coming in. After a couple of additional times, fold the towels again to make the islands even smaller. Then remove one towel at a time until only a single towel is left. All of the children should have at least one opportunity to ask others for help during the game.

Step 7. Group process: Tell the children that the game is now over. Have them sit on their chairs or the floor facing the front of the room, and tell them that it is time to discuss the game.

- *Group process questions.* First, ask the children what they needed to do to play the game. Emphasize the importance of asking for help and helping others. Second, ask the children how they felt when the music was playing. Third, ask the children how they felt when the music was turned down lower and lower. Fourth, ask the children how they felt when the music was off. Fifth, ask the children for examples of when they needed help from others. Sixth, ask the children how they felt when they needed help. Seventh, ask the children how they felt when others helped them. Eighth, ask the children how they felt when they helped others.
- *Motivational system.* In front of the group, review each child's efforts toward each of the three group goals. Give one sticker award for each group goal accomplished (allow 10 minutes). This activity involves two therapists. The first therapist calls each child up to receive his or her stars (one to three stars) and helps the child place the star(s) on the group star chart. The group claps at the end for each child. The other therapist helps each child choose stickers to place into the sticker book one at a time (see Reddy, 2012, for more example group sessions).

Parent Training Group

Concurrent with the children's group training, parents are provided group training in CAMP. The parent training group program is based on ADHD behavioral intervention literature (Reddy et al., 2015a), Barkley's (1997) parent training model, and Hanf's (1969) two-stage program for child noncompliance. The parent group is designed to provide an intensive parent training and support group experience. Parents are trained on techniques to promote their children's social and behavioral needs in the home and at school. The five primary objectives of the program are to (a) increase parents' applied knowledge of ADHD and awareness of their child's strengths and weaknesses; (b) teach and systematically maintain the use of behavioral techniques in the home, at school, and in public places; (c) improve interactions between parents and children; (d) teach parents effective methods for managing anger and stress; and (e) enhance parents' collaboration with school personnel and knowledge of special education law.

Group Structure and Sessions

The parent group runs for 10 consecutive weeks and concurrently with the children's group. The concepts and skills taught in the parent training group build on each other and compliment the skills taught in the children's training group. Handouts outlining behavioral techniques and strategies are distributed weekly to reinforce concepts and skills taught. Weekly homework assignments also are distributed to promote parents' skills in implementing techniques that complement their children's training. Parents are encouraged to take notes, ask questions, and provide advice and support to other group members. At the conclusion of each session, a brief summary of the skills taught to the children during that session is provided. Each session is briefly described, as follows.

During Session 1, parents are welcomed to the program and praised for obtaining early intervention services. The program goals and issues of confidentiality are discussed. An overview of the social, behavioral, learning, and neurocognitive processes associated with ADHD is presented. The rules, behavioral techniques, and structure of the child group training are described. Parents are encouraged to review their children's performance (i.e., group sticker chart) at the end of each session. Parents also are asked to complete a family weekly schedule and list their family rules for the next session.

During Session 2, family weekly schedules are assessed in the context of factors that affect children's symptoms and parental stress. Parents are encouraged to review their family rules and revise them in behavioral terms. The technique *Giving Effective Commands* is taught via a detailed handout (see Reddy, 2012). Parents are asked to practice the technique twice a day in preparation for the next session.

For Session 3, the Giving Effective Commands homework is reviewed, and parents are trained on *Game Cards*, a technique to structure daily routines (e.g., morning, evening) and enhance parent–child interactions. Parents are taught key concepts in child management (e.g., negative or positive consequences must be immediate, specific, consistent). In addition, a group exercise on the characteristics of parents' "best and worst bosses" is conducted and then compared with their characteristics as parents (i.e., bosses). Parents are also trained on *Using Positive Attention* to promote child compliance (see Reddy, 2012). For homework, parents are told to implement the positive attention technique for 10 minutes, twice a day.

During Session 4, parents are encouraged to continue implementing all previous techniques, and are trained on the technique *Teaching Your Child to Not Interrupt You*. Parents are asked to identify and define in behavioral terms two behaviors they wish to improve in their children. The benefits of a token economy system are reviewed. Parents are asked to revise their family rules and list privileges their children could earn for the next session. The *Use of Time-Out* as a positive technique for self-control is also introduced. Parents are encouraged to model the Use of Time-Out in the home and are told to practice the Teaching Your Child to Not Interrupt You technique once a day until the next session.

For Sessions 5 and 6, the steps for designing and implementing a token economy system are reviewed. Parents are asked to begin implementing their token economy systems at home (end of Session 6).

During Session 7, the parents review initial successes of the token economy systems and discuss the benefits and specific steps for graphing children's performance across time. As an extension to the token economy system, the techniques *Managing Behavior in Public Places* and *Time-Out in Public Places* are taught.

Session 8 reviews homework and discusses methods for *Managing Parental Stress*. Parents are asked to implement two stress management techniques during week. Examples of techniques may include taking 10 minutes to sit alone, listen to soft music, or read a book or a magazine.

During Session 9, homework is reviewed and strategies for *Managing Parental Anger* are introduced. In addition, strategies for *Fostering Positive Peer Relationships* through adult supervised, structured, play opportunities are presented. Parents are asked to set up structured play dates for their child before the next session.

During Session 10, termination is discussed, and strategies for promoting home and school collaboration are outlined. A brief overview of special education laws and regulations is provided.

Training

The parent training group should be implemented by qualified professionals who have training in child development, child psychopathology, social learning, and behavior modification. This program includes techniques designed for parents of children with behavioral difficulties who have language and/or general cognitive functioning above 3 years.

The third component of CAMP is individual parent and teacher BC. The critical elements and implementation processes are summarized, as follows.

Home and School Behavioral Consultation

A modified version of Bergan and Kratochwill's (1990) four-stage BC model was used (Reddy, Fabiano, Barbarasch, & Dudek, 2012). BC is an indirect problem-solving model in which the consultant works in a collaborative manner with the consultee (i.e., parent, teacher), who works directly with the client (i.e., child). The BC model includes several features: (a) the consultee is an active participant throughout the problem-solving process; (b) the client is involved to varying degrees in the consultation process; (c) the consultant provides knowledge and skills to the consultee; (d) the model links all stages of the consultation decision making to empirical evidence; (e) problems are described as a discrepancy between existing and desired behaviors; (f) environmental factors affect behavior; and (g) plan effectiveness and goal attainment are emphasized, rather than client deficits (Bergan & Kratochwill, 1990).

In CAMP, parents are assigned the same consultant as the classroom teacher. BC is provided separately to parents in their home and to teachers at school. Parents and teachers are encouraged to communicate and collaborate through face-to-face visits, telephone calls, and use of home–school daily notes. On average, four to five consultation sessions are provided to parents, and three to four consultation sessions are provided to teachers.

Four Stages of the BC Model

The BC model in CAMP includes four stages: problem identification, problem analysis, plan (treatment) implementation, and problem evaluation. *Problem identification* entails defining goals to be achieved, specifying the measures of client performance to be used (e.g., tests, direct observation), establishing and implementing data collection procedures, and determining the discrepancy clause between current performance and desired performance. *Problem analysis* involves choosing and conducting an analysis procedure (i.e., analysis of skills and/or analysis of conditions), developing plan strategies (i.e., broad action plans) and tactics (i.e., specific procedures, events, and materials to be used), and determining procedures for evaluating performance during plan implementation. *Plan implementation* includes the preparation to carry out the plan and monitoring of the plan implementation. Resources and constraints involved in implementing the plan are examined. *Problem evaluation* consists of evaluating treatment data and determining whether the goals have been achieved and the plans were effective. Postimplementation planning (i.e., strategies to continue and generalize treatment gains) is then conducted.

Training

BC requires professionals to be knowledgeable and trained in behavioral techniques, consultation methods, and data collection. Coursework and supervised training in consultation are needed.

EVIDENCE AND REPLICATION FOR CAMP

CAMP has been evaluated through experimental and quasi-experimental design studies (e.g., Reddy, 2010, 2012; Reddy et al., 2001, 2005; Springer & Reddy, 2010). These investigations used five inclusion criteria: (a) children were ages 4½ years to 8½ years; (b) enrolled at a preschool or elementary school; (c) diagnosed with ADHD by a pediatric neurologist, psychiatrist, and/or psychologist; (d) met the *Diagnostic and Statistical Manual of Mental Disorders* (4th ed.; *DSM–IV;* American Psychiatric Association, 1994) criteria for ADHD; and (e) exhibited clinically elevated scale scores (1.5 standard deviations above the mean) on several standardized child assessment measures. The three exclusion criteria used were (a) children whose parents were recently separated or in the process of divorce, (b) children who had experienced other significant losses in the past 12 months (e.g., death of sibling or parent), and (c) children who had been sexually and/or physically abused within the past 18 months.

A multimethod, multisource assessment approach (child, parent, teacher) including behavior rating scales (e.g., Achenbach, 2009, System of Empirically Based Assessment Child Behavior Checklists), parent stress inventories (e.g., Parenting Stress Index; Abidin, 1995), family efficacy scales, and child self-report measures was used to evaluate the effectiveness of CAMP. In several studies, assessment instruments were administered in the home and school before the start of the program, at program completion, and at 4-month follow-up.

The efficacy of CAMP was measured through two approaches: statistically and clinically meaningful differences. First, statistical or reliable change was observed between and within intervention groups across time periods (e.g., repeated measures analysis of covariances and planned comparisons with Dunn-Bonferonni correction). Second, clinically meaningful effects of CAMP were assessed using three methods: (a) between-group effect sizes (ESs; Glass, McGaw, & Smith, 1981), (b) within-group ESs (Smith & Glass, 1977), and (c) Jacobson and Truax's (1991) reliable change index.

Overall, CAMP results revealed statistically significant and clinically meaningful improvements in parents' functioning (stress reduction) and in child behavior in the home and at school at program completion (e.g., Reddy, 2010, 2012; Reddy et al., 2001, 2005; Springer & Reddy, 2010). In investigations that included three treatment conditions (i.e., CAMP, child and parent training group, and child group training only), statistically reliable and clinically meaningful reductions in children's externalizing behavior in the home were found across all three conditions. Overall, parents reported that their children exhibited less hyperactivity, oppositional, and/or problem behaviors. As expected, CAMP participants demonstrated the greatest reduction, followed by participants in the child and parent training group condition, and then the child group training only condition. Gains were maintained at 4-month follow-up. Moreover, CAMP teachers reported greater reductions in student externalizing behaviors at program completion and follow-up than those in the other two conditions.

Improvements in children's social competence in the home and in the classroom also were found. In the home, child group training participants exhibited small clinical improvements (i.e., ESs ranging from .24 to .27), child and parent training group participants yielded statistically significant and moderate clinical improvements (i.e., ES of .59), and CAMP participants demonstrated statistically significant and large clinical improvements (i.e., ESs from .80 to 1.84). Gains were sustained at follow-up. Generalization of gains to the classroom also was noted. Groups exhibited statistical and clinical (i.e., ESs from .22 to 1.31) improvements, with the greatest level of generalization occurring in CAMP. Improved parental efficacy was also found. All conditions exhibited reductions in parental stress.

At program completion, CAMP children exhibited statistically significant improvements and large positive clinical effects (i.e., ES of .90) on internalizing behavior. At follow-up, the child group training condition exhibited small clinical improvements (i.e., ES of .27), the child and parent training group condition had medium clinical improvements (i.e., ES of .40), and the CAMP condition displayed large clinical improvements (i.e., ES of .90). For improvements in internalizing behavior, generalizability of gains to the classroom was not found. Likewise, Jacobson and Truax's (1991) reliable change index was computed to assess the clinical significance of individual treatment-related outcomes at program completion. CAMP families exhibited the greatest percentage of reliable change and/or reliable change with recovery (below clinical elevated levels) for all of the measures. Moreover, CAMP families demonstrated the lowest percentage of no change/ deterioration on all of the measures.

In a modified CAMP program (i.e., no parent/teacher BC), Springer and Reddy (2010) evaluated the clinical significance of measuring between-session parental adherence on child and parent outcomes for 51 children (ages 4 to 8½ years). Three group treatment conditions, (a) child-only treatment (C1), (b) child and parent training (C2), and (c) C2 plus parent adherence measure (C3) were compared to assess the clinical significance of measuring parental adherence on child behavioral problems, socialization skills, and parental efficacy. Parent and child training with parent self-assessment of training adherence (C3) resulted in better outcomes on child and parent measures than the other two conditions (C1 and C2). In addition, results suggested that a multimodal group training program for young children with ADHD was favorable to child group training only.

Replication and transportability of any program are predicated, in part, by the appropriateness of the clinical population and treatment setting used. Comprehensive screening assessments are critical for ensuring the replication and transportability of efficacious programs. The CAMP screening process was used to determine whether children and families were appropriate for the program or would be better served by other forms of treatment.

CAMP was developed to provide intensive psychoeducational training for young children with ADHD, their parents, and classroom teachers. As a language-based program, CAMP was designed to treat children with ADHD who may have other processing disorders, such as speech/language difficulties, occupational and/or physical therapy needs (e.g., sensory integration, motor planning, fine/gross motor skills), and learning disabilities. However, this program may not be suited for children with limited or no language skills. Because CAMP is a new program, outcome investigations have been limited to a narrow scope of children and/or families. For example, previous investigations have been conducted with Caucasian, college-educated, middle-class families. Thus, it remains unanswered whether CAMP would be equally effective on children with ADHD from ethnically diverse, lower-middle class, and/or middle-class families. Moreover, the efficacy of CAMP for ADHD children with histories of physical abuse or general maltreatment is unknown. In addition, CAMP has been implemented at a university-based clinic, with consultation services provided in the home and at school. An apprenticeship approach was used to train personnel for this program; doctoral students facilitated the children's training group, parent training group, and consultation services, and they received weekly intensive individual and group supervision. Step-by-step training manuals and protocols were developed for training and dissemination. CAMP can be easily implemented in schools, agencies (e.g., Head Start), or outpatient clinics.

CONCLUSION

CAMP offers a promising intervention approach for children, parents, and teachers that can be replicated easily and transported to other settings (e.g., school, clinic, agency). This program uses CB-GPIs, in part, to promote ADHD children's social and behavioral skills. Given the complexity of ADHD children's social, behavioral, and cognitive needs, CB-GPIs alone cannot serve as the sole tool in treating this complex population. Thus, the success of CAMP or any program rests on the careful screening and selection of families for the program, sequencing of behavioral interventions, trainer and trainee adherence to the treatment protocol, and comprehensive outcome assessments used.

REFERENCES

Abidin, R. R. (1995). *Parenting stress index: Professional manual* (3rd ed.). Odessa, FL: Psychological Assessment Resources.

Achenbach, T. M. (2009). *The Achenbach system of empirically based assessment (ASEBA): Development, findings, theory, and applications.* Burlington: University of Vermont, Research Center for Children, Youth, and Families.

American Psychiatric Association. (1994). *Diagnostic and statistical manual of mental disorders* (4th ed.). Washington, DC: Author.

Baggerly, J., & Parker, M. (2005). Child-centered group play therapy with African American boys at the elementary school level. *Journal of Counseling & Development, 83,* 387–396. http://dx.doi.org/10.1002/j.1556-6678.2005.tb00360.x

Bandura, A. (1973). *Aggression: A social learning analysis.* Englewood Cliffs, NJ: Prentice Hall.

Barkley, R. A. (1997). *Defiant children: A clinician's manual for assessment and parent training.* New York, NY: Guilford Press.

Barkley, R. A. (1998). Attention-deficit/hyperactivity disorder. In E. J. Mash & R. A. Barkley (Eds.), *Treatment of childhood disorders* (2nd ed., pp. 55–110). New York, NY: Guilford Press.

Bay-Hinitz, A. K., & Wilson, G. R. (2005). A cooperative games intervention for aggressive preschool children. In L. A. Reddy, T. M. Files-Hall, & C. E. Schaefer (Eds.), *Empirically based play interventions for children* (pp. 191–211). Washington, DC: American Psychological Association. http://dx.doi.org/10.1037/11086-011

Bergan, J. R., & Kratochwill, T. R. (1990). *Behavioral consultation and therapy.* New York, NY: Plenum Press.

DuPaul, G. J., & Stoner, G. (2014). *ADHD in the schools: Assessment and intervention strategies* (3rd ed.). New York, NY: Guilford Press.

Ferland, F. (1997). *Play, children with physical disabilities, and occupational therapy.* Ottawa, Canada: University of Ottawa Press.

Garaigordobil, M., & Echebarria, A. (1995). Assessment of peer-helping program on children's development. *Journal of Research in Childhood Education, 10,* 63–69. http://dx.doi.org/10.1080/02568549509594688

Glass, G. V., McGaw, B., & Smith, M. L. (1981). *Meta-analysis in social research.* Beverly Hills, CA: Sage.

Goldstein, A. P. (1988). *The prepare curriculum: Teaching prosocial competencies.* Champaign, IL: Research Press.

Hand, L. (1986). *Comparison of selected developmentally oriented low organized games and traditional games on the behavior of students with emotional disturbance.* Unpublished master's thesis, Temple University, Philadelphia, PA.

Hanf, C. A. (1969, April). *A two-stage program for modifying maternal controlling during mother–child (M–C) interaction.* Paper presented at the meeting of the Western Psychological Association, Vancouver, Canada.

Hoag, M. J., & Burlingame, G. M. (1997). Evaluating the effectiveness of child and adolescent group treatment: A meta-analytic review. *Journal of Clinical Child Psychology, 26*, 234–246. http://dx.doi.org/10.1207/s15374424jccp2603_2

Jacobson, N. S., & Truax, P. (1991). Clinical significance: A statistical approach to defining meaningful change in psychotherapy research. *Journal of Consulting and Clinical Psychology, 59*, 12–19. http://dx.doi.org/10.1037/0022-006X.59.1.12

Orlick, T. (1988). Enhancing cooperative skills in games and life. In F. L. Smoll, R. Magill, & M. Ash (Eds.), *Children in sport* (pp. 149–159). Champaign, IL: Human Kinetics.

Perou, R., Bitsko, R. H., Blumberg, S. J., Pastor, P., Ghandour, R. M., Gfroerer, J. C., . . . the Centers for Disease Control and Prevention (CDC). (2013). Mental health surveillance among children—United States, 2005–2011. *Morbidity and Mortality Weekly Report, 62*(Suppl. 2), 1–35.

Reddy, L. A. (2010). Group play interventions for children with attention deficit/hyperactivity disorder. In A. A. Drewes & C. E. Schaefer (Eds.), *School-based play therapy* (2nd ed., pp. 307–329). Hoboken, NJ: Wiley. http://dx.doi.org/10.1002/9781118269701.ch15

Reddy, L. A. (2012). *Group play interventions for children: Strategies for teaching prosocial skills.* Washington, DC: American Psychological Association. http://dx.doi.org/10.1037/13093-000

Reddy, L. A., Fabiano, G., Barbarasch, B., & Dudek, C. (2012). Behavior management of students with attention-deficit/hyperactivity disorders using teacher and student progress monitoring. In L. M. Crothers & J. B. Kolbert (Eds.), *Understanding and managing behaviors of children with psychological disorders: A reference for classroom teachers* (pp. 17–47). New York, NY: Continuum International.

Reddy, L. A., & Goldstein, A. P. (2001). Aggressive replacement training: A multimodal intervention for aggressive children. In S. I. Pfeiffer & L. A. Reddy (Eds.), *Innovative mental health prevention programs for children* (pp. 47–62). New York, NY: Haworth Press.

Reddy, L. A., Newman, E., & Verdesco, A. (2015a). Attention-deficit hyperactivity disorder: Use of evidence-based assessments and interventions. In R. Flanagan, K. Allen, & E. Levine (Eds.), *Cognitive and behavioral interventions in the schools: Integrating theory and research into practice* (pp. 137–159). New York, NY: Springer.

Reddy, L. A., Newman, E., & Verdesco, A. (2015b). Use of self-regulated learning for children with ADHD: Research and practice opportunities. In T. J. Cleary (Ed.), *Self-regulated learning interventions with at-risk youth: Enhancing adaptability, performance, and well-being* (pp. 15–43). Washington, DC: American Psychological Association.

Reddy, L. A., Spencer, P., Hall, T. M., & Rubel, E. D. (2001). Use of developmentally appropriate games in a child group training program for young children with attention deficit hyperactivity disorder. In A. A. Drewes, L. J. Carey, & C. E. Schaefer (Eds.), *School-based play therapy* (pp. 256–274). Hoboken, NJ: Wiley.

Reddy, L. A., Springer, C., Files-Hall, T. M., Benisz, E. S., Hauch, Y., Braunstein, D., & Atamanoff, T. (2005). Child ADHD multimodal program: An empirically supported intervention for young children with ADHD. In L. A. Reddy, T. M. Files-Hall, & C. E. Schaefer (Eds.), *Empirically based play interventions for children* (pp. 145–167). Washington, DC: American Psychological Association. http://dx.doi.org/10.1037/11086-009

Reddy, L. A., Weissman, A. S., & Hale, J. B. (2013a). Neuropsychological assessment and intervention for emotion and behavior-disordered youth: Opportunities for practice. In L. A. Reddy, A. Weissman., & J. B. Hale (Eds.), *Neuropsychological assessment and intervention for youth: An evidence-based approach to emotional and behavioral disorders* (pp. 3–10). Washington, DC: American Psychological Association.

Reddy, L. A., Weissman, A. S., & Hale, J. B. (Eds.). (2013b). *Neuropsychological assessment and intervention for youth: An evidence-based approach to emotional and behavioral disorders*. Washington, DC: American Psychological Association. http://dx.doi.org/10.1037/14091-000

Reed, M., Black, T., & Eastman, J. (1978). A new look at perceptual-motor therapy. *Academic Therapy, 14*, 55–65.

Rennie, R. L. (2000). A comparison study of the effectiveness of individual and group play therapy in treating kindergarten children with adjustment problems. *Dissertation Abstracts International: Section A: Humanities and Social Sciences, 63*, 3117.

Ryan, A. M., & Patrick, H. (2001). The classroom social environment and changes in adolescents' motivation and engagement during middle school. *American Educational Research Journal, 38*, 437–460. http://dx.doi.org/10.3102/00028312038002437

Schneider, L. B. (1989). *The effect of selected low organized games on the self-esteem of kindergartners*. Unpublished manuscript, Leonard Gordon Institute for Human Development Through Play, Temple University, Philadelphia, PA.

Shen, Y. J. (2002). Short-term group play therapy with Chinese earthquake victims: Effects on anxiety, depression and adjustment. *International Journal of Play Therapy, 11*(1), 43–63. http://dx.doi.org/10.1037/h0088856

Smith, M. L., & Glass, G. V. (1977). Meta-analysis of psychotherapy outcome studies. *American Psychologist, 32*, 752–760. http://dx.doi.org/10.1037/0003-066X.32.9.752

Springer, C., & Reddy, L. A. (2010). Measuring parental treatment adherence in a multimodal treatment program for children with ADHD: A preliminary investigation. *Child & Family Behavior Therapy, 32*, 272–290. http://dx.doi.org/10.1080/07317107.2010.515522

Torbert, M. (1994). *Follow me: A handbook of movement activities for children*. New York, NY: Prentice Hall.

IV

EMPIRICALLY BASED PLAY INTERVENTIONS FOR DEVELOPMENTAL DISORDERS AND OTHER MODELS

10

THE EARLY START DENVER MODEL: A PLAY-BASED INTERVENTION FOR YOUNG CHILDREN WITH AUTISM SPECTRUM DISORDERS

KATHERINE S. DAVLANTIS AND SALLY J. ROGERS

In 1943, renowned American psychiatrist Leo Kanner published the first scientific paper describing "early infantile autism." Drawing from an entire career spent seeing children with developmental and psychiatric impairments, Kanner described a group of 13 children whose symptoms seemed similar to each other's and unique from all other diagnostic groups of children he had seen. He focused on the major differences that set this group apart: their lack of reciprocal, affective social interactions with others; their unique communication impairments; their resistance to change; and their repetitive, stereotypic, and ritualized play patterns. A variety of empirical studies conducted over the past 60 years has delineated additional cognitive and affective differences in play in autism. The effect of autism on the development of symbolic play is so profound that it has been one of the defining features of the disorder in childhood (American Psychiatric Association, 2000). Difficulty with play has been found to be a more prominent symptom very early in life than the

http://dx.doi.org/10.1037/14730-011
Empirically Based Play Interventions for Children, Second Edition, L. A. Reddy, T. M. Files-Hall, and C. E. Schaefer (Editors)

classic symptoms involving insistence on sameness and repetitive routines that Kanner emphasized (e.g., Bernabei, Camaigni, & Levi, 1998; Charman et al., 1997; Rutherford, Young, Hepburn, & Rogers, 2007; Williams, Reddy, & Costall, 2001).

This chapter describes the theory and research support of the Early Start Denver Model (ESDM; Rogers & Dawson, 2010). The ESDM treatment components, implementation processes, and transportability methods are presented along with illustrative case examples.

COGNITIVE ASPECTS OF PLAY IN AUTISM

The unique difficulty that children with autism have in symbolic play was highlighted in early work by Wing and colleagues (Wing, Gould, Yeates, & Brierly, 1977) and elaborated in a series of studies from Marian Sigman's laboratory at the University of California, Los Angeles. Beginning in the 1980s, that group demonstrated that young children with autism were uniquely impaired in symbolic play (Mundy, Sigman, Ungerer, & Sherman, 1986; Sigman & Ungerer, 1984; Ungerer & Sigman, 1981). Those play deficits were related to language comprehension and to general developmental levels, both concurrently and predictively (Sigman et al., 1999). Similar findings have been reported by many groups (e.g., Charman et al., 1997; Hobson, Lee, & Hobson, 2008; Lam & Yeung, 2012).

Autism-specific effects on functional play, which can be thought of as developmentally simpler than symbolic play, have been reported less consistently across studies. Some groups, particularly those that have studied the youngest groups of children with autism, have reported no group differences on functional measures (Charman et al., 1997; Naber et al., 2008). Those studies that have examined older preschoolers, however, have tended to report group differences (Libby, Powell, Messer, & Jordan, 1998; Trillingsgaard, Sørensen, Nemec, & Jørgensen, 2005; Williams et al., 2001).

The reason for the play deficits in autism is still an open question. Over the past 2 decades, symbolic play difficulties in autism have been attributed to a cognitive difficulty with metarepresentation associated with development of theory of minds (Lam & Yeung, 2012; Leslie, 1987; Varga, 2011). However, several findings have challenged the metarepresentational deficit theory (see Jarrold, 1997, for a detailed discussion of these views). One challenge involves the functional play difficulties in autism. Because functional play has no symbolic elements but, instead, involves handling toys in culturally defined ways (e.g., using a hairbrush to brush hair), this difficulty cannot be explained by the metarepresentational account because functional play does not require representing another person's mental state (Williams et al., 2001).

Conflicting findings in the symbolic play area also have challenged the metarepresentational theory. Some groups have reported no differences between children with autism and children with other developmental delays or typically developing children in their spontaneous acts of symbolic play (Dominguez, Ziviani, & Rodger, 2006; Morgan, Maybery, & Durkin, 2003; Thiemann-Bourque, Brady, & Fleming, 2012). Other groups have developed paradigms in which children with autism are presented with various objects and are requested to create, imitate, or identify specific symbolic transformations (Charman & Baron-Cohen, 1997; Libby, Powell, Messer, & Jordan, 1997; McDonough, Stahmer, Schreibman, & Thompson, 1997). In those studies, children with autism performed at equivalent levels of symbolic ability as clinical comparison groups. Those studies demonstrated that preserved symbolic capacities in autism have a common element that differs from other studies of symbolic play in autism: The adult requests a particular symbolic enactment. The performance of children with autism in those situations suggested that they are cognitively capable of symbolic representations but that they appeared to have difficulty in spontaneously generating the pretend play acts (Jarrold, 1997; McDonough et al., 1997).

Generativity, the ability to create novel actions spontaneously, is considered to be one of the executive functions that is markedly impaired in children with autism (Chan et al., 2009; Kleinhans, Akshoomoff, & Delis, 2005; Robinson, Goddard, Dritschel, Wisley, & Howlin, 2009). It has been suggested that autism-specific problems with generativity, rather than with symbolic processes per se, provide an alternative explanation for the symbolic play deficits that can address this contrast between impairment in spontaneous symbolic play but are not in elicited symbolic play (Jarrold, 1997). The generativity hypothesis also can account for the functional play differences that are apparent in autism (Jarrold, 1997; Williams et al., 2001). Two groups have tried to test these two theories against each other, and results have been inconclusive (Craig & Baron-Cohen, 1999; Rutherford & Rogers, 2003). Given the complex and sometimes contradictory findings involving play performance in children with autism spectrum disorder (ASD), this is clearly an area in which current theories do not contain all the evidence. Additional conceptual and empirical work is needed.

AFFECTIVE ASPECTS OF PLAY IN AUTISM

Interactive behaviors involved in play in autism have received far less attention. Unlike Kanner's descriptions of the aloofness and withdrawal of his patients, some groups have found that children with autism have demonstrated positive responses to playful adult initiations from school staff

(Jackson et al., 2003) and from parents (Kasari, Sigman, & Yirmiya, 1993). However, children with autism do not initiate social interactions anywhere near the frequency of children with other disorders or children with typical development (Landa, 2011), and they do not "send" smiles and positive expressions to other people as frequently or as clearly as children with other diagnoses (Ozonoff et al., 2010). Current intervention approaches, such as Floortime (Wieder & Greenspan, 2001), RDI (relationship development intervention; Gutstein, Burgess, & Montfort, 2007), SCERTS (Social Communication, Emotional Regulation, and Transactional Support; Prizant, Wetherby, Rubin, & Laurent, 2003), and ESDM (Rogers & Dawson, 2010), place special emphasis on physical types of social games because of the positive shared affect and communicative exchanges that such play fosters.

THE EARLY START DENVER MODEL

Key Treatment Ingredients and Design

The ESDM began as the Denver model in 1981. It was developed by Rogers and her colleagues at the University of Colorado Health Sciences Center as a developmentally based daily group intervention program that focused on play, relationships, and language development for young children with autism or other disorders of development, language, and behavior. The main features of the Denver model approach were (a) a focus on all developmental areas with specific emphasis on interpersonal, constructive, and symbolic play skills; (b) development of affectively rich and reciprocal relationships with others, including development of imitation skills; (c) development of symbolic language with particular focus on verbal language; (d) use of high-quality teaching strategies in small groups and individual teaching sessions that were delivered in carefully planned teaching episodes across the child's natural environments for 25 or more hours per week; and (e) positive behavior support approaches to unwanted behaviors. Rogers and Pennington (1991) described the underlying developmental model in a theoretical paper strongly influenced by Stern (1985). Rogers, Hall, Osaki, Reaven, and Herbison (2000) described in detail the theoretical orientation of the approach and the goals, beliefs, and treatment approach of the original Denver model, and early outcome papers suggested that the model accelerated development and improved autism symptoms and language progress (e.g., Rogers, Herbison, Lewis, Pantone, & Reis, 1986; Rogers & Lewis, 1989).

In 2002, Rogers and Geraldine Dawson at the University of Washington began to collaborate on designing an intervention model specific to the youngest children with ASD to be delivered through one-on-one treatment at home via parents and trained staff. Developed as part of Dawson's STAART [Studies to Advance Autism Research and Treatment] Center, the partners incorporated principles and practices from the Denver model and fused principles of applied behavior analysis and practices of pivotal response training into the model. Interval-based systems for gathering progress data within treatment sessions were developed to fit inside a play- and relationship-based delivery without disrupting the flow of interaction. In addition, the partners developed systematic procedures for making treatment decisions, established fidelity of implementation measures, updated and elaborated the curriculum, formalized assessment procedures, and developed systematic training procedures for staff. The new model was christened the Early Start Denver model, an intervention for toddlers with ASD as young as age 12 months.

The main vehicle for delivery of ESDM is the *joint activity routine* (Rogers & Dawson, 2010), a dyadic activity developed by the partners that involves four parts—setup, theme, variation(s), and closing—and is marked by many reciprocal social–communicative exchanges in which both partners initiate and respond to the other's bids. The adult provides many learning opportunities for the child within each joint activity, and these opportunities are specific to the child's developmental objectives. Joint activities are used to teach all types of skills, including social, communicative, fine motor, gross motor, and self-care skills (see the ESDM manual—Rogers and Dawson, 2010—for detailed descriptions of all aspects of the approach).

Although not all joint activities are play based (e.g., eating skills), the majority of teaching opportunities in ESDM are delivered inside social or object-based play activities because play is such a fundamental platform for early childhood development. In ESDM, the use of play as a core of treatment of autism in very young children recognizes the two types of play that are affected by autism: social–communicative and symbolic play. The social–communicative aspects of play typically present in the first year of life as affective exchanges between infants and adults through lap games. Bruner (1975), among others, recognized this type of ritualized social exchange as providing critical pragmatic foundations for the development of language. In ESDM, emphasis on this aspect of play is considered to provide the building blocks needed for social awareness of self and others as subjective beings with mental states and minds that can interface, and for development of intentional communication involving verbal and nonverbal behaviors.

In ESDM, affectively rich, dyadic play episodes that focus on the partnership rather than on object play are a crucial part of the therapy, and they occur throughout the child's day. Known as "sensory social routines," they are used heavily, especially in the beginning of treatment to establish a positive affective relationship between child and adult, increase social attention and orientation, create moments of interpersonal synchrony, and build gestural and vocal communication that intentionally communicates social goals involving initiating, responding to, and maintaining social interactions.

Case Example: Social–Affective Play

This is an example from a very first therapy hour: Twenty-month-old Amy and her parents entered the therapy room for the first time. Amy, completely nonverbal and very busy, was a darling blond with blue eyes and beautiful curls. She immediately started to fuss and pull on her parents to leave. Her new therapist had the parents sit down and asked them to become very boring for the next hour. Her therapist then pulled out a large rubber ball, so big it came up to Amy's waist, and approached Amy with the ball, patting on it so it made a lively sound. Amy reached her hands to the ball, and the therapist picked Amy up and sat her on the ball, holding her securely at the waist, facing her, and bouncing her rhythmically up and down with fairly big movements. Amy smiled and laughed, and, at times, the therapist got excellent eye contact in these smiles. Then the therapist introduced a chant: "A bounce, a bounce, a bounce, a stop," and then stopped moving Amy. Amy jiggled her body to repeat the movement, and her therapist said, "Oh, you want more bounce. Okay, let's bounce." Then she began the routine again, bouncing and chanting with shared smiles and eye contact for just a few seconds, and then stopping and waiting for Amy to respond. For the next two repetitions, the therapist reactivated the routine when Amy moved her body to continue the game. The therapist then added a variation: Amy needed to make and maintain eye contact while moving her body to continue the game. So she simply waited during the pause; after Amy moved her body up and down with no response from the therapist, Amy looked at her. The therapist immediately responded, "You want to bounce?" and bounced her.

Now Amy was using eye contact to share her pleasure during bouncing and to request that the activity continue, and in just a few minutes, the therapist had created a lovely, affectively rich, reciprocal routine in which both partners shared smiles and eye contact. It was an enjoyable activity: The child took major initiative to begin and continue the routine, and used eye contact and gestures to do so. Even though an object was involved, the activity functioned as a sensory social routine because the focus was on the two partners' interacting with each other, and the object provided the scaffold for this extended dyadic interaction.

Although social–affective play is critical for relationship building, dyadic engagement, communication development, constructive play with objects, and symbolic play with objects are important contributors to cognitive development, and symbolic play seems to be important for understanding self and others. Vygotsky (2000) suggested that symbolic play provides the young child with early experiences in the power of the mind and in the ability to let thought prevail over the environment—a critical quality for development of abstract thought. Piaget (1962) highlighted the role of symbolic play as an opportunity to review and master practice events in one's life, social roles, and rituals through repetition in play. Both of these qualities of symbolic play should be helpful for young children with autism as they develop language and the ability to represent and think about experiences, rather than being tied to the world of objects and sensations. Symbolic play routines can be helpful in teaching verbal preschoolers with autism social language conventions and social role behaviors. Moreover, symbolic play routines are a main source of play and an educational activity among typically-developing children in preschool settings. Teaching verbal and nonverbal children with autism to play appropriately with thematic play materials provides an important vehicle for their interactive play with peers. In ESDM, the interpersonal aspects of play and symbolic aspects of play are considered integral aspects of the curriculum.

Case Example: Symbolic Play

Tyler was a bright and lively African American 4-year-old with autism, a sturdy and smiling child who spoke in phrases and had excellent sensorimotor play skills. He did not use objects to represent other things, however, and so developing symbolic play skills was an immediate objective. Symbolic play came alive for Tyler when his therapist began to use dolls to act out his daily life in preschool. She named several of the small child dolls for Tyler and his five classmates, and gave the adult doll the teacher's name. The therapist then set the dolls in a circle and began the "hello circle" routine that Tyler knew so well from class. Tyler responded with excitement and delight as he picked up two of the dolls and began to sing the songs and have the dolls act out the movements from the circle time routine. Tyler then initiated another group routine from class with the dolls, and prompted his therapist to take the teacher role (i.e., "Dr. Sally, you be Jean"). Using pretend figures to act out his own life experiences was thoroughly enjoyable for Tyler, and his therapist found that similar scenarios could be used to prepare him for new events, such as his first trip to the dentist.

One of the most important pieces of work that was done with symbolic play for Tyler was to work on his fears. He had many fears, including that of the hair dryer. Using the dollhouse, family dolls, and props made from play dough, the therapist began to weave themes related to Tyler's fears into the pretend play. So, after a bath routine in the dollhouse, a hair dryer was needed to dry the dog, and then to dry the doll Tyler's hair. Hair dryer noises were made vocally to accompany the scene, and Tyler and his therapist blew air to simulate the dryer. The therapist had the doll react fearfully to the hair dryer and Tyler provided some of the script. Then the mother doll moved to comfort Tyler, and he was asked for her script. He had the mother doll provide comfort: "It's OK. It's just warm air to dry your hair. It won't hurt you" were the words he provided. This became a favorite play theme over the next few weeks, and his parents reported that, at home, he now wanted to touch the hair dryer, turn it on and off, and aim it at their hair. His parents went along with this play: wetting their hair a little and having Tyler dry it. They also used every opportunity to provide the hair dryer whenever anything got wet, so when Tyler got his sleeves wet or spilled water, or when their hands were wet, the parents got out the hair dryer. Within 2 weeks of the first play theme, Tyler no longer cried nor screamed when the hair dryer was running, and he was able to let his parents dry his hair. He would comfort himself as he had in the play scene: "It's OK. It's just warm air."

Setting and Sessions

The Denver model was originally developed for a daily, 12-month thera-peutic preschool; to be delivered in small groups of six children and three adults for several hours per day; and to be accompanied by parental interventions at home on targeted areas. In the past 15 years, the approach has been adapted for use in several different settings, including in inclusive preschools in which a child with autism attends with typically developing children, 1-hour-long weekly therapy sessions delivered by a professional trained as a generalist in ESDM that are accompanied by daily play at home delivered by a parent trained to use ESDM techniques, and intensive home intervention programs involving delivery by trained therapists and by parents. Once children reach age 3 years, a carefully planned half-day (inclusive) preschool experience is an important part of the overall treatment package. Regardless of the type of delivery, the goal is to provide a minimum of 25 hours per week of carefully structured treat-ment that follows ESDM practices across the various life settings of the young children with autism; this treatment is always accompanied by parentally deliv-ered home interventions for maintenance and generalization, and to work on skills that only occur at home. Although the ESDM practices for one-on-one teaching are carefully spelled out in the manual (Rogers & Dawson, 2010), fidelity of implementation measures and elaborated procedures are currently under development for those who want to carry out ESDM in group settings (Vivanti, Dissanayake, Zierhut, Rogers, & Victorian ASELCC Team, 2013).

Resources

To evaluate and build each child's individual learning plans, ESDM intervention involves an interdisciplinary team, including disciplines, such as early childhood special education, occupational therapy, speech/language therapy, clinical child psychology, and behavior analysis, and also parents. In a preschool, the educational team provides most of the treatment, and the other disciplines provide consultation and some individual therapy. In the therapy- and home-based models, one of the disciplinary professionals heads the team; the other disciplines are in a consultative role to the main therapist or team leader, and much of the intervention is delivered by assistants in intensive models involving 15 or more delivery hours. Assistants contribute greatly in the classroom and intensive home models. In all the scenarios, parents are an integral part of the treatment team, attending weekly or biweekly parent coaching sessions, reviewing child progress, helping the team identify the most important areas of intervention for daily life, and providing daily intervention at home within the many natural activities and joint activity routines that occur between parents and young children each day.

Treatment Delivery

Treatment is organized around a set of short-term learning objectives that are developed by the lead therapist and parent with input from the entire interdisciplinary team. These objectives are based on the ESDM curriculum tool, which covers the full range of developmental areas: cognition, play, receptive and expressive language, social interactions, fine and gross motor skills, and self-care. Each child has approximately 16 to 20 written objectives to be accomplished in a 12-week period. A set of learning steps that build from the baseline skill to the learning objective are developed for each, and these steps become both the teaching plan and the data system for measuring daily progress. In preschool, the teaching plans are developed in relation to the group activities and are embedded in group and individual classroom instruction. In home programs, the teaching plans are delivered in one-on-one sessions and are embedded into natural caretaking and play routines.

Process and Flexibility of the Treatment Delivery

The process of delivering ESDM is flexible. The basic tenets involve partnership with parents, focus on play, communication, positive affect, dyadic relationships, many learning opportunities, child-preferred activities, teaching in areas of development, and a carefully planned and organized learning environment. However, the materials and activities used and the types of structure can vary greatly from one child to the next, depending on each child's specific needs. The style of the teaching thus can vary, whereas the organization of the treatment—from assessment to objectives, to teaching steps, delivery, and data collection—is invariant. Delivery procedures and measures of delivery fidelity are thoroughly articulated in the ESDM treatment manual (Rogers & Dawson, 2010).

OUTCOME STUDIES

A variety of research designs have been used to test the efficacy of the model, including early pre–post groups designs, single-subject designs, and randomized controlled trials. Examples of each type are represented in this section.

Rogers et al. (1986)

This was the first of the outcome studies; it involved 26 preschool-age children diagnosed with autism, another pervasive developmental disorder (PDD), or another psychiatric diagnosis. An early childhood special education teacher, two assistants, and a consulting speech/language pathologist and child clinical psychologist delivered treatment in a classroom setting for 2¾ hours per day, 4 days per week. An assessment battery was administered before enrollment and after 6 months of daily intervention. This battery consisted of the Michigan Scales (Rogers et al., 1981), the Play Observation Scale (Rogers et al., 1986), and the Mother–Child Play Interaction Scale (Rogers & Puchalski, 1984). After treatment, children demonstrated considerable acceleration of developmental rates on the Michigan Scales in cognition, language, social/emotional, and fine motor skills. In terms of play, they demonstrated significant gains in symbolic play skills, specifically statistically significant increases in complexity of their use of symbolic agents in play, of representing objects symbolically, and in the number of symbolic schemas combined in play. In addition, the children demonstrated statistically significant gains in continuing play interactions, taking turns, and sharing play schemas with the experimenter. In terms of social interactions with parents, children demonstrated statistically significant increases in positive affect and number of social initiations toward their mother and significant decreases in episodes of negative affect in response to mothers' initiations. In addition, there was a significant increase in episodes of positive affect in response to maternal social initiations and a significant number of vocalizations. An examination of educational placements following Denver model intervention for 20 children revealed that 35% of the group were functioning in the normal range on all measures and went to nonspecialized settings (this was in the mid-1980s, before inclusion was a common educational practice), 30% were considered to have developmental difficulties but not significant social/emotional or autism-specific difficulties, and 35% continued to have difficulties focused in the social or emotional area, including autism.

Vismara, Colombi, and Rogers (2009)

Vismara, Colombi, and Rogers (2009) conducted a nonconcurrent multiple-baseline study to examine the effects of a 12-week, individualized

ESDM parent-training program (P-ESDM) involving eight toddlers with autism. The program included once-weekly, 1-hour, clinic-based parent training sessions over the course of 12 weeks, along with four follow-up sessions spanning and additional 3 months. Participants included children ages 10 months to 36 months who had been recently diagnosed with autism. Study goals were to assess parental acquisition of ESDM techniques and assess changes in child social communication behaviors as a result of the program. Via weekly training sessions, parents were taught to embed P-ESDM techniques into their ongoing family routines, including parent–child play and caretaking activities.

Data were gathered via probes of two 10-minute video samples each week: one of a play activity between parent and child, and one of a play activity between therapist and child. Parent mastery of ESDM techniques was assessed using the ESDM fidelity scale, a 14-item Likert-based rating system that evaluates use of key teaching techniques. Child social communication behavior was assessed via examination of the number of spontaneous functional verbal utterances and the number of imitative behaviors exhibited by children. Researchers used the child behavior rating scale (CBRS; Mahoney & Wheeden, 1998) to assess children's engagement across a five-point Likert-based rating system.

Researchers found that, for those parents who completed the training program, all but one acquired mastery of ESDM at or above an 85% criterion by the fifth or sixth training session. In addition, high levels of correct ESDM implementation were maintained at follow-up. In terms of child change, researchers found that once the intervention began, children increased their production of functional verbal responses and their use of imitative behaviors. These changes too were maintained through the follow-up period. Next, researchers found that children's number of spontaneous verbal utterances showed the largest gains once parents met mastery criteria of ESDM. Researchers also found that, on the CBRS, children increased their levels of attentiveness and social initiative behaviors over the course of the intervention.

Dawson et al. (2010)

Dawson et al. (2010) conducted a randomized controlled trial investigating the efficacy of ESDM for improving outcomes of toddlers diagnosed with ASD. The study included 48 children between the ages of 18 months and 30 months at the time of enrollment, all of whom had been diagnosed with ASD. Participants were randomly assigned to one of two groups: ESDM intervention or a control group. Participants assigned to the ESDM group received yearly assessments, 20 hours per week of in-home ESDM intervention provided by trained clinicians, ongoing parent training in the use of

ESDM techniques, and expected parent delivery of ESDM for at least 5 hours per week. Participants in the control group received yearly assessments, intervention recommendations and referrals, and services available in the community. All children were assessed by assessors blind to their group status after 1 year and 2 years of treatment.

After 2 years of treatment, children assigned to the ESDM group showed significant improvement in cognitive ability when compared with children assigned to the control group, as measured by the Mullen scales of early learning (MSEL; Mullen, 1995). Children who had received ESDM demonstrated a 17.6-point gain in MSEL scores, whereas those who had received community treatment demonstrated a 7.0-point gain. In addition, the ESDM and control groups differed significantly in their adaptive behavior after 2 years of intervention, as measured by the Vineland Adaptive Behavior Scales (VABS; Sparrow, Balla, & Cicchetti, 1984). Although participants in the ESDM group showed similar standard scores at the 1- and 2-year outcomes, participants in the control group showed, on average, an 11.2-point decline. Children who received ESDM were more likely to improve in diagnostic status by way of experiencing a change in diagnosis from autism to PDD-NOS [not otherwise specified] compared with children in the control group.

An electroencephalogram study (Dawson et al., 2012) examining response to social and nonsocial stimuli of the subjects compared to a group of age-matched children with typical development revealed that those children who had received ESDM showed normal patterns involving stronger responses to social over nonsocial stimuli, whereas the children with autism who received community interventions showed the opposite pattern than both the ESDM and typical groups showed. The community group demonstrated stronger responses to nonsocial over social stimuli, patterns demonstrated in previous studies by children with autism.

REPLICABILITY AND TRANSPORTABILITY TO OTHER SETTINGS

ESDM has been replicated in several different sites as part of multisite efficacy studies and as part of new treatment and research centers. The home-based one-on-one intervention has been replicated in a number of university settings, as reported in Vismara, Young, Stahmer, Griffith, and Rogers (2009), with sites demonstrating excellent fidelity of implementation by the trained therapists and also excellent fidelity of implementation by the parents trained by those therapists in replication sites. Two groups in Australia also have developed ESDM as a group-based model, and studies are now beginning to appear that are demonstrating positive effects on children's developmental rates in those settings too (Vivanti et al., 2013). The model appears somewhat easier to replicate in early intervention settings—in which the typical intervention tasks involving data management, evaluating child progress, and writing learning objectives are a normal part of professional practice—than in clinical practices, such as hospital-based speech and language clinics—in which little time is allotted for paperwork and there is a significant need to maximize billable hours. In those settings, it is sometimes difficult to set aside the time needed for the curriculum assessments, parent coaching, development of objectives, and data summary after sessions.

ESDM involves specific procedures for assessing children and developing and delivering an early intervention program. A variety of procedures have been developed to train others to use the model at high levels of fidelity of implementation, measure the quality and frequency of their implementation of the key interventions, teach the replication site staff members to monitor and evaluate their use of the new procedures, and measure the effects on children's behavior and development and on parent use of the techniques at home.

Vismara, Young, et al. (2009) conducted a study to determine how well the training package taught others to use the model. In a comparison of the effectiveness of distance learning versus live instruction for training community-based therapists in ESDM, they found that both methods were effective in teaching therapists to implement the model and to train parents. In conjunction with therapists' improvements in the use of the model, child and parent skill gains occurred over time for both methods of instruction. Thus, a variety of flexible training methods have been developed to disseminate ESDM across early intervention sites.

CONCLUSION

Several main points were discussed in this chapter. First, autism impairs the development of several aspects of play: the rich affective exchange that occurs between play partners, novelty and flexibility of object play, and use of symbolic play to act out personal life events and develop increasingly abstract thought. Thus, social–affective and cognitive aspects of play are affected. Second, the importance of play to children's emotional, cognitive, and social development is considered to be so important that focusing on play development is considered fundamental to appropriate education and intervention for young children with autism. Each of the best known intervention approaches for young children with autism directly addresses play as part of the intervention curriculum, and children with autism have consistently demonstrated their ability to learn and grow in play skills.

A comprehensive intervention approach for early autism, ESDM, specifically targets play. ESDM targets development in the cognitive and the social–affective aspects of play through the development of specific objectives that are addressed directly in group, home, and one-on-one work using didactic and naturalistic teaching methods. Outcome studies involving young children with autism treated via ESDM have demonstrated significant gains in symbolic play and significant changes in affective, reciprocal exchanges during play with their parents, in addition to significant gains in language, cognitive, and adaptive behavior compared with contrast groups.

Autism presents a significant impediment to young children's development of cognitive, affective, and social–communicative aspects of play. Yet, the impairment is not absolute, and the mechanisms by which autism impairs play development have not been elucidated. The empirical data have demonstrated the capacity of young children with autism to improve play skills, regardless of functioning level. Thus, the key variable in promoting progress appears to be quality of intervention, not capacity of the child. However, no studies have demonstrated that focusing on play alone results in significant and comprehensive changes in the developmental patterns and/or rate of young children with autism. Play is part, but only one part, of a comprehensive intervention approach.

REFERENCES

American Psychiatric Association. (2000). *Diagnostic and statistical manual of mental disorders* (4th ed., text rev.). Washington, DC: Author.

Bernabei, P., Camaigni, L., & Levi, G. (1998). An evaluation of early development in children with autism and pervasive developmental disorders from home movies: Preliminary findings. *Autism, 2,* 243–258. http://dx.doi.org/10.1177/1362361398023003

Bruner, J. S. (1975). The ontogenesis of speech acts. *Journal of Child Language, 2,* 1–19. http://dx.doi.org/10.1017/S0305000900000866

Chan, A. S., Cheung, M. C., Han, Y. M. Y., Sze, S. L., Leung, W. W., Man, H. S., & To, C. Y. (2009). Executive function deficits and neural discordance in children with autism spectrum disorders. *Clinical Neurophysiology, 120,* 1107–1115. http://dx.doi.org/10.1016/j.clinph.2009.04.002

Charman, T., & Baron-Cohen, S. (1997). Brief report: Prompted pretend play in autism. *Journal of Autism and Developmental Disorders, 27,* 325–332. http://dx.doi.org/10.1023/A:1025806616149

Charman, T., Swettenham, J., Baron-Cohen, S., Cox, A., Baird, G., & Drew, A. (1997). Infants with autism: An investigation of empathy, pretend play, joint attention, and imitation. *Developmental Psychology, 33,* 781–789. http://dx.doi.org/10.1037/0012-1649.33.5.781

Craig, J., & Baron-Cohen, S. (1999). Creativity and imagination in autism and Asperger syndrome. *Journal of Autism and Developmental Disorders, 29,* 319–326. http://dx.doi.org/10.1023/A:1022163403479

Dawson, G., Jones, E. J. H., Merkle, K., Venema, K., Lowy, R., Faja, S., . . . Webb, S. J. (2012). Early behavioral intervention is associated with normalized brain activity in young children with autism. *Journal of the American Academy of Child & Adolescent Psychiatry, 51,* 1150–1159. http://dx.doi.org/10.1016/j.jaac.2012.08.018

Dawson, G., Rogers, S., Munson, J., Smith, M., Winter, J., Greenson, J., . . . Varley, J. (2010). Randomized, controlled trial of an intervention for toddlers with autism: The Early Start Denver Model. *Pediatrics, 125,* e17–e23. http://dx.doi.org/10.1542/peds.2009-0958

Dominguez, A., Ziviani, J., & Rodger, S. (2006). Play behaviours and play object preferences of young children with autistic disorder in a clinical play environment. *Autism, 10,* 53–69. http://dx.doi.org/10.1177/1362361306062010

Gutstein, S. E., Burgess, A. F., & Montfort, K. (2007). Evaluation of the relationship development intervention program. *Autism, 11,* 397–411. http://dx.doi.org/10.1177/1362361307079603

Hobson, R. P., Lee, A., & Hobson, J. A. (2008). Qualities of symbolic play among children with autism: A social–developmental perspective. *Journal of Autism and Developmental Disorders, 39,* 12–22. http://dx.doi.org/10.1007/s10803-008-0589-z

Jackson, C. T., Fein, D., Wolf, J., Jones, G., Hauck, M., Waterhouse, L., & Feinstein, C. (2003). Responses and sustained interactions in children with mental retardation and autism. *Journal of Autism and Developmental Disorders, 33,* 115–121. http://dx.doi.org/10.1023/A:1022927124025

Jarrold, C. (1997). Pretend play in autism: executive explanations. In J. Russell (Ed.), *Autism as an executive disorder* (pp. 101–140). Oxford, England: Oxford University Press.

Kanner, L. (1943). Autistic disturbances of affective contact. *Nervous Child, 2,* 217–250.

Kasari, C., Sigman, M., & Yirmiya, N. (1993). Focused and social attention of autistic children in interactions with familiar and unfamiliar adults: A comparison of autistic, mentally retarded, and normal children. *Development and Psychopathology, 5,* 403–414. http://dx.doi.org/10.1017/S0954579400004491

Kleinhans, N., Akshoomoff, N., & Delis, D. C. (2005). Executive functions in autism and Asperger's disorder: Flexibility, fluency, and inhibition. *Developmental Neuropsychology, 27,* 379–401. http://dx.doi.org/10.1207/s15326942dn2703_5

Lam, Y. G., & Yeung, S. S. (2012). Cognitive deficits and symbolic play in preschoolers with autism. *Research in Autism Spectrum Disorders, 6,* 560–564. http://dx.doi.org/10.1016/j.rasd.2011.07.017

Landa, R. J. (2011). Developmental features and trajectories associated with autism spectrum disorders in infants and toddlers. In D. G. Amaral, G. Dawson, & D. H. Geschwind (Eds.), *Autism spectrum disorders* (pp. 213–228). New York, NY: Oxford University Press. http://dx.doi.org/10.1093/med/9780195371826.003.0014

Leslie, A. M. (1987). Pretense and representation: The origins of "theory of mind." *Psychological Review, 94,* 412–426. http://dx.doi.org/10.1037/0033-295X.94.4.412

Libby, S., Powell, S., Messer, D., & Jordan, R. (1997). Imitation of pretend play acts by children with autism and Down syndrome. *Journal of Autism and Developmental Disorders, 27,* 365–383. http://dx.doi.org/10.1023/A:1025801304279

Libby, S., Powell, S., Messer, D., & Jordan, R. (1998). Spontaneous play in children with autism: A reappraisal. *Journal of Autism and Developmental Disorders, 28,* 487–497. http://dx.doi.org/10.1023/A:1026095910558

Mahoney, G., & Wheeden, C. A. (1998). Effects of teacher style on the engagement of preschool aged children with special learning needs. *Journal of Developmental and Learning Disorders, 2,* 293–315.

McDonough, L., Stahmer, A., Schreibman, L., & Thompson, S. J. (1997). Deficits, delays, and distractions: An evaluation of symbolic play and memory in children with autism. *Development and Psychopathology, 9,* 17–41. http://dx.doi.org/10.1017/S0954579497001041

Morgan, B., Maybery, M., & Durkin, K. (2003). Weak central coherence, poor joint attention, and low verbal ability: Independent deficits in early autism. *Developmental Psychology, 39,* 646–656.

Mullen, E. M. (1995). *Mullen scales of early learning: AGS edition.* Circle Pines, MN: American Guidance Service.

Mundy, P., Sigman, M., Ungerer, J., & Sherman, T. (1986). Defining the social deficits of autism: The contribution of non-verbal communication measures. *Journal of Child Psychology and Psychiatry, 27,* 657–669. http://dx.doi.org/10.1111/j.1469-7610.1986.tb00190.x

Naber, F. B. A., Bakermans-Kranenburg, M. J., van IJzendoorn, M. H., Swinkels, S. H. N., Buitelaar, J. K., Dietz, C., . . . van Engeland, H. (2008). Play behavior and attachment in toddlers with autism. *Journal of Autism and Developmental Disorders, 38,* 857–866. http://dx.doi.org/10.1007/s10803-007-0454-5

Ozonoff, S., Iosif, A. M., Baguio, F., Cook, I. C., Hill, M. M., Hutman, T., . . . Young, G. S. (2010). A prospective study of the emergence of early behavioral signs of autism. *Journal of the American Academy of Child & Adolescent Psychiatry, 49,* 256–66.e1, 2.

Piaget, J. (1962). *Play, dreams, and imitation in childhood.* New York, NY: Norton.

Prizant, B. M., Wetherby, A. M., Rubin, E., & Laurent, A. C. (2003). The SCERTS model: A transactional, family-centered approach to enhancing communication and socioemotional abilities of young children with autism spectrum disorder. *Infants & Young Children, 16,* 296–316. http://dx.doi.org/10.1097/00001163-200310000-00004

Robinson, S., Goddard, L., Dritschel, B., Wisley, M., & Howlin, P. (2009). Executive functions in children with autism spectrum disorders. *Brain and Cognition, 71,* 362–368. http://dx.doi.org/10.1016/j.bandc.2009.06.007

Rogers, S. J., & Dawson, G. (2010). *Early start Denver model for children with autism: promoting language, learning, and engagement.* New York, NY: Guilford Press.

Rogers, S. J., Donovan, C. M., D'Eugenio, D., Brown, S. L., Lynch, E. W., Moersch, M. S., & Schafer, D. S. (Eds.). (1981). *Developmental programming for infants and young children* (Vol. 2). Ann Arbor: University of Michigan Press.

Rogers, S. J., Hall, T., Osaki, D., Reaven, J., & Herbison, J. (2000). The Denver model: A comprehensive, integrated, educational approach to young children with autism and their families. In S. L. Harris & J. S. Handleman (Eds.), *Preschool education programs for children with autism* (2nd ed., pp. 95–135). Austin, TX: Pro-Ed.

Rogers, S. J., Herbison, J. M., Lewis, H. C., Pantone, J., & Reis, K. (1986). An approach for enhancing the symbolic, communicative, and interpersonal functioning of young children with autism and severe emotional handicaps. *Journal of Early Intervention, 10*, 135–148.

Rogers, S. J., & Lewis, H. (1989). An effective day treatment model for young children with pervasive developmental disorders. *Journal of the American Academy of Child & Adolescent Psychiatry, 28*, 207–214. http://dx.doi.org/10.1097/00004583-198903000-00010

Rogers, S. J., & Pennington, B. F. (1991). A theoretical approach to the deficits in infantile autism. *Development and Psychopathology, 3*, 137–162. http://dx.doi.org/10.1017/S0954579400000043

Rogers, S. J., & Puchalski, C. B. (1984). Social characteristics of visually impaired infants' play. *Topics in Early Childhood Special Education, 3*, 52–56. http://dx.doi.org/10.1177/027112148400300409

Rutherford, M. D., & Rogers, S. J. (2003). Cognitive underpinnings of pretend play in autism. *Journal of Autism and Developmental Disorders, 33*, 289–302. http://dx.doi.org/10.1023/A:1024406601334

Rutherford, M. D., Young, G. S., Hepburn, S., & Rogers, S. J. (2007). A longitudinal study of pretend play in autism. *Journal of Autism and Developmental Disorders, 37*, 1024–1039. http://dx.doi.org/10.1007/s10803-006-0240-9

Sigman, M., Ruskin, E., Arbelle, S., Corona, R., Dissanayake, C., Espinosa, M., . . . Zierhut, C. (1999). Continuity and change in the social competence of children with autism, Down syndrome, and developmental delays. *Monographs of the Society for Research in Child Development, 64*, 1–114. http://www.jstor.org/stable/3181510

Sigman, M., & Ungerer, J. A. (1984). Cognitive and language skills in autistic, mentally retarded, and normal children. *Developmental Psychology, 20*, 293–302. http://dx.doi.org/10.1037/0012-1649.20.2.293

Sparrow, S. S., Balla, D. A., & Cicchetti, D. V. (1984). *The Vineland adaptive behavior scales: Interview edition.* Circle Pines, MN: American Guidance Service.

Stern, D. N. (1985). *The interpersonal world of the human infant.* New York: Basic Books.

Thiemann-Bourque, K. S., Brady, N. C., & Fleming, K. K. (2012). Symbolic play of preschoolers with severe communication impairments with autism and other developmental delays: More similarities than differences. *Journal of Autism and Developmental Disorders, 42*, 863–873. http://dx.doi.org/10.1007/s10803-011-1317-7

Trillingsgaard, A., Sørensen, E. U., Nemec, G., & Jørgensen, M. (2005). What distinguishes autism spectrum disorders from other developmental disorders before the age of four years? *European Child & Adolescent Psychiatry, 14*, 65–72. http://dx.doi.org/10.1007/s00787-005-0433-3

Ungerer, J. A., & Sigman, M. (1981). Symbolic play and language comprehension in autistic children. *Journal of the American Academy of Child Psychiatry, 20*, 318–337. http://dx.doi.org/10.1016/S0002-7138(09)60992-4

Varga, S. (2011). Winnicott, symbolic play, and other minds. *Philosophical Psychology, 24*, 625–637. http://dx.doi.org/10.1080/09515089.2011.559621

Vismara, L. A., Colombi, C., & Rogers, S. J. (2009). Can one hour per week of therapy lead to lasting changes in young children with autism? *Autism, 13*, 93–115. http://dx.doi.org/10.1177/1362361307098516

Vismara, L. A., Young, G. S., Stahmer, A. C., Griffith, E. M., & Rogers, S. J. (2009). Dissemination of evidence-based practice: Can we train therapists from a distance? *Journal of Autism and Developmental Disorders, 39*, 1636–1651. http://dx.doi.org/10.1007/s10803-009-0796-2

Vivanti, G., Dissanayake, C., Zierhut, C., Rogers, S. J., & Victorian ASELCC Team. (2013). Brief report: Predictors of outcomes in the early start Denver model delivered in a group setting. *Journal of Autism and Developmental Disorders. 43*, 1717–1724.

Vygotsky, L. S. (2000). Play and its role in the mental development of the child. In J. Bruner, A. Jolly, & S. Sylva (Eds.), *Play: Its role in development and evolution* (pp. 537–554). New York, NY: Basic Books.

Wieder, S., & Greenspan, S. I. (2001). The DIR (developmental, individual-difference, relationship-based) approach to assessment and intervention planning. *Zero to Three, 21*, 11–19.

Williams, E., Reddy, V., & Costall, A. (2001). Taking a closer look at functional play in children with autism. *Journal of Autism and Developmental Disorders, 31*, 67–77. http://dx.doi.org/10.1023/A:1005665714197

Wing, L., Gould, J., Yeates, S. R., & Brierly, L. M. (1977). Symbolic play in severely mentally retarded and in autistic children. *Journal of Child Psychology and Psychiatry, 18*, 167–178. http://dx.doi.org/10.1111/j.1469-7610.1977.tb00426.x

11

INTEGRATED PLAY GROUPS MODEL: SUPPORTING CHILDREN WITH AUTISM IN ESSENTIAL PLAY EXPERIENCES WITH TYPICAL PEERS

PAMELA WOLFBERG

The *integrated play groups (IPG) model* is an empirically based intervention that was created out of profound concern for the many children on the autism spectrum who are missing out on the joy and benefits derived from play experiences. Over the past half century, the vital role of play for children's development, socialization, and cultural participation has received substantial attention (Elkind, 2007; Miller & Almon, 2009). Contrary to the commonly held belief that play is largely superfluous, something children do to merely pass the time, researchers have noted that play is as basic and pervasive a natural phenomenon as sleep (Brown & Vaughn, 2009). Play with objects and with people is fundamental for children to make sense of their sensory, physical, and social encounters in everyday life. From an early age, play with other children is of profound relevance for gaining entry into peer groups and participating in the play culture. The social and imaginary worlds that children create together, apart from adults, is the essence of play culture—and it is within this realm

http://dx.doi.org/10.1037/14730-012
Empirically Based Play Interventions for Children, Second Edition, L. A. Reddy, T. M. Files-Hall, and C. E. Schaefer (Editors)

223

that children of diverse ages and abilities acquire indispensable skills that support social communicative competence and linguistic, cognitive, emotional, and creative growth (Corsaro, 2004; Wolfberg, 2009; Wolfberg et al., 1999).

CONUNDRUM OF PLAY FOR CHILDREN WITH AUTISM

Without explicit guidance, children with autism are at high risk for being deprived of consistent play experiences that foster developmental growth and meaningful peer relationships. *Autism* refers to the broad definition of *autism spectrum disorder (ASD)*, a neurodevelopmental disability characterized by clinically significant and persistent problems in social communication and interaction accompanied by restricted, repetitive patterns of activities and interests (American Psychiatric Association, 2013). Across the autism spectrum is variability; symptoms range from mild to severe and may change over the life span.

Acknowledging the unique differences of individuals, it is noted that, collectively, children with autism share remarkably similar struggles that place them at a distinct disadvantage when it comes to play (both with and without other children). Consistent with current diagnostic criteria, Lorna Wing (1978), in her seminal work, noted impairments in social interaction, communication, and imagination as hallmarks of the autism condition. These core features are inextricably linked to challenges in the spontaneous development of representational and social forms of play (for an overview of research on play in autism, see Wolfberg, 2009).

Within the representational domain, children with autism present with a specific impairment in the symbolic dimension of pretend play that extends to functional play. Compared with developmentally matched peers, their play manifests in less diverse and complex forms. They exhibit unusual fascinations that involve intense fixations on objects, activities, or themes, such as gazing at a shiny surface, collecting and lining up bottles according to size, echoing a television commercial, or describing the inner workings of a washing machine. They often repeat such play routines with little variation, thus giving the appearance of being devoid of purpose and meaning.

Persistent challenges also are evident in the social domain of play with peers. Capacities to enter, coordinate, and sustain social play with peers clearly are compromised by communication challenges. Within the context of free play with peers, prevalent patterns or profiles are revealed. Children with an aloof profile tend to avoid or withdraw from peers. Those with a passive profile show a subtle interest in peers by watching or imitating them, sometimes from afar. Children with an active-odd profile show an obvious interest in being with peers by approaching them in an idiosyncratic fashion.

As eloquently described by Wibke Jonas (2012), a researcher in Sweden and mother of a child with autism,

> the social and imaginary play that typically developed children show us is difficult to stimulate—when you leave your child [with autism] at daycare or school . . . at a birthday party . . . you see almost all children playing together in groups . . . and then you find your child alone, riding his or her bike on the yard, sorting play cards, with an adult, or doing whatever, but [by] himself. . . . You feel that your child is excluded and an outsider. (p. 1)

Maximizing the Potential of Children With Autism to Play

An enduring myth is that children with autism are innately incapable and devoid of any proclivity to play and socialize with peers, yet strong evidence has revealed a different picture. Indeed, these children have the same intrinsic drive and many similar capacities for play and socialization as typical children. What differs is that they convey their interests and abilities in ways that are uniquely their own (Boucher & Wolfberg, 2003; Jordan, 2003).

The idiosyncratic nature of play in children with autism frequently is too ambiguous for others to recognize and decipher in a constructive manner. Perceived as showing limited social interest or peculiar behavior, children with autism are likely to be neglected or rejected by peers who lack knowledge or experience with this population (Sterzing, Shattuck, Narendorf, Wagner, & Cooper, 2012). Research has suggested that after repeated failed attempts to engage peers, children with autism cease initiating and withdraw into solitary activity (Wolfberg, 2009; Wolfberg & Schuler, 1993, 2006). Thus, the transactional nature of experiences with peers shape the extent to which children with autism gain entry into the peer culture and reap the benefits afforded by play. As put by Jonas (2012):

> Playing, as an interaction between children can be like a dance. "There are routines, standards and missteps, there is give and take, there is learning, and there are often vast differences in motivation and skill level." A child must learn to be an adept partner, being sensitive to the needs and intentions of the other child so that fun and pleasure and development can occur. "This dance can be beautiful, it can be awkward, it can be difficult." To learn this dance is extremely important for children on the autism spectrum. [Quotes are from Barrett & Fleming, 2011.] (p. 1)

For children with autism to meet their potential for play, they need specialized intervention that closely considers the unique nature of their development and sociocultural experience. The IPG model aims to address core challenges in children with autism by maximizing their development and intrinsic motivation, which are supported through mutually engaging play experiences with typical peers. Conceptually, while embedded within a framework of sociocultural theory, the intervention encompasses developmental and ecological features (Vygotsky, 1966, 1978). Inspired by Rogoff's (1990) cross-cultural research, the notion of *guided participation* reveals the mutual benefits of engaging in culturally valued activity (in this case, play) with the guidance, support, and effort of social partners who differ in skill and status. Thus, another aim of the IPG intervention is for typical peers to gain empathy, understanding, and acceptance of the unique ways in which children with autism express themselves and relate to others in play.

KEY TREATMENT INGREDIENTS FOR THE IPG MODEL

IPG Intervention Parameters

An IPG intervention brings together children with autism (novice players) and typically developing peers (expert players) in small groups led by an adult facilitator (IPG guide). Originally designed for children from preschool through elementary age (approximately ages 3–11 years), extensions of the IPG model are being applied to diverse age groups while incorporating innovations, such as movement, drama, art, filmmaking, and other culturally valued activities.

Each IPG is customized for an individual child with autism in coordination with the child's education and therapy plan. Parents and key professionals collaborate as a team in the process. The team makes a determination if an IPG intervention is appropriate for an identified child. To be eligible, a child must be at least 3 years old and be receiving support services through an individual family support program, individual education program, or its regional equivalent. An IPG intervention may be deemed appropriate if the team agrees that the child (a) presents developmental delays or differences that affect his or her capacity to spontaneously play and socialize with peers, and (b) will potentially benefit from an intensive, inclusive, peer play intervention to address challenges in these areas.

Each IPG includes three to five participants; the number of expert players exceeds the number of novice players. Novice players include children of diverse abilities across the autism spectrum, whereas expert players comprise typical peers, including siblings, who are competent in social communication and play, and have expressed interest in participating. Consideration is given to selecting players with the potential of forming long-lasting friendships beyond the IPG setting. Thus, it is ideal to recruit peers from the child's natural social network. Recruiting familiar peers offers advantages from the start, but familiarity can also evolve as a part of the IPG experience. Groups may include children of a similar age or mixed ages, both of which offer benefits. There is no distinct advantage to same- or mixed-gender groups other than to provide divergent sociocultural experiences.

IPG intervention programs are delivered in settings that support natural opportunities for inclusive play. To date, they have been successfully run in school, at home, and in community and clinical venues. To foster continuity and secure attachments, the same group of children meets on a regular and frequent basis. Each program generally runs for 12 weeks, meets twice a week for either 30- or 60-minute sessions. Many school run programs meet for 30-minute sessions during natural social breaks, such as lunch and recess, whereas programs that take place after school hours or in other venues hold longer sessions.

Within the respective site, a specially designed play area is developed to serve as the primary meeting space for an IPG. It is optimal for a permanent space to be designated that is available for regular and extended use. Play areas may be set up in classrooms, therapy rooms, family rooms, or outdoor playhouses in warmer climates. They are purposefully restricted in size with clearly defined boundaries, explicitly organized with visual supports (i.e., picture-word icons, schedules, labels) and thematically arranged. Play areas include a range of developmentally and age-appropriate play materials that have high social and imaginative potential, and correspond to the interests of all of the players, including the unique fascinations of a particular child with autism. Play activities may include pretending, constructing, movement, interactive games, art, music, drama, video, and other creative pursuits.

In preparation for the IPG program, advanced opportunities are provided for the children (novice and experts) and adults to participate in "autism demystification" activities (Wolfberg, McCracken, & Tuchel, 2014, p. 177). The purpose of these activities is to foster understanding, acceptance, and empathy for people with autism in a sensitive and age-appropriate manner. Corresponding to a philosophy of respect for diversity and inclusion, these activities are offered to integrated groups and never identify to the group that a particular child has autism. A puppet presentation designed for younger children and a simulation game designed for older populations are offered through a partner organization, Friend 2 Friend Social Learning Society. Supplemental activities, such as book sharing, discussions, role-plays, and related games, are carried out to reinforce concepts over the course of the intervention.

IPG Provider Qualifications and Preparation

Qualified IPG providers include experienced professionals—such as educators, psychologists, speech-language pathologists, occupational therapists, and home-based interventionists—who receive advanced preparation as an IPG master guide to practice independently or as a part of a school, community organization, or clinic. Training is provided through participation in the IPG master guide apprenticeship program offered by the Autism Institute on Peer Socialization and Play (see http://www.autisminstitute. com). This noncorporate collective of independent professionals and family members is devoted to advancing the principles and practices of the IPG model through training, research, and global outreach.

The IPG master guide apprenticeship program is grounded in a comprehensive, competency-based curriculum, as documented in the IPG field manual (Wolfberg, 2003). Following completion of a 2-day introductory IPG seminar, candidates participate in advanced training and field supervision over the course of two 15-week semesters. Each semester, candidates implement at least one 12-week IPG that includes one or two children on the autism spectrum. Each semester consists of start-up support to initiate IPG interventions at respective sites, monthly group training providing in-depth coverage of each phase of the IPG model, monthly individual candidate supervision by a qualified IPG field supervisor, and evaluations (mid-term and final) based on videotaped observations and independent fidelity checks.

Throughout their apprenticeship, candidates are monitored on their progress as they develop a portfolio that provides detailed documentation, including reflection log, completed field exercises, data binders comprising IPG assessments and summative reports for each child with autism, written feedback from supervisors based on individual supervision, and the results of the mid-term and final evaluation. An online blog offers a collective space for candidates to reflect; share stories; exchange ideas, strategies, resources, and materials; and engage with one another within and across other sites.

On successful completion of their apprenticeship, IPG master guides demonstrate knowledge and skill in the design and delivery of IPG interventions that support children representing diverse ages, abilities, socioeconomic groups, languages, and cultures. As qualified IPG providers, individuals and organizations become professional partners as members of the collective.

IPG Intervention Delivery Process

Effective delivery of the IPG intervention is contingent on sensitive assessment, which provides the IPG guide with an intimate understanding of each novice player's unique potential. The IPG model includes a comprehensive set of assessment tools that serve to guide decisions for identifying realistic and meaningful goals, selecting appropriate intervention strategies, and evaluating children's progress. To document children's development and experiences over time, quantitative and qualitative data are collected and analyzed. Data sources include in vivo and videotaped observations; interviews with parents, key professionals, and children; and artifacts produced within the context of the IPG. The assessment framework encompasses developmental profiles of children's social and symbolic dimensions of play, social communication with peers, play preferences, and diversity of play. Social validation and generalization of acquired skills across settings and play partners are further evaluated as a part of the assessment process.

Delivery of the IPG intervention involves multiple layers of systematic support for guiding children in social and imaginary play experiences. Routines, rituals, and visual supports are incorporated to capitalize on the distinctive ways in which children with autism think and learn. Play sessions are organized in a highly predictable manner with opening and closing routines that surround a period of guided participation in child-centered play. This period of guided play reinforces opportunities for children to play freely while forming an inclusive play culture. Play experiences center on mutually engaging materials, activities, and themes, which reflect the unique interests, developmental capacities, and sociocultural experiences of novice and expert players.

The premise of guided participation is to enable novice and expert players to initiate and incorporate desired activity into socially coordinated play while stimulating novice players to practice novel and increasingly complex forms of play. Ultimately, novice and expert players are encouraged to mediate their own play activities with minimal adult guidance. Like the overlapping petals of a lotus flower, guidance participation involves the application of a set of key practices.

The practice of *nurturing initiations* relies on being attuned to the conventional, subtle, and obscure way in which children may express their interests in play. Play initiations may be directed to oneself, peers, and materials while conveyed through action and dialogue. No matter how unusual, all such expressions are interpreted as purposeful, adaptive, and meaningful attempts to participate in play. For example, a child who repeatedly gets in and out of a box may be indicative of an interest in playing hide-and-seek with the other children. To nurture such initiations requires recognizing, interpreting, and responding to each attempt. In this way, the child's initiations are catalysts for novice and expert players to find common ground in play while building on the novice player's social and symbolic play repertoire.

Scaffolding play involves modulating assistance to match and slightly surpass the child's capacity to independently engage in play with peers within what Vygotsky (1978) referred to as the *zone of proximal development* (ZPD). The art of scaffolding play involves a delicate balance of knowing when to step in and out, and when to speak and remain silent to support rather than intrude on the natural flow of the play experience. At times, an intensive level of support may be required whereby the adult's role is much like that of a stage director: directing and modeling ways in which the children may engage in the play. As the children gradually become more competent playing together, the role shifts to that of an interpreter and coach who offers subtle suggestions, poses questions, makes comments, and uses gestures and visual supports. Once the children become fully engaged in reciprocal play, the adult withdraws to the periphery of the group and stands by as a secure base while allowing the children to play on their own.

Supporting the children to effectively elicit another's attention and sustain joint engagement is central to the practice of *guiding social communication*. Both verbal and nonverbal modes of communication are used as strategies. Using visual cue cards and posters of what to do and what to say, discussion, role-play, and incidental (i.e., in-the-moment) techniques assist children in learning how to invite and join peers in play, and how to maintain and expand on play interactions. The children are guided to recognize, interpret, and respond to each other's verbal and nonverbal cues as meaningful and purposeful acts. Expert players learn how to attune to nuanced communication that may be expressed by the children with autism. Simultaneously, novice players gain skill in communicating in a more effective and conventional manner. The intent is for these skills to become a natural part of the children's repertoire without relying on adult guidance or the presence of visual cues.

The practice of guiding play in the ZPD involves an assortment of techniques that maximize the novice player's developmental capacity to engage in play experiences with peers. The idea is to nudge the child just slightly beyond his or her present capacity within the ZPD. A continuum of development is reflected in the methods used to guide the children—that is, orientation, imitation and mirroring, parallel play, joint focus, join action, role enactment, and role-playing. The intent is for the children to be fully immersed in play experiences with peers, even if initial participation is minimal. With repeated exposure, novice players may perform actions and roles that they only gradually grow to fully comprehend. For instance, a child who has an affinity for lining up objects may take on the role of a store clerk who stacks the shelves while his peers pretend to go shopping.

IPG SESSION CASE EXAMPLE

The following IPG session features Bea, a 7-year-old girl formally diagnosed with ASD. Bea participated in an IPG intervention as a part of an after-school program. The IPG meets twice weekly for 1-hour sessions. IPG master guide Lina, who has a background in clinical psychology, leads the sessions. Bea, the only novice player, participates in the group with four expert players: Franco, Jessica, Kiki, and Rollo, all of whom are close in age to Bea.

Based on assessments, Bea was observed to engage primarily in functional play in a limited number of activities. She displayed a passive social play style, spending much of her time as an onlooker or in parallel play. Her spontaneous communication was relatively limited, and she relied on others to prompt her to use verbal and nonverbal means to initiate and respond to others. The focus of the intervention was on extending Bea's development in the following areas: symbolic-pretend by role-playing real and invented scripts with dolls, self, peers and/or imaginary characters; common focus play by engaging in joint action, mutual imitation, and reciprocal exchanges with peers; social–communicative competence by increasing the rate and quality of spontaneous initiations and responses using more effective verbal and nonverbal means; and increasing the number or variety of play interests.

Opening Ritual

As each child enters the playroom to begin the session, the child picks up his or her personalized name tag that displays the child's photo alongside a picture icon used to symbolize the IPG. Hanging on one wall is a poster that the children illustrated in a previous session after they had self-selected the name Awesome Kids Group. Lina calls the children to gather in a circle on the rug and systematically leads the children through a familiar opening ritual. A plastic microphone, which is used as a "talking stick," is passed from one child to the next to signal the child's opportunity to speak. Lina guides the children step by step as she reviews a series of neatly arranged visual supports: "check-in" board on which each child places his or her name tag and says hello; "Things to Remember in Play Group" poster that lists guidelines for expected behavior: "Be kind to each other," "Be kind to the toys," "Stay in the play area," "Ask if you need a break," "Include each other"; and "schedule" board that lists the session sequence: hello, play, cleanup, snack, and goodbye. Lina next asks the children to discuss what they would like to play together. They then sing a song and do a cheer that they made up about the Awesome Kids Group.

Guided Participation in Play

In this session, Franco and Rollo choose to pair up and play with puppets while Jessica, Kiki, and Bea agree to play a combination of store and house. Bea passively watches Jessica and Kiki from a distance as they begin preparations. Jessica quickly approaches Bea and asks her if she wants to play store, to which Bea smiles and responds affirmatively and repeats, "Play store."

Lina presents a set of "role-tags" that depict the various grocery store roles and asks the three girls to choose what they would like to be. Jessica abruptly chooses cashier; Kiki rejects the roles and announces that she will wait in the house for the groceries to be delivered to her. As it happens, Kiki has a cold that day and chooses to rest on throw pillows. Apparently unclear as to her options, Lina offers Bea the choice of the role of shopper or bagger. Jessica intercedes by taking the role-tag from Lina and showing it to Bea and saying, "Bagger." Bea responds by taking the role-tag, slipping it on, and saying, "Bagger." Lina suggests that perhaps the puppets can be shoppers, to which Franco and Rollo agree and begin loading up a grocery cart with play food.

Lina helps the children set up a table bag to serve as the checkout stand complete with a cash register and a shopping bag. Jessica readily takes her place at the cash register. Bea follows, but then wanders off to look at the other children. Jessica begins to call her, "Bea, Bea . . . ," but Bea does not respond. Lina holds up a social communication cue card that visually depicts two children in close proximity and has the written words "stand close." Jessica responds by getting up and moving physically close to Bea. She then points to Bea's role-tag and asks, "Bea, who are you?" to which Bea looks and responds, "Bagger." Jessica takes Bea by the hand and leads her to her spot at the checkout stand, saying, "Okay, then you need to stand here and bag."

Next, the boys begin unloading the groceries on the table while Jessica scans them across the cash register. Bea watches passively and then wanders off again. Noticing this, Jessica calls out, "Oh no, we lost our bagger again." To redirect the players, Lina, using the microphone as a prop, models while saying, "We need a bagger, we need a bagger." Jessica follows suit by taking the microphone and repeating, "We need a bagger, we need a bagger." Bea takes notice and moves back to her previous spot.

Meanwhile, Franco takes over the role of cashier by scanning the groceries and handing them to Jessica, who then hands them to Bea to bag. Bea places the first item in the bag but then cannot keep up with the rapid rate of the new cashier. Lina suggests that Jessica place the items on the table one by one to give Bea a chance to catch up. With each new item, Jessica speaks into the microphone, "Put it in, bagger, put it in bagger . . . ," to which Bea responds by putting the item in the bag and saying, "Check!" The children establish a rhythm in which Rollo unloads the groceries, Franco scans the item, Jessica passes the item on to Bea, and Bea places it in the bag. After several minutes, Franco announces the price, "100 dollars!" Bea responds a moment later, "100 dollars!" After Rollo pays, the children disperse and begin mulling around Kiki with the newly bought items.

Still in her resting place at home, Kiki calls out, "It's my birthday, okay?" Simultaneously, Bea spontaneously heads over to a shelf and takes down a doctor's kit and sits beside Kiki. Lina comments, "Is the birthday girl sick? Are you the doctor?" Bea opens the doctor kit and dumps the paraphernalia onto the floor. Placing the stethoscope over her ears, she moves in close to

Kiki, who motions with her hand to place the end of the stethoscope on her chest. Bea follows suit, to which Kiki and Bea exchange reciprocal smiles and a giggle. Jessica and Franco sit beside Bea. They take turns modeling how to use the different doctor instruments. Rollo picks up a toy shot and pretends to stick himself, and exclaims, "Ow, ow, ow!" Bea picks up another toy shot and begins to press it into the doctor kit box. Seeing this action, Jessica guides Bea's hand over to Kiki's arm and says, "No, it goes here. Give her a shot." Bea imitates this action and pushes the toy shot into Kiki's arm several times as the three girls giggle.

After some time, Kiki announces it is time for the birthday party. Throughout this episode, Bea sits quietly, watching the children who surround her on all sides. Jessica and Kiki begin organizing a pretend cake using a plastic container; Franco and Rollo begin singing, "Happy birthday to you . . . cha-cha-cha!" When they reach the end of the song, Kiki pretends to blow out the candles. Next, Jessica, Franco, and Rollo yell at the top of their lungs: "Happy birthday!" Several moments later, Bea, with a huge smile, suddenly bursts out at the top of her lungs: "Happy birthday!"

Closing Ritual

The play session closes with cleanup, a shared snack, and a discussion. Each child takes a turn speaking into the microphone to tell the group what they had fun playing. Jessica tells the group, "I had fun playing grocery store. Bea's turn. Have a nice day" and then passes the microphone to Bea. Bea holds the microphone, and Lina prompts her: "Did you have fun playing today?" Bea responds, "Yes, I think so, I'm really sure . . ." After a moment, Lina next asks, "What did you like playing?" Jessica interrupts, "Grocery store, right?" to which Bea repeats, "Grocery store" and then adds, "Doctor, Jessica's turn." Bea attempts to pass the microphone back to Jessica. To redirect her, Lina points to Rollo, and asks Bea, "Whose turn is it?" Bea affirms, "Rollo's turn" and passes the microphone to him. The discussion concludes with what the children might like to play next time; Bea chooses doctor, and the others unanimously agree. The expert players offer possible variations on the theme, including an emergency hospital for animals, to which Bea shows excitement when Kiki hands her a stuffed dog. The session concludes with an Awesome Kids Group goodbye cheer.

IPG INTERVENTION RESEARCH SYNOPSIS

The therapeutic benefits of the IPG intervention for children with autism of diverse ages, abilities, languages, cultures, and socioeconomic groups have been documented in more than 2 decades of research. This body of research includes a series of experimental and exploratory studies that have been carried out by, as well as replicated and extended the work of Wolfberg and colleagues. Although most have been published in peer-reviewed journals and research reports (Bottema-Beutel, 2010; Julius et al., 2012; Lantz, Nelson, & Loftin, 2004; Mahnken, Baiardo, Naess, Pechter, & Richardson, 2004; Richard & Goupil, 2005; Wolfberg, 2009; Wolfberg, DeWitt, Young & Nguyen, 2014; Wolfberg & Schuler, 1992, 1993; Yang, Wolfberg, Wu, & Hwu, 2003; Zercher, Hunt, Schuler, & Webster, 2001), unpublished studies also have produced promising outcomes (Antipolo & Dichoso, 2003; Gonsier-Gerdin, 1993; Mikaelan, 2003; O'Connor, 1999; Schaefer & Atwood, 2003). External reviews of this work have further garnered support for the IPG model as an established evidence-based intervention (see, e.g., American Speech-Language-Hearing Association, 2006; DiSalvo & Oswald 2002; Iovannone, Dunlop, Huber, & Kincaid, 2003; National Autism Center, 2009).

To a large extent, experimental studies have examined the effect of the IPG intervention on the social, communication, and play development of the novice players, whereas exploratory studies have examined possible influences that have shaped the children's developmental growth and sociocultural experiences. The attitudes, perceptions, and experiences of the expert players also were examined in some studies, whereas social validation measures assessed parent perceptions of the IPG intervention and its effect on their children.

Collectively, research outcomes have shown consistent evidence that the children with autism produced more spontaneous, diverse, and complex play over the course of the IPG intervention. Relative to initial developmental levels, there were noted decreases in isolate and stereotyped patterns of play that corresponded to advances in more socially coordinated (i.e., parallel, common focus, common goal) and representational play (i.e., functional, symbolic pretend). Also documented were improvements in communication and language that corresponded to social advances. The research evidence further revealed that advances in social interaction, communication, and play were maintained after withdrawal of adult support. The accumulated evidence has further suggested that the intervention yielded generalized and socially valued gains because noted improvements carried over to different settings, social partners, and activity contexts. Benefits for expert players also were supported by evidence that documented greater awareness, compassion, and acceptance of individual differences as portrayed by the children with autism. Moreover, mutual friendships were noted to develop between some novice and experts players that carried over to other social contexts within the school, home, and community.

As Wolfberg and Schuler (2006) noted in an earlier discussion of research on the IPG model,

Consistent with [other] play related intervention studies . . . these cumulative findings suggest that children with ASD are capable of improving their social interaction, communication and play with explicit adult guidance and peer mediated support. The system of support provided through guided participation in play with typical peers apparently helped to arouse and nurture the children's social and symbolic growth. Immersion in joint play with more competent peers allowed for the fine tuning of imitation skills, the practice of more advanced forms of play and language and the contextualization of stereotypic behavior (including echolalic speech) that might otherwise have been perceived as deviant. . . . Commensurate with claims made by Vygotsky (1978) and Bruner (1990), one might speculate that social reciprocity propels symbolic growth within the context of culturally relevant activity. The IPG model created a cultural milieu with the potential to counteract the deficits in imagination and symbolic thinking that may be secondary to limited social experience in children with ASD. (p. 214)

Replication and Transportability of the IPG Model

Drawing on research and practice to date, the IPG model has continued to evolve and has been transformed by new developments in an ever-expanding field of autism. Contributing to these efforts are many innovative individuals who have adapted the IPG intervention to diverse treatment contexts and populations that represent a broader age range. The common thread that runs through these approaches is joint engagement in mutually enjoyed experiences that are playful in nature and valued by the peer culture. The following is an overview of research-based approaches to date.

An approach combining sensory integration (SI) therapy with the IPG intervention was developed for use by occupational and physical therapists in clinical settings (Fuge & Berry, 2004). *SI therapy* centers on enhancing children's organization and processing of sensory information using a variety of methods of stimulation (e.g., vestibular, tactile, proprioceptive, visual, auditory, gustatory, olfactory) as building blocks for functional skills. These skills are not taught but are allowed to emerge spontaneously as foundations develop. For therapy to be most productive, the combined approach creates an atmosphere that is relaxed, mutually supportive, and playful. Activities are designed to be intrinsically motivating and child-centered to capitalize on the child's attention and motivation, and the child's innate drive to move, explore, and learn through pleasurable experiences. In addition to targeting play, goals and objectives focus on such areas as postural responses, concept development, and fine motor development. Appropriate space and equipment are critical to success, whereby activities selected for children of differing ages and abilities revolve around spontaneous interests.

The integrated drama groups (IDGs) intervention, an adaptation of the IPG model, was developed for a range of ages (Neufeld & Wolfberg, 2009). Similar to an IPG, an *IDG* comprises novice and expert players; the idea is that the children teach and learn from each other. Each group is led by a trained facilitator who has experience working with individuals on the autism spectrum and has a background in theater arts. Each 1-hour session consists of a period of dramatic play, improvisation, and scene work with selected materials and props; a cool-down; and a reflective period to discuss what occurred during the session, followed by a period of free play/ unstructured activity. Although an adult facilitates the group, the ideas for the improvisation and dramatic roles and games that are played as a part of the group come from the children themselves. The ideas arise from the unique interests and abilities of the novice and expert players. In an improvisation scene, the children generate the seed of the idea (i.e., a story, a movie, a real-life challenge). The adult then offers the children a basic idea of how the scene might flow and allows the children to determine for themselves what to say and how to go about carrying out the story to its end. Thus, similar to an IPG, play and imagination are central to the shared experiences of novice and experts in an IDG.

Another adaption of the IPG model is *integrated teen social groups* (ITSGs), which are designed to support high-quality social experiences within a framework that provides a loose structure suitable for many settings and a range of participants and themes (Bottema-Beutel, 2010).

Although participants include a higher number of teens who are typically developing to those on the autism spectrum, a central premise is equal footing between them. The adult facilitator maintains a balanced role that is respectful of teen peer culture, which, by its very nature, may defy expectations of the adult world. The facilitator applies strategies to support the participants in planning and executing activities around a common theme on which the group agrees in advance, such as creating comic books, making jewelry, playing a board game, or editing a video. During the initial stages, the adult may need to make suggestions and help design the activities, but the participants gradually take on more of the responsibility as they become more cohesive as a group. Reflecting the interests of participants, activities include a variety of roles so members with different strengths can find meaningful ways to participate. Moreover, the activities are consistent with the cultural expectations of the respective setting. If an ITSG is taking place in a summer camp, for example, the activities might include modifications of games, sports, and team-building experiences at the camp. A core aspect of the ITSG experience is for the participants to understand and appreciate each other's different contributions to the activities that they plan and carry out together.

CONCLUSION

To date, IPG programs have been successfully established in diverse settings (i.e., school, home, community) at the regional, national, and international levels. Yet, despite best efforts, there is an unprecedented need to expand program development so that it meets the ever-increasing demand to support growing numbers of children with autism and their families around the world. From a developmental, sociocultural, and human rights perspective, a need that is paramount is to prepare educators, therapists, parents, and others with the knowledge and skill to implement effective, research-based interventions that explicitly support children with autism to successfully participate in inclusive peer play experiences. Thus, future directions for replication and expansion of the IPG model are focused on global outreach. It is hoped that such efforts will help to raise awareness as they support children with autism in essential play experiences with typical peers.

REFERENCES

American Psychiatric Association. (2013). *Diagnostic and statistical manual of mental disorders* (5th ed.). Arlington, VA: Author.

American Speech-Language-Hearing Association. (2006). *Guidelines for speech-language pathologists in diagnosis, assessment, and treatment of autism spectrum disorders across the life span.* Retrieved from http://www.asha.org/policy

Antipolo, L., & Dichoso, D. (2003). *The effects of integrated play groups with sensory integration on the play and social skills of children with sensory integrative dysfunction* (Unpublished master's thesis). San Jose State University, San Jose, California.

Barrett, J., & Fleming, A. S. (2011). Annual research review: All mothers are not created equal: Neural and psychobiological perspectives on mothering and the importance of individual differences. *Journal of Child Psychology and Psychiatry, 52,* 368–397. http://dx.doi.org/10.1111/j.1469-7610.2010.02306.x

Bottema-Beutel, K. (2010). The negotiation of footing and participation structure in a social group of teens with and without autism spectrum disorder. *Journal of Interactional Research in Communication Disorders, 2,* 61–83.

Boucher, J., & Wolfberg, P. J. (2003). Play [Editorial]. *Autism, 7,* 339–346. http://dx.doi.org/10.1177/1362361303007004001

Brown, S., & Vaughn, C. (2009). *Play: How it shapes the brain, opens the imagination, and invigorates the soul.* New York, NY: Penguin.

Bruner, J. S. (1990). *Acts of meaning.* Cambridge, MA: Harvard University Press.

Corsaro, W. A. (2004). *The sociology of childhood* (2nd ed.). New York, NY: Sage.

DiSalvo, C. A., & Oswald, D. P. (2002). Peer-mediated interventions to increase the social interaction of children with autism: Consideration of peer expectancies.

Focus on Autism and Other Developmental Disabilities, 17, 198–207. http://dx.doi. org/10.1177/10883576020170040201

Elkind, D. (2007). *The power of play: How spontaneous, imaginative activities lead to happier, healthier children.* Cambridge, MA: Da Capo Press.

Fuge, G., & Berry, R. (2004). *Pathways to play: Combining sensory integration and integrated play groups.* Shawnee Mission, KS: AAPC.

Gonsier-Gerdin, J. (1993). *Elementary school children's perspectives on peers with disabilities in the context of integrated play groups: "They're not really disabled, they're like plain kids."* Unpublished manuscript prepared as a pilot study in the context of the joint doctoral program in Special Education, in the Department of Graduate Studies in Education at the University of California, Berkeley, and the Department of Special Education at San Francisco State University, San Francisco, California.

Iovannone, R., Dunlop, G., Huber, H., & Kincaid, D. (2003). Effective educational practices for students with autism spectrum disorders. *Focus on Autism and Other Developmental Disabilities, 18*, 150–165.

Jonas, W. (2012, September 20–21). *Welcoming address.* Paper presented at the meeting of the Integrated Play Groups Research Seminar, Autism Foundation with the University of Stockholm, Sweden.

Jordan, R. (2003). Social play and autistic spectrum disorders: A perspective on theory, implications and educational approaches. *Autism, 7*, 347–360. http://dx.doi.org/ 10.1177/1362361303007004002

Julius, H., Wolfberg, P., Losch-Jahnke, I., Neufeld, S., Matthes, E., Nguyen, T., & Schade, F. (2012). *Integrated play and drama groups for children and adolescents on the autism spectrum* [Final report submitted to the TransCoop Research Project, Alexander von Humboldt Foundation with the Flora Family Foundation and Mendelson Family Foundation]. Unpublished manuscript, San Francisco State University, San Francisco, California, and University of Rostock, Rostock, Germany.

Lantz, J. F., Nelson, J. M., & Loftin, R. L. (2004). Guiding children with autism in play: Applying the integrated play group model in school settings. *Exceptional Children, 37*(2), 8–14.

Mahnken, H., Baiardo, C., Naess, M., Pechter, R., & Richardson, P. (2004, May). *Integrated play groups and sensory integration for a child diagnosed with ASD: A case study.* Poster presented at the American Occupational Therapy Association annual conference, Minneapolis, MN.

Mikaelan, B. (2003). *Increasing language through sibling and peer support play* (Unpublished master's thesis). San Francisco State University, San Francisco, California.

Miller, E., & Almon, J. (2009). *Crisis in the kindergarten: Why children need to play in school.* College Park, MD: Alliance for Childhood.

National Autism Center. (2009). *National standards project report—Findings and conclusions: Addressing the need for evidence-based practice guidelines for autism spectrum disorder.* Randolph, MA: Author.

Neufeld, D., & Wolfberg, P. J. (2009). From novice to expert: Guiding children on the autism spectrum in integrated play groups. In C. E. Schaefer (Ed.), *Play therapy for preschool children* (pp. 277–299) Washington, DC: American Psychological Association.

O'Connor, T. (1999). *Teacher perspectives of facilitated play in integrated play groups* (Unpublished master's thesis). San Francisco State University, San Francisco, California.

Richard, V., & Goupil, G. (2005). Application des groupes de jeux integres aupres d'eleves ayant un trouble envahissant du development [Implementation of integrated play groups with PDD students]. *Revue Québécoise de Psychologie, 26*(3), 79–103.

Rogoff, B. (1990). *Apprenticeship in thinking: Cognitive development in social context.* New York, NY: Oxford University Press.

Schaefer, S., & Atwood, A. (2003). *The effects of sensory integration therapy paired with integrated play groups on the social and play behaviors of children with autistic spectrum disorder* (Unpublished master's thesis). San Jose State University, San Jose, California.

Sterzing, P. R., Shattuck, P. T., Narendorf, S. C., Wagner, M., & Cooper, B. P. (2012). Bullying involvement and autism spectrum disorders: Prevalence and correlates of bullying involvement among adolescents with an autism spectrum disorder. *Archives of Pediatrics & Adolescent Medicine, 166,* 1058–1064.

Vygotsky, L. S. (1966). Play and its role in the mental development of the child. [Original work published 1933]. *Soviet Psychology, 5*(3), 6–18.

Vygotsky, L. S. (1978). *Mind in society: The development of higher psychological processes.* Cambridge, MA: Harvard University Press.

Wing, L. (1978). Social, behavioral, and cognitive characteristics: An epidemiological approach. In M. Rutter & E. Schopler (Eds.), *Autism: A reappraisal of concepts and treatment* (pp. 27–45). New York, NY: Plenum Press.

Wolfberg, P. J. (2003). *Peer play and the autism spectrum: The art of guiding children's socialization and imagination.* Shawnee Mission, KS: Autism Asperger.

Wolfberg, P. J. (2009). *Play and imagination in children with autism* (2nd ed.). New York, NY: Teachers College Press, Columbia University.

Wolfberg, P. J., DeWitt, M., Young, G. S., & Nguyen, T. (2014). Integrated play groups: Promoting symbolic play and social engagement with typical peers in children with ASD across settings. *Journal of Autism and Developmental Disorders.* http://psycnet.apa.org/doi/10.1007/s10803-014-2245-0

Wolfberg, P. J., McCracken, H., & Tuchel, T. (2014). Fostering play, imagination and friendships with peers: Creating a culture of social inclusion. In K. D. Buron & P. J. Wolfberg (Eds.), *Learners on the autism spectrum: Preparing highly qualified educators and related practitioners* (2nd ed., pp. 174–201). Shawnee Mission, KS: AAPC.

Wolfberg, P. J., & Schuler, A. L. (1992). *Integrated play groups project: Final evaluation report* (Contract No. HO86D90016). Washington, DC: Department of Education, Office of Special Education and Rehabilitative Services.

Wolfberg, P. J., & Schuler, A. L. (1993). Integrated play groups: A model for promoting the social and cognitive dimensions of play in children with autism. *Journal of Autism and Developmental Disorders*, *23*, 467–489.

Wolfberg, P. J., & Schuler, A. L. (2006). Promoting social reciprocity and symbolic representation in children with ASD: Designing quality peer play interventions. In T. Charman & W. Stone (Eds.), *Social & communication development in autism spectrum disorders: Early identification, diagnosis, & intervention* (pp. 180–218). New York, NY: Guilford Press.

Wolfberg, P. J., Zercher, C., Lieber, J., Capell, K., Matias, S. G., Hanson, M., & Odom, S. (1999). "Can I play with you?" Peer culture in inclusive preschool programs. *Journal for the Association of Persons With Severe Handicaps*. *24*, 69–84.

Yang, T.-R., Wolfberg, P. J., Wu, S.-C., & Hwu, P.-Y. (2003). Supporting children on the autism spectrum in peer play at home and school: Piloting the integrated play groups model in Taiwan. *Autism*, *7*, 437–453.

Zercher, C., Hunt, P., Schuler, A. L., & Webster, J. (2001). Increasing joint attention, play and language through peer supported play. *Autism*, *5*, 374–398.

12

CHILD PARENT RELATIONSHIP THERAPY: THEORY, RESEARCH, AND INTERVENTION PROCESS

NATALYA A. LINDO, SUE C. BRATTON, AND GARRY L. LANDRETH

The development of filial therapy by Bernard and Louise Guerney in the early 1960s represented a major shift in the field of play therapy (B. Guerney, 1964). In response to a lack of effective mental health services for children and families, the Guerneys developed a model for training parents in client-centered play therapy skills to use with their children in supervised play sessions (L. Guerney, 2000). The Guerneys recognized the influence that parents have on their children's development and established filial therapy as a means to teach parents strategies for facilitating their children's healing and increasing overall family functioning (Andronico, Fidler, Guerney, & Guerney, 1967; B. Guerney, 1964).

In the Guerneys' original filial therapy model, a group of six to eight parents met weekly with a trained play therapist for an undefined period that sometimes extended beyond 1 year (Andronico et al., 1967; B. Guerney, 1964). In an effort to increase parent participation and reduce financial and

http://dx.doi.org/10.1037/14730-013
Empirically Based Play Interventions for Children, Second Edition, L. A. Reddy, T. M. Files-Hall, and C. E. Schaefer (Editors)

241

time constraints, Garry Landreth refined the Guerneys' model and developed a time-limited, structured, 10-session training program (Landreth, 2012). Landreth and Bratton (2006) formalized the 10-session training format in their text *Child Parent Relationship Therapy (CPRT): A 10-Session Filial Therapy Model* to distinguish the model from other filial therapy approaches. The CPRT protocol was manualized by Bratton, Landreth, Kellam, and Blackard (2006) to provide practitioners and researchers with a tool for ensuring integrity in implementing the intervention.

CPRT (Landreth & Bratton, 2006) is an empirically supported treatment for children presenting with a broad range of concerns and focuses on strengthening the parent–child relationship to help parents better understand and respond to their children's social, emotional, and behavioral needs. Similar to the Guerneys' model, caregivers are taught child-centered play therapy (CCPT) principles, attitudes, and skills to use during weekly, supervised play sessions with their children. CPRT is based on the premise that parents have more emotional significance to a child than a therapist does and the belief in parents' capacity to become therapeutic agents in their children's lives. Although most parenting programs focus on behavioral change of the child, CPRT focuses on changing the parent through increased parental confidence and effectiveness.

CRITICAL COMPONENTS OF THE INTERVENTION

Central to the success of CPRT is the requirement that treatment providers are first trained in CCPT principles and skills, and then trained and supervised in the 10-session CPRT treatment protocol (Bratton et al., 2006) to ensure treatment fidelity. The treatment manual includes the training protocol, therapist's guide, parent notebook, supplemental resources, and a CD-ROM containing all parent training materials to print for each CPRT group.

In CPRT, a group of six to eight parents typically meets once per week for 2 hours, although CPRT has been used successfully in more intensive formats. The small-group format of the CPRT model requires a delicate balance of didactic and support group components aimed at maximizing parents' success in learning and applying the CPRT skills. Initial treatment goals include creating an environment of safety, acceptance, and encouragement while helping parents normalize their experiences through sharing with other group members. Parents are given information about child development, CCPT philosophies, techniques, and skills that positively influence the parent–child relationship. Parents also receive specific assignments to facilitate learning and to practice new skills (Landreth & Bratton, 2006).

Equipped with developmentally responsive ways of communicating, parents are able to strengthen their relationship with their children.

The CPRT model involves a supervision component in which parents video record their 30-minute play sessions with their children and receive feedback from the therapist and the group members. During these special play-times, parents set up a specific group of toys in a designated area of their home and conduct weekly, child-led play sessions (B. Guerney, 1964; Landreth & Bratton, 2006). During the group process component of CPRT, parents directly experience the interpersonal relationship skills (e.g., empathy, encouragement, reflective responding) that they are learning to apply with their own children (Landreth & Bratton, 2006).

INTERVENTION PROCESS: A CASE ILLUSTRATION

CPRT is designed as a preventative approach and a treatment intervention for children presenting with a range of social, emotional, and behavioral problems. Investigators have found support for its efficacy with a variety of populations. The following case illustration represents the CPRT process with a specialized population: non-offending parents of sexually abused children; it was selected to demonstrate the flexible use of the treatment model to meet the needs of specific populations of parents. Readers may refer to Landreth and Bratton (2006) and Bratton et al. (2006) for more detailed descriptions of the traditional CPRT training content and treatment process, including comprehensive transcriptions of a CPRT group from Session 1 through Session 10.

Background Information

At the time of intake for CPRT, Mrs. A was a 28-year-old Caucasian mother whose 5½-year-old daughter, Laura, was believed to have been sexually abused. The preschool had reported suspected abuse to child protective services (CPS) when Laura was 5 years old. Although the medical exam and initial forensic interview were inconclusive, CPS concluded that, at a minimum, Laura had experienced sexual abuse characterized by oral sex. CPS suspected but was unable to confirm that Laura's stepfather, who had been in her life since she was 2 years old, was the perpetrator. Mr. A denied the abuse. Mrs. A allowed him to continue to live with them until a court order issued 3 months later stated that he could not have contact with Laura and therefore had to move out of their home.

Based on the recommendation of CPS, Laura started play therapy at an agency that specialized in childhood sexual abuse. After 6 months of individual play therapy, during which Mrs. A participated in regular parent consultations,

Laura's therapist referred Mrs. A for CPRT at the same agency. She believed that although Laura had been making progress in play therapy, her strained relationship with her mother was a barrier to her optimal growth. In particular, Mrs. A's limited ability to provide emotional support and comfort appeared to be a major source of distress for Laura. Mrs. A's insistence that she did not need counseling to cope with the abuse was of concern to Laura's therapist; however, she believed that her consistency in bringing Laura to play therapy and her willing participation suggested that she would be committed to the considerable parental investment required in CPRT. Other factors that pointed to CPRT being a good fit for Mrs. A included her expressed sense of being powerless to help her child, feelings of guilt that she had not initially believed Laura, and a lack of social support (Mrs. A had no contact with family members and had no friends, other than at work). Thus, following an initial assessment of mother and child's readiness to participate in CPRT, which included a play observation, the CPRT therapist determined that Mrs. A would begin CPRT with five other mothers whose children had experienced sexual abuse, while Laura continued to receive play therapy. Although atypical for children in CPRT, the decision to continue play therapy for Laura was determined to be necessary.

Sessions 1–3: Learning CPRT Principles and Skills

Establishing an atmosphere of safety, acceptance, and encouragement is the top priority in Sessions 1 to 3, especially for this population of parents who need opportunities to share and normalize their experiences. Still, the CPRT model requires that the therapist be mindful of balancing parents' need for support with teaching the foundational CCPT attitudes and skills in preparation for parents to begin their play sessions with their child after Week 3. To ensure success in skill attainment, CPRT relies heavily on demonstration and role-play of skills. Beginning skills include following the child's lead, reflecting feelings, and reflecting verbal and nonverbal content of child's play. More important, parents are taught that, during the weekly 30-minute special playtime with their child, they are to focus their full attention and convey a genuine interest in and acceptance of their child by communicating these four messages: (a) I am here, (b) I hear you, (c) I understand, and (d) I care (Landreth & Bratton, 2006). This attitude and expression of acceptance on the parent's part is at the core of developing a closer and more secure parent–child bond and facilitating healing within the child.

During Session 1, Mrs. A shared little in the group, but she seemed less anxious as the session progressed. Her nonverbal communication indicated that she was able to connect with the other parents' experiences and feelings. Mrs. A participated more during didactic activities. She seemed to need the structure provided by the therapist to feel safe to speak up.

Session 2 began with parents' sharing their homework assignment to notice and reflect four different feelings expressed by their child over the past week. Although Mrs. A had participated in the feeling practice exercise the week before, she reported that Laura did not express any feeling other than "happy." Mrs. A's difficulty in acknowledging Laura's more negative feelings continued to be problematic. As other parents described times when their children had expressed anger and sadness, she listened but seemed closed off. Later, when it was time to role-play CCPT skills, Mrs. A seemed uncomfortable, particularly when it was her turn to role-play the child.

Mrs. A arrived early to Session 3, as did another mother whose abuse story was similar in that, initially, neither had believed that their husband could have abused their child. For the first time, Mrs. A was able to verbally acknowledge her guilt. The other mother affirmed her feelings and let Mrs. A know that she had felt ashamed and afraid that she had damaged her relationship with her child, but that she had worked hard to repair the relationship and forgive herself. By this point, other parents had arrived to the group and shared similar feelings. This interchange appeared to be a pivotal point for Mrs. A. She now seemed more open to showing her vulnerability and feelings in the group, and stated, "It's a relief to be able to tell someone how ashamed I am that I didn't believe Laura and to find out that I'm not the only one makes me feel like maybe I'm not such a horrible mother."

Although this experience appeared beneficial to Mrs. A, it also seemed to bring up feelings that she had likely repressed. She seemed preoccupied during most of Session 3, and, again, struggled during role-play of skills, particularly in the role of the child. Session 3 review and role-play of CCPT skills are critical because parents typically conduct their first play session with their child during the week between Sessions 3 and 4. The therapist pulled Mrs. A aside after the session was over and let her know that she was aware that tonight's session had been difficult. After they discussed Mrs. A's feelings, it was agreed that, for the next several weeks, Mrs. A would conduct her play sessions with Laura at the clinic—with the therapist available for support and feedback. This arrangement allowed the therapist to review CCPT skills one-on-one with Mrs. A.

Mrs. A brought Laura in for the play session as scheduled. Knowing that the therapist would be there if she needed her, she seemed to feel less anxious, although she expressed some concern that Laura would act aggressively, as she had in the past. During the play session, Mrs. A was able to follow Laura's lead and appeared genuinely interested. She continued to have difficulty reflecting feelings, but because Laura was enjoying her time with her mother, Laura expressed little aggression and did not direct any at her mother. The one time that Laura pounded the punching bag several times, Mrs. A seemed to have difficulty with the activity but remained relatively calm. The therapist was able to offer encouragement by emphasizing the CCPT skills that Mrs. A had demonstrated (e.g., allowing Laura to lead her play, her focused attention and interest, and what appeared as greater acceptance of Laura's angry feelings). The therapist also was able to help Mrs. A see the connection between Laura's enjoyment of having her mother's full attention and her reduced need to act out. Although the therapist attempted to briefly explore Mrs. A's reaction when Laura was hitting the punching bag, Mrs. A was resistant and said that it had not bothered her. Because Mrs. A expressed concern that she was not as good at the CCPT skills as the other mothers, it was agreed that she would wait until Session 6 to show her video to the entire group and that the therapist would continue to meet with her at the clinic for her weekly play session with Laura.

Sessions 4–10: Group Process of Supervised Play Sessions

Skill refinement through supervision and processing of parent–child play sessions is the major activity in Sessions 4 through 10. Each session begins with all parents sharing their experiences during the special playtimes with their children; the majority of the time is spent viewing videos and giving feedback to the two parents of focus for that week. The use of video playback holds parents accountable, facilitates greater insight as parents view themselves, provides more opportunities for vicarious learning, allows parents to see the effect of the play session on their children, and permits the therapist to reinforce skills demonstrated and suggest alternative responses and actions, when needed. Perhaps more important, viewing play sessions within the group format permits the therapist to offer parents support and encouragement in a more concrete and meaningful manner, and also provide opportunities to build group cohesion because parents are able to share their struggles and receive support from other parents. In Sessions 4 through 8, foundational skills continue to be emphasized along with the added skills of limit setting, choice-giving, encouragement, and self-esteem–building responses. To ensure success during this practice phase, parents are restricted to practicing the CCPT skills only during the 30-minute play sessions, thus avoiding feelings of failure that inevitably arise when parents try to apply their new skills too quickly to daily problems that arise. In the final two sessions, parents are helped to generalize and apply their new skills to everyday interactions with their children.

In Session 4, Mrs. A seemed relieved as she heard other parents express their nervousness during their first play session, especially when she saw that they struggled to use the new skills. Although she gave only minimal feedback about her session, she seemed to gain strength from seeing others supported in their struggles. During her weekly play session with Laura, Mrs. A demonstrated progress in reflecting Laura's verbal and nonverbal play content. She appeared slightly more relaxed, but feelings continued to be a source of difficulty.

CPRT Session 5 was particularly difficult for Mrs. A. During informal sharing, one mother shared her fear that her own experience of sexual abuse as a child was keeping her from responding to her child's abuse story in a healthy manner. Because that parent had worked on this issue in her own therapy, she was able to show a high level of insight. Mrs. A was noticeably quiet during and after this interaction. The therapist was aware of a change in Mrs. A's affect but sensed that she needed more time before she would be ready to openly process her feelings.

Mrs. A kept her appointment to conduct her third play session with Laura before CPRT Session 6. The therapist spent 10 minutes going over reflection of feelings, especially the importance of reflecting Laura's feelings of anger or sadness. The therapist explained that Laura needed to know that her mom accepted her even when she felt really angry, that it was okay for Laura to feel mad about the abuse, or sad that she does not get to see her friends from the old neighborhood, or even that she is confused about how she feels about her stepfather—maybe mad at him for what he did, but also remembering the fun things that they did together and missing him. Mrs. A appeared thoughtful and replied, "I never thought of it that way . . . I thought it was best for her to not dwell on the negative stuff."

During her play session with Laura, Mrs. A showed continued progress in mastering the CCPT skills. For the first time, Mrs. A was able to reflect some of Laura's feelings. Laura's play was noticeably more focused. About 15 minutes into the session, Laura started to play with the dollhouse. She placed the baby doll all alone in the bedroom and the mother figure in the living room, and said that the baby was crying. Mrs. A made several appropriate responses, including "She feels sad." As Laura's play became increasingly intense, Mrs. A's body language conveyed acceptance and a genuine interest in Laura and her play. Although her response rate was slower than what is desired, Mrs. A was able to respond to Laura's feelings several times throughout the play sequence. The therapist knew that this play session had been important for both mother and child, and reflected that to Mrs. A afterward. Mrs. A was obviously affected by her experience with Laura. She knew that Laura's play had been meaningful, although she could not explain why. What she said next was profound: "I could feel her [Laura's] sadness . . . how alone she felt." The therapist was able to spend a few more minutes with Mrs. A to reflect on what seemed like a significant moment with her daughter. For what was likely the first time since the disclosure of the abuse, Laura was beginning to express her feelings in the presence of her mom, knowing that her feelings were accepted and valid. Equally important, Mrs. A was able to witness

Laura's perception of her experience and better understand how she was feeling. The plan to provide extra support to Mrs. A seemed to be paying off.

Session 6 began with Mrs. A's expressing that she was nervous about showing her video. Group members offered encouragement by remarking on their own struggles in remembering how to respond. Mrs. A had her video set to the beginning of Laura's dollhouse play and said that she knew Laura's play was important. Group members too could see that Laura's play was meaningful and commented on Mrs. A's ability to be fully with Laura throughout that play. As the therapist processed the experience and the other mothers offered their support and understanding, Mrs. A again shared that "I could really feel her [Laura's] sadness . . . how alone she felt." At that point she began to cry, saying that she knew "how that baby was feeling" because she now realized that was how she had felt as a child. She chose not to share details but disclosed to the group that she had been sexually abused as a child. She further shared that she had never told anyone else. The therapist was careful to respect her privacy but, at the same time, provide acceptance and validation for Mrs. A's feelings and the courage it took for her to share her experience.

Following the group session, Mrs. A stayed to talk to the therapist in private and said that she knew that she needed to work through what had happened to her as a child. As a result, Mrs. A began weekly personal counseling at the same time her daughter received play therapy. Given Mrs. A's disclosure and the likelihood that the next several weeks would be difficult, the therapist decided to continue to monitor the weekly play sessions. Over the remaining CPRT sessions, Mrs. A came to realize that she had been afraid of Laura's feelings because they mirrored her own repressed feelings that she did not believe were valid or acceptable. She was aware of the reciprocal effect between her self-acceptance and her ability to accept her daughter's feelings and needs, and the effect on Laura's behavior.

In Session 10, as parents described changes in themselves and in their children, Mrs. A was the first to share:

> Laura knows that I'm here for her when she needs me. . . . It means so much to me that I am able to say that. . . . Since starting our play sessions, she has opened up and was able to tell me things that she was afraid to tell me before. . . . It has helped me feel like I can help my daughter recover from the abuse . . . that she will grow up healthy and normal.

In describing changes in Laura, Mrs. A reported that her aggression had decreased significantly, as had their power struggles. She stated that the limit-setting and choice-giving strategies had been helpful but that learning to acknowledge and accept her daughter's feelings had made the "real difference." She remarked on how much closer she felt to Laura. With tears in her eyes, she described the new nighttime ritual that Laura called "cuddle time," adding it was hard to tell who enjoyed it most. This was in stark contrast to the bedtime power struggles that Mrs. A had shared with group members in their first session together.

Undoubtedly, Mrs. A's individual counseling was a factor in her demonstrated insight into herself, her daughter, and their relationship; yet, the support she received from group members seemed to be a significant force in Mrs. A's acceptance of her feelings regarding her abuse experience. The skills she learned and was able to apply in play sessions with Laura also seemed important to Mrs. A's growing confidence in her ability to understand and respond to Laura's needs. In this complicated case, several treatment factors likely affected the successful outcome. But when asked what she believed had made the biggest difference, Mrs. A had a ready answer: "My relationship with Laura. . . . She now knows I love her, no matter what."

The preceding case illustration provides a glimpse into the content and intervention process of the CPRT protocol in that it shows how a stronger parent–child relationship served as the vehicle for change for both parent and child. In the current authors' experience, change within the parent is often the most significant factor in children's growth and healing. Therefore, we chose to focus primarily on how change was facilitated within the parent through the group process and parent–child play sessions. Other components not specifically addressed in the case study include collaboration between Laura's play therapist and the CPRT therapist; supplemental systemic services, such as teacher consultations; and follow-up. We encourage CPRT therapists to take a holistic approach to intervention and ensure that they consider the multiple contexts of both parent and child.

THE EVIDENCE BASE FOR CPRT

CPRT is a well-researched child therapy intervention model. More than 40 studies have examined its effects on diverse populations of children and their caregivers; 35 of those studies were controlled outcome studies that collectively provide strong empirical support for the protocol. The vast majority of studies have reported statistically significant beneficial outcomes and moderate-to-large treatment effects on reducing children's behavior problems, decreasing parental stress, and enhancing parental empathy (Bratton, Landreth, & Lin, 2010). Meta-analytic findings have indicated an overall large treatment effect for CPRT and have suggested that relative to traditional play therapy, treatment outcomes were stronger when parents were involved fully in the delivery of the play therapy intervention (Bratton, Ray, Rhine, & Jones, 2005; Landreth & Bratton, 2006).

The majority of CPRT outcome research has focused on the effect of training parents as therapeutic agents for their children who demonstrate social–emotional or behavioral problems. Recognizing the significance that teachers hold in young children's lives, a growing body of research has demonstrated the benefits of a teacher-adapted CPRT model, child–teacher relationship training (CTRT; Morrison & Bratton, 2010); and a few studies have investigated the effect of training student mentors in CCPT skills to use with children deemed at risk for school failure. CPRT has demonstrated positive effects with a range of populations, including sexually abused children; children whose mothers or fathers are incarcerated; children who live in domestic violence shelters; and children diagnosed with learning differences, attachment disorders, pervasive developmental disorders, chronic illness, and adjustment disorders. Furthermore, CPRT has demonstrative beneficial, controlled outcomes with nondominant populations, including Hispanic, Hispanic immigrant, African American, Native American, Chinese immigrant, Korean, Korean immigrant, and Israeli. Consistent with the diversity of CPRT participants, CPRT studies were conducted in various settings, including public and private schools, community agencies, hospitals, Head Start programs, churches, prisons, shelters, and a Native American reservation. Table 12.1 presents a concise summary of selected CPRT studies. Because of space limitations, 20 outcome studies representative of the body of CPRT research were selected for inclusion on the basis of the following criteria: published or in-press; experimental ($n = 10$) or quasi-experimental ($n = 10$) research design; CPRT was compared with a no-treatment, active-control, or comparison group; and treatment integrity ensured through use of a protocol.

REPLICATION, IMPLICATIONS, AND CONCLUSION

The large number of controlled outcome studies demonstrating the efficacy of CPRT provides support for its viability as a treatment for children presenting with a range of emotional and behavioral difficulties. CPRT is a consultation model that positions the parent as the therapeutic agent under a mental health professional's supervision. The strong empirical support for CPRT indicates that parents can be effective change agents for their children. Furthermore, meta-analytic research results have suggested that treatment outcomes are stronger when parents are fully involved in the delivery of play therapy interventions than outcomes for traditional play therapy (Bratton et al., 2005). Landreth and Bratton (2006) proposed key

TABLE 12.1
Child Parent Relationship Therapy (CPRT) Controlled Outcome Research: Selected Studies

Authors	Participants/methods	Findings
Baggerly & Landreth (2001)	$N = 29$ at-risk kindergarteners; random drawing to treatment groups $C = 14$ no-treatment wait list $E = 15$ children received 10 weekly, 20-minute play sessions from CPRT-trained fifth-grade mentors who were directly supervised by professionals trained in play therapy and CPRT protocol.	Compared with the control group, parents of experimental group children reported a statistically significant reduction in their kindergarteners' internalizing behavior problems over time; although not statistically significant, teachers and parents reported a greater reduction in overall behavior problems of children who were receiving CPRT and an increase in self-esteem following 10 supervised play mentoring sessions with their fifth-grade mentors compared with the control group.
Bratton & Landreth (1995)	$N = 43$ single parents of 3- to 7-year-olds identified with behavioral concerns; random drawing to treatment groups $C = 21$ no-treatment waitlist $E = 22$ CPRT CPRT group received 10 sessions of CPRT training (1/week, 2 hours) and conducted 7 play sessions with their children (1/week, 30 minutes)	Between-group differences over time revealed that parents in the CPRT group demonstrated a statistically significant increase in empathic interactions with their children as directly observed by independent raters; CPRT parents also reported a statistically significant gain in parental acceptance and statistically significant reductions in parent–child relationship stress and in their children's behavior problems compared with the control group over time.
Carnes-Holt & Bratton (2014)	$N = 61$ adoptive or foster-to-adopt parents of 2- to 10-year-olds; random drawing to treatment groups $C = 29$ no-treatment waitlist $E = 32$ CPRT CPRT group received 10 sessions of CPRT training (1/week, 2 hours) and conducted 7 play sessions with their children (1/week, 30 minutes)	Adoptive parents reported statistically significantly greater improvement demonstrated by CPRT children across time on their total behavioral problem and externalizing behavior problem in comparison with children in no-treatment control group; in addition, adoptive parents in the CPRT group also reported a statistically significantly greater reduction in parent–child relationship stress from pre- to posttreatment compared with adoptive parents in the no-treatment control group. *(continues)*

TABLE 12.1

Child Parent Relationship Therapy (CPRT) Controlled Outcome Research: Selected Studies   (Continued)

Authors	Participants/methods	Findings
Ceballos & Bratton (2010)	$N = 48$ immigrant Hispanic parents of Head Start children identified with behavioral problems; random drawing to treatment groups C = 24 no-treatment waitlist E = 24 CPRT CPRT group received 11 sessions of culturally adapted CPRT training (1/week, 2 hours) and conducted 7 play sessions with their children (1/week, 30 minutes); CPRT curriculum translated and sessions conducted in Spanish.	Compared with the control group over time, CPRT-trained parents reported statistically significant improvement in their children's externalizing and internalizing behavior problems, and parent–child relationship stress; CPRT showed a large treatment effect on all dependent variables; 85% of children in the CPRT group moved from clinical or borderline behavior problems to normal levels; 62% of parents reported a reduction from clinical levels of parenting stress to normative functioning; findings were discussed in light of culturally relevant observations.
Chau & Landreth (1997)	$N = 34$ immigrant Chinese parents of 2- to 10-year-olds; parents assigned to treatment groups based on random drawing and parents' schedules C = 16 no-treatment waitlist E = 18 CPRT CPRT group received 10 sessions of CPRT (1/week, 2 hours) and conducted 7 play sessions with their children (1/week, 30 minutes)	Compared with the control group over time, parents in the CPRT group demonstrated a statistically significant increase in empathic interactions with their children as directly observed in play sessions by independent raters; from pre- to posttreatment, parents in the CPRT group also reported a statistically significant increase in parental acceptance and a statistically significant decrease in parent–child relationship stress compared with the control group.
Costas & Landreth (1999)	$N = 26$ nonoffending parents of sexually abused 5- to 9-year-olds; assigned to treatment groups based on random drawing and location C = 12 no-treatment waitlist E = 14 CPRT CPRT group received 10 sessions of CPRT training (1/week, 2 hours) and conducted 7 play sessions with their children (1/week, 30 minutes).	Between-group differences over time revealed that parents receiving CPRT demonstrated statistically significant gains in empathic interactions with their children as rated by objective raters, acceptance of their children, and improvement in parent–child relationship stress; although not statistically significant, CPRT-trained parents reported a marked improvement in their children's behavior problems, anxiety, emotional adjustment, and self-concept.

Glover & Landreth (2000)	$N = 21$ Native American parents of 3- to 10-year-olds living on a reservation in the western United States; parents assigned to treatment groups based on their location on the reservation $C = 10$ no-treatment waitlist $E = 11$ CPRT CPRT group received 10 sessions of CPRT training (1/week, 2 hours) and conducted 7 play sessions with their children (1/week, 30 minutes).	Compared with the control group over time, parents in CPRT group demonstrated a statistically significant increase in their empathic interactions with their children as directly observed in play sessions by independent raters, and their children also demonstrated a statistically significant increase in desirable play behaviors with their parents (independent raters); CPRT-trained parents also reported an increase in parental acceptance and a decrease in parent–child relationship, and their children reported increased self-concept, although these results were not statistically significant.
Harris & Landreth (1997)	$N = 22$ incarcerated mothers of 3- to 10-year-olds; randomly assigned to treatment groups within cycles based on mothers incarceration schedule $C = 10$ no-treatment waitlist $E = 12$ CPRT CPRT group received 10 sessions of CPRT (2/week, 2 hours) and conducted 7 play sessions with their children at the jail during visitation (2/week, 30 minutes).	Compared with the control group over time, mothers in the CPRT group demonstrated a statistically significant increase in their empathic interaction with their children as directly observed by independent raters and reported statistically significant gains in their parental acceptance and a statistically significant decrease in their children's behavior problems.
Helker & Ray (2009)	$N = 24$ Head Start teachers (12 teacher–aide pairs) of at-risk preschoolers ($n = 32$) identified with behavior problems; teachers assigned to treatment groups based on random drawing and teachers' schedules $C = 12$ (6 pairs) active control $E = 12$ (6 pairs) CTRT CTRT group received teacher-adapted, 10-session CPRT protocol followed by 8 weeks (3/week, 15 minutes) of in-class coaching.	Between-group differences over time revealed that CTRT-trained teachers/aides demonstrated a statistically significant greater use of relationship-building skills in the classroom and a statistically significant relationship between CTRT-trained teachers/aides' higher use of relationship-building skills in the classroom and students' decrease in externalizing behaviors; experimental group children demonstrated a statistically significant decrease in externalizing problems from pre- to mid- to posttreatment when compared with children in the active control group.

(*continues*)

TABLE 12.1

Child Parent Relationship Therapy (CPRT) Controlled Outcome Research: Selected Studies   *(Continued)*

Authors	Participants/methods	Findings
Jones, Rhine, & Bratton (2002)	$N = 31$ junior and senior high school students enrolled in year-long peer mentoring courses; 1 class was randomly drawn to receive the CPRT protocol, and the other class was assigned to a traditional peer assistance and leadership course titled PALs (children randomly drawn to treatment groups). C = 15 PALs course E = 16 adapted CPRT (to fit the year-long course structure) Both groups of mentors received training during their class time and conducted approximately 20 play sessions (1/week, 20 minutes) with children (ages 4–6 years) who were identified as at-risk by teachers.	Compared with high school mentors receiving the PALs course, mentors trained in the adapted CPRT protocol and directly supervised each week by professional play therapists demonstrated a statistically significant increase in empathic interactions with children as directly observed by objective raters; according to parent report, children in the CPRT group demonstrated statistically significant reductions in internalizing and total behavior problems from pre- to posttesting compared with children in the PALs group; parents of children in the CPRT group also reported marked improvement in their children's externalized behavior problems, but between-group differences were not statistically significant.
Kale & Landreth (1999)	$N = 22$ parents of 5- to 10-year-olds with learning difficulties; random drawing to treatment groups C = 11 no-treatment waitlist E = 11 CPRT CPRT group received 10 sessions of CPRT training (1/week, 2 hours) and conducted 7 play sessions with their children (1/week, 30 minutes).	Results indicated statistically significant improvement in parental acceptance and reduction in parent–child relationship stress from pre- to posttesting for the CPRT-trained group compared with the no-treatment control; although not statistically significant, parents trained in CPRT reported greater improvement in child behavior problems compared with the control group.
Kidron & Landreth (2010)	$N = 27$ Israeli parents of 4- to 11-year-olds; assigned to treatment groups based on parents' schedules C = 13 no-treatment waitlist E = 14 CPRT CPRT group received 10 sessions of CPRT training (1/week, 2 hours) and conducted 7 play sessions with their children (1/week, 30 minutes).	Compared with control parents, the CPRT group demonstrated a statistically significant increase pre- to post-treatment in empathic interactions with their children as rated by observers blind to study and reported a statistically significant reduction in parent–child relationship stress compared with the control group over time; CPRT parents also reported a statistically significant reduction in their children's externalized behavior problems.

Study	Sample/Method	Results
Landreth & Lobaugh (1998)	$N = 32$ incarcerated fathers of 4- to 9-year-olds; random drawing to treatment groups C = 16 no-treatment waitlist E = 16 CPRT CPRT group received 10 sessions of CPRT training (1/week, 1.5 hours) and conducted 8–10 play sessions with their children during weekly family visitation at the prison.	Compared with the control group over time, fathers in the CPRT group reported a statistically significant increase in their parental acceptance toward their children and a statistically significant reduction in parent–child relationship stress; in addition, children whose fathers were in the CPRT group reported a statistically significant increase in their self-esteem from pre- to posttesting.
Lee & Landreth (2003)	$N = 32$ immigrant Korean parents of 2- to 10-year-olds; random drawing to treatment groups C = 15 no-treatment waitlist E = 17 CPRT CPRT group received 10 sessions of CPRT training (1/week, 2 hours) and conducted 7 play sessions with their children (1/week, 30 minutes).	Between-group differences over time revealed that parents in the CPRT group demonstrated a statistically significant increase in their empathic interactions with their children as directly observed by independent raters and reported a statistically significant increase in their parental acceptance toward their children, as well as a statistically significant reduction in parent–child relationship stress.
Morrison & Bratton (2010)	$N = 24$ Head Start teachers (12 teacher–aide pairs) of at-risk preschoolers identified with significant behavior problems; teachers assigned to treatment groups based on random drawing and teachers' schedule; children ($n = 52$) assigned to treatment group based on teachers' group assignment C = 12 (6 pairs) active control E = 12 (6 pairs) CTRT CTRT group received teacher-adapted, 10-session CPRT protocol followed by 8 weeks (3/week, 15 min) of in-class coaching.	According to teacher reports, children whose teachers received CTRT demonstrated statistically significant reductions in externalizing and total behavior problems compared with the active control group across three points of measure; treatment effects were determined to be large; CTRT also showed a moderate treatment effect on reducing children's internalizing problem behaviors compared with the active control group; 84% of the children who received CTRT moved from clinical or borderline behavior problems to normal levels of functioning.

(continues)

TABLE 12.1
Child Parent Relationship Therapy (CPRT) Controlled Outcome Research: Selected Studies (Continued)

Authors	Participants/methods	Findings
Sheely & Bratton (2010)	N = 23 low-income African American parents of Head Start children identified with behavioral problems; random drawing to treatment groups C = 10 no-treatment waitlist E = 13 CPRT CPRT group received 10 sessions of CPRT training (1/week, 2 hours) and conducted 7 play sessions with their children (1/week, 30 minutes).	Findings indicated that when compared with the no-treatment control group, the CPRT group demonstrated statistically significant improvements over time in children's overall behavior problems and parent–child relationship stress; treatment effects were large; cultural considerations were discussed in light of the findings.
D. M. Smith & Landreth (2004)	N = 24 teachers of deaf and hard-of-hearing 2- to 6-year-olds; classrooms assigned to treatment groups based on stratified random drawing to ensure that groups were equal regarding children's age C = 12 no-treatment waitlist E = 12 CPRT CPRT teachers received 10 training sessions (1/week, 2 hours) and conducted 7 play sessions with identified students (1/week, 30 minutes).	Between-group differences over time revealed that children in the CPRT group made statistically significant improvement in behavior problems and social–emotional functioning; compared with control teachers, CPRT-trained teachers demonstrated statistically significant gains in their empathic interactions with students (direct observation by blinded raters) and also reported statistically significant increases in acceptance of their students.
N. Smith & Landreth (2003)	N = 44 4- to 10-year-olds; witnesses of domestic violence E1 = 11 children of mothers who were receiving CPRT E2 = 11 children in individual play therapy E3 = 11 children in sibling group play therapy C = 11 children in no-treatment comparison (E2 and C, Kot, Landreth, & Giordano,1998; E3, Tyndall-Lind, Landreth, & Giordano, 2001) CPRT group received 12 sessions (1.5 hours) of CPRT training over 2 to 3 weeks and conducted an average of 7 play sessions (30 minutes) with their children.	Compared with the no-treatment control over time, CPRT-trained parents reported statistically significant decreases in their children's behavior problems and children in the CPRT group reported a statistically significant increase in self-esteem; in addition, CPRT parents demonstrated a statistically significant increase from pre- to posttreatment in their empathic interactions with their children (direct observation by blinded raters); results across treatment groups revealed no statistically significant differences between interventions.

Study	Method	Results
Tew, Landreth, Joiner, & Solt (2002)	$N = 23$ parents of hospitalized, chronically ill 3- to 10-year-olds; parents assigned to treatment groups based on parents' schedule C = 11 no-treatment waitlist E = 12 CPRT CPRT group received 10 sessions of CPRT training (1/week, 2 hours) and conducted 7 play sessions with their children (1/week, 30 minutes).	Compared with the control group, CPRT-trained parents reported a statistically significant reduction in parent–child relationship stress and in their children's behavior problems; CPRT parents also reported a statistically significant increase in parental acceptance compared with control parents over time.
Yuen, Landreth, & Baggerly (2002)	$N = 35$ immigrant Chinese parents of 3- to 10-year-olds; random drawing to treatment groups C = 17 no-treatment waitlist E = 18 CPRT CPRT group received 10 sessions of CPRT training (1/week, 2 hours) and conducted 7 play sessions with their children (1/week, 30 minutes).	Between-group differences over time revealed that parents in the CPRT group demonstrated a statistically significant increase in empathic interactions with their children as directly observed in play sessions by independent raters; statistically significant between-group results in favor of CPRT also were found for increased parental acceptance, a reduction in parent–child relationship stress, and reduced child behavior problems.

Note. Treatment groups are denoted by C = control or comparison and E = experimental.

training components that are critical to the overall success and effectiveness of CPRT:

- the requirement that treatment providers are first trained in CCPT principles and skills, and then trained and supervised in the 10-session CPRT treatment protocol;
- the requirement that parents conduct weekly, video-recorded play sessions with their children and receive close supervision by the CPRT-trained therapist; and
- the structured use of the video-recorded play sessions and supervised role-play within the group format so that parents receive support and feedback on their use of the CPRT skills.

The strong research base for CPRT has implications for child therapists who are ethically responsible for accountability to their clients. All major mental health professional organizations in the United States have called on their members to use interventions that have empirical support. However, practitioners often struggle to identify evidence-based interventions that are applicable to their practice setting and populations. CPRT's manualized protocol contributes to its ease of replication by practitioners and researchers. Research findings have supported its efficacy with a range of populations, settings, and presenting concerns, thus demonstrating CPRT's transportability across settings and its potential for successful application with a variety of clinical populations. The use of CPRT cross-culturally is strongly indicated by the overwhelmingly positive findings from research with several nondominant groups. The focus on the family and the uniqueness of each individual positions this intervention as especially responsive to cultural variables.

The empirical support for CPRT holds implications for managed care providers and practitioners, especially in light of the current trend toward brief therapy and short-term interventions. CPRT was designed to increase parent participation and reduce financial and time constraints. It can be provided in a time-limited and group format and, therefore, aligns with managed care stipulations while it enables practitioners to provide effective care. Moreover, it is plausible to suggest that training parents in CPRT serves a preventative function by equipping parents with skills that can be infused into their daily interactions with their children, thereby helping them respond to difficulties in the parent–child relationship long after treatment has ended. On the basis of the evidence, child therapists should strongly consider the use of CPRT in their practice when clinically appropriate. Cases exist in which the presenting concerns or parent or child characteristics would dictate another course of action, such as the use of play therapy with a trained professional over CPRT, or as supplement to CPRT, as demonstrated in the case illustration for this chapter. Providing therapists use clinical judgment in treatment planning, the question is not whether to include parents in their child's therapy—it is when and to what extent.

CPRT research has increased in methodological rigor over its relatively short history by investigating clearly defined populations and target behaviors, and the use of randomized controlled trials with adequate sample size. Replication of well-designed studies by independent researchers is needed to move CPRT further toward recognition as an evidence-based treatment. Nevertheless, the robust findings for CPRT's effectiveness with a variety of problems and populations suggest that if a child and a parent are both suitable candidates, CPRT should be strongly considered as the treatment of choice.

REFERENCES

Andronico, M. P., Fidler, J., Guerney, B., Jr., & Guerney, L. F. (1967). The combination of didactic and dynamic elements in filial therapy. *International Journal of Group Psychotherapy, 17,* 10–17.

Baggerly, J., & Landreth, G. L. (2001). Training children to help children: A new dimension in play therapy. *Peer Facilitator Quarterly, 18*(1), 6–14.

Bratton, S. C., & Landreth, G. L. (1995). Filial therapy with single parents: Effects on parental acceptance, empathy, and stress. *International Journal of Play Therapy, 4*(1), 61–80.

Bratton, S. C., Landreth, G. L., Kellam, T. L. T., & Blackard, S. (2006). *Child–parent relationship therapy (CPRT) treatment manual: A 10-session filial therapy model for training parents.* New York, NY: Brunner-Routledge.

Bratton, S. C., Landreth, G. L., & Lin, Y.-W. D. (2010). Child parent relationship therapy: A review of controlled-outcome research. In J. N. Baggerly, D. C. Ray, & S. C. Bratton (Eds.), *Child-centered play therapy research: The evidence base for effective practice* (pp. 267–294). New York, NY: Wiley.

Bratton, S. C., Ray, D. C., Rhine, T., & Jones, L. D. (2005). The efficacy of play therapy with children: A meta-analytic review of treatment outcomes. *Professional Psychology: Research and Practice, 36,* 376–390. http://dx.doi.org/10.1037/0735-7028.36.4.376

Carnes-Holt, K., & Bratton, S. C. (2014). The efficacy of child parent relationship therapy for adopted children with attachment disruptions. *Journal of Counseling & Development, 92,* 328–337.

Ceballos, P. L., & Bratton, S. C. (2010). Empowering Latino families: Effects of a culturally responsive intervention for low-income immigrant Latino parents on children's behaviors and parental stress. *Psychology in the Schools, 47,* 761–775.

Chau, I., & Landreth, G. L. (1997). Filial therapy with Chinese parents: Effects on parental empathic interactions, parental acceptance of child and parental stress. *International Journal of Play Therapy, 6*(2), 75–92.

Costas, M., & Landreth, G. (1999). Filial therapy with nonoffending parents of children who have been sexually abused. *International Journal of Play Therapy, 8*(1), 43–66.

Glover, G. J., & Landreth, G. L. (2000). Filial therapy with Native Americans on the Flathead Reservation. *International Journal of Play Therapy, 9*(2), 57–80.

Guerney, B., Jr. (1964). Filial therapy: Description and rationale. *Journal of Consulting Psychology, 28*, 304–310. http://dx.doi.org/10.1037/h0041340

Guerney, L. (2000). Filial therapy into the 21st century. *International Journal of Play Therapy, 9*(2), 1–17. http://dx.doi.org/10.1037/h0089433

Harris, Z. L., & Landreth, G. L. (1997). Filial therapy with incarcerated mothers: A five-week model. *International Journal of Play Therapy, 6*(2), 53–73.

Helker, W. P., & Ray, D. (2009). The impact of child teacher relationship training on teachers' and aides' use of relationship-building skills and the effect on student classroom behavior. *International Journal of Play Therapy, 18*(2), 70–83.

Jones, L., Rhine, T., & Bratton, S., (2002). High school students as therapeutic agents with young children experiencing school adjustment difficulties: The effectiveness of a filial therapy training model. *International Journal of Play Therapy, 11*(2), 43–62.

Kale, A. L., & Landreth, G. L. (1999). Filial therapy with parents of children experiencing learning difficulties. *International Journal of Play Therapy, 8*(2), 35–56.

Kidron, M., & Landreth, G. (2010). Intensive child parent relationship therapy with Israeli parents in Israel. *International Journal of Play Therapy, 19*(2), 64–78.

Kot, S., Landreth, G. L., & Giordano, M. (1998). Intensive child-centered play therapy with child witnesses of domestic violence. *International Journal of Play Therapy, 7*(2), 17–36.

Landreth, G. L. (2012). *Play therapy: The art of the relationship* (3rd ed.). New York, NY: Brunner-Routledge.

Landreth, G. L., & Bratton, S. C. (2006). *Child parent relationship therapy (CPRT): A 10-session filial therapy model.* New York, NY: Routledge.

Landreth, G. L., & Lobaugh, A. (1998). Filial therapy with incarcerated fathers: Effects on parental acceptance of child, parental stress, and child adjustment. *Journal of Counseling & Development, 76*, 157–165.

Lee, M., & Landreth, G. L. (2003). Filial therapy with immigrant Korean parents in the United States. *International Journal of Play Therapy, 12*(2), 67–85.

Morrison, M. O., & Bratton, S. C. (2010). Preliminary investigation of an early mental health intervention for Head Start programs: Effects of child teacher relationship training on children's behavior problems. *Psychology in the Schools, 47*, 1003–1017.

Sheely, A. I., & Bratton, S. C. (2010). A strengths-based parenting intervention with low-income African American families. *Professional School Counseling, 13,* 175–183.

Smith, D. M., & Landreth, G. L. (2004). Filial therapy with teachers of deaf and hard of hearing preschool children. *International Journal of Play Therapy, 13*(1), 13–33.

Smith, N., & Landreth, G. L. (2003). Intensive filial therapy with child witnesses of domestic violence: A comparison with individual and sibling group play therapy. *International Journal for Play Therapy, 12*(1), 67–88.

Tew, K., Landreth, G. L., Joiner, K. D., & Solt, M. D. (2002). Filial therapy with parents of chronically ill children. *International Journal of Play Therapy, 11*(1), 79–100.

Tyndall-Lind, A., Landreth, G. L., & Giordano, M. A. (2001). Intensive group play therapy with children witnesses of domestic violence. *International Journal of Play Therapy, 10*(1), 53–83.

Yuen, T. C., Landreth, G. L., & Baggerly, J. (2002). Filial therapy with immigrant Chinese parents in Canada. *International Journal for Play Therapy, 11*(2), 63–90.

V

FINAL COMMENTS

13

FUTURE DIRECTIONS FOR EMPIRICALLY SUPPORTED PLAY INTERVENTIONS

SUE C. BRATTON AND DEE C. RAY

Recent advances in mental health care for children reflect the need for services to be integrated into everyday environments, including primary health care facilities (Substance Abuse and Mental Health Services Administration [SAMHSA], 2013) and schools (National Association of School Psychologists [NASP], 2014). The goal of integrated health care is to provide quality medical, behavioral, and mental health services in one setting. Integrated health care models focus on accountability procedures, including the use of evidence-based assessment and intervention. Major mental health professional organizations in the United States, including the American Psychological Association (APA), American Counseling Association (ACA), and National Association for Social Workers (NASW), have called on their members to ethically use interventions for which there is research support (ACA, 2014; APA, 2010; NASW, 2008). In a climate of managed health care and cost control, the field of child mental health has placed increased emphasis on the requirement to show empirical

http://dx.doi.org/10.1037/14730-014
Empirically Based Play Interventions for Children, Second Edition, L. A. Reddy, T. M. Files-Hall, and C. E. Schaefer (Editors)

evidence of the effectiveness of an intervention. As a result, agencies, private practitioners, and schools are facing growing pressure to use interventions with an evidentiary base to support their use for specific childhood disorders.

Although play is noted as important for children's holistic development (Perry & Szalavitz, 2006; Russ & Niec, 2011) and is the means through which children communicate and make sense of their worlds (Landreth, 2012), current standards of care require the substantiation and evidentiary support for the use of play in mental health intervention. Since the early 1900s, mental health professionals have embraced the value of play in child therapy because of its developmental and healing properties (Schaefer & Drewes, 2014). An abundance of research literature dating back to the 1940s supports the effectiveness of play therapy interventions (Bratton & Ray, 2000; Bratton, Ray, Rhine, & Jones, 2005; Ray & Bratton, 2010). Research on play-based interventions has expanded beyond traditional play therapy approaches to include interventions in which play is vital to the treatment process (Reddy, Files-Hall, & Schaefer, 2005; Russ & Niec, 2011). Over the past 2 decades, the field of child psychotherapy has experienced an upsurge in research production, largely resulting from an increased emphasis on evidence-based treatments (EBTs) and practices (Chorpita et al., 2011; Kazdin & Weisz, 2003; Weisz & Kazdin, 2010) and national focus on the shortage of mental health services tailored to children (President's New Freedom Commission on Mental Health, 2003). Despite public attention on the significant problems in providing for children's mental health care, the number of children who go untreated continues to increase (Centers for Disease Control [CDC], 2013; Mental Health America [MHA], 2013). Estimates indicate that up to 20% of children have a diagnosable mental health disorder (MHA, 2013) and less than one fourth of these children receive appropriate help (National Center for Children in Poverty [NCCP], 2014). One possible explanation is the lack of empirically supported interventions that are responsive to children's developmental needs (Bratton, 2010).

EBT is used broadly to indicate an intervention that has been tested in studies and found to show evidence of beneficial effects (Weisz & Kazdin, 2010), whereas research-supported play interventions are referred to specifically as *empirically based play interventions* (EBPIs). Our goal for this chapter is to provide an update on the current status of EBPIs and recommendations to advance the field in the areas of research, practice, and advocacy.

PRESENT STATUS

The initial edition of the present text (Reddy et al., 2005) was the first book to focus exclusively on empirically supported play-based interventions for children. Since this landmark publication, the numbers of EBTs for children that have been identified and disseminated have grown substantially (Chorpita et al., 2011; Weisz & Kazdin, 2010), although these interventions have focused scant attention on play-based treatments. Government agencies and professional groups created websites dedicated to disseminating information regarding EBTs for childhood disorders (National Center for Education Evaluation [NCEE], 2014; SAMHSA, 2014; Society of Clinical Child and Adolescent Psychology [SCCAP], 2014), yet, again, play-based interventions are underrepresented. Of the existing books on EBTs for children, other than Reddy et al. (2005), we found only two additional volumes that focused exclusively on research support for play interventions: Russ and Niec (2011) and Baggerly, Ray, and Bratton (2010). However, over the past decade, authors dedicated to reviewing play therapy intervention research have produced multiple meta-analyses (Bratton et al., 2005; Lin & Bratton, 2015; Ray, Armstrong, Balkin, & Jayne, 2015) and comprehensive systematic reviews (Bratton, 2010; Bratton, Landreth, & Lin, 2010; Landreth, 2012; Ray, 2011; Ray & Bratton, 2010), while responding to criticism that play therapy is not supported by sound scientific research (Baggerly & Bratton, 2010).

Bratton et al. (2005) conducted the most comprehensive meta-analysis of play therapy outcomes to date: It included 93 studies from 1953 to 2000 that were categorized into humanistic and nonhumanistic (i.e., behavioral) for the purpose of analysis. Bratton and colleagues calculated an overall effect size (ES) of .80 standard deviation, which indicated that treated children demonstrated greater improvement by approximately two thirds of one standard deviation compared with children in control groups. The researchers reported moderate-to-large ESs for internalizing (ES = .81), externalizing (ES = .79), and combined problems (ES = .93). Both humanistic play therapy (ES = .92) and nonhumanistic play therapy approaches (ES = .71) were considered effective. Lin and Bratton (2015) conducted a comprehensive meta-analysis of 52 controlled outcome studies using child-centered play therapy (CCPT, see Chapter 3, this volume). The findings from hierarchical linear modeling revealed a statistically significant overall ES (47), which indicated a moderate treatment effect for CCPT interventions. Ray et al. (2015) reviewed 23 controlled studies that evaluated the effectiveness of CCPT conducted in elementary schools. Meta-analysis results were explored using a random effects model for mean difference and mean gain ES estimates. Results revealed statistically significant effects for outcome constructs, including externalizing problems ($d = 0.34$), internalizing problems ($d = 0.21$), total problems ($d = 0.34$), self-efficacy ($d = 0.29$), academic progress ($d = 0.36$), and other behaviors ($d = 0.38$).

We have identified five comprehensive reviews of play therapy research published since 2010. Ray and Bratton (2010) reviewed 25 studies from 2000 to 2009 in which play therapy was conducted by a mental health professional and aspects of experimental design were used. The authors noted that, compared with their previous review of 6 decades of play therapy research (see Bratton & Ray, 2000), methodological rigor and research productivity had made significant gains in the 21st century. Ray and Bratton (2010) concluded that play therapy research shows strong evidence to support its use for a range of childhood disorders. Bratton et al. (2010) offered a comprehensive review of 32 child parent relationship therapy (CPRT, see Chapter 12, this volume) controlled investigations from 1995 to 2009. CPRT is a manualized, 10-session filial play therapy model in which caregivers provide weekly play sessions to their children under the direct supervision of a specially trained play therapist. The majority of these studies resulted in statistically significant positive outcomes on reducing child behavior problems, decreasing stress in the parent–child relationship, and increasing parents' empathic behavior with their children.

Bratton (2010) reviewed 51 school-based play intervention outcome studies, published from 1990 to 2009, in which a mental health professional or a specially trained and supervised paraprofessional conducted the intervention. The majority of investigations reported statistically significant findings on target problems compared with no treatment or an alternative treatment. Bratton (2010) concluded that school-based play therapy offered an accessible and effective early mental health intervention to treat children suffering with a range of social, emotional, and behavioral problems.

Landreth (2012) and Ray (2011) included comprehensive research reviews in their respective textbooks on CCPT. Landreth included 53 studies from 1995 to 2010 that used a CCPT or CPRT protocol, a control or comparison group, and standardized measurements. Ray reviewed 62 studies from 1947 to 2010 that followed the CCPT protocol. Landreth and Ray independently concluded that CCPT can be considered an EBT for diverse populations of children who present with a range of disorders and presenting issues.

For the purposes of this chapter, we searched and reviewed individual controlled outcome studies conducted since 2000, and found 111 studies that identified play therapy or a play-based component of treatment as a research variable. Of the 111 controlled outcome studies, 69 were categorized as randomized controlled trials (RCTs). Not only is the number of studies conducted since 2000 impressive—it exceeds the total research production from the previous 6 decades—but the review revealed a substantial increase in methodological rigor, which adds to the credibility of the evidence. In addition to the increased use of experimental research designs, protocols were developed, measures for fidelity of implementation were put into place, and training for intervention was detailed. For several EBPIs reviewed, use of standardized assessments, objective raters, multiple informants, and blinded assessors provided additional indicators of adherence to rigorous research procedures.

Consistent findings among individual studies, meta-analyses, and systematic reviews indicate the efficacy of therapeutic play interventions for children presenting with a range of social, emotional, behavioral, and academic issues, particularly for younger children who are underrepresented in nonplay EBTs (Weisz & Kazdin, 2010). Play intervention researchers over the past 10 years have responded to challenges issued by reviewers of play therapy research (Bratton et al., 2005) and play interventions (Files-Hall & Reddy, 2005), including increased use of RCTs and treatment protocols, clearly stated target problems, assessment of quantifiable outcomes, focus on time-limited interventions, adaptations to multicultural populations, involvement of parents and teachers as agents of change, and application in practice settings. Clearly, the status of EBPIs in the 21st century has been elevated. However, to meet the criteria for EBTs (SCCAP, 2014), several interventions reviewed for this chapter would benefit from an increase in well-designed RCTs that result in peer-reviewed publications and broad dissemination. Additional limitations in the contemporary empirical base are addressed in the following section and suggestions are offered to advance the field.

FUTURE DIRECTIONS

The field of play-based interventions offers new directions for research, practice, and advocacy. The chapters in this volume and published studies offer practitioners and the public an appreciation of the depth and breadth of childhood disorders and conditions that can benefit from the use of play interventions. Overall, the results are encouraging. Yet, the review also revealed challenges that researchers and advocates for play interventions need to address. We offer the following recommendations:

- Expand and strengthen evidence base of play interventions.
- Define and specify role of play in intervention.
- Examine mediators and moderators of play intervention outcomes.
- Expand evidence for meaningful clinical change in practice settings.
- Examine effects of caregiver involvement as a component of play interventions.
- Increase research on play prevention and wellness models.
- Disseminate research findings to increase professional and public awareness.

Expand and Strengthen the Evidence Base

Researchers must continue to build the base of evidence for therapeutic play modalities. Fortunately, researchers have access to excellent resources that outline current criteria for rigorous research design and methodology that will lead to recognition of a play intervention as evidence-based practice (Nathan & Gorman, 2007; Nezu & Nezu, 2008; Rubin & Bellamy, 2012; SCCAP, 2014). Although various systems for evaluating and categorizing study rigor exist, Nathan and Gorman (2007) proposed a six-level classification system that has been widely used in psychosocial research. Type 1 studies are considered most rigorous; use a randomized, prospective clinical trial; and adhere to stringent methodology (Nathan & Gorman, 2007). Such studies are characterized by the use of treatment protocols, treatment fidelity checks, active control or comparison groups, clearly identified inclusion and exclusion criteria, accepted diagnostic methods, blinded assessments, a priori power analysis to determine adequate sample size, psychometrically sound measurements, and clearly described statistical methods.

Increased use of RCTs is the most notable improvement in recent play intervention research. However, the majority of reviewed RCTs compared the effects of a play intervention with a waitlist control group and concluded that the treatment was superior to no treatment. Designing RCTs that use an active control or comparison group to examine treatment effects would strengthen the evidence base for EBPIs by controlling for the effect of attention. The strongest design would involve the comparison of an EBPI with a well-established child therapy protocol (SCCAP, 2014). Comparing experimental treatment to a similar comparison treatment or placebo provides greater assurance that assessors can be blinded to participants' group assignment, particularly when teachers and parents are the source of measurement. The low number of EBPIs that used blinded assessments represented a significant weakness in the reviewed research.

Use of protocols, or manuals, allow practitioners and researchers to replicate the intervention and are essential to establishing treatment fidelity. The good news is that the development of play intervention protocols has markedly increased. Yet, protocols often fail to adequately describe important treatment elements, such as the role of play in intervention, theoretical framework, developmental rationale, and therapist training requirements. In addition, for several interventions reviewed, procedures to ensure adherence to protocol were not described or were unclear. We recommend that researchers incorporate treatment fidelity procedures, such as use of protocol checklists and randomized viewing of video-recorded treatment sessions by an objective rater trained in the protocol.

The use of standardized measures in play intervention research has improved over the past decade. However, to increase confidence in findings, it is critical that researchers consistently use psychometrically sound measurements. Several excellent resources have described child assessments appropriate to a range of target research outcomes (Files-Hall & Reddy, 2005; Gitlin-Weiner, Sandgrund, & Schaefer, 2000; Russ & Niec, 2011). A major limitation in existing EBPI research is the failure to use multiple sources of measurement of target outcomes. Use of multiple informants, especially well-trained, blinded raters, permits greater confidence in the findings. However, it is important to acknowledge that this practice is limited by the availability of standardized measures that reliably measure the target problem and include forms for multiple informants (e.g., parents, teachers, direct observation for independent raters, child self-report).

As demonstrated in this volume, individual RCTs demonstrate beneficial outcomes on a variety of target disorders and outcomes. Noticeably absent are replication and follow-up studies. To provide credible evidence for an intervention with specific populations and outcomes, researchers must replicate well-designed intervention studies, preferably with independent teams of researchers. Demonstrating the beneficial effects of a play intervention in two Type 1 studies (Nathan & Gorman, 2007) can elevate the treatment to the designation of evidence based for the outcome of interest (Chorpita et al., 2011). Follow-up studies are needed to assess maintenance of gains, and they can provide useful information regarding adequate length of treatment relative to participant characteristics. Long-term follow-up studies allow for the examination of the premise that early play-based intervention prevents future problems.

In general, play intervention research has answered the challenge issued by proponents of the evidence-based movement to conduct research in real-world settings (Kazdin & Weisz, 2003; Weisz & Kazdin, 2010) through the abundance of research conducted in school settings. However, research needs to be expanded to explore the transportability of interventions to a wider variety of practice settings. Encouraging collaboration between researchers and practitioners is one way to extend rigorous research into real-world settings. Researchers bring experience in rigorous methodology, whereas practitioners lend their expertise in the clinical needs of the clients they serve and in the challenges inherent in conducting investigations in practice settings.

Play intervention practice and research benefits from increased communication and collaboration among professionals from various disciplines (e.g., child development, early childhood education, infant mental health, child psychology, child counseling, child psychiatry, parent education, family studies, neuroscience, child life, pediatric medicine, child health and recreation). Possible research ideas that could result from multidisciplinary collaborations are unlimited. For example, using imaging technologies and functional brain mapping, play intervention researchers and medical researchers could collaborate and directly explore the effects of play on children's brains (Gaskill & Perry, 2013), particularly for children presenting with a history of early complex trauma. Play researchers in child development and mental health disciplines could partner to design research to explore the relationships between such variables as types and quality of play behaviors and treatment outcomes. Collaboration also provides the opportunity for integration of health services in singular settings, thus providing a holistic approach to serving children.

Role of Play in Intervention

The role of play in the lives of children and in therapy for children remains controversial. This volume, as well as other recent literature (Brown & Vaughan, 2009; Elkind, 2007; Gaskill & Perry, 2013; Russ & Niec, 2011), emphasizes the importance of play and its relationship to elements of child development and mental health. However, Smith (2010) noted that the current culture operates under a "play ethos" in which there is "a strong and unqualified assertion of the functional importance of play, namely that it is essential to adequate (human) development" (p. 28). Although Smith questioned the acceptance of the play ethos because of the assumption of correctness and lack of empirical support, others have highlighted research that supports correlations between children's play, brain development, and overall functioning (e.g., self-regulation, emotional expression, cognitive development, interpersonal relationships).

Because the research on the role of play in children's development and mental health remains inconclusive, it is logical that the role of play in therapeutic intervention also is unclear. Any attempt to discuss the function of play in therapy must first address the essential question, What is play? There is general agreement in the literature that play is voluntary, intrinsically motivated, satisfying, and flexible, and has no goal or immediate purpose (Gaskill & Perry, 2013; Krasnor & Pepler, 1980; Landreth, 2012). Incorporating play materials into therapy does not ensure that these key elements of play are present. According to Gaskill and Perry (2013), the therapy process can be undermined when a mismatch occurs between the therapist's selection of play activities brought into therapy and the child's play needs (i.e., the interaction may not be voluntary, intrinsically motivated, or satisfying for the child).

In a review of the historical and current literature on play, Ray (2011) concluded that play has six functions in therapy: fun, symbolic expression, catharsis, social development, mastery, and release of energy. Ray emphasized children may use play for different purposes while in therapy, depending on their unique needs. Child mental health interventions often integrate play as a way of communicating with children. There seems to be consensus in mental health that play is a natural form of communication for children, yet much of the research is unclear about the extent and purpose of play as used in intervention. The CCPT literature (Landreth, 2012; Ray, 2011) cites play as the means of communication between therapist and child to build a relationship. According to Knell (2009), cognitive–behavioral play therapy uses play as a developmentally appropriate means to model or educate children. Interventions that have traditionally incorporated play as one component of treatment (e.g., The Incredible Years [IY], parent–child interaction therapy [PCIT]; see Chapters 7 and 8, this volume) lack specificity in the function of play for intervention. Recently, interventions have integrated play into EBTs that traditionally relied on verbal means of communication (e.g., trauma-focused cognitive–behavioral therapy; see Chapter 5), yet researchers are less articulate about the role of play in these interventions.

The one common factor among mental health interventions is that play has not been studied as an isolated variable in therapeutic outcome. Russ and Niec (2011) emphasized the lack of knowledge regarding the effect of play on outcome in clinically based practice. Researchers have yet to isolate play as a component of treatment to understand its role in emotional and behavioral change. We highly recommend that researchers begin to theoretically and empirically support the use of play. First, the rationale and role of play should be well-defined for play therapy, play-based treatments, and interventions that integrate play components. To fully implement treatment, practitioners should have an understanding of why play is used and what role it serves in intervention. In addition, theory drives research design; hence, to statistically explore the variable of play, its use needs to have a sound rationale. Furthermore, play needs to be studied apart from and in correlation to other components of therapy. Jent, Niec, and Baker (2011) encouraged researchers to consider the following guidelines when incorporating play into intervention: how play fits with intervention program goals; how play matches the ages of children for whom a program is designed; mechanisms within intervention that are likely to bring about change (i.e., the therapeutic powers of play; see Schaefer & Drewes, 2014); and identification of empirical links between those mechanisms and play (i.e., how does play affect outcome?).

Mediators and Moderators of Change

Researchers are challenged to examine variables that affect the strength of treatment outcomes. Possible variables of interest include therapeutic relationship, therapist training, amount and type of play, treatment intensity and duration, and parent involvement. Using the example of exploring how play works as a mechanism of change, study designs must first define components of treatment and procedures to measure those components with valid and reliable methods. Typically, this goal is met through the recognition and exploration of moderator and mediator variables. *Moderators* are characteristics that influence the extent to which change occurs, and *mediators* are processes through which change occurs (Kazdin & Nock, 2003). The purpose of studying moderating and mediating variables is to test theories underlying treatment and identify effective treatment actions (MacKinnon, Lockhart, Baraldi, & Gelfand, 2013). For the purposes of play interventions, understanding relationships, such as correlation between age and engagement in symbolic play (i.e., moderator) or the effect of frequency of play on outcome (i.e., mediating), is essential to understanding the role of play in therapy.

To clarify this point, the following is an example of how the study of play as a mediator variable can be helpful to the future of play-based interventions. In PCIT (McNeil & Hembree-Kigin, 2011), there are several components to treatment, such as teaching and coaching child-directed interaction to parents, and teaching and coaching parent-directed interaction. The teaching component involves training parents to facilitate certain play interactions, whereas the coaching involves teaching parents, via bug-in-the-ear, how to respond during play interaction with their children. Exploration of play as a mediating variable could possibly include the comparison of these interactions with play and without play in relationship to a child's disruptive behaviors. This type of design would allow the researcher to isolate the variable of play as a therapeutic factor in treatment. We recommend that play researchers design research that explores play and other mediators of interest in relationship to outcome, child characteristics, family characteristics, and therapeutic relationship. Increasing the complexity of research design helps build a theoretical and empirically supported rationale for the importance of play in child intervention.

Evidence for Meaningful Clinical Change in Practice Settings

Consistent with the evidence-based movement, matching intervention to a specific set of symptoms or diagnosis continues to be emphasized by scholars. Although this practice is helpful in ensuring that practitioners use treatments that are empirically supported, the problem is the real-life application of EBT for children who are often challenged by multiple internal and contextual obstacles. The majority of treated children do not present with a single diagnosis or issue (Angold, Costello, Farmer, Burns, & Erkanli, 1999), and even disorders that present with very different symptomology, such as depression and conduct disorder, frequently coincide (Weisz & Kazdin, 2010). In reviewing disorders among preschool children, Egger and Angold (2006) found that the risk of having comorbid psychiatric disorders increased 1.6 times with each additional year from age 2 years through age 5 years. They concluded that comorbidity seems to be a central feature of psychiatric disorders in preschoolers and older children. That children regularly present with multiple and complex contexts and behavioral symptoms suggests the need to investigate interventions that are effective in treating co-occurring disorders. Furthermore, to prevent subsequent and multiple disorders, Copeland et al. (2013) suggested that intervention and prevention programs for children should focus on multiple factors, including genetic risk and environmental exposures.

The concept of impairment, a key component of all diagnostic disorders, represents the effect a child's labeled disorders or behavioral symptoms have on the child and others who come into contact with that child. In the "real world" of therapy, child impairment is the key initiator for adults to seek mental health services for children in need (Angold et al., 1999). Ray, Stulmaker, Lee, and Silverman (2013) explored the construct of impairment as a focus of CCPT. They suggested that impairment may be a productive outcome to pursue in researching play therapy intervention, rather than the study of specific diagnoses. We suggest that researchers of play-based interventions would benefit from matching intervention and research design to a broader definition of outcomes that encompass the complexity of real-life child therapy. While still meeting standards for evidence-based practice, play researchers need to consider the effect of interventions on the holistic functioning of the child.

Effects of Caregiver Involvement

Contemporary literature on neurobiology emphasizes that working within the child's system to foster secure attachment relationships is an essential component to the therapeutic process, especially for young children (Gaskill & Perry, 2013; Siegel & Bryson, 2011). Given the nature of children's developmental needs and dependency on parents and the systems in which they live, involving caregivers (e.g., parents, teachers) to enhance treatment outcomes seems logical. Meta-analyses and systemic reviews of play therapy research support this view; treatments produced better outcomes when parents and other caregivers were involved. Four of the five reviewed EBPIs with the strongest evidentiary base (i.e., PCIT, CPRT, IY, child–parent psychotherapy) require full parent participation as a primary component of the change process. Initial studies on teacher-adapted models of CPRT, PCIT, and IY have shown promising results for training teachers to deliver play interventions. Overall, findings from rigorous studies have shown that caregiver-delivered play interventions facilitated positive change in the child's behavior, in the caregiver–child relationship, and in the caregiver. However, in some instances, caregivers or children may be unsuitable candidates for interventions in which caregivers are the primary therapeutic agents or when caregivers are unable or unwilling to invest the significant time commitment.

Despite the strong support for including caregivers in the therapeutic process, we found no studies that examined caregiver involvement as a mediator of treatment outcome in play interventions. A few interventions reviewed for this chapter mentioned parent involvement, but the parents' role in the intervention was often unclear. We propose development of EBPI protocols that specify varying doses of caregiver participation. Researchers could then compare the play intervention with parent involvement to the same intervention without parent involvement. For example, to explore effect of parent involvement as a component of an EBPI such as CCPT, research could investigate 50 minutes of weekly CCPT without caregiver involvement compared with 30 minutes of CCPT plus 20 minutes of a parent component (e.g., consultation, skill training, emotional support). To examine the type of parent participation as a mediator of outcome, researchers could compare an unstructured, parent support component with a parent component in which parents were taught play-based skills to practice at home during special play times with their children. Protocols must specify such things as the caregiver's role, the therapist's role (e.g., coach, teacher, trainer, supervisor), length and timing of parent component, the role of play in the parent component, fidelity checks for caregiver and therapist component, and the setting (i.e., clinic, home, or school) in which the caregiver component is delivered to the child. The training delivery method (e.g., bug-in-the-ear; video or live supervision; homework via books and DVD materials; group or individual format) as a mediator of outcome is another needed area of investigation.

Prevention and Wellness Models

The EBT movement has influenced research to focus primarily on maladaptive behaviors and childhood disorders. Research in child development and neurobiology has indicated that play is uniquely suited to facilitating children's normal development and overall health (Gaskill & Perry, 2013; Perry & Szalavitz, 2006; Russ & Niec, 2011). From a wellness and preventative perspective, research is needed to examine interventions that positively affect children's holistic development and adaptive functioning on a day-to-day basis. A few therapies reviewed for this chapter focused on prevention, yet examining the effects of wellness-focused play interventions is an area of research that has been largely ignored. We encourage play researchers to test prevention models in settings in which large numbers of children have daily access to services, such as schools, day care centers, and summer camps.

A challenge to researching play-based wellness models is a shortage of appropriate measurements to assess children's adaptive functioning and strengths, such as creativity, problem solving, and self-control. Files-Hall and Reddy (2005) identified a few strength-based assessments in their comprehensive review of psychometrically sound child measurements, and Gitlin-Weiner et al. (2000) and Russ and Niec (2011) provided descriptions of several play-based assessments focused on adaptive functions.

An additional challenge to the expansion of prevention play programs is a lack of resources, mainly insufficient number of professionals trained to provide for children's mental health needs. In light of estimates that fewer than one fourth of U.S. children with significant mental health problems receive appropriate services (MHA, 2013; NCCP, 2014), extending the use of play interventions to promote children's health will require creative solutions. One solution is to increase the use of trained therapeutic agents (i.e., non-mental health professionals) to deliver services and integrate play into children's day-to-day activities. Researchers investigating the efficacy of this approach are cautioned to develop protocols that clearly specify requirements for training and ongoing supervision relative to children's mental health needs and agents' prior experiences, and that describe screening criteria for children's participation in the program. The use of treatment agents and other paraprofessionals in play-based wellness programs has the potential to significantly affect our nation's overburdened child mental health care system. One specially trained child mental health professional could train and supervise numerous treatment agents (e.g., parents, teachers, speech therapists, school nurses, occupational therapists, mentors), thereby greatly increasing the number of children receiving preventative services. Not only are more children helped in a delivery model that includes varied treatment agents, caregivers and other frontline service providers can be made aware of early symptoms that indicate a child's need for professional intervention before problems become more serious. Appropriate early referrals may offer one means of closing the gap in the current crises in children's mental health care.

Disseminate Evidentiary Support and Research

For any mental health treatment to be widely used in practice, it must be regarded as effective by practitioners and those who pay for services, including clients, third-party payers, and public and private entities that fund community agencies. In this era of EBT, a strong empirical base is commonly viewed as the path to widespread acceptance and use of an intervention. In reality, other factors, including practitioners' education and training in specific interventions and their clinical success in applying interventions with clients, also affects perceived effectiveness.

Another issue that seems pertinent to a greater recognition of EBPIs is the need to distribute existing research findings to professionals across disciplines. Outside of textbooks focused exclusively on play therapy (O'Connor & Braverman, 2009; Schaefer, 2011) and play interventions (Reddy, 2012; Reddy et al., 2005), the majority of EBPIs reviewed in this volume are noticeably absent in the literature on evidence-based child therapies. For example, in a review of contemporary texts written by authorities on EBTs for children (Kazdin & Weisz, 2003; Weisz & Kazdin, 2010) and play intervention experts (Russ & Niec, 2011), we found no mention of empirical support for play therapy interventions based on humanistic principles. Weisz and Kazdin (2010) remarked on the lack of nonbehavioral treatment models in the research literature, specifically identifying "psychodynamic, client-centered, and humanistic" (p. 560). Yet, it is evident from the preceding chapters on CCPT (see Chapter 3) and CPRT (see Chapter 12) in this volume—both treatment modalities are grounded in the principles of person-centered theory—that these interventions are supported by a solid base of experimental research. The lack of acknowledgment of the existing play therapy and play intervention research is puzzling and suggests that the challenge for play intervention researchers and advocates goes beyond the directive to increase production of rigorous research.

To respond to this challenge, we must first understand the nature and scope of the problem. One strategy would be to survey members of all major mental health professional associations to determine information, such as the use of play interventions by practitioners, academics, and researchers; knowledge of existing empirical support for specific therapeutic play modalities; and education and training in EBPIs in graduate-level studies and postgraduate training. Specifically, we need to determine respondents' knowledge of role of play in child development and their training and supervised practice in therapeutic play interventions. Does use of play intervention in practice or research vary according to such things as professional affiliation, program of study, degree, theoretical orientation, and depth of training and experience? What is the relationship between these variables and respondents' knowledge of empirical support for play therapy and play intervention? Answers to these questions and others can guide further actions we suggest, as follows.

It is imperative that researchers and academics take a more aggressive role in widely disseminating research findings to professionals outside of their discipline through conference proceedings, peer-reviewed journals, professional association magazines, newsletters, and so on. For EBPIs that meet specified criteria, scholars can submit documented research findings to entities such as SAMSHA, SCCAP, and NCEE to be evaluated for inclusion in the listing of evidenced-based interventions on their respective websites. Armed with the impressive data contained in this text, advocates for play intervention must take every opportunity to speak up regarding the solid research support for the use of play in children's therapy.

Next, the efforts to advance the status of play and play intervention will benefit from increased communication and collaboration among scholars and practitioners from related disciplines (e.g., child development, early childhood education, infant mental health, child psychology, child counseling, child psychiatry, parent education, family studies, pediatric medical health care, neuroscience, child life). One course of action would be to convene a multidisciplinary symposium of play intervention researchers, leaders, and advocates with an overarching goal to inform, collaborate, and disseminate research findings. Activities could include research presentations from various disciplines and cross-disciplinary discussion groups to share ideas, address concerns, and propose solutions to promote widespread recognition of EBPIs. A possible outcome could be an interdisciplinary white paper that summarizes multiple perspectives on the importance of play in children's holistic development and multidisciplinary research support for the beneficial, preventative, and treatment effects of play on children's health and well-being. This type of white paper could be used as a basis for articles distributed to professional association newsletters and websites, and for informational fliers distributed to consumers, media outlets (e.g., parent magazines, television infomercials, news broadcasts) and other entities, such as foundations that fund child-related services and research.

An additional strategy for increasing collaborations among play intervention advocates is the creation of interest networks within major mental health organizations (e.g., APA, ACA, NASW, American Association for Marriage and Family Therapy). These networks would provide greater opportunities to share research and establish cross-disciplinary alliances. The Association for Play Therapy, the only mental health professional association to focus exclusively on the practice of play therapy, could expand the scope of its membership to include play and play intervention scholars to bring together a diverse group of play advocates and researchers with the long-term goal of interdisciplinary collaboration and research.

There is a need for individual play therapists and play-based organizations to market the facts about the practice of play therapy and the evidentiary support for play-based interventions. Brief explanations, definitions, and general statements of research findings can be distributed directly to parents, courts, legislators, and service organizations. As individual play therapists interact with others to build their practices, they can build a grassroots support network for the use of play in their communities.

CONCLUSION

The use of play in mental health treatment dates to more than 100 years ago; however, play therapy interventions have a history of criticism for their lack of scientific evidence (Baggerly & Bratton, 2010; Bratton et al., 2005; Russ & Niec, 2011) The present book disputes this myth with a compilation of the most empirically supported play-based interventions in the field of child mental health. Substantial progress has been made in proving the utility of play-based approaches in the treatment of a range of childhood disorders and difficulties that interfere in children's normal development. Specifically, EBPIs demonstrate beneficial outcomes on social skills and social adjustment; self-concept; language and academic achievement; trauma symptoms; internalizing problems; functional impairment; caregiver–child relationships; and a range of externalizing behavior problems, including ADHD symptoms, aggression, conduct problems, and disruptive behaviors. This text provides a much-needed and timely resource for child therapists, educators, researchers, and academics who advocate for the developmental and healing properties of play. Therapeutic play interventions provide a viable solution to address the shortage of early mental health services (MHA, 2013; NCCP, 2014) and the scarcity of well-established treatments identified to work with young children (SCCAP, 2014; Weisz & Kazdin, 2010). It is our hope that current and future researchers dedicated to providing empirical support for play interventions will find our recommendations useful in designing and disseminating research, and in expanding the practice of EBPIs to promote children's holistic development.

REFERENCES

American Counseling Association. (2014). *American Counseling Association code of ethics*. Retrieved from http://www.counseling.org/docs/ethics/2014-aca-code-of-ethics.pdf

American Psychological Association. (2010). *Ethical principles of psychologists and code of conduct (2002, Amended June 1, 2010)*. Retrieved from http://www.apa.org/ethics/code/index.aspx

Angold, A., Costello, E. J., Farmer, E. M., Burns, B. J., & Erkanli, A. (1999). Impaired but undiagnosed. *Journal of the American Academy of Child & Adolescent Psychiatry, 38*, 129–137. http://dx.doi.org/10.1097/00004583-199902000-00011

Baggerly, J., & Bratton, S. (2010). Building a firm foundation in play therapy research: Response to Phillips (2010). *International Journal of Play Therapy, 19*(1), 26–38. http://dx.doi.org/10.1037/a0018310

Baggerly, J. N., Ray, D. C., & Bratton, S. C. (Eds.). (2010). *Child-centered play therapy research: The evidence base for effective practice*. Hoboken, NJ: Wiley. http://dx.doi.org/10.1002/9781118269626

Bratton, S., & Ray, D. (2000). What the research shows about play therapy. *International Journal of Play Therapy, 9*(1), 47–88. http://dx.doi.org/10.1037/h0089440

Bratton, S. C. (2010). Meeting the early mental health needs of children through school based play therapy: A review of outcome research. In A. A. Drewes & C. E. Schaefer (Eds.), *School-based play therapy* (2nd ed., pp. 17–58). New York, NY: Wiley. http://dx.doi.org/10.1002/9781118269701.ch2

Bratton, S. C., Landreth, G., & Lin, Y. (2010). Child parent relationship therapy (CPRT): A review of controlled outcome research. In J. N. Baggerly, D. C. Ray, & S. C. Bratton (Eds.), *Child-centered play therapy research: The evidence base for effective practice* (pp. 267–294). Hoboken, NJ: Wiley.

Bratton, S. C., Ray, D., Rhine, T., & Jones, L. (2005). The efficacy of play therapy with children: A meta-analytic review of treatment outcome. *Professional Psychology: Research and Practice, 36*, 376–390. http://dx.doi.org/10.1037/0735-7028.36.4.376

Brown, S., & Vaughn, C. (2009). *Play: How it shapes the brain, opens the imagination, and invigorates the soul*. New York, NY: Penguin.

Centers for Disease Control. (2013). *Children's mental health—New report*. Retrieved from http://www.cdc.gov/Features/childrensmentalhealth/

Chorpita, B. F., Daleiden, E. L., Ebesutani, C., Young, J., Becker, K. D., Nakamura, B. J., . . . Starace, N. (2011). Evidence-based treatments for children and adolescents: An updated review of indicators of efficacy and effectiveness. *Clinical Psychology: Science and Practice, 18*, 154–172. http://dx.doi.org/10.1111/j.1468-2850.2011.01247.x

Copeland, W. E., Adair, C. E., Smetanin, P., Stiff, D., Briante, C., Colman, I., . . . Angold, A. (2013). Diagnostic transitions from childhood to adolescence to early adulthood. *Journal of Child Psychology & Psychiatry, 54*, 791–799. http://dx.doi.org/10.1111/jcpp.12062

Egger, H. L., & Angold, A. (2006). Common emotional and behavioral disorders in preschool children: Presentation, nosology, and epidemiology. *Journal of Child Psychology & Psychiatry, 47*, 313–337. http://dx.doi.org/10.1111/j.1469-7610.2006.01618.x

Elkind, D. (2007). *The power of play: Learning what comes naturally*. Philadelphia, PA: Da Capo Press.

Files-Hall, T. M., & Reddy, L. A. (2005). Present status and future directions for empirically based play interventions for children. In L. A. Reddy, T. M. Files-Hall, & C. E. Schaefer (Eds.), *Empirically based play interventions for children* (pp. 267–279). Washington, DC: American Psychological Association. http://dx.doi.org/10.1037/11086-013

Gaskill, R. L., & Perry, B. D. (2013). The neurobiological power of play: Using the neurosequential model of therapeutics to guide play in the healing process. In C. A. Malchiodi & D. A. Crenshaw (Eds.), *Creative arts and play therapy for attachment problems* (pp. 178–194). New York, NY: Guilford Press.

Gitlin-Weiner, K., Sandgrund, A., & Schaefer, C. (Eds.). (2000). *Play diagnosis and assessment*. New York, NY: Wiley.

Jent, J. F., Niec, L. N., & Baker, S. E. (2011). Play and interpersonal processes. In S. W. Russ & L. N. Niec (Eds.), *Play in clinical practice: Evidence-based approaches* (pp. 23–50). New York: Guilford Press.

Kazdin, A. E., & Nock, M. K. (2003). Delineating mechanisms of change in child and adolescent therapy: Methodological issues and research recommendations. *Journal of Child Psychology & Psychiatry, 44*, 1116–1129. http://dx.doi.org/10.1111/1469-7610.00195

Kazdin, A. E., & Weisz, J. R. (Eds.). (2003). *Evidence-based psychotherapies for children and adolescents*. New York, NY: Guilford Press.

Knell, S. M. (2009). Cognitive–behavioral play therapy. In K. J. O'Connor & L. D. Braverman (Eds.), *Play therapy theory and practice: Comparing theories and techniques* (2nd ed., pp. 203–236). Hoboken, NJ: Wiley.

Krasnor, L. R., & Pepler, D. J. (1980). The study of children's play: Some suggested future directions. *New Directions for Child and Adolescent Development, 1980*(9), 85–95. http://dx.doi.org/10.1002/cd.23219800908

Landreth, G. L. (2012). *Play therapy: The art of the relationship* (3rd ed.). New York, NY: Routledge.

Lin, Y.-W., & Bratton, S. C. (2015). A meta-analytic review of child-centered play therapy approaches. *Journal of Counseling & Development, 93*, 45–58.

MacKinnon, D. P., Lockhart, G., Baraldi, A. N., & Gelfand, L. A. (2013). Evaluating treatment mediators and moderators. In J. S. Comer & P. C. Kendall (Eds.), *The Oxford handbook of research strategies for clinical psychology* (pp. 262–286). New York, NY: Oxford University Press.

McNeil, C. B., & Hembree-Kigin, T. L. (2011). *Parent–child interaction therapy* (2nd ed.). New York, NY: Springer.

Mental Health America. (2013). *Position statement 42: Services for children with mental health conditions and their families*. Retrieved from http://www.mentalhealthamerica.net/positions/childrens-services

Nathan, P. E., & Gorman, J. M. (Eds.). (2007). *A guide to treatments that work* (3rd ed.). New York, NY: Oxford University Press.

National Association of School Psychologists. (2014). *An overview of school-based mental health services*. Retrieved from http://www.nasponline.org/advocacy/overview_sbmh.pdf

National Association of Social Workers. (2008). *Code of ethics of the National Association of Social Workers*. Retrieved from https://www.socialworkers.org/pubs/code/code.asp

National Center for Children in Poverty. (2014). *Children's mental health*. Retrieved from http://nccp.org/publications/pub_929.html

National Center for Education Evaluation. (2014). *What works clearinghouse*. Retrieved from http://ies.ed.gov/ncee/wwc/

Nezu, A. M., & Nezu, C. M. (Eds.). (2008). *Evidence-based outcome research: A practical guide to conducting randomized controlled trials for psychosocial interventions*. New York, NY: Oxford University Press.

O'Connor, K. J., & Braverman, L. D. (Eds.). (2009). *Play therapy theory and practice: Comparing theories and techniques* (2nd ed.). Hoboken, NJ: Wiley.

Perry, B. D., & Szalavitz, M. (2006). *The boy who was raised as a dog and other stories from a child psychiatrist's notebook: What traumatized children can teach us about loss, love, and healing*. New York, NY: Basic Books.

President's New Freedom Commission on Mental Health. (2003). *Achieving the promise: Transforming mental health care in America final report* (DHHS Publication No. SMA-03-3832). Rockville, MD: U.S. Department of Health and Human Services.

Ray, D. C. (2011). *Advanced play therapy: Essential conditions, knowledge, and skills for child practice*. New York, NY: Routledge.

Ray, D. C., Armstrong, S. A., Balkin, R. S., & Jayne, K. M. (2015). Child-centered play therapy in the schools: Review and meta-analysis. *Psychology in the Schools, 107–123.*

Ray, D. C., & Bratton, S. C. (2010). What the research shows about play therapy: Twenty-first century update. In J. N. Baggerly, D. C. Ray, & S. C. Bratton (Eds.), *Child-centered play therapy research: The evidence base for effective practice* (pp. 3–32). New York, NY: Wiley.

Ray, D. C., Stulmaker, H. L., Lee, K. R., & Silverman, W. K. (2013). Child centered play therapy and impairment: Exploring relationships and constructs. *International Journal of Play Therapy, 22*(1), 13–27. http://dx.doi.org/10.1037/a0030403

Reddy, L. A. (2012). *Group play interventions for children: Strategies for teaching prosocial skills*. Washington, DC: American Psychological Association. http://dx.doi.org/10.1037/13093-000

Reddy, L. A., Files-Hall, T. M., & Schaefer, C. E. (Eds.). (2005). *Empirically based play interventions for children*. Washington, DC: American Psychological Association. http://dx.doi.org/10.1037/11086-000

Rubin, A., & Bellamy, J. (2012). *Practitioner's guide to using research for evidence-based practice* (2nd ed.). Hoboken, NJ: Wiley.

Russ, S. W., & Niec, L. N. (Eds.). (2011). *Play in clinical practice: Evidence-based approaches*. New York, NY: Guilford Press.

Schaefer, C. E. (2011). *Foundations of play therapy*. Hoboken, NJ: Wiley.

Schaefer, C. E., & Drewes, A. A. (Eds.). (2014). *The therapeutic powers of play: 20 core agents of change* (2nd ed.). Hoboken, NJ: Wiley.

Siegel, D. J., & Bryson, T. P. (2011). *The whole-brain child: 12 revolutionary strategies to nurture your child's developing mind*. New York, NY: Delacorte Press.

Smith, P. K. (2010). *Children and play: Understanding children's worlds*. West Sussex, England: Wiley-Blackwell.

Society of Clinical Child and Adolescent Psychology. (2014). *Effective child therapy.* Retrieved from http://www.effectivechildtherapy.com/

Substance Abuse and Mental Health Services Administration. (2013). *Integrating behavioral health and primary care for children and youth.* Retrieved from http://www.integration.samhsa.gov/integrated-care-models/13_June_CIHS_Integrated_Care_System_for_Children_final.pdf

Substance Abuse and Mental Health Services Administration. (2014). *National registry of evidence-based programs and practices.* Retrieved from http://www.nrepp.samhsa.gov/

Weisz, J. R., & Kazdin, A. E. (Eds.). (2010). *Evidence-based psychotherapies for children and adolescents* (2nd ed.). New York, NY: Guilford Press.

INDEX

ABC (attachment and biobehavioral catch-up), 99
Abused children, 164, 169–173. *See also* Integrated play therapy for traumatized children
ACA (American Counseling Association), 265
Academic readiness coaching, 143
Acceptance, 19, 57–58
Active listening, 19
ADHD. *See* Attention-deficit/ hyperactivity disorder
Adverse childhood experiences, 18
Affect, 207–208, 210–211. *See also* Emotions
Agencies, 108
Agents of change in play therapy, 4
American Counseling Association (ACA), 265
American Psychological Association (APA), 8, 28, 265
Animal-assisted therapies, 107
Anxiety, 126. *See also* Cognitive–behavioral play therapy; Separation anxiety
APA (American Psychological Association), 8, 28, 265
Assertiveness, 24
Assessment, 80
Association for Play Therapy, 4
Attachment, secure, 275
Attachment and biobehavioral catch-up (ABC), 99
Attachment-based therapy, 99–100
Attachment problems, 152–153
Attention-deficit/hyperactivity disorder (ADHD), 139, 150–151, 164. *See also* Child ADHD Multimodal Program
Austin, J., 89
Autism spectrum disorders, 164. *See also* Early Start Denver Model
Axline, V. M.
 and child-centered play therapy, 59
 development of nondirective play therapy by, 19, 57, 120–121

and medical play therapy, 118
relational focus of, 140

Baggerly, J., 183, 251, 257, 267
Baker, S. E., 273
Barkley, R. A., 192
Bay-Hinitz, A. K., 183
Beck, Aaron, 77
Behavioral consultation (BC), 182, 194–195
Behavioral/directive play therapy, 5–6
Behavioral disorders, therapy for. *See* Parent-child interaction therapy
Behavior control, 24
Berg, B., 78
Bergan, J. R., 194
Bermudez, J. M., 108
Bibliotherapy, 83
Blackard, S., 242
Blanco, P. J., 66, 69
Bolig, R., 118, 120, 130
Boyle, C. L., 162
Brain development, 18
Brain mapping, 272
Bratton, S. C.
 and child-centered play therapy, 66, 67
 and child parent relationship therapy, 242, 250–252
 and child parent relationship therapy-, 254–256
 and empirically based play interventions, 267, 268
 meta-analysis of play therapy research by, 6, 124
Briggs, K. M., 90, 106
Bruner, J. S., 209

Cames-Holt, K., 251
CAMP. *See* Child ADHD Multimodal Program
CBPT. *See* Cognitive–behavioral play therapy
CBRS (child behavior rating scale), 215
CBT. *See* Cognitive–behavioral therapy
CCPT. *See* Child-centered play therapy

Trauma-focused cognitive–behavioral
    therapy (TF-CBT), 97–99, 106
Traumatized children, therapy for. *See*
    Integrated play therapy for
    traumatized children
Treatment for Adolescents with
    Depression Study (TADS), 78
Tsai, M.-H., 68

Unconditional positive regard, 19, 59,
    121
Upchurch, J., 120
U.S. Department of Education, 29
U.S. Department of Health and Human
    Services (DHHS), 96

Valle, L. A., 162
Van der Kolk, B. A., 97
Vineland Adaptive Behavior Scales
    (VABS), 216
Vismara, L. A., 214–217
Vygotsky, L. S., 229

Wang Flahive, M., 67
Webb, J. R., 118
Weissberg, R. P., 30
Weisz, J. R., 7
Welch, K. K., 66
Wellness models, 276–277
Wilson, C., 89
Wilson, G. R., 183
Winer Elkin, J. I., 30
Wing, L., 206, 224
Wolfberg, P. J., 234–235
Worchel, F. F., 120

Yale-Brown Obsessive-Compulsive
    Scale, 80
Young, G. S., 216, 217
Young, M. R., 126
Yuen, T. C., 257

Zimmer-Gembeck, M. J., 163
Zone of proximal development (ZPD),
    229–230

ABOUT THE EDITORS

Linda A. Reddy, PhD, is a professor of school psychology at Rutgers University. She received her doctorate in school psychology from the University of Arizona. Dr. Reddy has published more than 70 manuscripts or book chapters on attention-deficit/hyperactivity disorder (ADHD), group play interventions, school interventions, and testing. She is a fellow of the American Psychological Association (APA) and 2014 president of APA Division 16 (School Psychology). Dr. Reddy is the author of *Group Play Interventions for Children: Strategies for Teaching Prosocial Skills* (2012), lead editor of *Neuropsychological Assessment and Intervention for Emotional and Behavior Disordered Youth: An Integrated Step-by-Step Evidence-Based Approach* (2013), and lead author of the *Classroom Strategies Scales*. She is the recipient of research and service awards, and has received more than $43 million in funding for her work. A licensed psychologist in New Jersey, Dr. Reddy has extensive clinical experience working with children with emotional, behavioral, and neurocognitive difficulties, and with families and schools.

Tara M. Files-Hall, PhD, is a licensed clinical child psychologist, certified school psychologist, and registered play therapist in Florida. She received her doctorate in clinical psychology from Fairleigh Dickinson University.

Dr. Files-Hall has extensive clinical experience evaluating and treating children and adolescents, and consulting with parents, teachers, and school systems; and has advanced training in play therapy through the Association for Play Therapy, Inc. She has numerous publications and professional presentations on efficacy of play-based interventions and behavioral treatments for children with emotional and behavioral issues, including ADHD. Dr. Files-Hall maintains her private practice at Family C.O.P.E. (Center of Psychotherapy/Psychiatry and Evaluation) in Sarasota, Florida, where she conducts individual, play, and family therapy; conducts psychological evaluations; and provides school-based consultation to elementary, middle, and high schools.

Charles E. Schaefer, PhD, is an emeritus professor of psychology and former director of the Center for Psychological Services at Fairleigh Dickinson University. He is the cofounder and board member emeritus of the International Association for Play Therapy, and is the founder of the Play Therapy Training Institute in New Jersey. He received his doctorate in clinical psychology from Fordham University. With more than 40 years of experience working with children and parents, Dr. Schaefer has received numerous awards for his clinical and research work on child development, parenting, and play therapy; has published more than 60 books and numerous articles and book chapters on play-based interventions; and serves on several journal editorial review boards. He was the former director of psychology at The Children's Village in Dobbs Ferry, New York. He maintains a private practice for children and their families in Hackensack, New Jersey.